# STUDIES IN IMPERIALISM

general editor John M. MacKenzie

Established in the belief that imperialism as a cultural phenomenon had as significant an effect on the dominant as on the subordinate societies, Studies in Imperialism seeks to develop the new socio-cultural approach which has emerged through cross-disciplinary work on popular culture, media studies, art history, the study of education and religion, sports history, and children's literature. The cultural emphasis embraces studies of migration and race, while the older political, and constitutional, economic and military concerns will never be far away. It will incorporate comparative work on European and American empire-building, with the chronological focus primarily, though not exclusively, on the nineteenth and twentieth centuries, when these cultural exchanges were most powerfully at work.

## *Unfit for Heroes*

The resettlement and rehabilitation of the British Empire's servicemen and women after World War I presented post-war administrations with a host of acute social, political and economic problems. One of the more expensive solutions advanced by reconstruction planners was the resettlement of returning veterans on the land.

This detailed study not only examines the dominions' attempts to meet the daunting challenges of the post-war world, but also the political manoeuvres and economic initiatives which formed the basis of a new period in Anglo-dominion relations. Soldier settlement was seen as the economic cornerstone of a new and dynamic post-war society. The participation of British veterans provided the foundation for the more ambitious empire migration strategy developed by the imperial architect Leo Amery.

Drawing together previously untapped primary sources, this study explores important social and economic aspects of the transition of Anglo-dominion relations between the onset of World War I and the beginning of the Great Depression.

Kent Fedorowich is Lecturer in British Imperial History at the University of the West of England, Bristol

# STUDIES IN
# IMPERIALISM

# Unfit for heroes

## RECONSTRUCTION AND SOLDIER SETTLEMENT
### IN THE EMPIRE BETWEEN THE WARS

Kent Fedorowich

**MANCHESTER UNIVERSITY PRESS**
Manchester and New York

Distributed exclusively in the USA and Canada by
ST. MARTIN'S PRESS

Copyright © Kent Fedorowich 1995

*Published by* Manchester University Press
Oxford Road, Manchester M13 9NR, UK
*and* Room 400, 175 Fifth Avenue, New York, NY 10010, USA

*Distributed exclusively in the USA and Canada*
*by* St. Martin's Press, Inc.,
175 Fifth Avenue, New York, NY 10010, USA

*British Library Cataloguing-in-Publication Data*
A catalogue record for this book is available from the British Library

*Library of Congress Cataloging-in-Publication Data*
 Fedorowich, Kent, 1959–
  Unfit for heroes : reconstruction and soldier settlement in the
 empire between
the wars / Kent Fedorowich.
   p.  cm. — (Studies in imperialism)
  Includes bibliographical references and index.
  ISBN 0–7190–4108–2
  1. Agricultural colonies—Commonwealth countries—History—20th
century.  2. Veterans—Commonwealth countries—History—20th
century.  3. Reconstruction (1914–1939)—Commonwealth countries.
4. Agricultural colonies—Great Britain—Colonies—Africa—History.
5. Veterans—Great Britain—Colonies—Africa—History.
6. Reconstruction (1914–1939)—Great Britain—Colonies—Africa.
I. Title.  II. Series: Studies in imperialism (Manchester, England)
HD1516.C723F43  1994
333.3'1—dc20                                             94–27753
                                                            CIP

ISBN 0 7190 4108 2 *hardback*

Photoset in Trump Medieval by
Northern Phototypesetting Co. Ltd., Bolton
Printed in Great Britain by
Biddles Ltd, Guildford and King's Lynn

# CONTENTS

CONTENTS

# GENERAL EDITOR'S INTRODUCTION

Some years ago it was predicted that British imperial history would inevitably break down into a series of national histories. There were a number of reasons for this prophecy: political, diplomatic and constitutional history, the conventional over-arching themes of imperial studies, seemed to have reached a methodological and analytic impasse; the economic relations of empire had to a large extent become subsumed in global models, if not lost in an ideological labyrinth; and to a certain extent the abandonment of 'imperial history' seemed a politically correct parallel to the retreat from empire itself. On the other hand, national histories seemed to be a necessary concomitant of an era of decolonisation that involved not only the granting of independence to Asian and African states but also the progressive repatriation of constitutional and legal frameworks to the old 'dominions'.

It is now apparent that this prediction was unnecessarily pessimistic. A national historiography has played its part in the cultural self-confidence of state-building. Many more national histories will be written, but it has become apparent, in what some regard as a post-nationalist age, that the study of the complex relationships established by the British Empire has a new lease on life. Such studies no longer concentrate upon the centrifugal effects of metropole upon periphery, but deal in the interactive character of empire, particularly in its social, cultural, intellectual and military forms.

Kent Fedorowich's book well exemplifies this trend. Research on soldier settlement has to be set within the wider history of emigration and immigration. It needs to be understood in the context of the culture of 'ruralism', the anti-industrial agrarian myth which swept the English-speaking world in the early twentieth century. And it has to be interpreted through the repeated and fundamental contradictions of the imperial experience: benefits to the mother country in relieving social tensions; the social and economic development of the dominions; or the enhancement of imperial bonds.

Fedorowich's research spans not only British social history, but also that of Canada, South Africa, Australia and New Zealand, as well as touching on settlement elsewhere in the Empire (for example in Kenya). Soldier settlement, which has sometimes been studied in its national setting, can only be fully understood in its widest dimensions. Only then can its combination of high hopes and failure, its adaptation and frustration through the different conditions of the four dominions, and the hazards it faced through the extreme swings of the economic cycle, be fully understood. This book is an excellent example of the 'new' imperial history.

John M. MacKenzie

# ACKNOWLEDGEMENTS

The research for this book has taken me to three continents and seemingly countless archives, libraries and record offices. It has been a rewarding and enjoyable adventure in which I have made many acquaintances, both personal and professional, and cemented a few lasting friendships. In the course of researching and writing this work I have been ably assisted by many talented professionals. The librarians and staff of the following collections were very understanding: the National Archives of Canada, Ottawa; the Public Archives of Ontario, Toronto; the Public Archives of Manitoba, Winnipeg; the Saskatchewan Archives Board, Saskatoon and Regina; the Glenbow-Alberta Archive, Calgary; the McGill University Libraries, Department of Rare Books and Special Collections, Montreal; and the Robarts Library, University of Toronto. I would also like to give a special thanks to Glenn Wright of the National Archives for his invaluable assistance while on a brief sojourn to Ottawa in 1987.

Australia proved extremely rewarding. In Canberra, thanks must go to the librarians, archivists and their staffs at the Australian Archives, the Australian War Memorial, and the National Library of Australia; and to Mr Tom Roberts, office manager at the national headquarters of the Returned Services League of Australia who gave me permission to consult their papers at the National Library of Australia. In addition, I must thank the Australian Archive in Brighton, Melbourne, which contains official military documents. Special mention must be noted for the co-operation received at the Archive Office of New South Wales, Sydney; the Archive Office of Tasmania, Hobart; the Battye Library and Western Australian Archive, Perth; the Queensland State Archive, Brisbane; the South Australian Archive, Adelaide; the Victorian Public Record Office, Melbourne; the La Trobe Library, Melbourne, and the Mitchell Library, Sydney.

South Africa provided a rich and previously untapped source of primary material. More importantly, the librarians and staff of the Jagger Library, University of Cape Town; the Cape Archives Depot and South African Library, Cape Town; the Cory Library for Historical Research, Rhodes University, Grahamstown; the National English Literary Museum, Grahamstown; the Killie-Campbell Africana Library, University of Natal, Durban; the Johannesburg Public Library; the Central Archives Depot and Transvaal Archive Depot, Pretoria; and the National War Fund, Johannesburg, were always forthcoming and eager to help. A special thanks must be expressed to Anna Cunningham of the William Cullen Library, University of the Witwatersrand, Johannesburg, and Maryna Fraser of the Barlow Rand Archive whose expertise and genuine interest were much appreciated.

British librarians and archivists were very supportive and co-operative as well. I am indebted to the House of Lords Record Office; the Public Record Office, Kew and Chancery Lane, London; the British Library; the India Office Library;

ACKNOWLEDGEMENTS

the Imperial War Museum; the National Army Museum; the British Library of
Political and Economic Science; the Greater London County Record Office; the
Department of Palaeography and Diplomatic, Durham University; the
Wiltshire Record Office, Trowbridge; the Norfolk Record Office, Norwich; the
Modern Records Department, University of Warwick; the University of
Sheffield Library; the Institute of Commonwealth Studies, London; the
Bodleian Library and Rhodes House Library, Oxford; the National Registry of
Archives, London; and the National Archives of New Zealand, Wellington. A
very special thanks must be expressed to Donald Simpson and his successor as
librarian, Miss Terry Berringer, for their able assistance at the Royal Commonwealth Society Library; the institution where I first started this project. I
am equally grateful to the Warden and Fellows of New College and to the Keeper
of Western Manuscripts at the Bodleian Library for permission to consult and to
quote from the Milner Papers, to Lord Delamere for permission to examine and
to quote from the Hewins Papers, and to Julian Amery MP for permission to
consult and to quote from the Leo Amery Papers and Diaries. Finally I would
like to thank the editors of *Histoire sociale – Social History*, *Journal of
Imperial and Commonwealth History*, *War and Society* and Manchester University Press for permission to use portions of material I have previously
published with them.

Throughout my research and travels I have been generously supported by a
series of fellowships, scholarships and travel grants. They include the B. J.
Sanderson Fellowship, University of Saskatchewan; the Overseas Research
Scholarship administered by the Committee of Vice-Chancellors and Prin-
cipals, the Department of National Education, South Africa; the Australian War
Memorial, Canberra; and the research committee of the Faculty of Humanities
at the University of the West of England, Bristol. I am eternally grateful to Dr
Duff Spafford of the Department of Economics, University of Saskatchewan,
who suddenly produced much needed funding at a critical time during the
research for my doctoral thesis.

Many friends and relatives throughout England, Australia, Canada and South
Africa contributed in one way or another to this work. Their hospitality,
friendship and moral support has been unending and deeply appreciated. However, there are a few individuals who deserve special mention. Dr Stephen
Constantine, University of Lancaster, has provided me with a tremendous
amount of insight into emigration history. His grasp of the subject matter and
his knowledge of its broader aspects and implications have been extremely
useful. Dr Dane Kennedy, University of Nebraska, has been an enthusiastic
sounding board for a variety of ideas. I learned much about South Africa, its rich
sources and troubled history from long conversations with Eric Haynes, Richard
Bouch and Chris Tapscott. Professor Michael Roe, University of Tasmania, Dr
Joe Powell, Monash University, Dr Carl Bridge, University of New England,
Professor Peter Dennis and Dr Jeff Grey, Australian Defence Force Academy,
University of New South Wales, were of invaluable assistance regarding
Australian sources and historiography. Anita Burdette and Bill Russell, archives
officers at the Canadian High Commission in London, and Dr Rae Fleming were
a constant source of help regarding Canadian archival material. I would also like

## ACKNOWLEDGEMENTS

to thank John Barnes of the Government Department, London School of Economics, for his friendly advice and help in gaining access to the Amery Papers.

I also welcome this opportunity to express my sincerest thanks to Dr Robert Boyce, who supervised my doctoral thesis on which this book is based; and for his guidance, constructive criticism, and above all, patience during those labourious years. A mention must be made to my long-suffering colleagues in the School of History at UWE, Bristol; in particular Dr Martin Thomas whose painstaking editorial comments helped me to clarify many issues and ideas. Finally, I am indebted to my wife Gudrun whose love, support and assistance has been my greatest asset.

# LIST OF ABBREVIATIONS

| | |
|---|---|
| AIF | Australian Imperial Force |
| ANV | Army and Navy Veterans |
| CEF | Canadian Expeditionary Force |
| CPR | Canadian Pacific Railway |
| CSB | Closer Settlement Board |
| DRC | Dominons Royal Commission |
| EIO | Emigrants' Information Office |
| ELSC | Empire Land Settlement Committee |
| GWVA | Great War Veterans' Association |
| IUX | International Union of Ex-Servicemen |
| IVC | Imperial Veterans in Canada |
| MHC | Military Hospitals Commission |
| NMEL | Naval and Military Emigration League |
| NUX | National Union of Ex-Service Men |
| NZRSA | New Zealand Returned Soldiers' Association |
| OSC | Oversea Settlement Committee |
| RCI | Royal Colonial Institute |
| RSL | Returned Servicemen's League |
| SSB | Soldier Settlement Board |

*For Nell and Stuart Dyson*

# INTRODUCTION

Over five million service personnel were demobilised by Great Britain and her four self-governing dominions after World War I. For some their reintroduction to civilian life was straightforward and uneventful, and many simply returned to the jobs they had occupied before the war. For others their readjustment to civilian life was difficult, full of despair and bitter disappointment. Similarly, the repatriation, resettlement and rehabilitation of the empire's servicemen and women presented British, dominion and colonial post-war administrations with a host of social, political and economic problems. There was an overwhelming official conviction that reconstruction would be a daunting challenge which had to be met with the greatest possible energy, efficiency and decisiveness in order to ensure the economic recovery and political viability of the nation and empire. Moreover, solutions developed by the imperial and dominion authorities were seen as fundamental to the establishment of a new and dynamic post-war society and empire. Soldier settlement was one of these solutions.

Two Canadian scholars have argued that the demobilisation of large citizen armies was at once one of the greatest, and yet one of the most ignored, social processes of the twentieth century.[1] Despite the fact that a large university library could be filled to capacity with the material on war and warfare, it seemed remarkable how little there is on topics such as demobilisation, repatriation and rehabilitation of military personnel. The subject has attracted increasing academic interest of late, particularly among social rather than military historians, but the coverage remains patchy. Consequently, the field still possesses enormous scope for research and publication today. Soldier settlement was an important component of certain of the principal Allied combatants' post-war reconstruction strategies after both world wars. However, here too only a few writers have examined the question with any thoroughness.

The purpose of this book is to explore in greater detail the issue of soldier settlement. Using a comparative framework, the book examines two parallel but complementary themes: the settlement of British soldiers in the overseas or 'white' dominions (Australia, Canada, New Zealand and South Africa) between 1915 and 1930; and the resettlement of dominion soldiers in their countries of origin and the problems they encountered. This, in turn, allows for a better understanding of the difficulties faced by British veterans. Although the primary focus is the resettlement of British ex-servicemen overseas in the post-World War I era, it is first necessary to analyse previous attempts at an imperial soldier settlement policy and to discuss the motives behind these schemes. One must place soldier settlement within the larger context of imperial migration prior to 1914 in order to elicit the changes in attitude and policy which occurred after the armistice. Such an examination calls forth other questions which also must be addressed. We need, for example, to understand changes to Anglo-dominion relations that were consequent upon the incorporation of British ex-service personnel into a host of overseas soldier settlement programmes. To undertake such an investigation one must also unravel the internal responses of the dominion governments to British settlement proposals. What, for example, were the political, economic and social ramifications of these imperial initiatives? Did imperial soldier settlement lead to a fundamental transformation in Anglo-dominion relations? What bearing did attempts to find the 'right type' of British soldier settler have upon future imperial migration and settlement policy?

Until recently, soldier settlement was seen as just another facet of dominion land settlement policy; a logical extension of a tried and proven method to enhance the economic development of the 'white' dominions. Recent research, however, has introduced a new dimension to our understanding of soldier settlement policy: that of social control.[2] The attempt by the conservative and reactionary forces of postwar society to use soldier settlement to de-fuse social unrest is an important theme which needs further analysis. For it must be emphasised that soldier settlement was already deeply subsumed within the backward-looking and archaic ideology of the yeoman farmer and the agrarian myths which flourished in Britain before World War I. These questions of social engineering and popular myths of national character must be examined within an imperial framework as well.

Why did the British government, which had steadfastly refused to intervene in the migration field prior to 1914, suddenly embark upon a vigorous programme of state-aided migration after 1918? The war galvanised the British government into committing itself to a large-scale free passage scheme for its ex-service personnel between 1914 and 1922. What is not fully understood is the pressure private interest groups, such as the Royal Colonial Institute and ex-servicemen's organisations, brought to bear on the imperial and dominion governments. The internal tensions and debates within the higher echelons of the respective bureaucracies and the changes in attitude and policy formulation that resulted have attracted equally sparse attention. Similarly, the impact of key imperial and national visionaries on soldier settlement policy, notably men such as L. S. Amery, who stamped his personal mark on the free passage scheme in the attempt to establish a landed imperial yeomanry overseas, has until now not been fully explained. This study addresses these issues and reveals how soldier settlement became a vehicle for a new era in empire co-operation and economic development.

## Notes

1 Desmond Morton and Glenn Wright, *Winning the Second Battle*, Toronto, 1987.
2 Marilyn Lake, *The Limits of Hope: Soldier Settlement in Victoria 1915–38*, Melbourne, 1987.

# CHAPTER ONE

# Past policies and precedents, 1650–1914

'Colonisation by discharged soldiers', pronounced *The Veteran* in 1918, 'is as old as time itself'.[1] And so it is. Throughout ancient history disbanded soldiers played a key role in the settlement and development of expanding empires. The Romans, for instance, expanded and consolidated their empire by employing a system of military colonisation. Tacitus, the Roman historian and chronicler, recorded in his *Annals* the failure of one such Roman soldier colony.[2] Security was the principal reason the ancients settled disbanded soldiers on farms on the frontier. The settlement of a loyal, trained and disciplined garrison force bolstered the defence capability of a frontier territory and could be used as a militia in times of internal strife. Land was also a convenient form of payment for services rendered; a reward for the hardship and sacrifices soldiers encountered on campaign. A third reason for soldier settlement was often to supplement civilian efforts to develop the economic potential of a newly acquired territory.

In North America during the struggle between the colonial empires of France and England, the settlement of French and British forces in their respective colonies became an important facet of colonial defence policy. After the expulsion of the French from Quebec in 1763 the British government maintained this policy in Canada in order to meet the very real threat of American aggression. Similarly, British soldiers stationed in New Zealand, Australia, South Africa and India were encouraged to settle in these territories upon receipt of their discharge to meet increased demands from colonial settlers who were constantly threatened by attacks from hostile, indigenous tribes or from incursions, real or imagined, from rival imperial powers.

After 1815 a change of emphasis emerged with regard to soldier settlement. Social and economic considerations had always been closely associated with the strategic factors, and both the French and British had employed soldier settlement as a supplement to their respective colonial development policies in North America. However, government expenditure and assistance had been small. Defence rather than development remained paramount, though many government officials realised that the development argument gave soldier settlement wider popular appeal. But with the return to peace in 1815 the drastic cut-back in military expenditure and manpower led to spiralling unemployment, in response to which the British government launched the first large-scale, government-assisted emigration scheme to Canada and South Africa, in which a small number of soldiers participated. British governmental intervention into the migration field, albeit on a very limited scale, demonstrated the increasing importance of soldier settlement as a tool of colonial development and social relief. By 1914 the arguments for soldier settlement on the grounds of imperial defence and of empire development had reached a level of equality. Moreover, the linkage of soldier settlement with imperial development allowed empire migration enthusiasts the opportunity to use soldier settlement as a vehicle for the formulation of a more ambitious post-World War I migration policy across the empire. To understand this change of emphasis, the present chapter is mainly devoted to the colonial and imperial soldier settlement programmes in Canada and South Africa prior to 1914, since their experiences provide the most numerous and detailed accounts of soldier settlement policy.

## Resettling disbanded and discharged soldiers, 1650–1900

Prior to the British occupation of Quebec in 1763 the French colony of New France operated under a *seigneurial* system of land tenure. The *seigneur* was a private individual, usually possessing considerable standing and influence in the community, who received concessions of land from the Crown. In return, the *seigneur* was obliged to settle a required number of tenants or *habitants* on his concession. The *seigneur* was the civil and military leader of the community and as a rule the largest landowner. He possessed wide-ranging powers and rights which governed all aspects of the colony's social, economic and political life, the most important being the right to collect rents on land, levy fees on the transfer of tenure and charge tithes on his tenants' produce. The entire system was closely regulated and tightly knit with everyone knowing exactly his or her function within the community.

The *seigneurial* system provided a systematic approach to colonisation in New France along feudal guidelines imposed from Versailles. It was a land settlement rather than a land tenure system and though reflecting the social and political ideals of French society it was primarily conceived as a military solution to the problems of colonial defence.[3] Soldiers were encouraged by the grant of free land to settle in the colony, but they were disbanded rather than discharged because disbandment did not exempt them from future military duties. Consequently, these veterans provided an important contribution to the reinforcement and strengthening of the colony's defences, and contributed to its economic growth and prosperity. The architects of the *seigneurial* system believed that if enough soldiers were disposed to settle in New France its defence would be ensured. Settlements were established along the St Lawrence River and its major tributaries to defend the colony's navigable communications network from Indian attack or British incursions from the thirteen American colonies or the smaller Canadian settlements. The largest and most notable soldier settlement project in New France was initiated in the late 1660s by veterans of the Carignan-Salières regiment who established themselves along the Richelieu river as a buttress against the Iroquois.[4]

British soldier settlement in Nova Scotia, New Brunswick and Ontario followed the pattern earlier set in New France. Detachments of troops were disbanded in these colonies with the express hope that they would increase the productivity of the colonies and provide a first-rate militia for colonial defence. The strategic port of Halifax had been populated by disbanded soldiers in 1749 and was the first major British example of a conscious soldier settlement plan.[5] Following the conclusion of the American Revolutionary War in 1783 the presence of a large, restless and potentially dangerous enemy on the southern borders of its North American possessions posed a troublesome and taxing problem to the British government: how best to defend an already long and exposed border? The expulsion of France from Quebec had eliminated one component from the problem but it contributed another by extending the border area which needed defending. One solution was the settlement of disbanded regiments on the south bank of the upper St Lawrence River which, to a certain extent, relieved the problem of defending Quebec from attacks launched from upstate New York. The United Empire Loyalists (American colonists loyal to the Crown who had fought with the British as militia and fled to Canada after the American Revolutionary War) were also placed along the St Lawrence and the St John River in New Brunswick in order to provide a trustworthy pool of irregulars.[6]

In the years prior to the War of 1812 a large number of Americans, other than Loyalists, migrated north and settled in southern Ontario. Canadian politicians became alarmed at this influx of settlers because, being unmistakably anti-British in temperament, they posed a real threat to the colony's internal security and could not be trusted in time of war. The British government reacted by instituting a settlement policy designed to inculcate a sense of loyalty among the new arrivals. Wherever possible discharged soldiers were settled amongst the American settlers to act as a deterrent against rebellion and insurrection. The gravity with which the British authorities regarded this problem was clearly demonstrated by the generous grant of land for each soldier and the liberal financial concessions for stocking and outfitting each homestead.[7]

Official demands for the reduction of the army estimates after the Napoleonic Wars forced the British government to initiate a programme of severe military retrenchment. This aggravated the growing unemployment that accompanied the deep depression which followed peace. What remained to be done with these ex-soldiers? One imperial publicist believed the veterans provided an excellent source of manpower for the development of the colonies and advocated their emigration to these territories.[8] The British government agreed but instead of initiating a military emigration policy it began immediately to disband and discharge soldiers stationed in Canada. Partly as a reward for military service, partly as an encouragement to permanent settlement and colonial development, and more importantly as a cost-cutting measure, discharged soldiers wishing to stay in Upper Canada were encouraged to settle as farmers. Lieutenant-General Sir G. Drummond, Administrator of Upper Canada, was given full responsibility by the British government to encourage, assist and advise the new settlers. Gifts of freehold land were granted to officers and men, with concessions varying from 100 acres for a private to 1,200 acres for a Lieutenant-Colonel. Several new townships were established along the strategically important lake and river networks of the Ottawa river with a small party travelling further west to take up land near Fort Douglas in the Selkirk settlement of Manitoba. A similar but smaller scheme existed for discharged naval officers along the north shores of Lakes Erie and Ontario.[9]

There were many obstacles preventing the conversion of theory into practice regarding Britain's military settlement policy between 1812 and 1854. Despite the British government's assumption that discharged soldiers and sailors made good settlers, the evidence strongly suggested that the contrary was true. 'Unused to agricultural labour and inexperienced in pioneer life, (the soldier settler) had neither the resourcefulness nor the industry to succeed on the frontier'.[10] The disbanded soldier of 1815 was no different from his predecessor who had fought during the Seven Years War (1756–63) or the American Revolutionary War. Hardened by war, adventurous and restless, he was ill-prepared for the drudgery and tedium of farming. Yet the British government was more determined than ever after 1812 to make the military land grant a permanent feature of its colonial settlement policy.[11]

The strategic motive dominated the minds of British and colonial officials alike during the post-Napoleonic period. This was borne out by the fact that military settlements were located at strategic points along the Canadian-American frontier or at sites which straddled important communications routes. If an area happened to combine the advantages of both strategy and agricultural potential it was sheer good fortune. More often than not, if an area proved suitable, it took much back-breaking work to clear and prepare the land for cultivation. Poor roads, inadequate supplies, inaccessibility to markets and lack of capital compounded the plight of the soldier settler.[12] It was no wonder many of these men saw salvation in the land speculator.

The British authorities displayed an astonishing tenacity in their adherence to the idea that ex-soldiers made excellent colonists, capable of improving the productivity of a colony during peacetime and defending it in time of war. Of course distance played a pivotal role, as one Canadian historian has pointed out: 'It was easy enough to sit in a London club and draw a picture of a beautiful little Utopia somewhere out in America where the citizens were the best of soldiers and the most industrious of pioneer farmers at one and the same time'.[13] When reports of large-scale failure and abject misery were despatched by colonial administrators in Canada the reservations about the policy which surfaced in London were more than 'offset by a strong sense of obligation to those who had risked life and limb' for their country.[14]

The idea of military settlement as a viable colonisation and imperial defence policy persisted throughout the 1820s and 1830s. However, it was becoming evident that despite the noble claims made by its promoters that military settlement strengthened the physical and economic bonds of empire, the imperial government wanted above all to save money. The worst example of military settlement which combined attempts to reduce Treasury expenditure with the promotion of imperial defence was the settlement of British Army pensioners in Canada during the 1830s. Legislation was passed in 1830 which allowed all non-commissioned officers and privates entitled to a pension from the Chelsea Hospital and desirous of emigrating the opportunity to commute their pension into a final cash settlement to a sum not exceeding four years' pension.[15] The War Office laid down a rigorous set of conditions and qualifications that each pensioner and his family had to meet to ensure maximum success. Age, physical fitness and additional capital were the basic criteria used to select prospective settlers. Free passage and free land grants of between 100 and 200 acres were included as an added inducement for the pensioners.

The entire scheme was a fiasco. Of the 1,500 pensioners who landed in Upper Canada between 1830 and 1839 only 158 were reported to be supporting themselves in 1844.[16] In its haste to reduce pension payments the War Office ignored its own selection criteria, and those selected were old, infirm, unskilled and unsuited to tackle the harsh realities of life as pioneers. Government support and supervision were negligible. Ill-equipped for farming, many veterans squandered their commuted pensions and quickly became destitute. The larger towns and cities seemed to offer an opportunity for the veteran to start afresh, but with no money or skills he had to throw himself on the mercy of local relief agencies. This aroused the disgust of local taxpayers, and according to one colonial administrator disgraced the colony of Upper Canada and discredited the colonial government. Governor Aylmer of Quebec was particularly acerbic when he condemned the pensioner settlement scheme on the grounds that the men lacked application and resourcefulness, having squandered their commuted pensions: 'It has been found generally that these men are persons of irregular and disorderly habits and extremely improvident in matters connected with their own welfare.' The Imperial government, reluctant to accept responsibility for the disaster, eventually acknowledged its obligations to the poverty-stricken pensioners in 1840. Relief supplies were issued and a small weekly allowance was authorised. But it was too little too late.[17]

Undeterred, Earl Grey, the Colonial Secretary in Lord John Russell's administration, revived the idea of pensioner settlements in 1846. The scheme, like its predecessors, encountered its share of difficulties, but it succeeded because of good planning and supervision. Pensioners were carefully selected for their character and determination. They were concentrated in large groups near urban areas which ensured easy and proper supervision, and they were given sufficient capital for their agricultural pursuits. Settlement near urban areas possessed the added benefit of allowing the colonial authorities to assemble the pensioners quickly in times of civil unrest. Similarly, it gave the pensioner direct and easy access to domestic markets. Once again the parallel objectives of cutting military expenditure and developing colonial society provided the impetus for Grey's policy, and by 1853 all British regulars west of Kingston had been withdrawn and replaced by 750 pensioners on active and reserve status. An overall reduction in Canada of 3,000 regulars was achieved between 1847 and 1853, in part made possible by Grey's military settlement programme. Furthermore, the use of pensioners on active duty as troops or police allowed Canadian authorities time to make the transition between dependence on British troops for continued security to self-reliance on Canadian resources and manpower.[18]

From a strategic standpoint it was South Africa which received the British government's closest attention in the post-Napoleonic period.

Continual unrest on the eastern frontier of the Cape Colony between Cape colonists and the Xhosa nation had been a major source of concern ever since British occupation of the Cape Colony in 1806. The latest series of Xhosa raids in 1819 clearly demonstrated British weakness and insecurity on the eastern frontier. In the face of this threat, and as an attempt to alleviate the domestic unemployment problem, the British government offered free passages and land to men who would settle in the Albany district of the eastern frontier.[19] Each man who recruited parties of ten or more men was granted 100 acres per settler, and a total of 4,000 settlers arrived at the Cape in 1820. The settlement party consisted largely of farmers and artisans, victims of post-war unemployment, interspersed with a few professional people, soldiers, teachers and clergy.[20]

Security along the eastern frontier remained a constant problem in the Eastern Cape throughout the mid-nineteenth century, and this prompted another attempt by the British government to consolidate its position. The Albany settlement was further reinforced in 1856 by a large contingent of German soldiers disbanded from the British-German Legion.[21] These soldiers had been recruited for service in the Crimean War, but became a financial burden once the war was over and the British government hoped that their settlement in Africa would satisfy demands for military retrenchment at home and colonial pleas for improved security on the turbulent eastern frontier. The terms of settlement were quite generous, but disciplinary problems arising from a disparity of numbers between men and women limited the success of the scheme.[22]

Like her colonial cousins, New Zealand also witnessed several small-scale experiments in military colonisation in the nineteenth century. In 1851 the imperial government decided that it would be advantageous to grant special land concessions to those retired British officers who had participated in the internecine conflict with the Maoris, a fiercely proud and warlike native people. The policy's main objective was the improvement of the colony's internal security through the settlement of Britons in areas where the native population was disaffected. Agricultural development and the use of scrip as a payment for services rendered were also employed to justify the settlement policy, but in reality they were of secondary importance. Security remained the paramount objective. The Maoris were seen as a constant source of trouble by the settlers throughout the 1850s and 1860s. This resulted in the enactment of a series of regulations designed to entice retiring military and naval personnel to stay and settle in the colony, principally on the North Island. In all, 7,692 military and naval personnel were awarded land grants under the multifarious provisions established between 1851 and 1892.[23]

Between 1830 and 1870 the debate on colonial defence and the changing nature of imperial responsibility was integral to the larger question of Britain's future relationship with her overseas possessions. As successive British administrations wrestled with ideas for reducing the overall expenditure on imperial forces overseas, military settlement and the land grant system attracted increased criticism. It was argued that group settlements were costly, ineffective and unnecessary. A large number of influential businessmen, politicians and political economists, known collectively as the Manchester School, saw little use in spending vast sums of money in overseas territories which did little to justify their possession. A political empire based on the direct control and administration of territory found no justification within *laissez-faire* economics. Therefore the maintenance of large and expensive military garrisons or settlements overseas was an unnecessary burden.

W. E. Gladstone, a former Chancellor of the Exchequer in Lord Palmerston's administration and a future British Prime Minister, was one of the imperial garrison system's most ardent critics. Taking Canada as his example, he argued that as long as the colony relied on Britain for its defence it would never achieve true nationhood.[24] Like many other free traders, he believed that the acquisition of self-government implied a concomitant responsibility for new duties such as defence. It fostered self-reliance and self-confidence in the colony; essential qualities which would relieve Britain of the financial burden of colonial defence and release garrison troops for home defence or continental duty. He therefore considered Canadian demands for continued maintenance of a large British garrison in the colony as inconsistent with their parallel demands for increased responsible government.

On becoming Prime Minister, Gladstone championed the doctrine of *laissez-faire* economics. Upon assuming office in 1868 one of his first priorities was the rapid dismantlement of the remnants of the garrison system. Edward Cardwell, Secretary of State for War and the architect responsible for sweeping military reforms during this period, proposed to reduce the imperial garrison in Canada by 10,000 men. However, the Riel Rebellion of 1870 in Manitoba, and delays in the refortification of Quebec prevented the withdrawal of imperial troops from central Canada until 1871.[25] Nevertheless, the reforms fulfilled Gladstone's election promise to adopt a policy of colonial retrenchment. More importantly, Cardwell's policies demonstrated Britain's determination to readjust and respond to the worsening diplomatic and military situation in Europe.

The entire policy caused great anxiety throughout Canada. Many Canadians believed that Britain was abandoning her imperial responsibilities and exposing Canada to eventual American annexation. This did not happen, but fear of American annexation, particularly of Manitoba and the North-West territory, was a motive force to Canadian post-confederation settlement and economic development in western Canada. Deemed a wasteful and fruitless exercise, attempts at military colonisation were apparently abandoned by the British government in 1867. Not so in Canada.

In 1870 the new province of Manitoba was created and Sir Garnet Wolseley was despatched with a force of British regulars and Ontario militia to reinforce Canadian political authority in the region. When the adventure was completed the Canadian government offered scrip to each member of the expedition as a reward for services rendered. The scrip granted each soldier the right to claim 160 acres of land, the majority of which was taken along the Red River. The Canadian government hoped the expedition would stave off any American annexationist designs on western Canada. Similarly, the settlement of British regulars and Canadian militia was intended to act as a deterrent against pro-American agitation or native unrest. However, most of the soldiers promptly sold their scrip to hungry land speculators and returned to eastern Canada.[26]

In 1885 the North-West territory was engulfed by rebellion and an expeditionary force was despatched to quash it. The campaign was successful and the veterans of the North-West Rebellion, like their predecessors in 1870, became eligible for land grants. The terms were generous and consisted of two adjacent quarter sections totalling 320 acres. For those who did not want to become settlers, scrip was awarded valued at $80. Obviously, the proposed compensation was a patriotic response for services rendered and inconveniences suffered in putting down the insurrection. Once again, security on the frontier was a key factor in determining policy. However, there was a subtle but important shift in emphasis away from military strategy towards economic development which was illustrated by the doubling of the land grant. The success of the military operation had demonstrated Canada's determination to protect its sovereignty in the region. But long-term security could only be maintained through an effective economic strategy in which large-scale settlement was an important component. Canadian politicians therefore saw soldier settlement as supplementing the overall development strategy. It was designed to open up the vast regions of the Canadian west 'to the young men of that soldiery who have seen the North-West, who know its advantages, and desire to settle there. It is of great importance . . . to that country and to the whole Dominion, that a considerable portion of that body should take up their habitation in the North-West, to which they have gone as loyal soldiers and as supporters of the supremacy of the law and of the Government of Canada'.[27] Unfortunately for Canada's nation-builders, the added inducement of an extra 160 acres did not prove as attractive to the campaign's victors as the scrip.

Soldier settlement in Canada was scarcely more important or extensive after 1867 than before. What was markedly different about it after confederation was that land grants ignored rank and reflected a more systematic governmental approach to colonisation and the economic development of the Canadian prairies. As noted above, there was a change in emphasis. Whereas prior to 1870 strategic presumptions dominated economic considerations as the primary motive for military settlement, the emphasis had shifted in favour of the latter by the 1880s. The initiation of a free homestead system after confederation was dictated by the necessity to safeguard national interests, promote western expansion and realise the goal of a transcontinental dominion 'against the march of "manifest destiny" south of the border'. Therefore the emphasis on land selection was shifting from military strategy and defence to planned settlement and agricultural productivity, with these economic motives becoming rather more prominent as the century progressed.[28]

The abandonment of military colonisation by the British government in 1867 did not mean that the issue had disappeared from the British domestic political arena. Some politicians and senior service officers continued to raise the issue of military colonisation in the late Victorian era in the context of armed forces reform. The Crimean War had demonstrated gross inadequacies in the recruitment, training and organisation of the British Army. To rectify these problems, a number of measures were initiated, the most sweeping being those introduced in 1870 by Edward Cardwell, the Secretary of State of War. One of his most significant initiatives was the introduction of a revised system of short service 'with the colours'. Although the initial term of service in the regular army remained fixed at twelve years, the Army Enlistment Act of 1870 provided that soldiers could serve the first six years with the colours and then transfer to the reserves for the remainder. Recruitment was central to these changes. The introduction of short service enlistment would not only allow for the creation of a large and effective reserve, but the reformers anticipated that the new system would attract a better quality of recruit. However, there were problems. A shorter enlistment period increased the annual demand for recruits. Likewise, it meant that more men were being discharged every year, which some critics argued 'allowed experienced men to leave the army sooner'. This had the additional effect of increasing the number of ex-soldiers in the civilian labour market.[29]

As the imperial government grappled with the problems of military efficiency, enlistment and administration, it was apparent that pensions, post-service employment and the successful reintroduction of the soldier into civilian life were becoming increasingly important issues. Government investigations conducted in 1876–77 and 1894–95 left no doubt as to the difficulties encountered by many ex-servicemen.[30] Nevertheless, apart from providing a small and inadequate pension, and reserving a few clerical positions in certain government departments, the state avoided further responsibility by hiding behind the mantle of *laissez-faire* liberalism. Officials argued that a number of private charities and agencies already existed, such as the National Association for the Employment of Reserve and Discharged Soldiers (established in 1885), which provided welcome assistance to unemployed or destitute ex-servicemen and their families.[31] This attitude was reinforced by the findings of a select committee which delved into employment opportunities for retired soldiers and sailors in 1895. In addition, the Marquis of Lansdowne, the Secretary of State for War, emphasised the isolation many veterans experienced upon their return to civilian life and observed that society tended to regard all ex-servicemen as a 'peculiar class of men segregated from the rest of the community'.[32]

## National efficiency, the second Anglo-Boer War and reconstruction, 1900–14

The increasing interest in the welfare of the ex-soldier, army pensioner and reservist evident in Britain between 1900 and 1914 stemmed from the experience of the second Anglo-Boer War. The military catastrophes suffered by British arms in the opening stages of the conflict jolted an overconfident and complacent people. It provided an impetus for critical national self-examination and spawned numerous political, social and philanthropic organisations and societies aimed at reforming and improving Britain's national ideal. As George Bernard Shaw, the playwright and social critic, observed, 'Whatever else the war may do or undo, it at least turns its fierce searchlights on official, administrative and military perfunctoriness'.[33] 'National Efficiency' became the battle cry and catch-phrase for such critics. Tariff reform, compulsory military service, the Boy Scout movement, state-assisted emigration, eugenics and, more broadly, the concept of social imperialism were promoted as means of rebuilding Britain's resolve and national character.[34]

The dominions were also concerned with the condition of their own national fabrics during this period. Imperial defence, military reform and compulsory military service occupied the attention of a growing number of colonial politicians and empire-minded interests keen to reinforce the physical bonds of empire.[35] Compounding these issues was a deep-seated fear in the dominions that their Anglo-Saxon heritage would be diluted by the uncontrolled influx of 'racially inferior' immigrants from southern and eastern Europe and Asia. Such xenophobia reinforced Australian efforts to prevent the 'yellow peril' from gaining a foothold. The rigorous implementation of the 'White' Australia policy, which effectively barred the vast majority of Asiatics from entering the dominion, was paralleled by Canada's hardening nativistic attitudes towards recently arrived eastern European immigrants. To an increasing number of Canadians, these peasants clad in sheepskin coats were unassimilable and, moreover, untrustworthy. Demands were made for a more selective immigration strategy directed at promoting British migration and restricting the influx of these 'dangerous' foreigners. The resignation in 1905 of Clifford Sifton, the Liberal Minister of the Interior and architect of Canada's 'open door' policy, signalled this reorientation in immigration policy. Meanwhile, as the debates were waged over the dilution of the dominions' Anglo-Saxon heritage and the empire's military unpreparedness, the largest ever trans-oceanic migration of British subjects to the dominions was proceeding. It was an event whose significance was not lost on empire migration enthusiasts, military reformers or dominion and imperial politicians alike.[36]

Canada was the only dominion to provide a repatriation programme for its veterans who had fought in the second Anglo-Boer War. In 1908, Canada enacted the Volunteer Bounty Act which authorised the award of two adjoining quarter sections or 320 acres of dominion lands to Canadian volunteers who had served with the Canadian contingents or with British forces during the South African conflict. The usual fees levied for homestead entry and land patents were waived. However, each applicant was obliged to meet the homesteading provisions pre-scribed under the Dominion Lands Act of 1872. Under these provisions, each applicant was required to submit a homestead entry before 31 December 1910, and begin residence and cultivation on his claim within six months after the deadline. Alternatively, the applicant could surrender his rights to the homestead and receive scrip valued at $160, later increased to $500 in 1912. Scrip, which was transferable, was issued by the Minister of the Interior on warrants issued by the Minister of Militia.[37] The final result was a tremendous windfall for prairie land speculators as the land grant system deteriorated into the worst form of military gratuity. The Canadian Liberals, in opposition after the election of 1911, sharply attacked R. L. Borden's Conservative government, condemning the cash bonus system as nothing more than a 'big rake-off' which allowed the speculator 'an opportunity to make money without the volunteer doing what the country intended should be done'.[38] For example, of the 1.25 million acres of scrip taken up in Saskatchewan, more than 95 per cent was patented by speculators and, in Alberta, the figure was even higher at 96 per cent: 'a tribute to the acquisitiveness of the speculator rather than to the pertinacity of the South Africa volunteer'.[39]

In addition to efforts to attract Canada's own Boer War veterans to the land, there were attempts to promote the immigration and settlement of discharged British soldiers, reservists and army pensioners. In December 1906, the volatile Sam Hughes, a future Conservative Minister of Militia, tabled a resolution calling for a veterans land settlement policy on the Canadian prairies. He asserted, as he had often done in the past, that the interests of Canada and the empire would be better served with the settlement of honourably discharged British soldiers and their families than by immigrants from eastern Europe. He lamented that private enterprise had not devised a system of introducing this very valuable immigrant to Canada when it was acknowledged by the railway companies interviewed by him that ex-soldiers made good foremen and section hands. Hughes urged that the government should subsidise a settlement programme on the prairies for these men.[40]

The Canadian government had in fact taken some interest in the issue since before the Boer War, but its undertakings had been limited to the distribution of emigration pamphlets to libraries at the regimental depots. After the conflict, the Canadian government launched a publicity campaign aimed at British ex-soldiers and reservists interested in emigrating to Canada, but refrained, much to Hughes's disappointment, from initiating a state-aided settlement programme specifically for British ex-servicemen. Rather, British ex-service migrants interested in agriculture were processed using existing dominion land settlement legislation.[41]

The newly founded Commonwealth of Australia did not offer any inducement for its veterans to settle as farmers after the war. However, intense public and parliamentary pressure was exerted upon the New Zealand government to give preferential treatment to those veterans wanting to farm upon their return from South Africa. The opponents of Prime Minister R. J. Seddon's government argued that an excellent opportunity existed for settling healthy, eager veterans who were prepared to venture limited amounts of capital in agriculture. Critics warned that such an opportunity should not be squandered, not least because the moral fibre of these valiant men was at stake. 'Such a policy would be far better than allowing them to knock about the hotels, drinking bad whiskey ... and knocking their cheques down, or competing with the workers of the city for employment'.[42] Even more galling for the opposition members were advertisements in English newspapers offering two million acres of freehold land to intending British immigrants when no land was available for returning New Zealand veterans. 'These young men had been appealing to the Government for land, but could not get it, and here was the Government pushing land on people in the United Kingdom who had not asked for it, and perhaps did not want it at all.'[43] Seddon was unmoved and made it clear in 1903 that no distinction or preferential treatment would be given to any prospective settler, 'whether returned troopers, or persons now resident in our colony, or persons of the farming class coming here from the Mother-country'.[44] Everyone would be given equal treatment.

South Africa was a special case and must be examined in the light of the British government's attempt to foster white racial harmony and create a new rural order in South Africa after 1902. The architect of Britain's reconstruction policy was Sir Alfred Milner, British High Commissioner for South Africa and Governor of the Cape and Transvaal between 1897 and 1905. For Milner, economic recovery was the key to a new and vigorous *British* South Africa.[45] His chief fear was Afrikaner nationalism which he regarded as the most dangerous and destabilising force in southern Africa. But to foster racial harmony, Afrikaners had to be encouraged to participate in the new industrial order and British immigrants had to be attracted and resettled in large numbers in the rural areas. The first duty of the reconstruction administration was therefore to 'settle and anglicise' South Africa using British emigrants and capital.[46] In order to offset Afrikaner political power, which was concentrated in the rural areas, Milner sought large numbers of loyal, English-speaking settlers to infiltrate the rural districts. The thousands of imperial troops awaiting demobilisation provided an obvious source. He readily admitted that it would be difficult to settle these men, who were for the most part agriculturally inexperienced. However, Milner believed that if they could be induced to stay, they would inculcate loyalty (or fear) among the rural Afrikaners, provide a firm foundation for additional settlement from Britain, and, because of their military experience, prove invaluable as a trained militia should the Boers attempt another insurrection.

Milner's policy failed miserably. Of the thousands of imperial troops who had fought in South Africa fewer than 2,000 participated in the government-sponsored resettlement programme. According to the novelist John Buchan, a member of Milner's reconstruction administration and attached to the Land Settlement Department between 1902–03, the conditions which were essential to success were found wanting.[47] For a start, the soldiers lacked the initial capital necessary to outfit a farm in South Africa properly and, as a result, they showed little enthusiasm for the project. Moreover, the work of the Land Department which was to co-ordinate British settlement work was agonisingly slow. Essential surveys, inspections and land purchasing were carried out neither quickly nor efficiently. The general muddle fostered discontent and impatience amongst the more enterprising soldiers and they soon lost interest, returned to Britain or sought employment elsewhere. By July 1902 very little had been accomplished. Despite a large injection of funds and the reorganisation of the entire settlement operation, the onset of a severe drought and a wide outbreak of cattle fever dampened official expectations and hampered further the efforts of those who had not already been 'choked off' by maladministration and unforeseen natural calamities.[48]

The lacklustre performance of Milner's military colonisation and assisted emigration schemes did not deter public interest or philanthropic action in securing a better life for the ex-soldier, army pensioner and reservist at home or overseas. As military reform and imperial defence became increasingly important political issues in Edwardian Britain, the plight of the British ex-servicemen and army pensioners attracted the attention of a growing number of philanthropists and social reformers. In fact, immediately before the outbreak of World War I there were more charitable societies and self-help associations than ever before devoted specifically 'to fight the inequalities suffered by British servicemen and their families'.[49] There was even an organisation which assisted ex-servicemen to emigrate to the overseas dominions.

The Naval and Military Emigration League, founded in November 1909, was the only British emigration society which dealt exclusively with former military personnel. Though lacking the reputation and connections of the earlier pioneering agencies, such as the East End Emigration Fund, the Salvation Army and the Self-Help Emigration Society, it sought to establish its presence through a determined propaganda and lobbying campaign. A vocal proponent of imperial defence, and an active participant in the intense public discussion of these years about greater defence co-operation and compulsory military service, the NMEL provided a useful channel through which several dominions, and especially Canada, were able to recruit British military specialists for their permanent forces.[50]

The general aim of the NMEL was to furnish ex-servicemen with information about employment and settlement opportunities in the dominions. The organisation was chiefly concerned with the welfare of enlisted men, particularly those with little or no pension money.

Although it did extend a helping hand to officers of limited means, the agency focused its attention upon ex-servicemen who were out of work and had no prospects in Britain. The League found jobs in the dominions for its clients and advanced the necessary money for passage and related expenses. It also endeavoured to operate on a self-supporting basis; recipients were encouraged to repay money that had been advanced. The League, in the words of its own literature, was not 'a commercial institution, and [would] not . . . under any circumstances, look to make a profit. At the same time, it [was] not a charity'.[51]

The majority of the ex-servicemen whom the League sent to Canada were found satisfactory, but the government was extremely disappointed by the very small percentage who turned to farming. As early as 1903, senior immigration officials had reported that ex-soldiers rarely made good farmers in Canada and those who did take up farming seldom remained on the land for any length of time 'as most of them do not seem to care for steady work'.[52] W. D. Scott, Superintendent of Immigration in Ottawa, reported that 'whether it is the earlier training and lack of initiative, I do not know, but in any case, they make poor farmers . . . They seldom take to agricultural work, preferring rather to stay in the cities where numbers of them can be found working as elevator men (and) janitors'.[53] This trend continued right up to the outbreak of war. Of the 314 subsidised ex-servicemen who arrived in Canada during 1913, only twenty-nine took up farming.[54] British Army pensioners proved to be particularly troublesome and the most embarrassing from the Department of Interior's viewpoint. After several disappointing placements, Scott warned the Canadian High Commission that army pensioners were better left in the mother country. 'Our employment Agents will scarcely touch any more charitable organisation or army pensioners . . . Almost without exception they complain that such men are worse than useless, owing to the trouble they give in being placed.' Superintendent Scott advised the government not to contemplate or initiate an increased absorption of the ex-soldier class.[55]

The outbreak of war in August 1914 effectively ended the NMEL's operations, but not before a total of 2,388 men, women and children had emigrated to the dominions under the League's auspices. Canada remained the favoured dominion, in part because of its geographical proximity, and it would seem that the Canadian government did more than any other dominion to assist British veterans. Certainly, Canada benefited from the recruitment of these professional soldiers into its permanent force. They made an important contribution to the dominion's ability to shoulder an increased burden of responsibility for its own defence successfully. Canada's increasing military capacity, in turn, served Britain's advantage both by reducing commitments for the

British forces, and improving the pool of potential reinforcements that might be available in the event of a major war in Europe or Asia. The collaboration by both governments with a philanthropic organisation to promote Canadian military development was also significant for it demonstrated the willingness of some officials to use private means to meet specialised emigration requirements, especially at a time when the British government steadfastly refused to intervene in any way in the promotion of everyday emigration.

However, the NMEL's achievements must not be overstated. Despite its network of local, voluntary committees and the endorsements from many prominent imperialists throughout the empire, it operated on a shoestring and failed to secure large-scale official support. Moreover, it failed to overcome Britain's commitment to *laissez-faire*. Indeed, the fear of a European war and the need to keep military reserves at home was the British government's overriding concern which, in the final analysis, was the greatest single factor limiting the NMEL's operations. In the end, it did little more than assist in recruiting a few specialists for the Canadian permanent force and gave a handful of veterans, who might not have had the chance otherwise, the opportunity to start a new life overseas. None the less, the NMEL's activities highlighted the growing importance which some elements of Edwardian society attached to the welfare of the empire's soldiery. Indeed, many of the debates which emerged on post-World War I soldier settlement, migration and post-service employment had been clearly rehearsed. What is most startling, however, is that these same lessons were 'forgotten' with the outbreak of war. That soldiers were less inclined to undertake agricultural work, for example, seemed to have been ignored by many politicians and officials who, in the latter stages of World War I, were determined to implement comprehensive soldier settlement policies throughout the empire upon its conclusion. It is to these schemes and the debates which surrounded their implementation that we now turn our attention.

## Notes

1 McGill University Libraries, Department of Rare Books and Special Collections, *The Veteran*, I, July 1918, p. 19. *The Veteran* was the national mouthpiece of the Great War Veterans Association (GWVA), the largest Canadian veterans' organisation created during World War I. The first issue was published in December 1917.
2 W. H. Warman, *The Soldier Colonists*, London, 1918, x. For an example of the quote used by Warman see Tacitus, *The Annals*, trans. John Jackson, IV, London, 1951, pp. 152–3.
3 W. L. Morton, *The Kingdom of Canada*, Toronto, 1963, p. 40; W. J. Eccles, *Canada Under Louis XIV 1663–1701*, Toronto, 1964, pp. 46–52; Robert England, 'Discharged and disbanded soldiers in Canada prior to 1914', *Canadian Historical Review*, XXVII,

1946, pp. 1–2.

4 Jack Verney, *The Good Regiment: The Carignan-Salières Regiment in Canada, 1665–1668*, London, 1991, especially the nominal roll in Appendix B, pp. 145–85.

5 C. P. Stacey, 'Halifax as an international strategic factor, 1749–1949', *Canadian Historical Association, Report*, 1949, pp. 46–55; J. S. Martell, 'Military settlements in Nova Scotia after the War of 1812', *Collections of the Nova Scotia Historical Society*, XXIV, 1938, p. 75.

6 Norman Macdonald, *Canada, 1763–1841 Immigration and Settlement*, Toronto, 1939, pp. 39–67; Paul Douglas Dickson, ' "We prefer trade to dominion": imperial policy and the settlement of the King's Royal Regiment', *Ontario History*, LXXXII, 1990, pp. 129–48; Christopher Moore, 'The disposition to settle: the Royal Highland Emigrants and Loyalist settlement in Upper Canada, 1784', *Ontario History*, LXXVI, 1984, pp. 306–25. For an examination of the United Empire Loyalists and their resettlement see Christopher Moore, *The Loyalists: Revolution, Exile, Settlement*, Toronto, 1984, pp. 118–95.

7 England, 'Discharged and disbanded soldiers', pp. 4–12.

8 Patrick Colquhoun, *Treatise on the Wealth, Power and Resources of the British Empire in every quarter of the World*, 2nd ed., 1815, pp. 422–31; R. Koebner, *Empire*, Cambridge, 1961, p. 292.

9 Public Records Office, London (hereafter PRO), Colonial Office Papers (hereafter CO), CO 43/23, Lord Bathurst, Secretary of State for War and the Colonies, to Drummond, 20 March and 31 May 1815. Eric Jarvis, 'Military land granting in Upper Canada following the War of 1812', *Ontario History*, LXVII, 1975, pp. 121–34; A. S. Morton, *A History of the Canadian West to 1870–71*, Toronto, n.d., pp. 592–3; W. A. B. Douglas, 'The blessings of the land: naval officers in Upper Canada, 1815–1841', in Adrian Preston and Peter Dennis, eds, *Swords and Covenants*, London, 1976, pp. 42–73.

10 R. G. Riddell, 'A study in the land policy of the Colonial Office, 1763–1855', *Canadian Historical Review*, XVIII, 1937, p. 394.

11 *Ibid.*, p. 393.

12 Helen I. Cowan, *British Emigration to North America, 1783–1837*, Toronto, 1928, pp. 65–95; George F. Playter, 'An account of three military settlements in eastern Ontario – Perth, Lanark and Richmond, 1815–20', *Ontario Historical Society Papers and Records*, XX, 1923, pp. 98–104; Martell, 'Military settlements in Nova Scotia', pp. 77–8.

13 A. R. M. Lower, 'Immigration and settlement in Canada, 1812–1820', *Canadian Historical Review*, III, 1922, p. 40.

14 Martell, 'Military settlements in Nova Scotia', p. 75.

15 J. K. Johnson, 'The Chelsea pensioners in Upper Canada', *Ontario History*, LIII, 1961, p. 274.

16 *Ibid.*, p. 276. Johnson estimates that 4,000 veterans commuted their pensions. The lion's share, 3,200, emigrated to British North America while the remaining 800 travelled to the Australian colonies.

17 *Ibid.*, pp. 279–85; PRO, War Office Papers (hereafter WO), WO 43/542/part 2/ff. 149, Aylmer to the Secretary of the Treasury, 10 July 1832; ff. 146–7, Aylmer to Viscount Goderich, Secretary of State for War and the Colonies, 20 August 1832.

18 G. K. Raudzens, 'A successful military settlement: Earl Grey's enrolled pensioners of 1846 in Canada', *Canadian Historical Review*, LII, 1971, pp. 392–3.

19 For a detailed examination of the Albany settlement see I. E. Edwards, *The 1820 Settlers in South Africa*, London, 1934. The colonial defence argument of Miss Edwards is re-examined in an excellent study of early nineteenth century British emigration policy by H. J. M. Johnston, *British Emigration Policy 1815–1830*, Oxford, 1972.

20 T. R. H. Davenport, *South Africa: A Modern History*, London, 1987, pp. 43–4; Monica Wilson and Leonard Thompson, eds, *The Oxford History of South Africa*, I, Oxford, 1969, pp. 278–9; A. J. Cook, 'Irish settlers in the Eastern Cape in the early nineteenth century', *Southern African-Irish Studies*, I, 1991, pp. 100–12.

21 Wilson and Thompson, *Oxford History of South Africa*, I, pp. 281–3; British Parlia-

mentary Papers (hereafter BPP), nos 2202 and 2352 of 1857 and no. 389 of 1858.

22 *Ibid.* K. P. T. Tankard, 'The Lady Kennaway girls', *Southern African-Irish Studies*, II, 1992, pp. 278–86; *idem*, 'Effects of Irish versus German immigration on the eastern frontier, 1857–1858', *Southern African-Irish Studies*, I, 1991, pp. 113–21.

23 W. R. Jourdain, *Land Legislation and Settlement in New Zealand*, Wellington, 1925, pp. 22–3; W. R. Mayhew, 'The Returned Services Association, 1916–1943', unpublished M.A. thesis, University of Otago, 1943, pp. 131–3. For an excellent insight into the turbulent relations between the British and Maori in the mid-nineteenth century see James Belich, *The New Zealand Wars and the Victorian Interpretation of Racial Conflict*, Auckland, 1988.

24 Nicholas Mansergh, *The Commonwealth Experience*, 2 vols, 2nd ed., London, 1982, I, p. 53 and pp. 145–6; C. P. Stacey, *Canada and the British Army*, London, 1938, pp. 125–6.

25 A. P. Thornton, *The Imperial Idea and Its Enemies*, 2nd ed., London, 1985, p. 24; Morton, *The Critical Years*, p. 250; Stacey, *Canada and the British Army*, pp. 207–8.

26 A. F. J. Artibise, *Winnipeg: A Social History of Urban Growth 1874–1914*, Montreal, 1975, p. 105.

27 Canada, *Debates of the House of Commons* (hereafter *Debates*), 1885, IV, p. 3376.

28 A. S. Morton and Chester Martin, *History of Prairie Settlement and 'Dominion Lands' Policy*, Toronto, 1938, p. 516; England, 'Discharged and disbanded soldiers', p. 17.

29 Brian Bond, 'Recruiting the Victorian army, 1870–92', *Victorian Studies*, V, 1962, pp. 331–8; *idem*, 'The effect of the Cardwell reforms in army organisation, 1874–1904', *Journal of the Royal United Services Institute*, CV, 1960, pp. 515–24; A. V. Tucker, 'Army and society in England, 1870–1900: a reassessment of the Cardwell reforms', *Journal of British Studies*, II, 1963, pp. 100–41; A. R. Skelley, *The Victorian Army at Home*, London, 1977, pp. 251–4 and 212.

30 BPP, *Report of the Select Committee on the Employment of Soldiers, Sailors, and Marines in Civil Departments of the Public Service* (c. 356), 1876; *Report of the Select Committee on the Employment of Soldiers, Sailors, and Marines in Civil Departments of the Public Service* (c. 1877); *Report of the Select Committee on Retired Soldiers' and Sailors' Employment* (c. 258); *Report of the Select Committee on Retired Soldiers' and Sailors' Employment* (c. 338), 1895.

31 Gwynn Harries-Jenkins, *The Army in Victorian Society*, London, 1977; Edward M. Spiers, *The Army and Society, 1815–1914*, London, 1980; Peter Burroughs, 'Promoting thrift, sobriety and discipline in the British army: the establishment of military savings banks', *Histoire sociale – Social History*, XIV, 1981, pp. 323–37. For a description of the British Army's pension system, its administration and shortcomings in the nineteenth century, see Skelley, *Victorian Army*, pp. 204–18. Also see Peter Reese, *Homecoming Heroes*, London, 1992, pp. 31–74, for an excellent overview of the plethora of associations which were established to help ex-servicemen and their families prior to 1914.

32 PRO, WO 33/70, Civil Employment of Discharged Soldiers and Army Reserve Men (1897); extract from a circular letter drawn up by the Secretary of State for War to various government departments, 27 June 1896.

33 Quotation cited in Geoffrey Searle, *The Quest for National Efficiency*, Oxford, 1971, p. 39.

34 For a detailed discussion on the development of British social imperialist doctrine and politics, see H. John Field, *Towards a Programme of Imperial Life*, Westport, Conn., 1982; Bernard Semmel, *Imperialism and Social Reform*, New York, 1960; Samuel Hynes, *The Edwardian Turn of Mind*, London, 1968. For the debate on social imperialism and assisted emigration, see H. L. Malchow, 'Trade unions and emigration in late Victorian England: a national lobby for state aid', *Journal of British Studies*, XV, 1976, pp. 92–116; *idem*, *Population Pressures: Emigration and Government in Late Nineteenth Century Britain*, Palo Alto, California, 1979; Desmond Glynn, ' "Exporting outcast London": assisted emigration to Canada, 1886–1914', *Histoire sociale – Social History*, XV, 1982, pp. 209–38; Keith Williams, ' "A way out of our troubles": the

politics of Empire Settlement, 1900–22', in Stephen Constantine, ed., *Emigrants and Empire*, Manchester, 1990, pp. 22–44; Stephen Constantine, 'Empire migration and social reform 1880–1950', in Colin G. Pooley and Ian D. Whyte, eds, *Migrants, Emigrants and Immigrants: A Social History of Migration*, London, 1991, pp. 62–83.

35 D. C. Gordon, *The Dominion Partnership in Imperial Defence, 1870–1914*, Baltimore, 1965; Richard A. Preston, *Canada and 'Imperial Defense'. A Study of the Origins of the British Commonwealth's Defense Organisation, 1867–1919*, Durham, NC, 1965; John Barrett, *Falling In. Australians and 'Boy Conscription', 1911–1915*, Sydney, 1979; Jeffery Grey, *A Military History of Australia*, Cambridge, 1990, pp. 67–86; Desmond Morton, *A Military History of Canada*, Edmonton, 1985, pp. 122–9; Carman Miller, 'Sir Frederick William Borden and military reform, 1896–1911', *Canadian Historical Review*, L, 1969, pp. 265–84; Desmond Morton, 'The Canadian military experience in the First World War, 1914–1918', in R. J. Q. Adams, ed., *The Great War, 1914–18*, London, 1990, pp. 79–100.

36 R. C. Brown and Ramsay Cook, *Canada 1896–1921: A Nation Transformed*, Toronto, 1974, pp. 54–74; Donald Avery, *'Dangerous Foreigners'. European Immigrant Workers and Labour Radicalism in Canada, 1896–1932*, Toronto, 1979, pp. 16–64; Stuart Macintyre, *The Oxford History of Australia*, IV, *1901–1942*, Melbourne, 1986, pp. 122–44; Avner Offer, *The First World War: An Agrarian Interpretation*, Oxford, 1989, pp. 81–214.

37 *Statutes of Canada*, 7–8 Edward VII, Chapter 67; 2 George V, Chapter 52, 1912.

38 Canada, *Debates*, 1911–1912, IV, col. 6450.

39 Morton and Martin, *'Dominion Lands' Policy*, pp. 424–5. Of the 1,063,360 acres of scrip available in Alberta, 1,017,303 acres were patented by land speculators.

40 Canada, *Debates*, 1906–07, I, cols 736–9.

41 Kent Fedorowich, 'The migration of British ex-servicemen to Canada and the role of the Naval and Military Emigration League, 1899–1914', *Histoire sociale – Social History*, XXV, 1992, pp. 75–99.

42 *New Zealand Parliamentary Debates* (hereafter *NZPD*), 1903, CXXIII, p. 34.

43 *Ibid.*, 1903, CXXVI, p. 265.

44 *Ibid.*, p. 258.

45 Donald Denoon, *A Grand Illusion: The Failure of Imperial Policy in the Transvaal Colony during the Period of Reconstruction 1900–1905*, London, 1973, p. 37; Shula Marks and Stanley Trapido, 'Lord Milner and the South African state', *History Workshop Journal*, issue 8, 1979, p. 69; Kent Fedorowich, 'Anglicisation and the politicisation of British immigration to South Africa, 1899–1929', *Journal of Imperial and Commonwealth History*, XIX, 1991, pp. 222–46.

46 House of Lords Records Office (hereafter HLRO), John St Loe Strachey Papers, S/15/2/8 and /6, Sir Percy Fitzpatrick to Strachey, 9 November and 7 August 1900.

47 PRO, CO 721/2/f. 39, minutes of a meeting between the Oversea Settlement Committee and Buchan, 11 March 1919. For an analysis of the insufficiencies and political implications of Milner's rural reconstruction policy see Denoon, *A Grand Illusion* and M. Streak, *Lord Milner's Immigration Policy for the Transvaal 1897–1905*, Johannesburg, 1970. Also see John Buchan, *The African Colony*, London, 1903, pp. 255–83; idem, *Memory Hold-The-Door*, London, 1940, pp. 109–11; Paul Rich, ' "Milnerism and a ripping yarn": Transvaal land settlement and John Buchan's novel "Prester John" 1901–10', in Belinda Bozzoli, ed., *Town and Countryside in the Transvaal*, Johannesburg, 1983, pp. 412–29. The participation of Canadian soldiers in Milner's settlement scheme is discussed by Carman Miller, *Painting the Map Red: Canada and the South African War, 1899–1902*, Montreal, 1993, pp. 368–90.

48 For a detailed examination of Milner's soldier settlement plans see Streak, *Milner's Immigration Policy*, pp. 26–40; BPP, 1901, Cd. 626, *Report of the Lands Settlement Commission, South Africa, 28 November 1900*; HLRO, Strachey Papers, S/3/2/2 and /13, Buchan to Strachey, 13 October 1901 and 16 June 1902; L. S. Amery Papers, Box C.25, Milner to Amery, 26 January 1903; Buchan to Amery, 6 April 1903; Milner to Amery, 20 May 1903. Although the land settlement experiment was a failure, settlers in the Orange River Colony had been more successful than their counterparts in the

Transvaal. Colin Murray, *Black Mountain: Land, Class and Power in the Eastern Orange Free State, 1880s to 1980s*, Edinburgh, 1992, pp. 52–84.

**49** Reese, *Homecoming Heroes*, p. 73.

**50** R. J. Q. Adams and Philip P. Pourier, *The Conscription Controversy in Great Britain, 1900–18*, London, 1987; Peter Dennis, *The Territorial Army, 1906–1940*, Woodbridge, Suffolk, 1987, pp. 4–37; Ann Summers, 'Militarism in Britain before the Great War', *History Workshop*, issue 2, 1976, pp. 104–23.

**51** National Archives of Canada (hereafter NA), Immigration Branch files of the Department of the Interior, RG 76, vol. 585, f. 821430, part 1, 'Objects of the Naval and Military Emigration League', 1910, p. 4.

**52** *Ibid.*, vol. 202, f. 87046, part 1, T. Southworth, Director of Colonisation, Toronto, to W. D. Scott, 17 January 1903.

**53** *Ibid.*, vol. 585, f. 821430, part 1, Scott to Frank Oliver, Minister of the Interior (1905–10), 10 December 1910; Scott to W. W. Cory, Deputy Minister of the Interior, 31 October 1910.

**54** *Ibid.*, Cory memorandum, 12 January 1914.

**55** *Ibid.*, vol. 202, f. 87046, part 1, Scott to J. Obed Smith, Assistant Superintendent of Immigration in London, 6 March 1910; E. Terrill, Government Employment Agent, Wooler, Ontario, to Scott, 25 April 1910.

# CHAPTER TWO

# Empire migration, soldier settlement and British wartime initiative, 1914–22

For many in the British Empire, the long struggle in Europe between 1914 and 1919 demonstrated the importance of imperial co-operation, unity and self-sufficiency, goals which were increasingly emphasised as the war intensified. The war presented the opportunity for governments to shed older, established conventions, proceed along new paths and experiment with fresh ideas. Some of these schemes were applied to social planning and reconstruction, some to 'constructive imperialism: a renewed determination to invigorate the Empire as a bastion of British ideals and a bulwark of democracy'.[1] The majority of these high-minded imperial projects either did not survive the war or never got beyond the drawing-board. However, there were a few tangible achievements. Foremost amongst them was the free passage scheme for British ex-servicemen and women which operated between 1919 and 1922 under the auspices of the Overseas Settlement Committee (OSC), a body established in January 1919 and itself a creation of wartime imperial co-operation. The ex-servicemen's scheme was, in part, a response to the emotional outpouring generated by the war which led the imperial government to reward its fighting men and women for the sacrifices they endured for 'King and Country'. But it would be an over-simplification to state that free passage was granted merely on the basis of services rendered. Its inauguration must also be seen in the light of Britain's wartime anxieties, its turbulent domestic political scene after 1918 and the imperial government's attempts to grapple with the complex problems of demobilisation, veterans' discontent, industrial regeneration and chronic unemployment. Moreover, the failure of the British government to launch a successful domestic colonisation scheme also had a direct bearing on the implementation of this empire migration project.

The outbreak of war effectively ended imperial migration for the next five years. 'Of course everything here is all war and excitement, and

[ 25 ]

consequently the matter of emigration has fallen very far into the background', reported W. W. Cory, Canada's Deputy Minister of the Interior in August 1914.[2] W. D. Scott, Superintendent of Immigration in Ottawa agreed. Policy discussions had been 'totally eclipsed by the war'. Conditions were so 'abnormal', he explained, that 'I scarcely know what to recommend'.[3] The Colonial Office used stronger imagery. Emigration was 'at present virtually dead and shows no signs of early revival'.[4] It emphasised that all emigration would be actively discouraged for the duration of the war, particularly in cases of persons of military age. '*All* emigration of persons capable of [war] work should be stopped', insisted Arthur Steel-Maitland, Parliamentary Under-Secretary for the Colonies, in 1915. Bonar Law, the Canadian-born Secretary of State, emphatically agreed.[5] Subsequently, all dominion governments dutifully adhered to the policy of disallowing the entry of British immigrants eligible for war work or military service.

Post-war imperial migration was not regarded as a major issue by the imperial government until the summer of 1916, but thereafter its close association with post-war reconstruction made it an increasingly important matter. There were two sources of pressure for positive state intervention in the resettlement, rehabilitation and retraining of British ex-servicemen, including a state-aided free passage scheme to the dominions. The first was the Royal Colonial Institute (RCI) which initiated and directed the campaign during the war. The second source resulted from the failure of the Board of Agriculture and the fledgling Ministry of Reconstruction to formulate an appealing and large-scale domestic colonisation scheme between 1915 and 1920.

Imperial migration had always been a prominent issue on the agenda of the RCI, but after the Boer War, and especially after the formation in 1910 of the Standing Emigration Committee representing voluntary emigration agencies and organisations, the RCI assumed a leading public role. It set out both to raise public awareness of the advantages of redirecting British emigrants to destinations within rather than outside the empire, and to impress upon the government the value of a state-aided imperial migration policy.[6] The RCI was not deterred from its purpose by the outbreak of war. As early as November 1914 the Standing Emigration Committee requested permission to send an official deputation to Lewis Harcourt, Bonar Law's predecessor as Colonial Secretary, to discuss the employment and emigration of ex-servicemen after the war.[7]

The Colonial Office promptly poured cold water on this initiative by playing down the importance of post-war emigration in general. Colonial Office officials were certain that the imperial government would not commit itself to any policy pronouncements until the final recommendations of the Dominions Royal Commission (DRC) had been tabled. 'An additional reason for going slow', minuted one official, 'is that no one can now foresee whether it will be desirable to encourage in any way the emigration of men after the war.'[8] Emigration, another Colonial Office official remarked, was not one of the first but one of the last expedients the government could implement. The nation could not afford to bleed itself of vital manpower during reconstruction. Furthermore soldier resettlement was 'only a small fractional part of the huge and infinitely more complex problem' of imperial post-war population adjustment. The Colonial Office was adamant that the RCI initiative could not be sanctioned. It was condemned by the bureaucrats as premature, inopportune and mischievous.[9]

Preoccupied with the immediate demands of the war it was obvious that the Colonial Office had neither the time, the inclination nor the enthusiasm for such an issue. It maintained that the imperial government had given no indication of changing its pre-war policy of 'neither encouraging (nor) discouraging emigration' after the war.[10] In fact, the Colonial Office was unsure whether post-war emigration even fell within its jurisdiction. The Board of Trade, it suggested, with its network of 400 employment exchanges nationwide, was better suited to undertake administrative responsibility once the government had chosen a policy. Officials of the Board of Trade were inclined to agree.[11]

Undeterred, the RCI pushed ahead for an audience. Its president at this crucial juncture, a former Governor-General of Canada, threw his customary energy and determination into the fray. An ardent social reformer with a keen personal interest in emigration, and a passionate disciple of imperial unity, Grey provided the RCI with strong leadership and unquestioned prestige during his five years in office (1912–17).[12] He was deeply concerned about the potential threat posed by large numbers of idle, restless, unemployed ex-servicemen on the nation's social and political stability after the war. Alarmed by recent political developments in Britain since the turn of the century, in particular the rise of socialism, Grey found a receptive audience at the RCI who shared the same deep concerns over the 'organic' nature of British society and empire. He and his RCI colleagues feared that demobilisation would bring unacceptably high levels of unemployment and ensuing political unrest which would accelerate socialism to the detriment of the *status quo*. 'It is obvious that when the war is over there will be thousands of ex-soldiers and sailors out of employment; industrious, disciplined men who if left to themselves may become a social and political menace.'[13] Like many others, he was convinced that the outdoor experience of British troops in the trenches would inculcate a strong spirit of adventure which 'will have taken so strong a hold as to make them most reluctant to return to the humdrum conditions of their old life'.[14] To harness this constructive but potentially dangerous energy and avert post-war political and social unrest, he advocated large-scale overseas soldier settlement projects which would guarantee work and a future for returning soldiers.

Reluctantly the government partially relented. Bonar Law, who had recently succeeded Harcourt as Colonial Secretary, and Lord Selborne, President of the Board of Agriculture, agreed to meet an RCI deputation on 22 July 1915, although the permanent officials at the Colonial Office wrote off the meeting as a complete waste of time.[15] The deputation was dominated by members of the reconstituted Standing Emigration Committee which had been given the unmanageable title of the 'After the War' Empire Land Settlement and Rural Employment Committee (ELSC). Formed in early 1915 and chaired by Earl Grey, the new committee was given the task of redrafting and reinvigorating Grey's earlier proposals into a new platform from which to carry on the fight for positive state intervention in the migration field.

Bonar Law appeared somewhat sympathetic to the deputation's entreaties. However, he made it absolutely clear that he would make no commitment nor issue any policy statement. Privately, however, he supported the pervasive Colonial Office tenet that the RCI's efforts were hasty, untimely and inappropriate. His carefully worded response was a masterful display of official intransigence sugared in a coating of public courtesy. Moreover, the discussion of overseas settlement was deflected by Law's emphasis on the Board of Agriculture's investigation of domestic soldier colonisation.[16] The RCI went away empty handed.

Undaunted, the RCI persevered. It kept post-war emigration and land settlement and, above all, the needs of the ex-servicemen in the forefront of the public's attention. On 10 February 1916 the RCI despatched Rider Haggard, imperial adventure novelist, agricultural reformer and active RCI member on a fact-finding mission to the dominions to canvass official opinions of plans to assist ex-servicemen to settle in the empire overseas after the war. The impact of Haggard's mission and the overwhelming response he received in most of the dominions exceeded even the most optimistic RCI expectations. The Colonial Office was also surprised by its success.[17] Immediately upon Haggard's return in late July, the RCI marshalled its forces for another assault on the government. Another deputation was formed and presented its views to Bonar Law and Lord Crawford, the President of the Board of Agriculture, on 10 August 1916. The deputation, led by the intrepid Earl Grey, applauded and endorsed the British government's examination of domestic soldier settlement, but repeated its previous demand for the establishment of an Imperial Migration and Land Settlement Board and reiterated the importance of assisting those British ex-servicemen and their families who wanted to migrate to imperial destinations after the war. According to Grey, land settlement was attracting growing popular support as an instrument of repatriation and post-war reconstruction not only in Britain but throughout the empire. It was thus time for the British government to formulate an imperial settlement policy. Once again Bonar Law's reply was polite but guarded.[18]

Almost simultaneously, the Reconstruction Committee, created in March 1916, requested the views of seven government departments, including the Colonial Office, on the specific issue of ex-service migration, and whether the government should encourage any form of emigration after the war.[19] The departments concerned unanimously accepted that if emigration was going to be encouraged it must go to the dominions, but they could agree on neither the principle itself nor the degree and type of assistance.[20] As for the Colonial Office, Terence Macnaghten, chairman of the Emigrants' Information Office, acknowledged the importance that the Reconstruction Committee and the Board of Trade attached to post-war emigration, but he remained sceptical. 'We are still ignorant of what the post-war conditions will be', he commented in June 1916, 'and whether it will be right to encourage or discourage emigration, or simply to pursue the neutral policy of the period before the war'.[21] By August, however, he was more hesitant. 'I am not at all clear what our policy in this Office is towards emigration, and I have no notion what the policy of H.M.G. is likely to be.'[22] At least Macnaghten now accepted that it was logical and 'safest for the Gov't to take the matter in hand, and guide such emigration . . . into the best channels'.[23]

Pressure from both inside and outside government to formulate some kind of policy became so intense during the summer of 1916 that the Colonial Office could no longer maintain its customary disdain for so-called amateur and uninformed opinion which had hitherto allowed it to evade the emigration issue. In September 1916 Bonar Law resolved to take some practical steps to tackle post-war ex-service migration. He emphasised the need to find employment at home for the largest number of British ex-servicemen. However, he admitted that some would emigrate no matter what kind of domestic arrangements were prepared. In order to ensure that they did not drift outside the imperial sphere 'from want of guidance and knowledge of the opportunities available to them in the Dominions' the first priority was the creation of a central authority to 'formulate plans and coordinate efforts'. Moreover, what he specifically wanted from the dominions was concrete and immediate information on the nature of their own land settlement and employment schemes for ex-servicemen.[24] The permanent officials at the Colonial Office, however, remained circumspect and demonstrated their intense hostility to organised emigration by a determined rear-guard action throughout the rest of 1916. While promising to establish a central body they plotted against attempts by the RCI to seek representation on it or to influence policy making.[25] Attempts to circumvent the RCI failed, however, when political events overtook the Colonial Office's departmental machinations.

In December 1916 Walter Long replaced Bonar Law as Colonial Secretary when Lloyd George became Prime Minister. Unlike his predecessor, Long was truly interested in the emigration issue and proved eager to forge ahead. Reminding the dominions of the urgency of the ex-service migration question, he prodded them (except New Zealand) for a response to Bonar Law's September telegram. The Canadian government promised an answer after the provincial premiers' conference in early January 1917. The Duke of Devonshire, Governor-General of Canada, reported that while the conference was interesting, revealing and was valuable in promoting an exchange of useful ideas, it had not arrived at any definite conclusions.[26] Australia, which was discussing the subject at an inter-state conference when Long's reminder arrived, also delayed its reply until January. It was more positive. British veterans would be granted unconditionally the same soldier settlement facilities as Australians. On the other hand, South Africa had not reached a decision and indications were that when it did it would be polite, non-committal and strictly limited to helping South African veterans. The idea of a central authority to co-ordinate post-war ex-service migration, however, fell on indifferent ears.[27]

Meanwhile, Long demanded the early formation of a consultative committee which would consider ex-servicemen and post-war migration, and he insisted that it should contain knowledgeable individuals from outside government.[28] To facilitate this Long appointed the emigration enthusiast and former Australian Governor-General, Lord Tennyson, as chairman of the Empire Settlement Committee. The committee that consequently took shape in early 1917 originally comprised twenty-five members, later expanded to thirty-three, representing a cross-section of British, dominion, state and provincial governments. Several outside interests, including the Salvation Army, were nominated to the committee.[29] The RCI was successfully denied official representation by the Colonial Office. However, the RCI was indirectly represented thanks to the inclusion of Rider Haggard as a committee member.

The committee's brief was to make recommendations as to the steps the British government should take in constituting the central body to facilitate the supervision and assistance of post-war emigration, to collate information that might be useful to intending emigrants and report on the necessary measures to be taken for settling ex-servicemen in the empire. Long had it in mind that, as he told Tennyson, the central body would probably emerge from his committee using the existing committee members.[30] The Tennyson committee agreed with the recommendations of the DRC's final report published in March but went one step further. The DRC supported the establishment of special machinery to assist ex-servicemen to select, purchase and settle on land in the overseas dominions. It did not, however, mention free passage as part of the package.[31] The Tennyson committee, however, supported the principle of free passage to the dominions for ex-servicemen and the provision of development capital for the various soldier land settlement schemes.[32]

Aware of the Tennyson committee's opinions and with the findings of the DRC before it, the Imperial War Cabinet, with little discussion, approved the New Zealand resolution that intending British emigrants be offered inducements to settle within the empire.[33] This pronouncement was significant: at last the British government had officially endorsed the need for limited state intervention in imperial migration matters. Nevertheless, it was only a general statement of principle without specific reference to free passage for British ex-servicemen. The British cabinet were content to let the Colonial Office proceed with drafting a post-war emigration policy based on the recommendations of the DRC and Tennyson committee reports. The permanent officials were, however, still convinced that British stock was needed at home. They regarded the development of post-war Britain as more important than overseas development, and they opposed any propaganda enticing ex-servicemen to emigrate to the dominions. Instead, Macnaghten argued, priority should be given to 'an attractive land settlement and general development programme in the UK'.[34] This is precisely what happened. From April 1917 the issue of free passage and overseas development assistance for British ex-servicemen after the war was submerged within the British government's pursuit of a domestic colonisation scheme and the Colonial Office's preoccupation with casting an all-encompassing Emigration Bill in 1918.

## Domestic soldier settlement and reconstruction

The chimera of a swift and speedy conclusion to the war drowned in the mud of Flanders. By the end of 1915 all combatants realised that their resources and manpower had to be mobilised for total war. Consequently, the state had to intervene in areas of social and economic policy hitherto confined to the domain of private initiative and enterprise. For many social imperialists the necessity of increased state intervention was perceived to be a tremendous political challenge which demanded social, economic and political reform immediately after the war was won. The return to normality therefore did not simply mean an attendant restoration of British society to its pre-war days. Instead, the war provided an opportunity for the construction of a new post-war social, economic and political order.[35]

The appalling casualty rates and the steady stream of wounded returning home were a daily reminder that it was becoming impossible for private charities and philanthropic organisations to cope with the enormous task of rehabilitation, retraining and re-employment of returning veterans. This prompted the British government in February 1915 to investigate these problems, in particular the employment and vocational opportunities available to disabled soldiers and sailors. In May 1915 the Murray committee, named after its chairman G. H. Murray and appointed by Herbert Samuel, President of the Local Government Board, recommended that the state should assume absolute responsibility for the care of the war disabled. This included the restoration of their health, the provision of training facilities should they wish to pursue a new trade and assistance in securing employment. One solution which was brought to the committee's attention, and which received its support, was the settlement of soldiers and sailors on the land.[36]

Indeed, home colonisation proved popular with British agricultural reformers and politicians alike.[37] Naturally, patriotism permeated the demands for a domestic soldier settlement scheme. Many believed that small-scale farming operations offered returning veterans the best opportunity of leading a healthy, fulfilling and productive life. Patriotism aside, there were also important strategic, social and economic arguments for resettling British ex-servicemen on small holdings, such as increased agricultural self-sufficiency, enhanced revival of British agriculture, fortification of the social fabric against revolution and reinforced political stability. Landholding ex-servicemen, trained with the necessary agricultural skills, would prove a welcome addition to the long and noble tradition of the British yeoman, representative and defender of a healthy, stable rural society.

Throughout 1915 and 1916 the Board of Agriculture received a growing number of enquiries from both within and outside Whitehall about the possibility of employing disabled veterans in agriculture and the establishment of small soldier settlement colonies. Lord Lucas, Selborne's predecessor at the Board of Agriculture, welcomed these enquiries, believing that disabled veterans could be used as a partial solution in relieving the chronic shortage of agricultural labour.[38]

Another member of the Murray committee and a leading agricultural reformer, Leslie Scott, agreed. 'My own belief is that the open air life of soldiering will create quite a new impetus towards agricultural life . . . Should the demand be larger it will obviously have to be considered in close connection with the purely agricultural question of increasing our output from the land'.[39]

This was precisely what concerned many leading politicians and agricultural reformers. From a strategic standpoint, it was vital that Britain reduce its dependence on imported foodstuffs by increasing domestic food production. The threat of an unlimited submarine campaign, actually unleashed in 1917, clearly demonstrated Britain's vulnerable supply lines and emphasised the need for greater agricultural self-sufficiency. This was certainly apparent to Sir Maurice Hankey, Secretary to the Committee of Imperial Defence, who stated that from the perspective of home defence, Britain's 'Achilles heel' was her dependence on imported foodstuffs and raw materials. However, this important national objective could only be achieved by safeguarding the supply of agricultural labour. The plan to resettle British ex-servicemen on small holdings was therefore developed within this context. Soldiers, both disabled and able-bodied, were seen by some permanent officials, politicians and agricultural reformers as the vanguard of a new development designed to increase Britain's rural population and revitalise a flagging agricultural sector.[40]

It was Selborne's foresight and energy which brought the idea of settling the disabled and discharged soldier on British farm land to the cabinet's attention.[41] Committed to reconstruction, he became one of the leading advocates for greater state control of the war effort, which he regarded as a positive force in shaping a new, vigorous and agriculturally self-sufficient post-war society.[42] Selborne shared Scott's concern for the plight of the ex-servicemen and his enthusiasm for employing them on the land. He appointed a departmental committee in July 1915, chaired by Harry Verney MP, a former parliamentary secretary at the Board of Agriculture (1914–15). Its objective was to consider and report on the requisite steps to promote the settlement and employment on the land in England and Wales of disabled and discharged ex-servicemen.[43] Selborne agreed with his Parliamentary Secretary, F. D. Acland, that the entire matter was 'clearly one of extreme interest and difficulty'.[44] Sydney Olivier, Permanent Secretary at the Board of Agriculture, emphasised the importance of having experienced men on the committee. The committee's 'real work should not be theoretical but practical and exploratory of the concrete material to be dealt with'.[45] It was argued that the information should be gathered by those most directly concerned with the small holdings movement in Britain and, in particular, men who had been closely associated with previous attempts at domestic colonisation and land settlement: experts who knew 'what kind of men, with what kind of assistance, and at what expense, can be settled upon such lands with any prospect of their becoming self-supporting'.[46] To Olivier's mind it was obvious that the government would be confronted with demands for some sort of home colonisation programme and it was necessary, therefore, to prepare for such an eventuality. Selborne concurred and stated that the Verney committee's recommendations should be completed for cabinet perusal as soon as possible.[47]

Early in March 1916 Prime Minister Asquith appointed a cabinet committee to consider whether land settlement should be made integral to the government's demobilisation policy. On 11 March Selborne presented a summary of the as yet unpublished Verney committee recommendations to this cabinet committee.[48] He readily admitted that a state-sponsored land settlement scheme for returning soldiers would be expensive. But he warned his cabinet colleagues that the dominions would no doubt launch an aggressive campaign to attract these men to settle overseas: '(S)urely it would be deplorable if such men had no opportunity of settlement in their native country.' British public opinion would condemn the government if no concessions were made for settlement at home.[49] Selborne proposed following the Verney committee's recommendations for the establishment of a co-operative colony system comprised of small allotments between three to five acres. He urged that because ownership or tenancy of small holdings was such a divisive political issue the land should remain under the complete control of the state. The Marquis of Crewe in his weekly cabinet summary to King George V reported that the veterans' resettlement colonies were 'in reality part of the great problem of reorganisation and of restoration after the war, bound up with all the social and commercial activities of the country.'[50]

Selborne was authorised to submit estimates to the Treasury for the establishment of three experimental colonies. These colonies were to be situated in different parts of the country in order to test the settlers' ability to adapt to a variety of soil, farming and climatic conditions. The Treasury would provide a 'modest outlay' of capital. Lord Lansdowne, a prominent landlord and chairman of the cabinet committee appointed to study Selborne's proposals, emphasised the importance of 'maintaining the purely experimental character of the schemes'. He stressed that the government should not hold out promises of a general allotment of land to disabled and discharged ex-servicemen. Selborne's instructions to his officials were more explicit:

The Cabinet desire that this policy shall not be spoken of as necessarily part of a larger policy, and stress is to be laid on the experimental and strictly limited character of the operation. No language is to be used which would lead every disabled or discharged sailor and soldier who wishes to settle on the land to think that he has a claim to have land provided for him. The establishment of these colonies is to be regarded as an experiment of a new type of settlement.[51]

The President of the Board of Agriculture succeeded in establishing his pioneering colonies which were provided for in the Small Holdings and Allotments Act of 1916.[52] Practical agriculturists attacked the Act as a trifling piece of legislation and a 'miserable little bill'.[53] R. E. Prothero MP, a leading agricultural reformer and a future president of the Board of Agriculture, believed that the initial capacity of 300 men was 'wholly inadequate'. His lack of confidence was justified in the face of press reports which estimated that 750,000 men would return to the land after the war. Nevertheless, these same critics agreed that if the legislation genuinely marked the beginning of a new development in British agricultural policy, this also made it a scheme worth fostering.[54]

Prothero, later Lord Ernle, realised that domestic colonisation would only relieve some of the pressure for soldiers wanting to farm:

[M]en who wish to settle on the land and to follow agriculture as an industry ought not to be driven, for lack of opportunity, out of this country. (However) if men are such adventurous spirits . . . they should have every facility given them within the Empire, and in that way the Mother Country and her children will build up between them a stronger Empire.[55]

In October 1917 he presented a detailed memorandum to the War Cabinet on the entire question of providing land for soldiers upon demobilisation. Demand for land would far outstrip supply. If these demands were not met immediately, or if no suitable settlement schemes had been installed before hostilities ended, dangerous rumblings of discontent would be aroused amongst returning veterans desirous of farming in Britain. It was essential to decide upon a policy immediately or else government inaction would contribute to the exodus of ex-servicemen eager to seek land overseas.[56]

Domestic settlement nevertheless proved an utter failure.[57] As mentioned above, despite detailed and exhaustive examination from as early as May 1915 by the Board of Agriculture and the Ministry of Reconstruction, other ministries chose to ignore the issue. Wartime inflation, speculation, limited resources and the Treasury's freeze on local spending made it extremely difficult for county councils to meet the demand for small holdings from returned veterans.[58] The sudden ending of the war on 11 November 1918 therefore caught the British government by surprise and without a home or overseas soldier settlement policy. The government was forced to provide an emergency grant of £20 million to the county councils for the acquisition of land and equipment. Further delays threatened when a general election was announced the day after the armistice. Prothero, now President of the Board of Agriculture, became deeply concerned that a number of candidates attempted to make political capital out of the issue which they knew little or nothing about. Worse still, he feared that strong pressure from an ill-informed public would force Lloyd George to endorse a misconceived policy on grounds of political expediency. Of Lloyd George's six major campaign speeches the first three dealt with domestic reconstruction in which agricultural reform and veteran resettlement were increasingly emphasised. Combined with the government's new housing policy, this was calculated to woo the veteran vote.[59]

As an electoral tactic, Lloyd George's appeal to the British public as a friend of the returned soldier was a shrewd piece of politicking. At the same time, it demonstrated that he was to some degree sensitive to veterans' problems. Nevertheless, the government was unprepared, despite continual warnings from the reconstructionists led by Prothero and C. Addison, Minister of Reconstruction, to deal quickly and effectively with the demands of its ex-servicemen. The charge of political expediency must be examined in the larger context of the events and atmosphere surrounding the 1918 election and its aftermath. The British government in the latter part of 1918 and the first six months of 1919 was confronted with widespread discontent in the armed forces. In part, the disgruntlement was fuelled by the chaotic demobilisation procedure. Confronted with growing unrest and impatience within the armed forces over the slowness of the demobilisation procedure, senior army officers in both France and Britain were faced with increasingly violent outbreaks of indiscipline. Similarly, it was reported by intelligence sources that the Navy was in danger of open mutiny.[60] Initially preoccupied with the general election most politicians chose to ignore these problems. However, as the disturbances escalated a growing number of politicians and ministers grew sensitive to veterans' issues, in particular domestic, and then overseas, soldier settlement. These domestic constraints revitalised the apparently moribund plans to assist ex-servicemen to emigrate.

According to some government ministers, indiscipline and mutiny were symptoms of a larger, more menacing and socially destructive disease – Bolshevism. 'There is undoubtedly, in this country', reported Sir Alfred Mond, the First Commissioner of Works in November 1918, 'a certain fever of revolutionary Bolshevist ideas.'[61] The Russian revolution had stimulated the growth of radical and revolutionary movements in Britain. Trade unionism, itself influenced by and supportive of the Russian revolution, had grown during the war as well. So, too, had the British government's domestic intelligence surveillance unit which monitored a variety of 'red', 'socialist' and 'anti-government' individuals and associations, including a number of ex-servicemen's organisations.[62] For the most part, veterans' leaders were level-headed and pragmatic individuals who sought legitimate redress of grievances using constitutional methods through established institutions and forms of protest. The National Union of Ex-Service Men (NUX) and the International Union of Ex-Service Men (IUX) were the exception. The Special Branch reported that James Cox, the national secretary of the IUX, rejected constitutional action and the IUX was 'an out and out revolutionary socialist organisation seeking to establish an industrial republic'. Moreover, it was unemployment, lack of proper housing and grievances over pension gratuities which fuelled the fires of most veteran discontent.[63] After a new and more acceptable demobilisation scheme was introduced in late January 1919 and soldiers were absorbed into the labour market, the unrest soon subsided. In hindsight, this challenge to authority may not have been critical, 'but it was unnerving'.[64]

## An administrative landmark in constructive imperialism

The period between 1919 and 1922 proved to be a crucial one for constructive imperialists throughout the empire. Their hopes were initially raised by the appointment in January of Lord Milner, the embodiment of the social imperial creed, as Colonial Secretary, and his disciple and close confidant, Leo Amery, as Under-Secretary. Stressing the need for 'a complete change' in the Colonial Office, determined to impose their will over the permanent officials and assert their authority, the new leadership eagerly launched itself into its responsibilities convinced 'that we must in time give it a new "orientation" '.[65] The distinguishing feature of the Milner-Amery partnership was that they possessed a clear set of imperial objectives,[66] leading the list of priorities of which was an aggressive empire migration policy.

The task of assisting ex-servicemen was a completely separate matter, according to Amery when he first took office in January: 'I had already at the (Oversea Settlement) committee hammered at any rate one point, namely that the treatment of ex-Service men is one of an award they are entitled to and has nothing to do with general emigration policy.'[67] Amery envisaged the free passage scheme as a limited venture restricted to a maximum of three years. However, there was an important qualification: 'In order . . . to avoid a mere stimulation of emigration in an undesirable form, this privilege should be strictly confined to *bona fide* settlers on the land, or those who can prove that they have a definite offer of other suitable employment.' As far as Amery was concerned the 'problem of the emigration of ex-service men is very largely an agricultural one'.[68] Indeed, permanent officials at the Colonial Office were unenthusiastic and seemed to regard the free passage scheme as the responsibility of another department such as the Ministry of Labour or the War Office.[69] Similarly, they acknowledged that some ex-servicemen would leave Britain no matter what the government's attitude or policy, but so far as they were concerned the free passage scheme was not an emigration scheme proper and therefore outside its jurisdiction or interest. Nor did they regard it as having any economic significance. It was simply a humanitarian gesture designed to lessen the financial burden of those wanting to make a new life for themselves and their families in the overseas empire.[70]

Amery's more immediate aim was to frame a new emigration bill which would enhance imperial unity, contribute to the economic well-being of the empire and offset the fiasco of Long's ill-conceived 1918 Emigration Bill. Despite his optimism, he encountered only delay, disappointment and frustration from a confused and divided cabinet between January and March 1919. He complained to Milner, who was then in Paris attending the peace talks, that he badly needed his support in the cabinet. Until Milner returned, the emigration bill would be 'left in the air'.[71]

The majority of the cabinet were convinced that the nation would shortly experience an intense period of prosperity and a tremendous shortage of labour. To promote emigration would therefore exacerbate the shortage, delay prosperity and hamper reconstruction. The Ministry of Labour strongly concurred. Milner and Amery were, however, equally convinced that if a new emigration bill was not forthcoming immediately the country would face serious economic and social distress, and Sir Auckland Geddes, Minister of National Service, agreed.[72] The cabinet ignored the argument. Amery struggled constantly to get his emigration bill discussed in cabinet, and on 7 February he saw Bonar Law, Lord Privy Seal, and ascertained that empire migration was to be included in the King's Speech. Four days later Amery went down to Parliament to hear the speech but, to his disappointment, Lloyd George had struck out its reference at the last moment. At a stormy cabinet meeting two weeks later the Prime Minister continued to vacillate, being sceptical about the entire issue. Meanwhile, Amery was being asked questions on emigration in Parliament of which he had to give 'evasive answers'. Growing impatient, he pressed Bonar Law in early March once again to put empire migration on the cabinet agenda and sent an additional note to the Prime Minister to prod him into action. Milner, who had returned from the peace talks, saw Amery several days later and reported that Lloyd George was 'still very sticky about the Overseas Settlement business'. After this further display of the Prime Minister's irresolution, they chose to concentrate on getting the finances for the more immediate task of assisting the emigration of ex-servicemen. The broader overseas settlement legislation would have to wait.[73]

Suddenly at the end of March, the War Cabinet decided to take up the question of assisting ex-servicemen to emigrate overseas, catching Amery off balance. Although he had prepared the necessary drafts complete with arguments, he had not supplied Milner with them. None the less, the cabinet was eager to push ahead and on 31 March it accepted, subject to Lloyd George's approval, the recommendations on free passages outlined by Amery in February.[74] Why the sudden rush to implement a policy which most of the cabinet were content to ignore? Unemployment had become the government's main problem. In March 1919 over 300,000 veterans were receiving unemployment benefits, and this was a factor in Lloyd George's sudden desire to implement Amery's free passage scheme.[75] Furthermore, the cabinet feared the revolutionary spirit which was sweeping the country, and in particular ex-servicemen. Assisted emigration could de-fuse the situation.

Amery wanted the government's offer of free passage to be open for three years beginning 1 January 1920. This allowed ex-servicemen ample time to choose between employment opportunities in Britain or the overseas empire. It was also designed to give the dominions time to establish the necessary administrative machinery, prevent a rush of applications swamping the Overseas Settlement Office and 'to meet the possible charge that we wish to hustle people out of the country'.[76] It was estimated that a three-year programme would assist no fewer than 405,000 ex-servicemen and their families at a cost of just over £6 million.[77] But three years were too long to promise, argued the Treasury. Austen Chamberlain, Chancellor of the Exchequer, thought it better to limit free passage to one year and reconsider its extension in light of the experience gained. On 8 April, Amery stood before Parliament during question time and announced the government's one year free passage grant for ex-servicemen and women which would begin on 1 January 1920. Pleased with the accomplishment, he realised that enormous difficulties yet lay ahead.[78] Its implementation would require the creation of an effective administrative structure and the willing co-operation of dominion authorities.

Sustained unemployment among British ex-servicemen provided the impetus for the extension of the ex-servicemen's free passage scheme. As unemployment intensified in the latter part of 1920 Milner and Amery were determined to get it extended for another year. In October Amery appeared before the newly formed cabinet committee on unemployment, chaired by Sir L. Worthington-Evans, to argue for the scheme's extension as 'a means of relieving abnormal unemployment during the coming winter', and Milner reiterated the point to the cabinet two weeks later. Money spent on assisted passages, he argued, also saved the Exchequer from the sustained burden of crippling unemployment benefits.[79] The Treasury nevertheless remained hostile to any suggestion of increased expenditure, particularly for the extension of the ex-servicemen's free passage scheme. As winter tightened its grip and unemployment rose, however, even a reluctant Treasury had to admit the need for limited action. In November the cabinet agreed with Milner's October memorandum and the Treasury sanctioned a one year extension of the free passage scheme. 'I am clear', wrote Chamberlain, 'that if the original policy was right this extension is still more right.'[80] In addition, the Minister of Labour, Dr T. J. Macnamara, previously sceptical of Amery's overseas settlement strategy, became a convert to it. In 1922 he explained to his cabinet colleague, Winston Churchill, that his concern stemmed from the tens of thousands of young, able-bodied but unemployed ex-servicemen who had been out of work for more than two years. 'I have been thinking that we ought to look to over-sea settlement as one of the methods of relieving the unemployment situation here. I know that we have hitherto hesitated to relate over-sea settlement and unemployment and it is only the present exceptional position and emergency that would warrant any other course.'[81]

The financial provisions of the scheme were not extended beyond December 1921 because of plans to introduce the broader Empire Settlement Act in early 1922. However, successful applicants were given until 31 December 1922 to make their sailing. The deadline was further extended until March 1923 for those few who had delayed their departure because of illness or bureaucratic problems.

What were the mechanics of the free passage scheme? Ex-servicemen and women who had enlisted for active duty and whose service began before 1 January 1920 were eligible under the scheme but not those who had served solely with dominion, colonial or Indian army units. Women were required to have served for not less than six months in a corps administered by a British government department. This not only included the women's branches of the armed forces but a variety of nursing services, the Women's Land Army, the Forage Corps and the

Forestry Corps. All concerned could obtain free third-class passages for themselves and their dependants to the nearest convenient port of the dominion or colony of their choice. The same privilege was extended to the widows and dependants of fallen ex-servicemen provided they fulfilled the criteria above and were drawing a pension from the imperial government.[82] The British government through the local officials of the fledgling Ministries of Labour and Pensions established the eligibility of applicants. Then, properly screened, applications were forwarded to the representative of the dominion or colony in which the candidate concerned wanted to settle. The onus was placed squarely on the dominions to evaluate each case individually and to judge whether the candidate was medically fit and properly suited for employment opportunities overseas.[83] Only when the OSC had received dominion approval would a third-class passage warrant be issued. Using a variety of advertising techniques the OSC worked hard to inform returning ex-servicemen of its services, the benefits of the free passage scheme and the employment opportunities which existed overseas. It seemed straightforward, but in practice it was far from being so.[84]

The final total of 86,027 fell far short of Amery's early 1919 estimate of 405,000.[85] Furthermore, it was evident that these numbers were neither going to make an appreciable impact on relieving Britain of its unemployment 'emergency' nor promote imperial co-operation, unity and self-sufficiency. To understand the varied reactions and responses of the dominions to the ex-servicemen's free passage scheme more fully, its shortcomings and the incorporation of British veterans in a host of overseas soldier settlement projects, it is necessary to examine dominion policies and attitudes in greater detail.

## Notes

1 John A. Schultz, 'Finding homes fit for heroes: the Great War and empire settlement', *Canadian Journal of History*, XVIII, 1983, p. 99.
2 NA, RG 76, vol. 5, f. 41, part 3, Cory to W. D. Scott, Superintendent of Immigration, 19 August 1914.
3 *Ibid.*, memorandum by Scott, 8 October 1914; Scott to Cory, 3 September 1914.
4 PRO, CO 323/726/52106, T. C. Macnaghten, chairman of the Emigrants' Information Office, to Lord Islington, Under-Secretary of State for India, 31 October 1916.
5 PRO, CO 323/693/52767, Steel-Maitland to Bonar Law, 2 November 1915; minute by Steel-Maitland, 19 November 1915.
6 Trevor Reese, *The History of the Royal Commonwealth Society, 1868–1968*, London, 1968, p. 161; Royal Commonwealth Society Archive (hereafter RCSA), 1910 Emigration Conference File, E. T. Scammell and A. R. Pontifex to James R. Boosé, secretary of the RCI, 7 February 1910; Scammell to Boosé, 1 and 10 March 1910; *Official report of the Emigration Conference held on May 30–31, 1910, convened by the Royal Colonial Institute*, London, 1910, p. 26; *The Times*, 14 May 1910.
7 PRO, CO 532/76/48673, Sir Arthur Pearson, newspaper proprietor and member of the Standing Emigration Committee, to F. G. A. Butler, senior Colonial Office official and

former chairman of the EIO, 26 November 1914.

8 *Ibid.*, minute by Butler, 27 November 1914; Butler to Pearson, 1 December 1914; RCSA, Empire Migration Committee, memorandum by Pearson, 21 December 1914.

9 PRO, CO 532/82/26960, minute by Macnaghten, 12 June 1915; quotation cited in Schultz, 'Fit for heroes', p. 102; CO 532/76/48673, minute by Macnaghten, 27 November 1914 and minute by Sir John Anderson, Permanent Under-Secretary of State for the Colonies, 30 November 1914.

10 PRO, CO 532/76/48673, minute by Macnaghten, 27 November 1914.

11 PRO, Ministry of Labour Papers (hereafter LAB), LAB 2/1230/LE 27353/2, memorandum by W. Windham, 17 November 1916.

12 Bodleian Library, Oxford, Round Table Papers, MSS. Eng. Hist. c. 777, paper entitled 'The Colonial Institute', 17 June 1912, no author; Harold Begbie, *Albert, Fourth Earl Grey, A Last Word*, London, 1917, pp. 11 and 81; Mary E. Hallet, 'The Fourth Earl Grey as Governor-General of Canada', unpublished Ph.D. thesis, University of London, 1969, pp. 23–5 and 82–5.

13 Schultz, 'Fit for heroes', p. 100; Joseph M. Fewster, 'Documentary sources concerning Australia in Durham University', *Durham University Journal*, new series, L, 1988, p. 65; PRO, CO 532/76/48673, Grey to Islington, 3 December 1914.

14 PRO, CO 532/82/2090, Grey to Islington, 23 December 1914.

15 For these negotiations see Schultz, 'Fit for heroes', pp. 101–2; PRO, CO 532/83/30739, minute by Anderson, 6 July 1915.

16 A full transcript of the interview appears in the RCI periodical *United Empire*, VI, 1915, pp. 680–90.

17 For details of the mission and the reaction of the official mind see D. S. Higgins, *The Private Diaries of Sir Henry Rider Haggard 1914–1925*, London, 1980, pp. 51–73; H. Rider Haggard, *The After-War Settlement and Employment of Ex-Service Men in the Oversea Dominions*, London, 1916; Peter Pierce, 'Rider Haggard in Australia', *Meanjin*, XXXVII, 1977, pp. 200–8; HLRO, J. C. C. Davidson Papers, f. 15, Sir Ronald Munro-Ferguson, Governor-General of Australia, to Bonar Law, 24 May 1916; PRO, CO 532/84/27819, minute by Macnaghten, 20 June 1916.

18 RCSA, Proceedings of the Deputation to the Secretary of State for the Colonies and the President of the Board of Agriculture, 10 August 1916, pp. 1–4.

19 PRO, Ministry of Reconstruction Papers (hereafter RECO), RECO 1/685, Nash circular to Boards of Agriculture and Trade, Local Government Board, Colonial Office, Scottish Office, Home Office, and the War Office, 11 August 1916.

20 PRO, RECO 1/683, War Office to Reconstruction Committee, 31 August 1916; RECO 1/684, Local Government Board to Reconstruction Committee, 6 September 1916; Board of Agriculture to Reconstruction Committee, 10 October 1916; PRO, Board of Trade Papers (hereafter BT), BT 13/70/E 30346, Board of Trade memorandum, 30 August 1916.

21 PRO, CO 532/89/26194, minute by Macnaghten, 5 June 1916.

22 PRO, CO 532/89/37065, minute by Macnaghten, 10 August 1916.

23 PRO, CO 532/89/38085, minute by Macnaghten, 15 August 1916.

24 PRO, CO 532/89/47507, Bonar Law to Governors-General of Canada, Australia and South Africa, and Governors of New Zealand and Newfoundland, 21 September 1916.

25 Schultz, 'Fit for heroes', p. 107.

26 Wiltshire Record Office (hereafter WRO), Walter Long Papers, WRO 947/609, Devonshire to Long, 12 January 1917.

27 PRO, CO 532/91/6463, Munro-Ferguson to Long, 3 February 1917; WRO 947/601, Lord Buxton, Governor-General of South Africa, to Long, 20 December 1916. New Zealand did not need prodding as Prime Minister Massey, who had been in Britain since October, discussed the matter with the Colonial Office direct. PRO, CO 532/85/46077, Lord Liverpool, Governor of New Zealand, to Bonar Law, 26 September 1916.

28 Schultz, 'Fit for heroes', p. 108.

29 BPP, Cd. 8672, *Empire Settlement Committee*, 1917. See PRO, CO 532/89/62468 for the detailed correspondence concerning the selection, constitution and format of the

committee. Hallam Tennyson, was the son of the famous poet Alfred, first Lord Tennyson.

30  PRO, CO 532/91/4023, Long to Tennyson, 16 January 1917.
31  BPP, Cd. 8462, *Dominions Royal Commission, Final Report*, 1917, pp. 83 and 92–4.
32  BPP, Cd. 8672, *Empire Settlement Committee*, pp. 24 and 21.
33  Ian Drummond, *Imperial Economic Policy 1917–1939*, London, 1974, pp. 50–1; PRO, Cabinet Office Papers (hereafter CAB), CAB 23/40, minutes of Imperial War Cabinet, 24 and 26 April 1917.
34  Schultz, 'Fit for heroes', p. 107; PRO, CO 532/98/28638, minute by Macnaghten, 12 June 1917.
35  R. J. Scally, *The Origins of the Lloyd George Coalition*, Princeton, NJ, 1975, p. 3; Kenneth Morgan, *Consensus and Disunity: The Lloyd George Coalition Government 1918–1922*, Oxford, 1979.
36  BPP, Cd. 7915, *Report of the Disabled Sailors and Soldiers Committee appointed by the President of the Local Government Board*, 1915; G. Wootton, *The Politics of Influence*, London, 1963, pp. 28–30.
37  Colonel Henry Pilkington, *Land Settlement for Soldiers*, London, 1911; Charles Bathurst, 'The land settlement of ex-service men', *Nineteenth Century and After*, LXXVIII, 1915, pp. 1097–113; F. E. Green, 'Home colonisation by soldiers and sailors', *Nineteenth Century and After*, LXXIX, 1916, pp. 888–905; 'Sailors and soldiers on the land', *Quarterly Review*, CCXXVI, 1916, pp. 135–51; A. D. Hall, *Agriculture After the War*, London, 1916; Warman, *The Soldier Colonists*; C. G. Woodhouse, 'Returning the soldier to civilian life', *South Atlantic Quarterly*, XVII, 1918, pp. 265–89.
38  PRO, Ministry of Agriculture, Fisheries and Food (hereafter MAF), MAF 48/25/L 4528, W. H. Beveridge, Director of the Labour Exchanges and Assistant Secretary in charge of the Employment Department at the Board of Trade, to E. J. Cheney, Parliamentary Secretary to the Board of Agriculture, 3 March 1915; Cheney to Beveridge, 10 March 1915; Lord Lucas to G. H. Roberts, 15 March 1915.
39  *Ibid.*, Scott to Selborne, 5 June 1915
40  British Library, William Ashley Papers, Add. MS. 42256, f. 253, extract of secret evidence given by Sir Maurice Hankey which was not published in BPP, Cd. 8277, *Part II of the Departmental Committee appointed by the President of the Board of Agriculture and Fisheries to consider the Settlement and Employment on the Land in England and Wales of Discharged Sailors and Soldiers*, 1916.
41  P. B. Johnson, *A Land Fit For Heroes*, Chicago, 1968, p. 13.
42  Bodleian, Lord Selborne Papers, Box 83, Selborne to Vaughan Nash, Secretary of the Reconstruction Committee, 15 May 1916.
43  BPP, Cd. 8182, *Introduction and Part I of the Final Report of the Departmental Committee appointed by the President of the Board of Agriculture and Fisheries to consider the Settlement and Employment on the Land in England and Wales of Discharged Sailors and Soldiers*, 1916.
44  PRO, MAF 48/25/L 4528, minute by Acland, 3 June 1915 and endorsed by Selborne, 4 June 1915.
45  *Ibid.*, minute by Olivier, 3 June 1915.
46  *Ibid.*
47  *Ibid*; minute by Selborne, 4 June 1915.
48  Bodleian, Selborne Papers, Box 82, Selborne to R. McKenna, Chancellor of the Exchequer, 1 March 1916; Bodleian, H. H. Asquith Papers, vol. 16, Selborne to Asquith, 11 March 1916.
49  PRO, CAB 37/144/35, 'Settlement and Employment on the Land of Discharged Sailors and Soldiers', 11 March 1916.
50  Quotation cited in Johnson, *Land Fit For Heroes*, p. 13.
51  PRO, CAB 41/37/13, Lord Crewe to King George V, weekly cabinet summary, 29 March 1916; MAF 48/25/L 4532, minute by Selborne, 29 March 1916.
52  PRO, CO 532/89/29051, Assistant Secretary, Board of Agriculture, to Steel-Maitland, 20 June 1916; 'Scheme for the land settlement of ex-service men', *Journal of the*

*Ministry of Agriculture*, XXIV, 1917, pp. 326–8.

53 RCSA, ELSC Correspondence and Memoranda, 'Proceedings of the meeting between the ELSC and members of Parliament held on 31 May 1916'; 'Memorandum on home settlement', n.d. (probably 1917–18).

54 PRO, MAF 53/7, no. 42, deputation of the County Councils Association, 28 November 1917; MAF 53/8, no. 5, testimony of Rowland Hunt MP; Lord Ernle, *Whippingham to Westminster*, London, 1938, pp. 265–6; Edith Whetham, *The Agrarian History of England and Wales*, VIII, *1914–1939*, Cambridge, 1978, pp. 66, 90 and 94; idem, 'The Agricultural Act, 1920 and its repeal – the "Great Betrayal" ', *Agricultural History Review*, XXII, 1974, pp. 36–49.

55 PRO, MAF 53/8, no. 34, Lord Ernle's reply to a deputation from the British Empire Land Settlement League, 5 June 1918.

56 PRO, CAB 24/28/GT 2225, 'Land Settlement', memorandum by Prothero, 2 October 1917.

57 A total of 253,000 acres had been acquired by September 1920 in England and Wales which was enough to settle 17,770 men. However, only 8,178 had been settled on allotments complete with houses and equipment. Approximately 24,000 candidates, including a small number of civilians, had been provisionally approved as suitable candidates but as of 1 December 1920, 14,858 were still without holdings. Between the autumn of 1920 and the end of 1921 the situation for the veteran small holder steadily worsened. The Ministry of Agriculture enthusiastically reported in June 1923 that just under 19,000 men had settled of which 11,000 had taken possession since the 1920 harvest. But it was under no illusion as to the future difficulties these men would face. Moreover, only 8,000 had derived any benefit from the high produce prices obtained in 1919 and 1920. PRO, MAF 53/11, no. 31, 23 September 1920; *Journal of the British Legion*, I, 1921, p. 64; 'Position and prospects of ex-service small holders', *Journal of the Ministry of Agriculture*, XXX, 1923, p. 246; PRO, MAF 48/47, Cabinet Land Settlement Policy, 1920. In Scotland 6,000 allotments were provided for civilian and soldier settlement. Leah Leneman, *Fit for Heroes? Land Settlement in Scotland after World War I*, Aberdeen, 1989, pp. 1–37.

58 BPP, Cd. 8182, *Introduction and Part I of the Final Report of the Departmental Committee ... Discharged Sailors and Soldiers*, 1916; Cd. 8277, *Part II of the Departmental Committee ... Discharged Sailors and Soldiers*, 1916; Whetham, *Agrarian History of England and Wales*, VIII, pp. 109–41.

59 WRO 947/586, Prothero to Long, 7 December 1918; Johnson, *Land Fit For Heroes*; L. Orbach, *Homes for Heroes*, London, 1977, p. 42; M. Swenarton, *Homes Fit For Heroes*, London, 1981, pp. 67–87; Morgan, *Consensus and Disunity*, pp. 26–45; S. Ward, 'The British veterans' ticket of 1918', *Journal of British Studies*, VIII, 1968, pp. 155–69.

60 S. R. Graubard, 'Military demobilisation in Great Britain following the First World War', *Journal of Modern History*, XIX, 1947, pp. 297–300; S. P. Mackenzie, *Politics and Military Morale*, Oxford, 1992, pp. 1–39; Brian Bond, *British Military Policy between the Two World Wars*, Oxford, 1980, pp. 10–34; W. Kendall, *The Revolutionary Movement in Britain 1900–21*, London, 1969, p. 188. Also see Keith Jeffery's excellent piece on Britain's post-war army in Ian F. W. Beckett and Keith Simpson, eds, *A Nation in Arms. A Social Study of the British Army in the First World War*, Manchester, 1985, pp. 211–34.

61 PRO, CAB 24/69/GT 6270, memorandum by Mond, 12 November 1918.

62 S. Ward, 'Intelligence surveillance of British ex-servicemen, 1918–1920', *Historical Journal*, XVI, 1973, pp. 179–80; Christopher Andrew, *Her Majesty's Secret Service*, New York, 1986, pp. 224–9.

63 PRO, CAB 24/96/CP 429, 'Revolutionary Organisations in the United Kingdom', report by the Home Office, 9 January 1920; PRO, Treasury Board Papers (hereafter T), T 172/1121, deputation from the National Federation of Discharged and Demobilised Sailors and Soldiers, 6 February 1920. For an examination of British ex-servicemens' organisations as pressure groups see Wootton, *Politics of Influence*.

64 Ward, 'Intelligence surveillance', p. 187; David Englander and James Osborne, 'Jack,

Tommy, and Henry Dubb: the armed forces and the working class', *Historical Journal*, XXI, 1978, pp. 593–621; David Englander, 'The National Union of Ex-Servicemen and the labour movement, 1918–1920', *History*, LXXVI, 1991, pp. 24–42.

65 Amery Papers, Box E.61, Amery to Lloyd George, 14 November 1918; Box 54, Folder B, Milner to Amery, 12 February 1919; original diaries of L. S. Amery, 20 March 1918. Although the diaries have been published by John Barnes and D. Nicolson, eds, *The Leo Amery Diaries*, 2 vols., London, 1980 and 1988, the majority of the overseas settlement material was omitted. Diary material not included in the published version will be cited as Amery diaries while published material will be cited as Barnes and Nicolson, *Leo Amery Diaries*.

66 Stephen Constantine, *The Making of British Colonial Development Policy 1914–1940*, London, 1984, p. 47; Wm. Roger Louis, *In the Name of God, Go! Leo Amery and the British Empire in the Age of Churchill*, London, 1992. This provides the best analysis yet of Amery's imperial outlook and philosophy.

67 Amery diaries, 14 January 1919.

68 PRO, CAB 24/75/GT 6846, 20 February 1919.

69 PRO, CO 532/146/10143, minutes by E. J. Harding and H. Lambert, junior Colonial Office officials, 17 and 18 February 1919; minute by G. V. Fiddes, Permanent Under-Secretary, 18 February 1919.

70 Drummond, *Imperial Economic Policy*, p. 56.

71 Amery Papers, Box 54, Folder B, Amery to Milner, 12 February 1919.

72 Barnes and Nicolson, *Leo Amery Diaries*, I, pp. 253 and 256–7; PRO, LAB 2/1229/ED 20058/4 secret memorandum, 3 February 1919; CO 721/3/f. 52, a Mr Phillips to Macnaghten, 30 January 1919.

73 HLRO, David Lloyd George Papers, F/39/1/9, Amery to Lloyd George, 1 March 1919; Barnes and Nicolson, *Leo Amery Diaries*, I, 11, 24, 25, 28 February and 10 March 1919, pp. 256–8; Drummond, *Imperial Economic Policy*, p. 60; Amery diaries, 4, 5 and 10 March 1919.

74 PRO, CAB 23/9, minutes of War Cabinet, 31 March 1919; Amery diaries, 31 March 1919.

75 S. Ward, ed., *The War Generation*, Port Washington, NY, 1975, p. 22.

76 PRO, CO 532/143/20660, Amery to Milner, 7 April 1919

77 PRO, CO 721/1, 'Note on the Cost of the Proposals Contained in the Memorandum of the Emigration Committee', n.d. In Dane Kennedy's article, 'Empire migration in post-war reconstruction: the role of the Overseas Settlement Committee, 1919–1922', *Albion*, XX, 1988, p. 415, the figure is misquoted as 450,000.

78 PRO, CO 532/143/20660, Chamberlain to Amery, 8 April 1919; Amery diaries, 8 April 1919; House of Commons Debates, *Hansard*, fifth series, CXIX, 1919, cols 1857–8.

79 PRO, CAB 27/115/CU 40, Amery to Worthington-Evans, 1 October 1920; Drummond, *Imperial Economic Policy*, p. 62.

80 Drummond, *Imperial Economic Policy*, pp. 62–4; PRO, T 161/73/S 5691/1, minute by G. C. Upcott, junior Treasury official, 4 October 1920; T 161/30/S 1710, minute by Chamberlain, 8 November 1920.

81 PRO, CAB 27/115/CU 14, memorandum on emigration by Macnamara, 11 September 1920; CAB 24/137/CP 4062, memorandum by Macnamara, 22 June 1922; CO 537/1036, Macnamara to Churchill, 19 June 1922.

82 PRO, T 161/86/S 6527/06, copy of an OSC information flyer on the ex-service free passage scheme.

83 G. F. Plant, *Oversea Settlement*, London, 1951, p. 73.

84 Kennedy, 'Empire migration', p. 406; Amery diaries, 9 April 1919.

85 Plant, *Oversea Settlement*, pp. 74–5.

# CHAPTER THREE

# Maintaining a tradition

Despite the fact that soldiers in the past had proven inadequate and ineffective settlers the Canadian government launched a determined soldier settlement policy in late 1915. As two Canadian historians remark, a post-war soldier settlement scheme was inescapable. 'It was unprecedented and therefore unthinkable that a war could end without some effort being made to settle soldiers on the land. Tradition, mythology, and concern about rural depopulation overruled memories of the waste and failure of "military bounty".'[1] Canadians simply assumed that returning veterans would be offered farms as they had previously; and soldiers themselves had no reason to think any differently from their civilian counterparts. Sir Robert Borden, Canada's wartime Prime Minister, reassured servicemen that it was the solemn intention of both the nation and his government to 'prove to the returned man (their) just and due appreciation of the inestimable value of the services rendered to the country and empire'.[2]

Canadians did not deny that defending democracy and empire was expensive. Nor did the daily sacrifices and hardships encountered by their troops go unnoticed or unappreciated. The enormous display of patriotic fervour, in particular from English-speaking Canada, was proof enough, and it quickly reinforced Canadian society's already strong sense of obligation and indebtedness to its fighting men.[3] In this extremely emotional and highly charged atmosphere soldier settlement was one constructive method of demonstrating Canada's recognition of these sacrifices. However, land as a reward for services rendered was not soldier settlement's only appealing attribute. Far from it. Underlying the patriotic rhetoric were practical political, social and economic considerations which dictated the pursuit of a comprehensive soldier settlement policy.

Soldier settlement remained an important supplement to the dominion government's predominant and traditional role in settling and developing the agricultural resources of western Canada. This was reiterated in a memorandum submitted to the Minister of the Interior, W. J. Roche, by the Superintendent of Immigration, W. D. Scott, during the formulation of soldier settlement policy in early February 1916. Scott argued that Canada was still fundamentally an agricultural country and therefore it was in the national interest to ensure that the largest possible proportion of those soldiers 'fitted for or willing to undertake agricultural work (be) induced or assisted to do so'.[4] Inevitably, it became one of the most expensive planks in Borden's reconstruction programme.

Walter Scott, Saskatchewan's first premier, heartily endorsed his unrelated dominion namesake's assessment.[5] The settlement of returned men on the land fulfilled the object of populating and developing the remainder of Canada's vast and empty fertile regions. He firmly believed that Canada's most urgent problem, next to the successful prosecution of the war, was the need to increase the country's agricultural population and production. 'That will be the chief problem after the war, as it was before the war, and as it is during the war,' he prophesied.[6] Soldier settlement provided a partial solution.

More significantly, soldier settlement 'represented the first indication that the Canadian government viewed the land as its principal solution to unemployment'.[7] As in Britain, many Canadians feared that when the war ended there would be many unemployed and dissatisfied veterans who, if left unsatisfied, could pose a threat to the political and social stability of the country. The threat of social unrest, which gripped every Allied government after 1918, therefore provided additional motivation for the Canadian government to act decisively over this potentially dangerous problem. A complementary but quite distinctive sentiment was the notion that agricultural communities were healthier and more stable, politically and socially, than urban ones. The rural myth was not unique to Canada for each Allied combatant possessed its own version of this ideal. In Canada, the rural myth was expressed in the popular social philosophy of the back-to-the-land movement; an agrarian backlash aimed at halting rural depopulation brought about by increased industrialisation and urbanisation and the subsequent destruction of society's moral fibre that it implied.

Senator Sir James Lougheed was appointed by Borden, in July and October 1915, to chair two commissions which not only initiated the development of a national soldier settlement plan, but spearheaded the government's entire demobilisation plans and its investigation into the larger issue of Canada's post-war reconstruction problems. Lougheed, a lawyer by profession, had been government leader in the Senate and

Minister without Portfolio since Borden's election victory of 1911. Ontario born, Lougheed had migrated west to Calgary and established one of the most successful law firms in western Canada. Extremely wealthy, Lougheed had married wisely, virtually inheriting his father-in-law's Senate seat in 1889. In July 1915, he was appointed chairman of the Military Hospitals Commission (MHC), the agency which provided retraining and rehabilitation for Canada's war disabled. Its major tasks included the reception and placement of wounded soldiers, the purchase, maintenance and management of convalescent hospitals and sanitaria, vocational training and the provision of artificial limbs.[8]

The provinces established their own Returned Soldiers' Aid Commissions to work in conjunction with the national authority, but the duties of the provincial commissions were narrowly defined as assisting able-bodied soldiers with employment problems. Ultimate financial responsibility for retraining and re-educating the disabled for future employment fell squarely on the shoulders of Ottawa. 'The war is a national undertaking', stated Premier William Hearst of Ontario, 'and there is no desire that we should shoulder responsibility that should properly rest elsewhere.'[9] Hearst was correct in stressing national responsibility for the incapacitated soldier and it became painfully obvious that the provinces were reluctant to assume the enormous monetary and administrative headaches rehabilitation implied. It was ironic that the provinces should so easily delineate dominion-provincial jurisdiction on this issue when, in education for example, both levels of government had fought each other so bitterly for control.

The provincial premiers were also worried that returned soldiers would add to the steady stream of people already leaving the rural areas for the cities. At the inter-provincial conference held in Ottawa in October 1915 the premiers voted unanimously in favour of supporting a soldier settlement scheme. However, they argued that the complexities of the issue were 'national' and therefore beyond the scope of provincial jurisdiction. They advised the national government to institute a special inquiry to investigate the matter.[10] Once again, Ottawa was forced to pick up the slack and frame a returned soldiers' agricultural resettlement scheme.

It seemed a natural progression to Borden to extend the chairmanship of the Natural Resources Commission to Lougheed in October. The new commission was in part created to placate a mayoral delegation drawn from Canada's major cities which had descended upon Ottawa in the spring of 1915. The delegation had complained bitterly about the chronic unemployment in the cities during the previous winter. They demanded money to boost municipal relief programmes and requested that the urban poor should somehow be relocated and re-established on the land.[11] Borden, while promising to study the matter, quickly realised that the combination of the two commissions under one person would go far to meet the parallel demands of the premiers and mayors to deal with rural depopulation. He resolved to exploit the mayors' protestations and use the Natural Resources Commission as a springboard to launch the government's examination of the wider issue of Canada's post-war problems. In light of the recommendations of the interprovincial conference the Commission appeared a perfect instrument through which to formulate a national soldier settlement plan. With Lougheed as its chairman the decision to develop such a plan was a foregone conclusion.

W. J. Black, the former principal of the Manitoba Agricultural College, was chosen as secretary of the Natural Resources Commission.[12] An experienced administrator, Black was a wise choice as he was familiar with the problems of western development and land settlement. Lougheed's foresight was again evident in the appointment of Ernest Henry Scammell as secretary to the MHC. Born in England, Scammell was the son of E. T. Scammell, founder and secretary of the Naval and Military Emigration League. The younger Scammell was 'one of those officials a wise organisation cherishes', as he possessed enormous amounts of energy and administrative expertise.[13] It was Henry Scammell, more than any other individual, who shaped and moulded Canada's demobilisation and rehabilitation policies.

The urgency with which Canadian politicians and civil servants viewed the problem of continuing rural depopulation, and the seriousness with which they viewed soldier settlement as a partial solution, was echoed by Henry Scammell. 'One difficulty to be faced', he reported, 'will be that men from the country districts will be inclined to congregate in the larger centres.' Conversely, 'large numbers of men who previously followed an indoor occupation, both those who are able-bodied and those who are partially disabled, will after their long open air life in the trenches, decide to find employment on the land.'[14] The young Scammell had reached the same conclusion as Sir Arthur Pearson, the blind publisher and founder of St Dunstan's Hostel for blind ex-servicemen in London's Regent's Park. Pearson regarded agriculture as a vital step in the retraining and rehabilitation of the disabled veteran. He was able to persuade many blind veterans that poultry farming provided a practicable occupational alternative.[15]

W. D. Scott felt duty bound to offer practical solutions in the face of the 'lunacy' propounded by 'theorists' such as Pearson. Scott completely disagreed with the idea that soldiers who had lost an arm or leg would not be hampered to any great extent in their efforts to farm; and confined his attention 'solely to those who upon return are physically fit, express a desire for a rural life and have the physical strength necessary for the hard work' farming demanded.[16] He divided the group into two categories, experienced and inexperienced. Inexperienced candidates would be administered through the Department of the Interior and its various agencies such as the Immigration and Dominion Lands Branch. They would be placed with reliable farmers at current wages for one year in order to gain the instruction, advice and experience necessary to manage their own farm.

Scott proposed that two sections in each township, as yet ungranted, be reserved exclusively for returned soldiers for a period of four years.[17] He singled out the Peace River District of northern Alberta as a specific target for future development and suggested that all the odd numbered sections be similarly reserved. Instead of the customary homestead grant of 160 acres, qualified soldiers should be allowed 320 acres. He recommended that full co-operation by the provinces should be solicited. Provincial authorities were to be encouraged to offer similar inducements on land administered by them or assist by purchasing improved land for resale to the soldier settler. Scott also advocated the immediate incorporation of a ' "Returned Soldier Colonising Society" directed by leading capitalists of (a) philanthropic and patriotic turn of mind'.[18] Funding for the scheme would be provided by the society through a flotation of bonds guaranteed by the central government. Advances up to $1,000 would be available to each homesteading soldier and used as a downpayment or an advance on a lien. Interest would be charged and no patent would be issued until the loan was repaid in full. Eligibility was limited to honourably discharged soldiers who had either enlisted in Canadian regiments or been domiciled in Canada prior to their enlistment with Allied units. Finally, candidates had to satisfy government selection officers that they possessed sufficient expertise and practical farming knowledge to succeed in their new vocation. In order to ensure success and foster greater responsibility and independence among the soldier settlers, Scott proposed that each settler be required to invest $200 of his own capital.

Scott pondered that should the flotation of a loan by the proposed soldiers' colonising society prove unfeasible the merits of the project might warrant direct government participation as the central loan agency. 'To loan $1,000 each to 20,000 soldier farmers', commented Scott, 'would take $20,000,000.'

> Consider the consequent benefit to the nation as a whole entirely outside of the patriotic aspect of providing for our soldiers. Fro(m) 1896 to 1911 the Dominion Government paid in bounties on pig iron, steel, lead and petroleum $20,000,000 from which the country receives no return except the stimulus to trade. If the spending of this money is justifiable, surely

the loaning of a like amount for at least as important a purpose needs no justification.[19]

Scott's suggestion that the Canadian government underwrite the financial burden of soldier settlement and undertake the leading role in policy formulation was reinforced when the British government made preliminary enquiries concerning Canadian soldier settlement policy in October 1915.

The Colonial Office had received a proposal for a privately sponsored colonisation scheme in Canada from a consortium in the fruit-growing Okanagan Valley of British Columbia. The Colonial Office immediately forwarded the proposal to Ottawa and were promptly told by the Canadian Governor-General, the Duke of Connaught, that the Minister of the Interior refused to encourage any colonisation schemes proposed by private individuals. The majority of the private colonisation ventures in the past had been motivated by self-interest and had failed miserably creating much hardship in the process.[20] The Canadian government made it absolutely clear, as it always had prior to the war, that it was definitely unwilling to prejudice the national interest by supporting, approving or endorsing privately sponsored schemes.

Lord Milner, however, approached the issue from a different tack. He had learned that Lionel Hichens, a former member of his 'kindergarten' and now the managing director of the shipbuilding giant Cammell Laird, was embarking for Canada to investigate that dominion's munitions industry. Hichens had been closely involved with land settlement in South Africa during the reconstruction period after the Boer War and was acquainted with its problems. Milner suggested that as he was going over on behalf of the Ministry of Munitions he could also investigate post-war land settlement in Canada in a private capacity.[21] Milner realised the British government did not want to give the impression that it supported the emigration of its soldiers after the war, but he warned Bonar Law that, as many soldiers would leave Britain after the war no matter what the government did to encourage them to stay, it was much better to see them settle in the dominions than 'drift off' to the United States or the Argentine. He warned that there would be nothing but 'appalling muddle and waste . . . in the hurry and scramble' upon the cessation of hostilities, unless the main principles of a land settlement policy had been carefully 'thought out and laid down beforehand'.[22]

Milner was convinced that it was essential for the dominions to make adequate preparations if they wanted to obtain the quality and quantity of British emigrants they had so eagerly sought prior to the war. He was anxious that the golden opportunity supplied by Hichens's visit to

Canada should not be squandered by either the imperial or dominion government. Hichens had cultivated a good relationship with Borden and his cabinet colleagues and this provided additional leverage. 'It is not a question of this Gov(ernmen)t doing anything or of dictating to Canada', explained Milner, 'but only of a shove-off, which may lead to their doing the right thing on their own account.' Bonar Law acquiesced and drafted a letter to Borden along the lines suggested by Milner.[23]

Borden's reply to the Colonial Secretary and the record of the meeting between Borden and Hichens has not survived. Nevertheless, the report by the Ontario Commission on Unemployment, released in early 1916, provided Milner, Bonar Law and the Colonial Office with an opportunity to analyse Canada's response to the question of British post-war migration and the employment of ex-servicemen after the war.[24] This Commission was originally appointed to examine the recurrent causes of permanent unemployment in Ontario. It was not empowered to investigate unemployment arising out of the war. However, from a British perspective, the report offered a few interesting ideas and impressed the chairman of the EIO, T. C. Macnaghten.[25]

One important result derived from the Commission's investigations was its recommendation for the establishment in London of an Imperial Migration Board. The Board would represent the British and those dominion, provincial and state governments interested in promoting and improving migration within the empire. Jointly funded by the participating governments, the central agency would be responsible for the collection and dissemination of accurate, impartial and up-to-date information concerning imperial labour markets, occupations, industries, travel costs and accommodation.[26] The advocacy of an aggressive intra-imperial migration and land settlement policy was intended to check the population drain to foreign countries so as 'to conserve British manhood for the development of British territory and the support and defence of British institutions against future contingencies'.[27] The Commission also recognised the need for an extensive review of the system of subsidising shipping and booking agencies. To increase efficiency, the report recommended more adequate inspection of immigrants; and to ensure greater success amongst newcomers, it stated that each immigrant should possess a minimal amount of cash upon landing. Above all, it alerted the Ontario government to its pressing moral obligation to discharged British and Canadian soldiers. It warned that a serious economic and social crisis would result after the war if steps were not taken during hostilities to formulate a comprehensive employment policy for these men before their return.[28]

Macnaghten was encouraged by the Commission's findings. That it supported an intra-imperial migration policy was 'a considerable advance on anything connected with post-war emigration which has yet reached us from the Dominions'.[29] Although he found nothing in the report to indicate that the Commission supported the granting of free land to ex-soldiers, or that its views had the endorsement of the Ontario government, it was clear that it had some influence. He remained cautious as to whether it was desirable to encourage emigration from Britain after the war, nor was he certain that the dominions really wanted British ex-soldiers. But, he admitted, the soldiers themselves would certainly demand the opportunity to emigrate and would doubtless receive the wholehearted support of the 'well intentioned' emigration enthusiasts. Macnaghten concluded that it would be 'difficult to check the emigration movement (and) keep it in the right channels in the absence of fuller information' hitherto received from the dominions.[30]

## The Rider Haggard mission, 1916

Macnaghten may have been encouraged by the unofficial statements uttered by one provincial agency, but, like the rest of the Colonial Office, he hardly expected the resounding support Rider Haggard received in the dominions during his mission. Haggard's tour captured the public's imagination and turned what was simply a fact finding mission into a tremendous public relations victory for the RCI over an intransigent British government.

Initially, the Council of the RCI confined the tour to Australia and New Zealand. George McLaren Brown, European General Manager of the Canadian Pacific Railway and an active member of the RCI's Empire Land Settlement Committee, was responsible for expanding the original itinerary. He argued that if Haggard confined his mission strictly to the Antipodes the imperial character of the mission would entirely disappear.[31] Furthermore, he strongly recommended that Haggard proceed to the Antipodes via South Africa and return to England via Canada. The ELSC forwarded the resolution to the Council which wholeheartedly endorsed McLaren Brown's suggestion at its first meeting in 1916. On 3 January, Haggard received his instructions to proceed to the four 'white' dominions.[32]

In mid-January, J. Obed Smith enquired about the mandate Haggard had been given on behalf of the RCI. He sought clarification as to whether the British government had delegated its authority to the RCI to enter into discussions with the Canadian government, or whether the authority had been invested in Haggard.[33] Sir Harry Wilson, honorary secretary of the RCI, replied that the British government had raised no objections to Haggard's mission in a private capacity as the RCI's honorary representative. He emphasised, however, that Haggard had 'full discretion' to discuss land settlement questions with the dominion and provincial governments.[34] The Assistant Superintendent of Emigration became increasingly hostile.

> I . . . quite fail to understand why there should be any attempt to educate the Canadian Government and our Department on business which has been their public duty for so many years . . . I do not quite see what advantage there would be in you discussing the matter with me, so long as neither the Home Government have invited the assistance of any outsiders in connection with business which is obviously the first duty of this Department.[35]

Canada had been settling thousands of people satisfactorily for years with no outside assistance. Did the RCI really believe it had anything different to offer? 'I have received no hint that our Department is at all unable to carry on its business here and in Canada', Smith commented acidly, 'without calling for the assistance of others.'[36] Wilson attempted to reason with Smith. He offered him an opportunity to discuss the matter in a friendly, rational manner, reiterating that the RCI had no intention of interfering with the practices and policies of the Canadian government.[37] Unfortunately, he failed to de-fuse Smith's anger. Shortly afterwards, Wilson terminated the correspondence, but the Assistant Superintendent of Emigration's intense hostility cast a dark shadow over the Canadian visit.

Smith had other reasons for either not supporting or encouraging Haggard's visit to Canada. In a personal letter to Cory, written in language reminiscent of similar Colonial Office vitriol, he confided that Haggard was the last person in the world to be sent on such a task.[38] His condemnation was based on a similar mission Haggard had undertaken in 1905 when he had investigated the Salvation Army colonies in the United States at the bequest of the then Colonial Secretary, Alfred Lyttelton. Haggard's findings had then been deemed impractical and dismissed in an official report of a departmental committee assigned to review his recommendations. Furthermore, Smith warned Ottawa that the RCI had a reputation for 'rushing in where angels fear to tread . . . It seems to forget so frequently that Governments, like ours, have their own views and their own machinery for carrying out Canada's policy.' The RCI had to learn that Canada was quite capable of conducting its own business without outside interference and that land settlement and post-war migration were 'too serious and of too great import to be peddled around [by] well-intentioned gentlemen [who] often create an atmosphere which does not facilitate the real work of negotiations between Governments.'[39]

Smith's scathing remarks generated deep concern at the RCI as it was feared that details of his reaction and subsequent encounter with Wilson would be conveyed to his superiors in Ottawa. To offset this potential danger, the RCI attempted to clarify their position to the Canadian High Commissioner, Sir George Perley. Wilson advised Perley that Sir Charles Lucas, a former EIO chairman and currently chairman of the Council of the RCI, was 'very anxious that there should be no misapprehension about [Haggard's] visit, which is purely private and unofficial'.[40] As a further reinforcement to the RCI's bridge-building exercise, Haggard called on Perley to inform him of the exact object of his visit and reassure him that he did not wish to compete, 'or in any possible way interfere with any existing Commission, Com-mittee, or Society concerned with immigration' to Canada.[41] Wilson's impromptu instructions to Haggard reflected the RCI's deep-seated concern over Canadian attitudes. Opposition in Canada was anticipated and if Smith's hostility was an indication of what Haggard could expect in Canada, the situation looked grim. It was thus decided that, if Haggard encountered any resistance from the dominion government upon arrival at Vancouver, he was to halt the inquiry immediately and limit his enquiries to those requested by the DRC before returning directly to England.[42]

When Haggard did arrive in Canada in late June he found no sign of any such opposition. By contrast, his reception in Victoria, British Columbia, 'was striking and indeed enthusiastic' and included front page coverage in the local newspaper.[43] He was met by the all too familiar host of local businessmen and civic dignitaries and by E. H. Scammell, who had been despatched by Lougheed to escort Haggard across Canada. The schedule was hectic and he was kept extremely busy in Victoria with numerous public speaking engagements. It was at the Veterans Club, of which Rider's brother Andrew was president, where Rider pointed out that during his tour he had encountered some 'very liberal ideas' as to the issue of soldier settlement but apparently 'hardly any plans of a concrete nature for translating these ideas into action'.[44] He warned his audiences of the necessity for the empire to marshal its resources, co-ordinate its policies and concentrate its energies in order to avoid duplication of settlement and migration work conducted by private agencies and governments. Haggard emphasised the need to draw up a 'working plan' which would be ready for operation once the war was over.[45]

The initial Canadian response was pleasantly surprising. Local, prov-incial and dominion authorities were willing to listen, co-operate and exchange ideas and information with the RCI representative. He received a warm reception, the outlook appeared encouraging and opposition was non-existent, but Haggard was very careful to explain that he had no 'special scheme' and that he was on a 'mission of enquiry'.[46] The *Vancouver World* reported that Haggard had the 'welfare of the empire at heart' and that his opinions, ideas and advice on land settlement questions were 'based on study and experience, of a very wide and varied character (which) must command respect'.[47] However, Haggard remained cautiously optimistic and followed Wilson's instructions to the letter.

The apparent change of heart by Canadian authorities was being monitored by Wilson in London. Just prior to Haggard's arrival in Canada, Wilson informed Haggard that the Canadians were aware of his progress in Australia and New Zealand. He also reported that he had received very favourable responses from Borden and Lougheed which took 'the sting out of our friend Obed Smith's dog-in-the-manger communications'.[48] McLaren Brown had worked diligently to counteract any damage Smith had inflicted and it was largely through his influence that the 'mischief' of the Assistant Superintendent was rectified.[49] As well, Henry Scammell had proved to be a loyal ally by dispelling any misapprehensions that arose in Ottawa. Wilson was satisfied that Smith's 'interference' had been effectively removed and that the RCI could 'confidently expect no further trouble in Canada'.[50]

Haggard's message was simple and straightforward. He was deeply concerned about the mass exodus of British subjects who settled in countries outside the empire. The loss of such large numbers of good British stock was tragic, unnecessary and had to be curtailed if the British empire was to remain a healthy, vibrant international power. Personally, Haggard did not favour the emigration of British citizens to any overseas destinations. 'But if they insist on leaving', he explained, 'we want to try and take care that they leave for some place where the British flag flies.'[51] Similarly, in a hot and sultry Regina, he hoped to see 'this empire of ours one house with many rooms, in each of which its citizens may wander, knowing that there he is at home'.[52]

Soldier settlement, he told his listeners, was an attempt to solve the problem of emigration erosion. He made it quite clear to provincial and national leaders that British veterans returning home after the war would find little or no support, financial or otherwise, from the British government or private institutions and charities. He hoped that if promises of free grants of land and financial assistance were forthcoming from the dominions, extra pressure would be exerted on British authorities to support the imperial project. At the same time Haggard made it perfectly clear that the RCI's ELSC was not in existence to advocate and promote emigration. None the less, it was fundamentally more important to prepare for the eventuality of post-war migration and set the wheel in motion than patiently wait for the British government to initiate a plan once hostilities ended.

The enthusiastic Canadian response was inspired by the same patriotic fervour which had inspired the mission. The press surrendered their front pages and gave detailed reports of Haggard's progress as he travelled across the prairies. The *Edmonton Journal* proclaimed that the success of the mission was 'vital' to Canada's future while other editorials demanded every effort be made to encourage and formulate Haggard's efforts into a constructive framework.[53] Congratulations flooded in and as the mission progressed eastwards across western Canada the offers of land and concessions increased. A. R. U. Corbett, Haggard's private secretary during the mission, was not surprised given the equally exuberant Australian response. For Corbett had predicted during the Australian leg of the tour that the Canadian authorities 'will of course want to go one better and it will be rather amusing'.[54] And so it was.

Some reservations were none the less expressed. Walter Scott, the premier of Saskatchewan, agreed that any soldier settlement scheme required careful settler selection. 'Not all ex-Service men will be found adapted for or willing to become farm settlers and it will not help the situation to send out men who should be foredoomed to failure.'[55] He pointed out that success would be determined by the degree to which the state could guarantee a fair start to the soldier settler. The implementation of a comprehensive advance loan policy embodied in the settlement scheme was imperative.

The Canadian Pacific Railway (CPR) took the opportunity of Haggard's visit to disclose its plans to provide farms on its extensive holdings in western Canada for returning veterans from Canada and Britain. These plans were provisional and consisted of two methods of settlement. A system of assisted colonisation would provide the returned soldier with the opportunity of selecting his own farm on unsold CPR land in predetermined districts. Building material, equipment and livestock would be provided by the company on a long-term repayment scheme. The second approach was the 'Ready Made Farm' system, in which farms would be built and fully stocked prior to the soldier settler's arrival. Groups of fifty or more farms would be constructed to form a colony in which a demonstration farm and a central stores depot would be located which would be administered by a CPR colony superintendent. Strict selection practices were advocated necessitated by previous experience.[56] The proposals had been under discussion since the beginning of 1916 but the chairman of the CPR's advisory committee, J. S. Dennis, notified his associates that Haggard should only receive a general outline and that none of the information should be published because of its highly tentative nature.[57]

Lougheed also supported the ready-made farm principle advocated by the CPR and J. H. Sherrard, President of the Canadian Manufacturers Association.[58] He too took the opportunity, supplied by Haggard's visit, to release the report of the Natural Resources Commission. The Commission's findings assumed that returning veterans who made their homes on the land stood a better chance of leading a healthier, more prosperous life compared to soldiers employed in urban areas. Farming experience was not essential because the proposed soldiers' colonies would be designed to provide the occupational and managerial expertise required. These colonies would provide schools, churches, stores and a central training farm for prospective settlers. Each colonist was entitled to 160 acres and loans to a maximum of $1,500.[59]

The premiers of Alberta, Saskatchewan and Manitoba cordially invited Haggard to discuss the mission. While offering their support, they reminded him, however, that the three prairie provinces had no control over Crown land. Nevertheless, as he swept across western Canada, the momentum he generated strengthened his position by the time he arrived in Ottawa for discussions with Borden and his cabinet. Haggard met with a cabinet sub-committee on 18 July 1916 composed of Sir Thomas White, Minister of Finance, Martin Burrell, Minister of Agriculture, T. W. Crothers, Minister of Labour and Lougheed. His proposals received a sympathetic ear and when he met with Borden the following day the Canadian Prime Minister stated that he had a 'very agreeable interview with him'.[60]

The Prime Minister also assured Haggard that a soldier settlement policy would be introduced to Parliament in the near future. He reassured him that everything would be done to promote the immigration and settlement of British soldiers. Haggard was pleased; the interview with Borden embodied all he sought,[61] but although he had much to be satisfied about, Haggard was not naive. He advised the RCI to remain cautious.

> Now, at any rate, they have given their public promise from which they cannot and will not wish to recede. In any event it seems to me wise to let the glory rest with them and not to claim too much for our efforts. Perhaps the chief value of these lay, not so much in my arguments, as in the fact that I was able to show them that they had the Provincial Governments and the population of Canada behind them in anything that they might choose to do. Of this there could be no doubt after the very remarkable success of the meetings which I addressed in the various Provinces – for remarkable it was.[62]

Unfortunately, certain establishment figures in Ottawa were not as enthusiastic about Haggard's mission. The Solicitor-General and future Minister of the Interior, Arthur Meighen, was not overly impressed: '(Haggard) laid before us nothing whatever except a very general desire that we do something substantial in the way of facilitating land settlement by British soldiers; which indeed anyone might have taken for granted.'[63] Meighen contrasted the lack of substance in Haggard's interview with the 'well digested . . . concrete and definite' settlement scheme recommended by the Natural Resources Commission.[64] However, the cabinet were unenthusiastic about Lougheed's report as well. Ministers lacked the confidence in group settlements exuded by the CPR and Lougheed because years of experience had taught successive dominion governments that group settlements spelled failure and hardship. Both Haggard and Lougheed were told by the Departments of Agriculture and the Interior that no vacant townships existed close enough to railways to make such a colony scheme viable.[65] It was evident that the Canadian government had its own ideas and would implement these ideas at its own pace. Thus, while the Canadian government was not forthcoming, and possessed some serious reservations about the Haggard mission, it had none the less been a congenial host.[66]

## Soldier settlement in 1917

It was the provinces, not the dominion government, that initiated the first soldier settler schemes. The polite dismissal of Haggard's mission by senior officials in Ottawa was not accepted by Howard Ferguson, Ontario's energetic and enthusiastic Minister of Lands, Forests and Mines. Ontario became the first province to respond with a land settlement scheme for returned soldiers in February 1917. The province arranged to transport interned enemy aliens to the clay belt of northern Ontario near Kapuskasing to clear the dense forest for soldier settlement. Enemy internees were busily employed doing the back-breaking work of land clearance and road building, providing the basis of a reward and a fresh start for returned servicemen who had been fighting against the internees' own countrymen.[67] The Kapuskasing scheme proved extremely popular and was touted as Ontario's response to the back-to-the-land movement which was then sweeping across Canada. In Ontario boosters painted an attractive picture of the resource potential of the north and the enormous economic benefits that could be derived from it. The development of 'New Ontario' or the 'true North' was being vigorously promoted and it had universal appeal. The pioneer settlement at Kapuskasing would be the important first step in the expansion and long-term exploitation of northern Ontario's natural riches.[68]

Once enough land had been cleared Ferguson proceeded with the colony. Five townships were set aside located between sixty and seventy miles west of Cochrane on the National Transcontinental Railway. Each settler was promised 100 acres (of which ten acres was pre-cleared) and a maximum of $500 in provincial loans for the purchase of livestock and machinery, repayable within twenty years at 6 per cent interest.[69] A small sawmill was erected to complement the initial farming operations and provide additional revenue from the lumber produced during the land clearing. Horses, farm implements, wagons, sleighs and other heavy machinery were set aside in a community pool to assist the settler during the early stages of settlement. A training school was established on the provincial government's demonstration farm at Monteith, thirty miles south of Cochrane. Instruction in agriculture, land clearing, stumping and logging was offered.[70]

The Kapuskasing colony was founded on a co-operative community basis and provisions were made for the erection of a village complete with a school, administrative building, general store and laundry facilities. Ferguson placed great emphasis on the endless supply of good pulp wood in the region which he saw as a valuable winter income supplement for the settlers. There was also an enormous amount of road and bridge construction planned for the area which ensured the economic viability of the new settlement. Patents would be granted as long as the settler cleared two acres each year to the equivalent of 10 per cent of the total acreage, resided continuously for three years and built a habitable home. Such economic diversity was sure to guarantee the project's success and the Department of Lands, Forests and Mines was confident that the greatest enemy of northern development – loneliness – would be defeated because of the communal and co-operative framework it had established in Kapuskasing. Every social amenity had been provided for including a gramophone, piano and billiard table.[71]

Isolation was categorised as the settler's gravest foe by land settlement experts and colonisation enthusiasts alike. According to their argument, drought and pestilence were deemed inconsequential compared with the dominion government's current system of settlement which effectively encouraged solitude and retarded rural progress. The Ontario scheme and the CPR's soldier colonies and 'Ready Made Farms' project illustrated that many people believed that successful agricultural development required co-operative methods and that the provision of social amenities to enhance social inter-action was considered essential.[72] Lougheed's report, released during Haggard's mission in 1916, testified that even some senior politicians had succumbed to the notion of soldier settlement colonies. The effect this idea would have on policy makers in Ottawa and the practicality of the soldier colony idea was another matter.

Ontario was particularly anxious to extend this settlement opportunity to all soldiers who had served in the British forces during the war.[73] In a despatch to the Colonial Office, the Duke of Devonshire, Governor-General of Canada, gave his endorsement of the settlement scheme and 'was particularly impressed with the enthusiasm' of the men who were on the land already cleared.[74] Ottawa also took notice of Ontario's initiative. Scammell recorded that Ontario was the only province to implement its land settlement legislation fully. He complained bitterly that the other provinces were quite content to sit back and wait for Ottawa to provide funding.[75]

The initiative displayed by Ontario was not lost on either the British or Canadian governments. Borden responded by sending requests for information to each of the provincial premiers and his cabinet colleagues.[76] The replies were enthusiastic but raised a number of problems. The Saskatchewan government had not, in practice, adopted any policy to secure or assist British soldiers planning to settle in Canada. Co-operation was forthcoming and interest was keen but owing to the fact that Crown land was under Ottawa's jurisdiction in Saskatchewan it was not the province's responsibility to finance or adopt such a land settlement policy. In fact, the Saskatchewan authorities had adopted a wait-and-see strategy. They would only be forthcoming with assistance once the dominion government had outlined its own policy.[77] Premier George Clark of New Brunswick informed Borden of his province's recently passed post-war settlement legislation and its ongoing attempts to establish prosperous, self-contained community settlements. The New Brunswick legislation was based on exactly the same foundation as Ontario's Kapuskasing project. The community settlement idea was aimed at those soldier settlers who required financial assistance, training and mutual support. Clark was confident of the scheme's success and reminded Borden that imperial soldiers who desired to settle in New Brunswick after the war, and who possessed sufficient capital to make their enrolment in the community settlement project unnecessary, could purchase a previously cultivated farm in a productive locality through the Farm Settlement Board.[78]

Premier Brewster of British Columbia, though very supportive, believed that his province would be burdened with the greatest share of responsibility in a national soldier settlement scheme.[79] The prairie provinces and the Maritimes had little or no public land to offer. It remained for Ontario, Quebec and British Columbia to take charge.

Legislation had been passed during the last session, based on a report submitted in March 1916 by the provincial Returned Soldiers' Aid Commission, which made provision for land on co-operative farm settlements for local soldiers.[80] However, no final settlement details had been worked out. Brewster entertained other reservations.

> It seems to me that before any comprehensive plan can be adopted for the Dominion as a whole there should be a convention called at Ottawa . . . to discuss not only the duties of the provinces in respect of returned soldiers and of citizens generally, but the relation which the Dominion should bear to collective responsibilities. There should be some clear line of demarcation of duty and responsibility as among the several bodies in whatever compact is proposed to be framed, and I do not think any government should commit itself to a programme until it is definitely known what all the other governments will do.[81]

Borden agreed, announcing to his provincial counterparts that his government had drafted some preliminary legislative proposals but that it was eager for provincial input. There was also the issue of the Colonial Office's December reminder concerning dominion plans for British ex-servicemen. The Prime Minister announced that an inter-provincial land settlement conference would be held in Ottawa on 10–12 January 1917 to discuss these issues.[82]

The conference had two main objectives: 'A full, free and frank' discussion and exchange of ideas and information between the dominion and provincial governments on how best to settle ex-servicemen after the war. More importantly, the question of inter-government co-operation and the 'satisfactory division of responsibility' with regard to increased loan facilities and the settlement of unused land under private ownership were key points under discussion.[83] The question of technical education was examined as well as the preferential employment of ex-soldiers in the civil service and on public works projects. However, it was universally recognised that the underlying objective behind the conference and the proposed legislation was the vital national necessity of increased agricultural production.[84] The Duke of Devonshire cabled Walter Long, Bonar Law's successor at the Colonial Office, informing him that the conference had been interesting and revealing. '[W]ithout arriving at any very definite conclusions there was a useful interchange of ideas and good results may be expected to follow'. Long was pleased because the Canadian conference coincided with his attempts to examine the issue of post-war migration embodied in the Tennyson committee.[85]

Shortly after the conclusion of the conference a cabinet committee composed of Roche, White, Burrell and Meighen were given the task of framing the appropriate legislation. Lougheed's absence was manifest. In May 1917 the Canadian government presented its legislation for the repatriation and re-establishment of its soldiers on the land to the Canadian Parliament. The Soldier Settlement Act of 1917 was enacted to provide returning veterans with the opportunity of establishing themselves on a homestead.[86] This particular approach to land settlement emphasised the Canadian government's commitment to open up huge new areas of land for agricultural purposes. Roche stressed that the aim of the legislation was now two-fold: 'to assist the returned soldier and increase agricultural production'.[87] Admittedly, if the legislation proved attractive to the returned soldier, Roche believed it might provide an important measure to counteract the exodus of Canada's rural population to the cities. In some government circles officials believed that soldiers, as a class, would prove no exception to the above rule. The tendency to migrate to the metropolis still alarmed a growing number of Canadians concerned about the future of the country's social fabric.[88] One thing was certain: while recognising the sacrifices Canadian troops had made during the war, the basic conception of the soldier settlement legislation was that it was not a military bounty. Rather, it was a plan for making brave men into competent farmers. As was repeatedly emphasised in Parliament, in order to ensure maximum success the entire scheme had to be placed on sound businesslike principles.[89]

The Act established a three-man Soldier Settlement Board (SSB) which was empowered to grant loans to a maximum of $2,500 at 5 per cent interest for twenty years for the acquisition of land, livestock and farm machinery. Loans could be applied to property already owned or leased by the returned soldier, or to lands he wished to purchase, or to the settlement of free dominion lands in the prairie provinces. In the case of dominion lands the Act authorised the reservation for soldier settlement of all undisposed-of land within fifteen miles of a railway. A free grant of 160 acres was allowed to each soldier applicant wanting to homestead in these reserves. In addition, the soldier could easily expand his operation and claim the standard homestead right of 160 acres providing he had not exhausted the privilege already. The beneficiaries of the Act were Canadians who had served overseas with the Canadian Expeditionary Force or as members of the imperial forces and soldiers who had served with the imperial forces and any self-governing dominion or colony. Provision was also made for agricultural instruction of the inexperienced soldier settler, but no specifics were outlined.[90]

Roche proudly informed Parliament that Canada was doing its utmost for the returned soldier and that its soldier settlement legislation was 'the most generous and practicable offer made by any British dominion'.[91] Liberal back-benchers, although not challenging the government's generosity, were sceptical of the legislation, in particular the type and location of the land being offered. Roche countered with the announcement that there were 6.5 million acres of available dominion land within ten miles of railways in western Canada. But he was forced to admit that not all of it was open prairie. A good portion was swampy marshland, thick scrub or dense forest which needed a large amount of money, time and back-breaking work to bring under cultivation.[92] This prompted one New Brunswick Liberal back-bencher, W. H. Pugsley, to proclaim that the legislation did not go far enough for these very reasons. The available land was concentrated in the remote north central regions of the prairies, two-thirds of which was in Alberta. Pugsley charged that the soldier settler should not be sent to these remote and isolated areas where he would very likely become discouraged and quickly abandon the homestead. He complained that it was highly doubtful that many soldiers wanted to lead the lonely life of a pioneer. 'Not one man in a thousand would be attracted by an invitation to settle on land in the Peace River country, six hundred miles north of the American boundary, where there are no settlers, no schools, churches or doctors'.[93] Pugsley suggested that the government exercise its right of expropriation and obtain land in established settlement districts for those who were not desirous of pioneer settlement.

All concerned agreed that returned soldiers should not receive preferential treatment regarding land settlement. They should be treated as 'ordinary individuals, not as extraordinary persons',[94] but this did not warrant throwing all caution to the wind. These men would need some kind of support. The primary fear echoed by one seasoned prairie politician, and supported by a Lands Branch official, was the inadvisability of the dominion government of embarking upon a settlement policy in which the majority of the participants were inexperienced. 'Unless a man evinces a desire to his own volition to go in for farming, and has had previous experience therein . . . legislation framed with this object in view is doomed to failure.'[95] Promises of agricultural training were extracted from Roche but it was evident from his cursory treatment of the subject that nothing concrete had been mapped out. For its part, the dominion government ignored the opposition's calls for caution and greater forethought.

From its inception it was evident that the Soldier Settlement Act of 1917 was aimed at achieving imperial self-sufficiency and cultural uniformity. Roche declared:

Fortunately for us . . . in this period of national crisis, we have had the preponderance of our population Canadian and British-born. It is there-

fore, in my opinion, of the greatest importance, not only from a senti-
mental but also from a national and economic standpoint, that we should
maintain, to as great an extent as possible, the British element in our
population . . .[96]

The response to this Act was disappointing for its architects as only
slightly more than 2,000 men took advantage of the scheme between
1917 and 1919.[97] The biggest problem was the type and location of the
dominion lands as the majority of the good and easily accessible land
had been culled by homesteaders long before the war. Although
thousands of productive, easily accessible acres remained unsettled
they were in the hands of individual and corporate speculators.
Dominion lands, located in the heavily forested and marshy inter-lake
region of Manitoba, on the northern fringes of the park belt, in the Peace
River country of north-western Alberta, or the semi-arid Palliser Tri-
angle were extensive but isolated and marginally productive.[98] Farming
operations in these areas demanded a large and immediate infusion of
investment capital. Clearing land was a costly and slow business which
consumed any initial returns likely to be gained in the early years, and
Ottawa's failure to incorporate the powers of expropriation into the
SSB's mandate proved to be a glaring mistake. In 1918 it was announced
that 85 per cent of the twenty-two million acres of vacant dominion
land in the west had been deemed unacceptable because it was either
agriculturally unsuitable or too far from the railway.[99] This effectively
halved Roche's initial estimate and, equally significant, this was an
admission of policy failure by the government. A new policy was
urgently needed.

## Notes

1 Morton and Wright, *Winning the Second Battle*, p. 100.
2 Quotation cited in H. C. Baker, *Homes for Heroes*, Saskatoon, 1979, p. 2.
3 R. M. Bray, ' "Fighting as an ally": The English-Canadian patriotic response to the
Great War', *Canadian Historical Review*, LXI, 1980, pp. 141–68. Also see Desmond
Morton, ' "Junior but sovereign allies": the transformation of the Canadian Expeditionary Force, 1914–1918', in Norman Hillmer and Philip Wigley, eds, *The First
British Commonwealth: Essays in Honour of Nicholas Mansergh*, London, 1980, pp.
56–67.
4 NA, R. L. Borden Papers, vol. 67, f. OC 312 (A), p. 34334, Scott to Roche, 2 February
1916.
5 In W. J. C. Cherwinski's article, 'The incredible harvest excursion of 1908', *Labour/le
travailleur*, V, 1980, p. 59, footnote 9, he has incorrectly concluded that W. D. Scott,
the Ottawa civil servant and Walter Scott, Saskatchewan's premier, were brothers.
According to Henry J. Morgan, *Canadian Men and Women of the Time*, 2nd ed.,
Toronto, 1912, pp. 1005–6, the two men had completely different parents and there is
no subsequent primary or secondary source which would indicate that they were
remotely related.

6  Provincial Archives of Ontario (hereafter PAO), pamphlet file, no. 57 – 1915, Premier Walter Scott, 'Agricultural population and production', p. 4.
7  James Struthers, *No Fault of Their Own: Unemployment and the Canadian Welfare State 1914–1941*, Toronto, 1983, p. 17; *idem*, 'Prelude to depression: the federal government and unemployment, 1918–29', *Canadian Historical Review*, LVII, 1977, pp. 277–93. For contemporary examples see the Commission of Conservation, 'Report of conference held at Winnipeg in conjunction with the second annual meeting of the Civic Improvement League of Canada, 28–30 May 1917', in *Urban and Rural Development*, Ottawa, 1917, pp. 83–8.
8  *Canadian Annual Review*, 1916, p. 379; J. A. Corry, 'The growth of government activities in Canada 1914–1921', *Historical Papers*, 1940, pp. 63–73.
9  PAO, Prime Minister's Office, RG 3, William Hearst Papers, Box 16, 'Memorandum of suggestions adopted at inter-provincial conference, Ottawa, October 1915: the problem of taking care of and providing employment for members of the Canadian Expeditionary Force who return to Canada during the period of the war'.
10  Morton and Wright, *Winning the Second Battle*, p. 18; PAO, RG 3, Hearst Papers, Box 16, 'Memorandum of suggestions'.
11  Morton and Wright, *Winning the Second Battle*, p. 14.
12  *Ibid.*, pp. 100–1.
13  *Ibid.*, p. 8.
14  Quotation cited in Morton and Wright, *Winning the Second Battle*, p. 101. Ernest Scammell, *The Provision of Employment for Members of the Canadian Expeditionary Force on Their Return to Canada and the Re-Education of Those Who Are Unable to Follow Their Previous Occupations Because of Disability*, Ottawa, 1916, p. 9. Also see Robert Rogers, 'Canada's problems during and after the war', *Addresses delivered before the Canadian Club of Montreal*, 1916–17, pp. 79–86; A. C. Flumerfelt, ' "The landless man" and "the manless land" of Canada', *ibid.*, pp. 179–83.
15  A. Pearson, *Victory Over Blindness*, London, c. 1920, pp. 151–7; T. B. Kidner, 'The disabled soldier', *Addresses delivered before the Canadian Club of Montreal*, 1916–17, p. 115; Major J. L. Todd, 'Returned soldiers and the medical profession', reprint from the *Canadian Medical Association Journal*, VII, 1917, pp. 1–13; Desmond Morton, 'Noblest and best: retraining Canada's war disabled, 1915–1923', *Journal of Canadian Studies*, XVI, 1981–82, pp. 75–85. In a pamphlet released by the Canadian Military Hospitals Commission entitled, 'The soldiers return: from "Down and Out" to "Up and In Again": a little chat from Private Pat', Ottawa, 1917, the fictional Private Pat relates a story of a one-legged soldier farmer who was as good as any healthy farmer; 'and I've seen a photo of a one-armed farmer pitching hay, no less!'
16  NA, Borden Papers, vol. 67, f. OC 312 (A), p. 34334, Scott to Roche, 2 February 1916.
17  A section of land is one square mile or 640 acres.
18  NA, Borden Papers, vol. 67, f. OC 312 (A), pp. 34334–5, Scott to Roche, 2 February 1916.
19  *Ibid.*
20  PRO, CO 532/78/50891, Duke of Connaught, Governor-General of Canada, to Bonar Law, 22 October 1915.
21  HLRO, Bonar Law Papers, BL/50/1/21, Milner to Bonar Law, 10 October 1915; John Grigg, *Lloyd George from Peace to War 1912–1916*, London, 1985, p. 270. The kindergarten was the name given to Milner's cadre of young Oxford graduates who were placed in key administrative positions in the reconstruction government during and after the second Anglo-Boer War.
22  HLRO, Bonar Law Papers, BL/50/1/21, Milner to Bonar Law, 10 October 1915.
23  *Ibid.*; PRO, CO 532/82/34985, Milner to Bonar Law, 15 October 1915; Bonar Law to Borden, 15 October 1915.
24  Ontario Legislative Assembly, *Sessional Papers*, XLVIII, part XIII, no. 55, Report of the Ontario Unemployment Commission, 1916.
25  PRO, CO 532/84/14032, minute by Macnaghten, 29 March 1916.
26  *The Times*, 4 March 1916.
27  *Ibid.*

**28** *Ibid.*
**29** PRO, CO 532/84/14032, minute by Macnaghten, 29 March 1916.
**30** *Ibid.*
**31** RCSA, ELSC minutes, 21 December 1915; Royal Commonwealth Society, 'Sir Rider Haggard's mission', *Library Notes*, new series, no. 190, April 1973, p. 2.
**32** Higgins, *War Diaries*, p. 49.
**33** RCSA, ELSC, Smith to Wilson, 11 January 1916.
**34** *Ibid.*, Wilson to Smith, 12 January 1916
**35** *Ibid.*, Smith to Wilson, 19 January 1916.
**36** *Ibid.*
**37** *Ibid.*, Wilson to Smith, 20 January 1916.
**38** NA, Borden Papers, vol. 171, f. RLB 130, pp. 93147–8, Smith to Cory, 12 January 1916. One Colonial Office official, Edward Harding, secretary of the DRC and one who had witnessed first hand Haggard at work as a DRC commissioner, was not impressed by him at all. 'I *think* he is of the temperament which has very ordinary Imperial ideas, and thinks they are extraordinary. Perhaps that is the result of being a Novelist with a really keen imagination.' RCSA, E. J. Harding Papers, Harding to his father, 9 September 1913.
**39** NA, Borden Papers, vol. 171, f. RLB 130, pp. 93146–8, Smith to Cory, 12 January 1916.
**40** RCSA, ELSC, Wilson to Perley, 4 February 1916.
**41** NA, Department of External Affairs, RG 25, G I, vol. 1186, f. 1225–16, Bonar Law to the Duke of Connaught, 7 February 1916; Borden Papers, vol. 67, OC 312 (A), pp. 34336–9, Haggard to Perley, 2 February 1916; Perley to Borden, 4 February 1916; Perley to Haggard, 4 February 1916.
**42** RCSA, ELSC, Wilson to Haggard, 8 February 1916.
**43** *Ibid.*, Haggard to Wilson, 4 July 1916.
**44** *Daily Colonist* (Victoria), 1 July 1916.
**45** *Ibid.*
**46** *Ibid.*, 30 June 1916. R. B. Bennett, Conservative MP for Calgary, Lougheed's law partner and soon to be appointed the RCI's honorary Canadian representative, similarly informed Borden of the apolitical nature of Haggard's mission and message. NA, Borden Papers, vol. 181, f. RLB 406, p. 99067, Bennett to Borden, 15 July 1916.
**47** *Vancouver World*, 28 June 1916.
**48** RCSA, ELSC, Wilson to Haggard, 30 March and 30 June 1916.
**49** *Ibid.*, Wilson to Haggard, 30 March 1916; 'Sir Rider Haggard's mission', p. 4.
**50** RCSA, ELSC, Wilson to Haggard, 4 May 1916.
**51** *Saskatoon Daily Phoenix*, 14 July 1916.
**52** *Leader* (Regina), 13 July 1916.
**53** Schultz, 'Fit for heroes', p. 105.
**54** RCSA, ELSC, Corbett to Wilson, 14 April 1916.
**55** Saskatchewan Archives Board (hereafter SAB), Walter Scott Papers, M1-IV-92 (4), p. 41381, Walter Scott to Haggard, 13 July 1916.
**56** Glenbow-Alberta Archive (hereafter GAA), Canadian Pacific Railway, Advisory Committee Papers, Box 36, f. 431, J. S. Dennis, Assistant to the President of the CPR, to Haggard, 10 July 1916.
**57** *Ibid.*, Advisory Committee minutes, 8 July 1916.
**58** NA, Borden Papers, vol. 67, f. 312 (A), pp. 34365–6, Sherrard to Borden, 8 March 1916.
**59** Morton and Wright, *Winning the Second Battle*, pp. 101–2.
**60** *Canadian Annual Review*, 1916, p. 381.
**61** NA, Borden Papers, vol. 181, f. RLB 406, p. 99071, Haggard to Borden, 20 July 1916.
**62** RCSA, ELSC, Haggard to Wilson, date unclear (July 1916).
**63** NA, Borden Papers, vol. 181, f. RLB 406, p. 99072, Meighen to Borden, 21 July 1916.
**64** *Ibid.*
**65** Morton and Wright, *Winning the Second Battle*, p. 102.
**66** RCSA, ELSC, Corbett to Wilson, 14 July 1916.
**67** Desmond Morton, 'Sir William Otter and internment operations in Canada during the First World War', *Canadian Historical Review*, LV, 1974, pp. 32–58.

68 Charles M. Johnston, *E. C. Drury: Agrarian Idealist*, Toronto, 1986, pp. 166–7; Joseph Schull, *Ontario Since 1867*, Toronto, 1978, pp. 228–9; *Canadian Annual Review*, 1916, p. 485.

69 PAO, RG 3, Hearst Papers, Box 16, memorandum entitled 'Land settlement and opportunities for returned soldiers in the province of Ontario', 6 February 1917.

70 *Ibid.*, Box 15, memorandum for the Ontario premier entitled, 'The land settlement scheme for returned soldiers and sailors', by H. M. Robins, Acting Deputy Minister of Lands, Forests and Mines, 5 November 1918, pp. 1–6.

71 *Ibid.*, p. 3.

72 Thomas Adams, 'Returned soldiers and land settlement', in Commission of Conservation, *Rural Planning and Development*, Ottawa, 1917, pp. 207–9.

73 PAO, RG 3, Hearst Papers, Box 16, 'Land settlement and opportunities', 6 February 1917.

74 PRO, CO 532/93/55672, Devonshire to Long, 25 October 1917. Devonshire was confident that northern Ontario was 'bound to have a great future both from its minerals and its agricultural opportunities'. Bodleian, Selborne Papers, Box 93, Devonshire to Selborne, 7 October 1917.

75 NA, Department of Veterans Affairs, RG 38, vol. 225, E. H. Scammell, Deputy Minister of the Department of Soldiers' Civil Re-establishment, to J. B. Allen, Assistant Secretary of the Privy Council, 15 March 1918.

76 NA, Borden Papers, vol. 67, f. OC 312 (A), pp. 34399–407, Borden to provincial premiers, 25 September 1916.

77 *Ibid.*, pp. 34421–2, Acting Premier of Saskatchewan to Borden, 3 October 1916.

78 PRO, CO 532/84/24495, New Brunswick, *Statutes*, 6, George V, Chapter 9, 'An act to provide for settlements after the war'; NA, Borden Papers, vol. 67, f. OC 312 (A), pp. 34423–6, Clark to Borden, 6 October 1916.

79 NA, Borden Papers, vol. 67, f. OC 312 (A), p. 34430, H. E. Brewster to Borden, 6 October 1916.

80 NA, Borden Papers, vol. 67, f. OC 312 (B), *Report of the British Columbia Returned Soldiers' Aid Commission, 29 November 1915* (1916).

81 NA, Borden Papers, vol. 67, f. OC 312 (A), p. 34429, Brewster to Borden, 6 October 1916.

82 *Ibid.*, p. 34448 and pp. 34450–6, Borden to provincial premiers, 30 December 1916.

83 *Ibid.*, vol. 67, f. OC 312 (B), p. 34494, memorandum, 8 January 1917; vol. 67, f. OC 312 (A), pp. 34467–8, statement of proceedings of conference given to the press, 11 January 1917.

84 *Ibid.*, vol. 67, f. OC 312 (A), pp. 34467–8, statement of proceedings, 11 January 1917; 'From War to Peace': *General Survey of Canada's Repatriation Plans*, Ottawa, *c.* 1919, p. 44.

85 WRO 947/609, Devonshire to Long, 12 January 1917; Long to Devonshire, 12 February 1917.

86 *Statutes of Canada*, 7–8, George V, Chapter 21.

87 Canada, *Debates*, 1917, II, p. 1162.

88 *Ibid.*; NA, Records of the Department of the Interior, RG 15, vol. 1127, f. 380452(1), memorandum by C. H. E. Powell, 22 February 1917.

89 Canada, *Debates*, 1917, II, pp. 1162–5.

90 *Canadian Annual Review*, 1917, p. 321; Canada, *Debates*, 1917, II, pp. 1157–66.

91 Canada, *Debates*, 1917, IV, p. 3619.

92 *Ibid.*, p. 3620; Morton and Wright, *Winning the Second Battle*, p. 103.

93 Canada, *Debates*, 1917, IV, pp. 3618 and 3621.

94 NA, RG 15, vol. 1127, f. 380452, Powell to Hume, 22 February 1917.

95 *Ibid.* J. G. Turrif, a seasoned Saskatchewan homesteader and a Liberal MP, warned that soldiers unaccustomed to farming, whether they were from Canada or any other part of the empire, could not possibly succeed under the government's proposal. Experience not money, he argued, was the key to a successful policy and for the inexperienced he advocated a system of extensive agricultural education. Canada, *Debates*, 1917, IV, pp. 3779–80.

**96** Canada, *Debates*, 1916, I, p. 910.
**97** James Eayrs, *In Defence of Canada*, Toronto, 1964, p. 49.
**98** E. C. Morgan, 'Soldier settlement in the prairie provinces', *Saskatchewan History*, XXI, 1968, p. 41.
**99** *Canadian Annual Review*, 1918, p. 588.

# CHAPTER FOUR

## Soldier settlement in Canada: a dominion responsibility

the 'returned man' is a curious specimen and difficult, he demands attention on every occasion.[1]

The sudden ending of hostilities in November 1918 and the need to repatriate Canadian veterans quickly made it imperative that Ottawa formulate a broader soldier settlement strategy which eliminated the oversights inherent in the 1917 legislation. Determined to maintain strong and effective central leadership in reconstruction planning, dominion policy makers were mindful that the new soldier settlement legislation could provide an important supplement to Canada's reactivated immigration and development strategy. However, the war had transformed Canadian society and Ottawa soon realised that it would have to take into account some of these new developments when redrafting pre-war policies or embarking upon new initiatives. This was particularly evident in the area of post-war immigration policy.

Before 1914 Canada's national immigration policy was based on an economic strategy designed to develop its primary resource sector. The emphasis on agriculture and Ottawa's firm control over all aspects of immigration, colonisation and settlement ensured the pursuit of a consistent economic development policy. The settlement on the land of its own ex-soldiers was a logical extension of this national strategy. It was not simply an emotional response which acknowledged the sacrifices of Canada's fighting men and rewarded them for their suffering. Rather, it was a calculated plan designed to open up vast new areas of land, expand agricultural production, enrich the social fabric and increase national wealth under the paternalistic control of the dominion government. However, the war had changed people's attitudes and perceptions towards a variety of ethnic groups. Patriotism and conformity to Anglo-Canadian orthodoxies had become fundamental conditions for social acceptance within Canadian society. No longer were immigrants considered suitable simply because they were obedient, hard-working and armed with the proper agricultural credentials. Participation in the war effort was the yardstick used by many Canadians to assess an immigrant's loyalty as was his willingness to adopt the Canadian way of life. Anything less branded him unfaithful and an enemy. Henceforth, ethnic groups once welcomed into Canadian society such as Germans, Hungarians and Ukrainians were either denied access to Canada or had severe landing regulations imposed upon them. The agriculturally industrious religious sects, notably Doukhobors, Hutterites and Mennonites, who had previously been invited to settle on the prairies, were now judged incapable of 'Canadianisation' and were excluded. Although social compatibility and the willingness to adopt the Canadian way of life increased in importance they did not supplant the need to attract a skilled work-force as the main criteria behind immigration policy in the immediate post-war years. As Canada's immigration policy became more restrictive, its architects nevertheless maintained that with a return to normality Canada would secure sufficient numbers of agricultural and industrial workers either domestically or from the preferred nations of the United States and Britain.[2]

The optimistic assumption that British immigration would return to its pre-war levels was quickly dispelled. And with it went the expectations of achieving a culturally homogeneous society rooted in the institutions of an Anglo-Saxon heritage. The campaign to reinforce Canada's Anglo-Saxon character through a selective immigration policy was a potent, ideological weapon in certain sectors of Canadian society. Nativist sentiment, fuelled by racial prejudice, ran high, particularly in western Canada where many Anglo-Canadian trade unionists and farmers had developed a hostile attitude towards 'alien' immigrants.[3] Anxieties and emotions intensified upon news of the Russian revolution in 1917 and during the increasingly turbulent, sometimes violent, labour unrest between 1917 and 1919. Veterans joined forces with trade unionists, farmers and various nativist associations to combat the largely imaginary threat from within. In many cases veterans spearheaded anti-alien agitation, and by 1918 one association, the Great War Veterans' Association (GWVA) had eagerly accepted national leadership on the alien question.[4]

## Veteran militancy and the 'alien' question

'Among the most important (national issues) are the settlement of our agricultural lands and the pressing problem of the alien population of Canada', proclaimed Dr A. M. Forbes, vice-president of the GWVA.[5] Forbes argued that a policy of agricultural reconstruction based upon the

[ 71 ]

resettlement of returning veterans would do more to stabilise Canadian society than any other reconstruction policy. Agriculture, he stated, was of greater importance to the future well-being of the nation than manufacturing. The only way to stop social erosion was to make the countryside, rather than the city, a more attractive place to live for native-born Canadians. 'No nation can be regarded as unhealthy when a virile peasantry, contented with rural employments . . . exists on its soil.'[6]

Underlying Forbes's argument was the stark realisation that Canada's urban population was fast expanding. The 1921 census revealed that fractionally more Canadians lived in the cities than in rural areas.[7] Urbanisation inexorably increased and during the 1920s most rural Canadians grudgingly accepted the fact. Nevertheless, the farmer as the ideal Canadian citizen remained a powerful myth in post-war Canadian society. Land was the element which best exemplified social stability, and the sturdy yeoman farmer symbolised progress, development and a robust society. The appeal of, even reverence for, the past and its ancient traditions was another important element in this conservative ideology. The basic components of class harmony, social stability and tradition were common to both Canadian and British agrarian myths. But unlike British conservatism's romanticisation of country life, Canadians did not necessarily equate the agrarian myth with the 'nonindustrial, non-innovative and nonmaterial qualities' inherent in the British 'country-side of the mind'.[8] As in the United States, the Canadian yeoman's purpose was 'to strengthen the fibre of [the] country by building into the basic industrial structure . . . the best blood and bones of [the] nation'.[9] But the basic issue remained social stability rather than modernisation.

The austere Arthur Meighen, Canada's Minister of the Interior and the next Prime Minister, illustrated the point when he introduced the Soldier Settlement Act of 1919. The primary purpose of the legislation was to secure settlers for the development of vacant prairie farm land,

> and to make settlers of those who have proven themselves the backbone of the nation in its trouble. We believe that we cannot better fortify this country against the waves of unrest and discontent that now assail us . . . than by making the greatest possible proportion of the soldiers of our country settlers upon our land.[10]

Most veterans proved to be willing defenders of the existing order for several reasons. As more soldiers returned from the trenches in 1918 the membership and organisation of the veterans' associations grew stronger and became more aggressive in their demands.[11] Many became disgruntled soon after their homecoming by the government's apparent slowness and inadequate resourcing of their return to civilian life.

Disappointment turned to anger as some veterans discovered that civilian jobs they had vacated during the war had been filled by people they considered to be aliens. Hardened by their war experience and conditioned by a 'friend or foe' attitude, veterans usually identified the alien immigrant with the enemy they had recently fought against in Europe. With the advent of Bolshevism it was easy to transfer their animosity for the enemy alien to Russian and East European immigrants.[12] Subsequently, one of the GWVA's primary objectives was 'to inculcate loyalty to Canada and the Empire'.[13]

Land settlement had been a major plank in the GWVA's platform since its foundation in 1917, and it became a serious bone of contention between the association and the dominion government. Between 1917 and 1919 the GWVA attempted to cajole Ottawa into allowing it an equal share in the supervision of its soldier settlement policy.[14] The government flatly refused such a partnership and quietly shelved soldier settlement in order to face the nationally divisive issues of conscription and railway subsidisation in 1917–18. It was not until January 1918, after Borden's electoral victory, that the government picked up the thread of soldier settlement once again, and the announcement of the three-man Soldier Settlement Board, which would administer Canada's soldier settlement scheme, was finally made in the same month. It did little to restore the GWVA's confidence in the central government since two of the three seemed unqualified or unsuitable. One appointment, claimed the *Veteran*, reeked of political patronage. The real hostility, however, occurred over Major E. J. Ashton's appointment. Although a CEF veteran, Ashton's real expertise, according to the *Veteran*, was not in veterans' administration but as a furniture dealer and undertaker in Regina. The GWVA was greatly angered because the government had not approached the association and sought its advice on possible candidates. It therefore vented its displeasure: 'Perhaps the Government is a government of farseeing prevision and fears that the scheme of settlement on outlying homesteads . . . may bring veterans to untimely graves and is providing for their skilful interment.'[15] Its own exclusion apart, it could find little fault with the acting chairman and former Superintendent of Lands for British Columbia, Samuel Maber.

## The Soldier Settlement Act of 1919

Although Ottawa ignored GWVA pressure for official representation on the SSB, Meighen agreed that new legislation was urgently needed. He also concurred with Roche, his predecessor at the Department of the Interior, on the urgency of immediately selecting SSB personnel. The delay, according to Meighen, had been due to the tremendous difficulty in finding capable men 'for this most perplexing and indeed stupendous work'. At the same time, he could not ignore the pressure from the western premiers who were demanding immediate action in time for spring seeding.[16]

Maber realised immediately that Roche's legislation was wholly inadequate and he urged Meighen to reserve *all* dominion lands within fifteen miles of the railway. He also knew that there was a scarcity of good arable land close to existing rail networks on the prairies. The probability of a large number of soldiers applying to the SSB therefore necessitated the reservation of a better class of land.[17] But this was not enough. Maber pointed out that the bulk of the available homestead land along existing railways was in northern Saskatchewan and north-western Alberta. Many surveyed townships in the Peace River district of north-western Alberta still remained isolated and without rail communications. The only lands suitable for soldier settlers elsewhere on the prairies were claims cancelled through default, abandoned homesteads or expropriated reserve land. These lands were scattered throughout the region, but Maber was confident that the area contained a number of good homesteads.[18] In April 1918, Meighen reacted to Maber's entreaties and reserved all remaining vacant dominion land within fifteen miles of the railway.

Slowly, portions of school lands, Indian reserve lands, grazing leases, Hudson's Bay Company and forest reserves were set aside exclusively for returned soldiers.[19] The GWVA exerted constant pressure on the government to expand its soldier settlement programme. In May the British Columbia chapter hastened the utilisation of Indian reserves for returned soldiers in exchange for grazing leases. Saskatchewan veterans complained that progress was unsatisfactory[20] and, once again, veteran nativism reared its ugly head when demands were made to expropriate the homesteads of 'enemy aliens' such as Mennonites and Doukhobors. Similarly, land locked up by the speculators and corporations did not escape the veterans' demand for expropriation either.[21] Condemning the soldier settler legislation of 1917 as inadequate, the veterans' associations charged the Conservative government with 'merely tinkering with a vast question'.[22]

A flurry of activity engulfed the Department of the Interior and the SSB in 1918. Between April and July a new set of land regulations was formulated and dominion land agents were notified of the new procedures and priorities.[23] Throughout July a series of orders-in-council was implemented reserving a variety of dominion lands. This included the forty-mile wide railway belt in British Columbia, remaining Doukhobor reserves and unsurveyed lands in the Peace River and Vermillion districts of Alberta. Maber was particularly anxious to secure the reservation of these unsurveyed lands as it had been reported that squatters were moving into the districts. He recommended that squatting by civilians before a survey was carried out should be prohibited.[24]

Indian reserves were singled out by the GWVA as a promising solution to the land shortage. Numerous branches across the prairies agreed that the Indians were not making full use of these lands and that they should be purchased from the Indian bands at a fair and equitable price.[25] At first, the dominion government balked at the idea, but once the severity of the land shortage became apparent the proposal attracted serious attention. Meighen was particularly anxious to secure these lands and he implored D. C. Scott, Deputy Superintendent of Indian Affairs, that it was of the utmost importance for the success of soldier settlement to do so.[26] Scott was sympathetic and wanted to co-operate, but he stressed that his department's first duty was to the welfare of the Indian and he reminded Meighen that land could not be legally taken without the Indians agreeing to a surrender. Once a fair valuation was agreed upon the surrendered land would be administered by the SSB. As custodian of the Indian lands he wanted to ensure that the department 'are getting fair prices for the Indians'. He also worried about the danger that the SSB might obtain the most desirable land, leaving the Indians with poorer sections. He therefore strongly advised that the government be prepared to take the land *en bloc*.[27]

It was clear that a revitalised soldier settlement policy would need provincial participation. John Oliver, the Premier of British Columbia, had recognised the need for such a role as it emerged that the number of applicants would far outstrip the insufficient amount of suitable dominion land available. Oliver implored Borden to call a national conference to discuss amendments to the 1917 Act. The Prime Minister complied and on 19 November 1918 a post-war conference convened in Ottawa to discuss land settlement, immigration and agriculture. High on the agenda were land reclamation, land expropriation and a comprehensive agricultural training and education programme for soldier settlers.[28]

J. A. Calder, one of the three Liberals in the coalition cabinet, warmly endorsed Oliver's initiative. Since his appointment as minister of the new Department of Immigration and Colonisation, post-war immigration and land settlement had received his undivided attention. Calder was a shrewd Saskatchewan Liberal who was just beginning to make his name in national politics. The Conservative party hierarchy distrusted him and thought him a 'slick and unscrupulous partisan'.[29] But according to the *Canadian Annual Review* he was the chief representative of western thought in Ottawa.[30] In September 1918 he toured the prairies where he announced to a reporter of the *Winnipeg Free Press*, western Canada's leading newspaper, that the dominion government had drafted a broad policy regarding immigration and land settlement in which it recognised the need for 'full and direct co-operation with the Provinces. It involves the settlement of privately-owned lands, abandoned farms, and leased farms, and the employment of Provincial and Federal credit'.[31] He elaborated upon this pronouncement during the dominion-provincial conference in Ottawa, where he stood in for Meighen. He agreed with Oliver that the re-establishment of war veterans provided an excellent opportunity to develop the nation's resources. 'The economic situation demands that all our resources must now be utilised', and this unquestionably meant bringing vacant and under-developed prairie land into immediate use. 'This matter affects all Governments, Federal, Provincial and Municipal and the Returned Soldier problem must be hooked up to the general question of speeding up production . . . particularly food production.'[32]

Calder was under no illusion that to bring millions of acres of wilderness under cultivation would require heavy investment. The creation of a large number of small holders who might one day purchase their own farm was believed to be money well spent, but nothing would be achieved using parsimonious half measures. It also meant that the feuding between the provinces and Ottawa would have to cease. The premiers agreed, promised their support and acknowledged that settling returned soldiers was a dominion responsibility.[33] Calder's announcement of the government's broad intentions had paved the way for Meighen to formulate new legislation.

The 1917 Act had restricted the soldiers' choice to dominion land in western Canada. Provinces such as Nova Scotia were outside the original scope of the 1917 Act and had to provide their own schemes. However, very little Crown land remained in Nova Scotia and what was left was isolated, costly and heavily forested making it extremely expensive to clear. Now that soldiers could purchase farms and pre-empt vacant and abandoned homesteads outside the prairie provinces, Canada's soldier settlement policy became truly national. Although most of the enquiries came from veterans from the three prairie provinces, and the majority of the vacant land was in this region, the Maritime provinces and Quebec were eager to help their returning heroes within the limited resources available.[34]

Meighen sketched out his plans to Borden on 11 December 1918. With a few minor adjustments over the winter it became the framework of the government's policy. In May 1919 Meighen introduced the new legislation which contained a number of changes to make the scheme more attractive and thus induce more men to settle.[35] All vacant dominion lands within a fifteen-mile radius of a railway in Manitoba, Saskatchewan, Alberta and the railway belt of British Columbia were reserved for soldier settlement. The SSB was instructed to focus its attention on lands held vacant by land speculators and was authorised to designate these lands as settlement areas. The Soldier Settlement Act of 1919 empowered the Board to purchase these lands at a price set by the Exchequer Court should the speculator refuse the Board's offer. The new Act extended the Board's power to expropriate land from forest reserves and acquire uncultivated Indian reserves and school lands.[36] More importantly, it allowed veterans the freedom to choose and purchase privately owned land with government assistance. By its location and fertility such private land was preferable to Crown land in the area.

The chief provision of the new Act, however, was a larger, more generous credit programme. The classes of assistance provided under the Act were as follows:

---

1   To aid in settlement on lands purchased through the Board:
    (a)   up to $4,500 for the purchase of land;
    (b)   up to $2,000 for the purchase of livestock, implements, and other equipment;
    (c)   up to $1,000 for the erection of buildings and other improvements.

2   To aid in becoming re-established on land already owned by them:
    (a)   up to $3,500 for the removal of encumbrances, the payment so advanced not to exceed 50 per cent of the appraised value of the land;
    (b)   up to $2,000 for the purchase of livestock, implements, and other equipment;
    (c)   up to $1,000 for the erection of buildings or other permanent improvements.

3   To aid in becoming established on dominion lands in the prairie provinces:
    (a)   up to $3,000 for the purchase of livestock and equipment, and the erection of permanent improvements.[37]

---

Interest was set at 5 per cent per annum, but loan charges for stock and equipment did not begin until the third year and were payable in four annual instalments, while loans for land and buildings were repayable in twenty-five annual instalments. As with land selection, soldier settlers under the new scheme were given the option of making their own offer when purchasing implements and livestock. Before any purchase was made, however, the SSB required an appraisal from its own officials to ensure the proper expenditure of public money. According to officials in Ottawa, by the end of 1920 the new purchasing procedure had saved the Canadian public over $3.6 million.[38] Eligibility was limited to those Canadian veterans who had served overseas with the CEF and those domiciled in Canada before the war who had seen action with imperial or Allied forces. Full benefit was extended to ex-servicemen from the British Isles and the self-governing or 'white' dominions.

The SSB took additional measures to protect its investment by providing preliminary agricultural training facilities and expert supervision. This emphasis on proper selection, training and monitoring reflected Ottawa's determination to remain in complete control of its soldier settlement policy. Its efforts to establish training facilities before demobilisation, both in England and Canada, reflected the importance that Meighen attached to soldier settlement as a vital component of Canadian post-war reconstruction. Meighen informed Sir Edward Kemp, Minister of the Overseas Military Forces of Canada (OMFC), that negotiations were under way in Canada regarding the use of agricultural facilities and institutions. It was to be a co-ordinated effort between the SSB and the dominion and provincial Departments of Agriculture. Inexperienced applicants would receive training at the various provincial agricultural colleges and schools of agriculture, and successful private farmers would also be canvassed and selected to participate in an apprenticeship programme.[39] However, special opportunities existed in Britain during demobilisation. It was estimated that demobilisation would take from nine to eighteen months and therefore, while waiting for passage home, training facilities could be established for practical instruction in Canadian farming techniques and land settlement under the auspices of the Khaki University in Britain.[40]

Meighen urged that the military authorities should co-operate by providing training farms, horses, equipment and qualified instructors. SSB officials stressed the need for brief, three-month courses which concentrated on the practical rather than the academic or scientific. Candidates were to familiarise themselves with the daily routine of farm life before being sent to farmers who would provide additional practical ground work and experience.[41] Preliminary meetings had already taken place between the SSB and the Ministry of Militia's Demobilisation Committee for the prompt implementation of the arrangements for agricultural instruction. In December 1918, Commissioner Ashton and C. F. Bailey, Ontario's Assistant Deputy Minister of the Department of Agriculture, were despatched to London to survey Canadian troops on the question of land settlement and the need for training facilities in agriculture.[42] A census undertaken in early 1918 confirmed that 105,000 Canadian soldiers out of a total of 400,000 men overseas had expressed a wish to settle on the land after the war. These figures were later revised by Meighen who reported that on the basis of 273,444 replies from members of the CEF, 87,771 had expressed an interest in farming and stock raising.[43]

Experience, training and temperament were not the only criteria for a successful soldier settler. Capital was essential and the SSB was favourably inclined to put a minimum capital requirement of $500 on any candidate accepted for land settlement. When the 1919 legislation was announced Canadian veterans were entitled to make a down payment of 10 per cent on the purchase price of land, stock and seed. Imperial ex-servicemen were required to pay 20 per cent of the amount paid for these commodities and were to spend sufficient time on Canadian farms to acquaint themselves with Canadian farming methods.[44] For those ex-imperials who had farming experience, one year with a Canadian farmer was deemed sufficient while for inexperienced ex-imperials the minimum was two years.

Meighen defended the new measures in the Canadian House of Commons by stating that they were not a gratuity or reward for the soldier. The legislation provided the foundation for a systematic approach to the colonisation of new territory. 'The primary and great principle of this Bill is to secure settlers on the lands of this country', he announced,

[The] class of citizen that counts the most in the determination of the stability of a country . . . is undoubtedly the basic class – – the agricultural class . . . Its purpose is to strengthen the fibre of this country by building into the basic industrial structure of the best blood and bones of our nation.[45]

The Minister of the Interior never tired of stressing the national scope of the land settlement issue. It was an enormous task requiring co-operation between all levels of government. Participation of private individuals such as well-trained agricultural experts, experienced and capable farmers and financial officers from banks and mortgage companies was also essential. Regional qualification and advisory boards sprouted up throughout the country staffed largely by local farmers, instructors from provincial agricultural colleges and public servants from provincial Departments of Agriculture who were familiar with local land prices, soils and farming practices. The SSB bureaucracy mushroomed to meet the increasing pressure from applicants who needed land appraisals, loan estimates, supervision, advice and information. The watershed for the SSB was reached in June 1920 when staff numbers rose from a few hundred to a peak of 1,579. In 1923 Ashton reported that the supervisory staff alone consisted of 150 trained agriculturists, all practical men, many of whom possessed degrees from agricultural colleges.[46]

The new legislation had an immediate impact on the number of applications handled by the SSB. In March 1919 only 400 were received, but between May and July the average was 400 per week and by August it was 600.[47] In its first annual report published in March 1921, the SSB proudly announced that during 1919 approximately 75 per cent of the applicants were granted qualification certificates while in 1920 just under two-thirds were successful. The aggregate number of soldier settlers was 25,443 of which 19,771 or 77 per cent received loans to purchase farms privately. Loans amounted to over $80 million.[48] The acreage and livestock statistics were even more impressive. The SSB held clear title to over 2.1 million acres of land, 360,000 acres on mortgage and first charge on over 980,000 acres for a grand total of 3.49 million acres. Of this, over 765,000 acres had been acquired from various forest reserves, grazing leases, Indian lands, Hudson's Bay reserve lands, Doukhobor reserves and school lands on the prairies. The SSB had liens on 119,000 horses, cattle, sheep and swine, as well as numerous pieces of farm machinery. Statistically, it was an impressive picture. Even more encouraging was the fact that 10 per cent of the loans had been repaid.[49]

Despite Meighen's insistence that soldier settlement was not a 'big loan venture', but a practical scheme based on sound business principles, the *Canadian Annual Review* dubbed Canada's soldier settlement programme 'the largest real estate and loan business in Canada if not in the British Empire'.[50] Prime farm land in 1919 was not cheap. In the prairie provinces it was selling for between $50 and $60 an acre, but elsewhere it was considerably cheaper, averaging between $16 an acre in New Brunswick, $33 in Ontario and $53 in British Columbia. However, for those veterans who did not claim dominion land but purchased privately owned land, their price per acre was considerably higher. And it was land purchasing which comprised over half the loan money spent by soldier settlers.[51]

For the immediate future soldier settlement proved to be a notable success. The SSB was convinced that the 1919 Act had an appreciable effect in stemming rural depopulation. It made an important contribution to the back-to-the-land movement. The successful settlement of over over 25,000 soldiers with their families had added more than 100,000 people to Canada's permanent agricultural population. This was indeed of national significance, reported the SSB, because if the scheme had not been launched 'a great proportion of them would be found in the crowded centres of population, increasing the difficulty of the problems of unemployment'.[52] The SSB's production figures for soldier settlers were indicative of the importance of the soldier settler to Canadian agriculture. Over $10 million of livestock had been purchased by the SSB for its clients who in turn had produced, in a very short space of time, 2.6 million bushels of wheat and 6.5 million bushels of oats, and other grains, feed and fodder valued at $13.9 million.[53] Even more impressive was the number of virgin acres brought under cultivation. Of the 4.8 million acres occupied by soldier settlers, 2.1 million was raw dominion land lying in the prairie provinces. The number of soldier grants issued in this settlement area by March 1921 was 8,772 with each farm averaging 240 acres. Of this untamed land the SSB estimated that 194,000 acres or 9.2 per cent had been broken by 1920 and it was believed that in 1921 an additional 300,000 acres or 14.2 per cent would be tamed for the first time. Indeed, the SSB was encouraged by these figures because 928,000 acres of soldier settlement land had been brought under cultivation nationwide by 1921.[54]

However, by 1920 soldier settlers were already confronting serious problems. The initial rush of applicants made it impossible to screen all undesirable and unsuitable applicants and this resulted in the inevitable approval of a higher number of these cases than would have been under ordinary circumstances. Despite Meighen's insistence that the liberal monetary provisions in no way constituted a military gratuity or 'big loan venture', they were exactly that. 'The very nature of the scheme itself', admitted Commissioner Ashton, 'involved the waiving in many ways of ordinary business margins of security.'[55] The most significant blow to the entire scheme was the sharp and sudden post-war deflation which began in 1920. The majority of settlement took place in 1919 and 1920 when the prices of land, stock and equipment were at a premium. However, by the time the majority of soldier settlers had brought enough acres under cultivation or had built up their herds, prices for agricultural products had plummeted. The SSB was the first to admit the surprising results of 1920: 'Considering the collapse of markets in the middle of threshing, it is felt that the showing is a remarkably good one.'[56] The cost-price squeeze ushered in a period of failure, foreclosure, abandonment and indebtedness which haunted soldier settlers and politicians alike throughout the inter-war period.[57]

## Problems on the prairies

As mentioned earlier, it was Ontario and British Columbia which initiated the first soldier settlement schemes. However, the Kapuskasing soldier colony in northern Ontario was also the first provincial scheme to be abandoned in 1920, and British Columbia's soldier settlement plans were equally disappointing.[58] The dominion government was understandably keen to avoid the glaring mistakes witnessed in these two provinces. Reclamation of swamp and timber land, a task which British Columbian authorities wanted the dominion government to assume, was considered outside its jurisdiction by Ottawa. The key to successful settlement was to settle people on land which was ready to farm close to transportation facilities and markets. Lands which offered the greatest chance of ultimate success were those suited for mixed farming. 'Skillful farmers who believed that they allowed for every contingency have often failed in their enterprise by over specialisation,' exclaimed the SSB.[59] It argued that the impulse towards mixed farming was not ill-considered, but was calculated on sound economic principles.

In 1914, Cory had considered it imperative for the government to make changes to its land policy because of falling homestead entries. The traditional areas of settlement along the older railway lines were filling up and the largest tracts of available arable land were concentrated on the northern fringe or park belt of the prairie provinces. It was this area, recommended Cory, where the dominion government should concentrate its settlement efforts. Each prairie province had a specific forest fringe region targeted for mixed farming by the SSB. In Alberta the enormous Peace River district several hundred miles northwest of Edmonton was reserved for soldier settlement. Land expropriated from the Porcupine Forest Reserve in north-eastern Saskatchewan was designated as a soldier settler reserve and the Carraganna district in north central Saskatchewan near Prince Albert was believed to have tremendous potential as well. Manitoba had much less park belt to offer, and what was available was concentrated in the inter-lake region between Lakes Winnipeg and Manitoba or was chiselled from the Riding Mountain Forest Reserve and the Turtle Mountain Forest Reserve in the western and south-western parts of the province.

The basic impediment to successful soldier settlement in the park belt was that government officials proved over-optimistic in their appraisal of the region's immediate agricultural potential. The land was generally productive, but it was heavily forested and demanded clearing, draining and breaking. Transportation facilities were either lacking or poorly developed.[60] The SSB was emphatic that it did 'not contemplate the settlement of soldiers as pioneers in remote locations or under isolated conditions, removed from markets, in virgin forest lands, or on lands not cultivable without reclamation or other development.' In October 1919, Maber reiterated this point to a special Parliamentary committee which was examining veterans' affairs. But it was blatantly clear well before the publication of the SSB's first report in March 1921 that Ottawa had indeed failed to meet its own criteria in certain regions. The very nature of Ottawa's expansion of homestead lands through the acquisition of Indian lands, school reserves, grazing leases, Hudson's Bay reserve lands and the withdrawal of land from forest reserves, the majority of which was concentrated in the park belt, made soldier settlement in these isolated and sometimes inaccessible northern areas nothing but heartbreaking.[61]

Speculation and squatting in the Peace River district had made it crucial for the dominion government to reserve what was left of the homesteading land within fifteen miles of the railway in this newly surveyed northern region.[62] According to E. J. Lyne, a Liberal member of the Alberta Legislative Assembly and party secretary for the provincial Liberals in Grand Prairie, located in the heart of the Peace River country, what frustrated soldier settlers most was the lack of transportation facilities. He complained bitterly to William Lyon Mackenzie King, the newly elected leader of the national Liberals, that settlers who were urged by Ottawa to settle in this vast northern territory had a right to adequate rail facilities. Despite the dominion government's promises, the soldier settlers had been constantly denied proper rail and road transportation. In several proposed sites for soldier settlers the minimum distance from the railhead was eighty miles![63]

Manitoba possessed some of the most marginal settlement territory under SSB supervision.[64] The inter-lake district sandwiched between Lakes Winnipeg and Manitoba had been singled out by the SSB as a promising development area, and another promising site was land north of Dauphin located in the park belt and to the west of Lake Manitoba. Further north lay another area deemed suitable near the Manitoba-Saskatchewan border at Swan River. The SSB had also studied the feasibility of slicing forest reserve land from the Riding and Turtle Mountain reserves, and, under pressure from the Manitoba executive of the GWVA, a few hundred acres were carved off from each forest reserve.[65] Generally speaking, the majority of this reserved land was heavily forested and stony, particularly in the inter-lake region. Although it was reported that the soil was productive, the enormous amounts of time, energy and money required to bring the land under cultivation proved too much for some.

Even for those who overcame these obstacles, natural calamities such as frequent and early frosts, hail, flooding and drought wiped out even the best and most determined soldier settlers.[66] One desperate

[ 83 ]

Canadian soldier settler in the inter-lake region near Ashern reported that his one workable well was frozen and in order to water his animals he had to melt snow in the house. He had drilled four wells during the summer and had struck solid rock at depths varying from four to twelve feet. Worse still, while drilling he had been forced to take his livestock two miles every day to water. Four of his soldier settler neighbours had suffered a similar fate and were talking of pulling out if the government did not send proper drilling equipment. Despite the hardship and complications, there were many private individuals keen to sell land to returning veterans in fertile southern Manitoba.[67]

Although Alberta claimed the largest share of Canada's soldier settlers, it was in Saskatchewan, the second highest benefactor, that soldier settlement was pursued with the greatest determination. In early 1916 the Saskatchewan branch of the Military Hospital Commission had advocated the preparation of machinery to give returning veterans an opportunity to engage in farming after the war.[68] The Saskatchewan Returned Soldiers Employment Commission, the provincial agency responsible for securing employment and generally assisting returning veterans, was one of the more active and conscientious provincial soldiers' aid commissions in Canada. It too advocated the need for immediate and adequate preparation for returning soldiers before demobilisation. And it argued that the re-establishment and rehabilitation of Canada's citizen soldiers was a national obligation. The Commission insisted that this obligation could only be met by inter-provincial co-operation co-ordinated by the national government.[69]

Land settlement was integral to the Saskatchewan government's commitment to the returned soldier. Agriculture was the life-blood of the prairie economy and in Saskatchewan farming was more important to the provincial economy than in Manitoba and Alberta, both of which were able to exploit other natural resources. Because Saskatchewan had the most arable land of the three prairie provinces it had more at stake in a successful land settlement policy. More settlers would ensure a healthy and vibrant rural economy, but at the same time the reliance upon such settlement exposed the underlying weakness within the province's economy. Saskatchewan's economic base was too weak to support large-scale diversification – or so its politicians argued. Until the province had been effectively settled such diversification was impossible, which meant that its economy would remain heavily dependent upon agriculture. A series of crop failures and low yields would dramatically affect the most carefully laid land settlement policies. People would become discouraged and abandon farming, or poor conditions might deter new settlers from settling which in turn would have a direct bearing upon future prosperity and development. It was therefore essential that Saskatchewan be settled quickly and that as many new acres as possible be brought into production. The provincial government was aware of the seriousness of the problem, as was the dominion government which was the custodian of the region's natural resources exercising responsibility for land settlement and development.

The 1918 annual meeting of the Saskatchewan Returned Soldiers Employment Commission pointed out that there was insufficient, high quality farm land for soldier settlement which was easily accessible. The Commission recommended that land for returned soldiers should be in districts already settled and adjacent to existing railway lines. If insufficient land were available in certain districts the Commission urged dominion authorities to acquire additional land through expropriation. This was essential because, according to the Commission's figures, 70 per cent of those Saskatchewan veterans who had returned by August 1917 had expressed a desire to settle on the land. The Commission also decided that the obligations for clearing wooded lands for soldier settlement in Saskatchewan clearly rested with the dominion government.[70] The provincial Liberal government, under the leadership of Premier William Martin, agreed. Martin's administration had committed itself to unlocking large areas of homestead land which had been staked out by land speculators. It was determined to push ahead and devise a policy which contributed to increased settlement in Saskatchewan. Despite the fact that the prime responsibility theoretically lay with the dominion government, Martin was anxious to co-operate and take the initiative.

Saskatchewan had the widest variety of settlement areas on offer. This included the greatest proportion of Hudson's Bay reserve land located in the province and large tracts of virgin farmland surrendered by Indian bands to the SSB. Saskatchewan also disposed of the largest amount of school lands. Almost 95,000 acres were appraised and transferred to the SSB by September 1921; the valuation totalled $1.375 million. Saskatchewan's contribution dwarfed that of its prairie neighbours: Alberta and Manitoba scraped up between 10–12,000 acres each valued at $150,000 and $152,000 respectively.[71]

Within Saskatchewan the largest single settlement project was the Porcupine Soldier Settlement. Created by an order-in-council in June 1919 it comprised 200,000 virgin acres which had been withdrawn from lands previously categorised for homesteading in the Pasquia and Porcupine Forest Reserves of north-eastern Saskatchewan. In order to establish a uniform settlement pattern, planners deemed 240 acres to be the optimum settlement unit when taking into account the type of country involved. Soldiers were entitled to the standard homestead grant of 160 acres but were encouraged in addition to purchase an adjoining eighty-acre allotment. The sale of these allotments was intended to offset SSB expenditure on development projects such as roads and bridges which would in turn facilitate the opening up of the region. 'To settle the timber lands', explained Commissioner Ashton, 'we need pioneers who must still bridge the period between establishment and production.' The Porcupine settlement was to be the perfect example of this.[72]

The land was certainly untamed. No provision had been made beforehand for housing, roads, bridges or preliminary clearing, and the settlement was carried out under the harshest pioneering conditions imaginable. The region was heavily forested with thick stands of poplar and dense scrub regularly interspersed with sloughs, swamps and marshes. According to several soldier settlers, figuratively at least, they had to carve their homes and farms out of an unyielding environment.[73]

Despite the extreme hardships involved, the pioneers steadily pushed the frontier back in this bleak region. Several communities slowly emerged and the transcripts of the few Canadian soldier settlers that have survived are a colourful reminder of modern day pioneering, homesteading and development. Nevertheless, the results were disappointing and Ottawa's role left a lot to be desired. On 2 July 1919, the first day veterans were allowed to ballot for their choice of claim, 131 veterans took the opportunity to claim a soldier grant. By December 1923, 175 had been established of which twenty-five properties had been abandoned. Of the remaining 150 veterans sixty were married and ninety remained bachelors. However, there were a number of absentee operators and only 100 of the 150 actually lived on their holding. Two years later the total number of soldier grant entries had reached 283 in the Porcupine Reserve involving 67,200 acres or 105 square miles of farm land. Advances totalled approximately $281,000.[74] To further facilitate settlement, land was obtained by the SSB in 1919 from the Hudson's Bay Company for the planning and development of the new townsite of Lens. In 1920 planning permission was given by Saskatchewan's Minister of Municipal Affairs and the townsite was resurveyed to provide a church, hotel, hospital, library, schools, recreational, industrial and residential districts. Lens was to be the model for new town planning in Canada,[75] but despite this, the idea, including the name, never caught on. Much of the plans remained on the drawing board and the development which took place at Prairie River evolved at a snail's pace.

The SSB was pleased to report that the Canadian settlers were of a good type: 'They now realise the proposition they are up against, and with remarkably few exceptions are applying themselves to the making of a real success.'[76] But did these settlers realise what they were getting themselves into? Complaints began to trickle in soon after the initial clearing. The dominion government had committed itself to completing a road from Prairie River to the settlement area by the autumn of 1919. However, it was not until the summer of 1925 that the first roads were built for cars. The first car in the Prairie River area was purchased and used by the SSB, but even then the community was not linked to the provincial network for several more years.[77]

Between 1919 and 1930 the SSB spent $60,000 draining sloughs, clearing bush, building bridges and local grid roads. But it was not enough and concern mounted over the years about the lack of settlers in the Porcupine Reserve.[78] Continued isolation induced by a lack of direct road and rail communications was a major factor; the weather was another. During 1920 drought and an early frost accounted for crop failures ranging from 15 per cent to total failure.[79] The collapse in the price of primary products worsened the situation and was in turn exacerbated by a succession of indifferent harvests until 1924 when very poor returns were again recorded. Although some soldier settlers made an early windfall by planting alfalfa for feed, the majority had banked on wheat, the big cash crop on the prairies, and were broke by the winter of 1924. Once again the SSB encouraged the more destitute to find work in threshing gangs, road crews and lumber camps to supplement their family income. Local supervisors even went as far as to obtain preference of employment for these men in some camps.[80]

The lack of efficient transportation facilities was not the only major complaint in the Porcupine Reserve. One disgruntled settler made allegations of corruption against the SSB supervisors who, he claimed, had lined their pockets at the expense of their clients. The purchase of the eighty-acre allotment was another bone of contention. After seeing his neighbour carve out 160 acres of bush on a soldier grant the same disenchanted settler thought the SSB should have given that neighbour the eighty acres as a reward for all his hard work. Instead, the government charged that neighbour $3 an acre which wiped out his cash reserve.[81] There were numerous cases of individual hardship, fortitude and perseverance but despite Ottawa's optimistic projections it was clear that this particular soldier settlement project fell far short of its objectives.

What about the British soldier settlers in this region? Indications are that there were none in the first settlement period between 1919 and 1925. However, many Canadian veterans who settled in the region had returned with English war brides. Mrs Mary McLenaghan, whose husband Ed was a field supervisor for the SSB in Kitscoty, Alberta and

Prairie River, Saskatchewan between 1920 and 1925, had nothing but the highest praise for these women who endured tremendous personal hardship adjusting to Canadian pioneer life.[82] It was during the civilian phase of settlement that British settlers trickled into the area. In the autumn of 1924 Ed McLenaghan was despatched to England to select more. Based in Liverpool, McLenaghan spent seven months interviewing and screening prospective applicants for the 3,000 British families settlement scheme, a joint venture undertaken by the Canadian and British governments to promote British agricultural settlement in Canada. Between thirty and seventy families settled on abandoned soldier settler property in the Prairie River district in 1927. '[L]ike most government schemes', complained one Canadian settler, 'the ones sent over to recruit these settlers were as unqualified as [those] they selected.'[83]

As a soldier settlement project the Porcupine Reserve was a failure. Of the 500 homesteads reserved for British and Canadian ex-servicemen only 150 were occupied by *Canadian* veterans and the region was thrown open to civilian settlement in 1926. But this, and the attempt to settle British families in 1927 were indications of the failure of the scheme. By the 1930s only a handful of the original soldier settlers still occupied their properties and, in addition, more than half of the British families had also abandoned their farms.

## Overseas operations

The appointment of Lieutenant-Colonel K. C. Bedson as the SSB's overseas representative in February 1919 coincided with Milner's reconstitution of the OSC.[84] The demand for information on Canadian soldier settlement schemes, assistance and legislation by Canadian and British veterans necessitated its creation. Headquartered in the Canadian emigration offices in London, Bedson co-ordinated his activities with J. Obed Smith. Their tasks were to disseminate literature, interview and screen prospective applicants and liaise between the SSB and the OSC.

The Colonial Office welcomed the appointment and was anxious to find out what further steps the Canadian government was taking to assist British veterans. Ashton reported that the 'sentiment in Canada is . . . that we need more Anglo-Saxons' and British ex-servicemen were seen as a vital component in solving the problem.[85] Personally, he was confident that Canada could absorb an almost unlimited number of men into her rural population provided they were willing to work. Capital was another matter. It was much more difficult to start farming without capital than it had been at the turn of the century. Even if a British soldier settler possessed capital, Ashton advised that he work at least a year, and preferably two, with an experienced farmer in the district in which he intended to settle.[86]

Ashton was encouraged by Bedson's preliminary reports. For example, Bedson interviewed a group of British ex-officers and was impressed by their analysis of the emigration issue. 'All seem very keen and willing to take up land and fully appreciate the amount of work that is required if they are to be successful.'[87] More importantly, they had independent financial means and were prepared to purchase land privately. At the same time, they wanted to take advantage of the SSB's offer of assistance in purchasing farm machinery and enrolling in courses at the various agricultural colleges. These were precisely the class of immigrant Ashton was seeking. He explained to the Minister of Immigration that this immigrant group was the 'most desirous and should receive prompt attention and hearty support'.[88] Bedson informed George Fiddes, Permanent Under-Secretary at the Colonial Office, that soldier settlement in Canada would be a guaranteed success provided the dominion government 'supplied funds and gave the men proper encouragement', especially during the winter when grain farming would be at a standstill and family income tight.[89]

Determined to do all it could for this class of settler, the dominion government was anxious to avoid publicity. The Department of Immigration wanted to make 'a definite yet not a public move towards encouraging (them) to settle'.[90] For one thing they did not want to be left open to charges of class distinction or favouritism regarding transatlantic accommodation. It was evident that because these settlers had private means they could depart for Canada during the forthcoming summer, thus avoiding a wait until the following spring. It was suggested that Smith have a quiet word with the steamship companies to allocate some cabin space for these men before the remainder of the Canadian forces were despatched home. In the light of the Canadian demobilisation riots earlier that year, Smith was reminded of the political sensitivity of such a move. If it was made public that these men had been allocated cabin space and had landed in Canada before the last Canadians had returned home the domestic political uproar it would cause would be intense and unforgivable. Nevertheless, the government considered rapid action essential fearing that these men would quickly lose interest. Quiet, firm encouragement was advised.[91]

The case of the ex-officers was the exception rather than the rule. The majority of British ex-soldiers eager to migrate had little or no capital and relied on the imperial government's implementation of its free passage programme announced in April 1919. Its announcement was shortly followed by a meeting at the end of the month between the OSC, representatives from the War Office, Admiralty, High Commissioners and Agents-General. The application procedure and the administrative framework were the major focus behind the first set of meetings. The burning question, however, was the method and the extent to which the various dominions wanted to carry out the selection process themselves.[92]

The Canadian response to the free passage scheme was one of cautious enthusiasm. The senior dominion was quite proud of its immigration machinery, the success of which over the years was the envy of its sister dominions. Assisted passage, however, was not a policy favoured by Canadian immigration officials nor one appreciated by the general public.[93] 'Canada will always welcome the man who can pay his way, and stand on his own feet, but the man in Canada who requires "public assistance" is regarded as a failure.'[94] The special assistance given to British settlers, reported Sir William Clark, Britain's first High Commissioner to Canada, was resented by many Canadians who had carved their homesteads out of the wilderness without any government assistance whatsoever. They had worked hard, made good and could not understand the reason for all the 'mollycoddling'.[95] Canadian authorities were confident that their vast immigration network, extensive experience and advantageous geographical position would prove as effective in attracting British emigrants to Canada after the war as it had before the outbreak of hostilities and that emigration would therefore resume even without government subsidies.[96] None the less, the offer of free passage to British ex-servicemen and women who had unselfishly defended the empire in its hour of need was a well-deserved exception to the general rule.

When the British government first announced its free passage grants the Canadian government made it abundantly clear that it would retain a firm and independent hand in its selection of overseas immigrants. A precise set of guidelines was formulated governing the type of immigrant Canada wished to encourage. As ever, agriculturalists remained the top priority. F. C. Blair, Secretary to the Department of Immigration and Colonisation, declared that Canada wanted a class of settler who immediately upon arrival became a producer and not merely a consumer: 'Rapidity of development in Canada at the present time depends almost entirely upon our own ability to develop the natural resources, establish new enterprises with fresh capital and develop further those already in existence.'[97] Canada did not want to attract or assist people who would compete against local labour, and nor did it wish to promote the incursion of non-agricultural labour. This was particularly important given the number of Canadian ex-servicemen who were still looking for work.[98]

For ex-imperials wanting to farm under the auspices of the SSB, Canada was only willing to help those who were physically fit, morally upstanding, and in possession of an honourable discharge. Furthermore such settlers had to provide a deposit of £200 as a surety before sailing. They also had to have the cash necessary to pay the 20 per cent down payment required under SSB regulations for non-Canadian veterans eligible for land, livestock, machinery and building materials obtainable through the board. The selection and medical examination of British soldier settlers would take place in the United Kingdom. Shortly after Bedson's appointment a two-man selection board was established and despatched to the United Kingdom. The panel travelled throughout the country appraising soldier applicants at the various regional emigration offices.[99] Only when the selection board was satisfied that an applicant was suitable did the OSC grant a free passage. However, non-agricultural veterans were eligible under the scheme provided they had assured employment in Canada. Free passage grants were also available to widows and children of deceased British veterans, women war workers and orphaned children of British ex-servicemen and women.[100]

Despite the establishment of an elaborate administration, preliminary reports indicated that the few British ex-servicemen and women who had already arrived in Canada during 1919 had no intention of pursuing farm work. Some, finding the SSB's monetary requisite too high, were scared off. Others, not wanting to farm under the SSB, simply lied about their intentions of embarking upon an agricultural career in order to claim a free passage. Instead, many possessed solid offers of employment through relatives and friends, and were screened and approved as essential but non-agricultural immigrants. A major source of trouble was that many British veterans, provided that they met government landing regulations, entered Canada as ordinary immigrants. Problems arose almost immediately as the economic climate in Canada worsened in 1920. To begin with, many of the ordinary ex-service immigrants possessed little or no money on arrival, became impoverished and quickly threw themselves upon the mercy of local charities. Those who arrived under the free passage scheme also began to find conditions difficult and destitution quickly blurred the distinction between assisted and self-financing ex-soldier migrants. In some regions of Canada it was mistakenly assumed that all poverty-stricken British veterans had travelled to Canada under the auspices of the free passage scheme thereby bringing the entire scheme into some disrepute.

Confusion persisted as the SSB and immigration officials tried to clarify the situation. In January 1920 the *Vancouver World* proclaimed that 3,000 ex-imperials were left scattered, stranded and impoverished throughout British Columbia: 'Arriving here in flocks without any properly authorised persons to advise them, these men are unable to take up land as they intended, some are stranded, others fit for charity', while Canadian authorities steadfastly refused to assume responsibility.[101] The Vancouver representative of the newly created Department of Soldiers' Civilian Re-establishment confirmed that the situation was rapidly deteriorating. The majority of the new arrivals were army pensioners with wives and families who had travelled to Canada independent of the free passage scheme. Many were disabled or mentally unfit and had no previous farm experience or no intention of farming. His view was substantiated by the Commissioner of Immigration in Vancouver, A. L. Jolliffe, who reported that of 150 recently disembarked British ex-servicemen and their families only two claimed farming experience. Approximately one-half were pensioners, many were partially disabled and suffered from a variety of medical problems including shattered limbs, tuberculosis and neurasthenia. Over one-third had applied for immediate financial aid. As the situation became more critical, local repatriation and immigration officials demanded the implementation of preventative steps to halt the entry of disabled imperial veterans, especially pensioners.[102] Officials in Toronto faced a similar dilemma. They reported that an increasing number of ex-imperials were eagerly looking for work, and clearly feared that these men would seriously interfere, if not compete, with the re-establishment of Canadian veterans.[103] Ex-imperials might also become a source of serious unemployment in regions where there was already a large, unskilled labour force. For example, the DSCR unit officer in Port Arthur, Ontario (the important grain handling terminus on Lake Superior), stated that the 400 to 600 registered ex-imperials in his area had found plenty of work. But it was a region which possessed plenty of handymen and unless some of the ex-imperials had special mechanical abilities a decline in the local economy was bound to hit these men particularly hard.[104]

As winter approached the Ontario Soldiers' Aid Commission complained that it was being overwhelmed by destitute ex-imperials and their families requesting assistance. Unable to find work these men were increasingly relying upon the Commission to provide money and shelter until they could obtain satisfactory employment. Its biggest complaint was the type of ex-imperial immigrant arriving in Ontario.

> Most of these men leave England with the intention of taking up farm work but for some reason or other drift to the cities and do not fulfil their original intention. The housing problem here in Toronto is as acute as the employment situation and we are finding it almost impossible to obtain situations, excepting as labourers, and as these men do not appear in any

way willing to leave the City, it would appear . . . that steps should be taken to stop sending these families out.[105]

The Commission warned that the situation would worsen with the onset of winter.

The various Canadian veterans' organisations found the problem of the ex-imperial equally trying. The GWVA, the Army and Navy Veterans (ANV) and the Imperial Veterans in Canada (IVC) came under increasing pressure to provide financial assistance to tide over British veterans until they secured employment. As the number of penniless British veterans grew, the financial strains of supporting their fellow British comrades began to show, particularly with the IVC who bore the brunt of the appeals from impoverished ex-imperials. A spokesman for the Vancouver branch of the IVC implored the Chief of the Imperial General Staff, Field Marshall Sir Henry Wilson, to bring home to British veterans 'the unpreparedness of this country to absorb them into its industrial and agricultural life'.[106]

Ottawa accepted the need for more drastic measures to stop the flow of destitute and agriculturally inexperienced ex-imperials into Canada, and in September 1920 displayed a tougher posture. Repeated warnings were despatched to the OSC that Canadian landing regulations would be strictly enforced. Safeguards, such as a more thorough medical examination at the port of disembarkation, were suggested. Disabled pensioners were singled out, and Ottawa insisted that the physically unfit be stopped at Canadian ports and deported before they became a public charge.[107] The SSB emphasised continually that only those ex-imperials selected and accepted by its overseas office would be eligible for the benefits under the 1919 Act.[108] If 'other Imperial ex-Service men should happen to arrive without a ticket or without money for meals, it will be entirely their own fault, because they have been warned time and time again not to leave . . . without being thus provided'.[109] In many cases, Canadian officials put the reasons for failure squarely on the shoulders of the ex-imperials themselves. They professed to believe that many had become destitute during the voyage by squandering their savings through gambling. They also assumed – without evidence – that the rigours of military life and routine had impaired the abilities of many British ex-servicemen to adjust to post-war civilian conditions: 'It seems to be a hard thing for ex-soldiers to get rid of the idea that they are no longer in the army and must shift for themselves. Most of them expect that upon arrival at a Canadian port they will be met by an official who will provide them with billets, rations, transportation, or cater to their needs until such time as they can find employment.'[110]

Amery was dismayed by Canada's increasingly hard-nosed attitude towards British ex-servicemen. Canada's eagerness to co-operate, as expressed by its Prime Minister Arthur Meighen in October 1919, had vanished. Rather, it had been replaced by stringent selection guidelines rigidly enforced in London and at Canadian disembarkation ports.[111] In an attempt to clarify dominion immigration policy, J. A. Calder, Minister of Immigration and Colonisation, met Milner and Amery in London in September 1920. When Calder broached the subject of extending the free passage scheme for another year Milner made it abundantly clear that the extension would be contingent upon a greater degree of 'corresponding action' on behalf of the dominions, in particular an equal share of the financial responsibility. Milner stressed that because of the already enormous demands placed upon the British taxpayer an increase in the expenditure on overseas settlement could only be defended if it was shown to be essential in the context of the larger imperial policy of empire development. He also raised the issue of the self-governing dominions' attitude towards its new British citizens. The dominions showed a tendency to regard the arrivals from the mother country 'too much from the point of view of the immediate utility of their labour and too little from the point of view of their potential value as citizens in the Dominions'.[112] New settlers had to be made welcome and not regarded as 'mere working hands (or) drudges'.[113]

Calder and Smith agreed that there was room for improvement in Canadian attitudes but the dominion government remained resolute in its determination not to relax its policy. 'Our difficulty is not to make Canada better known in the Mother Country', echoed F. C. Blair, 'but rather to make an intelligent selection of those who are anxious to migrate.'[114] Ottawa's main consideration, however, was not to flood the domestic labour market with unskilled non-agricultural immigrants. Moreover, the Colonial Office was convinced that the SSB was unlikely to expand its operations in Britain because 'men selected on this side are apt to regard themselves as entitled to special privileges in many directions, and this makes them somewhat difficult to deal with'.[115] As a result, the Colonial Office believed that the establishment in Britain of a system of testing farms or large agricultural training camps would probably be abandoned, and this did indeed occur. In June 1920, the dominion government decided in favour of a network of training and receiving stations for ex-imperials in Canada to be administered by the SSB.[116]

The policy of disengagement continued with the withdrawal of Colonel Bedson as the SSB's overseas representative and the termination of his post on 31 January 1921. No qualification certificates would henceforth be issued in Britain. Those wishing to emigrate under the privileges of the Soldier Settlement Act were 'invited to proceed . . . as ordinary emigrants in the ordinary way'.[117] Upon arrival they were to apply to the District Superintendent of the SSB in the area they wished to settle and obtain the necessary information and advice on how to qualify for the benefits of the Act. Enquiries from prospective soldier settlers would in future be handled by Smith in London. No clear reason was given for Bedson's recall but it was implied that the emigration officials could easily cope with the additional number of applicants.[118] In reality, the decision was made to cut costs and rationalise overseas operations because the anticipated rush of British applicants never materialised. The dominion government's conscious efforts to keep the number of ex-soldier migrants low and the enormous problems certain regions of the country were having with the new arrivals also influenced their decision. Furthermore, Bedson informed the OSC that the new procedure did not offset the requirement for the £200 deposit.[119]

The OSC regarded the decision to discontinue Bedson's services as a serious impediment to the aspirations of many ex-servicemen eager to settle in Canada. The Colonial Office firmly believed that the inability to obtain selection certificates in Britain would discourage many ex-soldiers who might have entertained the thought of emigrating and subsequently applied for selection in Britain. More importantly, in light of the hardship many ex-imperials had already encountered, they feared that a stronger sense of injustice would be created in the minds of those British ex-servicemen who proceeded to Canada and were rejected having met the expense of travelling across the Atlantic.[120] Macnaghten discussed at length with McLaren Brown and J. S. Dennis of the CPR the possibility of the CPR stepping in to take over the work previously done by Bedson. The CPR were quite prepared to do so if officially requested by the dominion government. Macnaghten agreed to write to the Canadian High Commissioner urging him to support the CPR plan while Dennis promised to take up the issue with the dominion government when he returned to Canada at the end of the month.[121] However, nothing came of the idea.

Of the 31.3 per cent or 26,905 British ex-servicemen and their families who arrived in Canada under the auspices of the free passage scheme, approximately two-thirds were women and children. The total number of ex-imperials who migrated is much higher but impossible to ascertain because the figures do not exist for those who entered Canada as ordinary immigrants. What is clear from the sketchy statistics which have survived is that the free passage scheme failed to bring large numbers of ex-imperial agricultural immigrants. For example, of the 1,382 applicants approved in the period October-December 1921, only 136 were classed as agricultural. The majority had experience in shipbuilding, railways, engineering, construction, metal working, electricals and commerce. Similarly, of the sixty-five female ex-service applicants in the same period only eight were classified as agricultural and were categorised as inexperienced farm hands.[122] The number of British farm applicants chosen through the SSB in London was minimal. In its first annual report, the SSB reported that 'some hundreds' of ex-imperials had been examined and selected but no specific figure was cited. Four months after the ex-imperial guidelines were announced Commissioner Ashton reported that 159 ex-soldiers had paid the £200 deposit and had been granted selection certificates, but owing to shipping shortages in the spring of 1920 only fourteen had managed to sail. According to SSB records 340 ex-imperials were selected in 1920 as suitable for farming in Canada, but only 266 actually reported to the Board upon arrival. Of these, 134 withdrew their deposit before or during training and only a paltry sixty-nine were assisted under the OSC free passage scheme.[123]

## The watershed

Although the war had effectively halted immigration it spurred a phenomenal expansion of the Canadian agricultural sector. Over 92,000 homestead entries were recorded during the conflict and between 1916 and 1921 a total of 40,000 new farms were established on the prairies alone.[124] The dominion census of 1921 best illustrates the growth which occurred. Since the 1911 census the total number of farms increased by 28 per cent, total farm acreage by 52.5 per cent and total improved farm acreage by an amazing 95.3 per cent.[125] The major factor behind this expansion was wartime demand which stimulated higher prices during and immediately after the war. For example, in 1917 wheat was fixed at $2.21 a bushel, thrice its pre-war level, and by 1919 it had reached $2.38.[126]

Unfortunately, the short-term gains were derived at the expense of the agricultural sector's long-term stability and future prosperity which held disastrous consequences for soldier settlement. The Allies' insatiable appetite for Canadian wheat and the sharp rise in world wheat prices created a dangerous investment cycle on the prairies. Although Canadian farmers responded patriotically to the dominion government's plea for increased food production, the primary demand was for wheat. As demand and prices rose, farmers pressed more land into wheat production, often in addition to purchasing land or renting it from those neighbours who had enlisted. Official estimates demonstrated that the extension of the total area of farm crops in Canada between 1914 and 1918 had increased from 33.4 million acres to 51.4 million acres, an increase of 53.8 per cent.[127] Though this was a staggering accomplishment it held ominous implications. Prairie farmers had staked their future in the production of a single cash crop which made them extremely vulnerable to market fluctuations. This vulnerability was also reflected in prairie wheat acreage statistics. Between 1914 and 1918 wheat acreage increased from 9.3 million to 16.1 million, out of a national total in 1918 of 17.3 million, the largest on record.[128] This meant that 93 per cent of Canada's wheat production in 1918 was concentrated in the three prairie provinces. Wheat was indeed king but only if prices remained high.

Farmers continued to stake their immediate prosperity on wheat because it was easier and quicker to expand grain acreage compared to a similar expansion in livestock production. Not only was grain farming the 'path of least resistance' for expanding prairie farmers, but high prices were a much better stimulus which could accomplish more for the back-to-the-land movement than the best run propaganda campaign.[129] The dependence on a single staple for export was extremely perilous; something the Canadian government had both recognised and attempted to rectify prior to the war through the promotion of mixed farming. If a balance between grain and livestock could be struck between a larger number of farmers it would cushion their losses and create a degree of income stability when one or the other markets were weak. Specific wartime demand and high grain prices impeded such a practical approach. Besides, it was easier to obtain farm credit for grain farming because capital investment in the livestock industry was more expensive owing to the need to build and maintain the facilities to manage an efficient operation.[130]

Inflation also kept pace with rising wheat prices. Benefits obtained from increased cultivation and the bullish grain market were quickly absorbed by rising production and labour costs, additional investment and inflation. As a result, many farmers went into debt in anticipation that the boom times would continue after the war. However, over-capitalisation and over-expansion were not the only consequences faced by prairie farmers who persisted in pursuing the cultivation of a single crop during the war.

The high costs incurred did not make prairie farmers more efficient. In fact, many farmers, attracted by high grain prices, abandoned proved dryland farming techniques of summerfallowing, fall tillage and crop rotation. Inevitably, the desire to maximise profits and 'cash in' led to increased soil exhaustion. Plant diseases, such as rust, began to make inroads and this reduced crop yields in many western areas. The situation was further aggravated between 1916 and 1918 by drought and frost which reduced yields even more and contributed to soil infertility. After the record bumper crop of 1915, in which wheat yields averaged 29.3 bushels per acre, successive yields steadily declined until 1919 when the worst yield of 9.7 bushels per acre was recorded.[131] Of course, as long as prices remained artificially high and more land was brought under cultivation the drop in yields could be offset. Farmers would still be able to pay their expenses and maintain a comfortable living standard. However, they had sacrificed the long-term productivity of the land for short-term monetary gains. The farmer had resorted, in the words of the *Canada Year Book*, to 'extensive rather than intensive agriculture'.[132]

Wheat prices remained buoyant in 1919 at $2.38 per bushel. Dominion officials must have felt optimistic when framing the Soldier Settlement Act of 1919 because the generous credit terms, in combination with high prices, would ensure a high success rate amongst soldier settlers and a quick return on their investment. The enormous demand for soldier settlement literature, the keen interest amongst returning veterans and the initial rush of applicants during the summer of 1919 seemed to justify the dominion government's confidence. There was no better stimulus to settlement than high prices.

Prior to the 1920 harvest, all indications were that the Canadian government's firm lead had started to pay handsome dividends. 'This is more or less the beginning of things', explained Major John Barnett, chairman of the SSB, in September 1920, 'in as much as a survey of next season's breaking indicates that at least 500,000 acres of new land will (have been) broken' since the SSB's establishment.[133] Preliminary production and freight receipts for 1920 demonstrated that the 10,000 producing soldier settlers had already generated $3 million in rail and shipping revenue while producing crops valued at $10 million. Barnett estimated that with 250,000 acres of new soldier settlement land under cultivation in 1921 and twice the number of soldier settlers, freight receipts would double by the end of the 1922 fiscal year.[134] In fact, close to 190,000 new acres were brought into production, raising the aggregate amount of new acres to 600,000. At the end of the 1921 fiscal year soldier settlers occupied 5.23 million acres. Even with the collapse of the market price for grain during the middle of the 1920 harvest, veterans brought in farm receipts totalling $12.7 million.[135]

The highwater mark was 1920. SSB officials were mildly surprised that even with the market collapse and the high labour and threshing costs, 9,372 settlers of the 12,174 obligated to meet their first loan payment by 1 November 1920 had done so in whole or in part. Approximately $2.3 million was due of which 53.9 per cent or $1.24 million was collected. In addition, soldier settlers were urged to make payments above the minimum required in order to reduce their debt load as soon as possible. Prepayments amounting to a little over $1 million were subsequently received.[136] Collections had gone exceedingly well given the economic circumstances, and it was with a great deal of pride and gratification that the results obtained 'placed the stamp of guarantee upon soldier settlement work'.[137] The self-congratulation proved premature.

From the SSB's inception in 1918 to 31 March 1921 a total of 1,470 cases of abandonment were reported compared with 329 who repaid their loans in full. However, the SSB considered 7 per cent as a norm for the amount of adjusted or salvaged claims. The adjustment figures were broken down into three categories, of which fraud, misrepresentation and dishonesty made up a small number of cases. Just under one-third were attributed to causes beyond the control of the settler, such as death, recurring illness or disability due to war service and crop failure. The SSB placed the blame for failure unfairly but squarely on the shoulders of the struggling settler. It cited poor temperament, bad management and abandonment for no apparent cause as factors for discontinuance.[138] Certainly, these matters did play a role, but to claim that failure was largely due to personal attributes or flaws was preposterous. The major causes of failure were economic, such as high prices for land, stock and equipment at a time when commodity prices were plummeting. Most veterans had arrived too late to reap the benefits of wartime profits, but still had to pay inflated wartime prices and pay off their growing debts from falling incomes.[139] By March 1923, 3,285 soldier settlers or 14.5 per cent had discontinued farming. A year later the total had climbed to 21.5 per cent or 5,203. The SSB acknowledged the fact that poor land, crop failure and low farm prices contributed to the growing number of abandonments but it still maintained as late as 1924 that the personal factor was a major reason for failure.[140]

There was no question that the boom and bust of 1920–21 was a major contributory factor behind the failure of many a brave soldier settler. The price of wheat was less than half the 1919 price and reached only $1.11 per bushel in 1921.[141] But it was not *the* major factor: many soldier settlers were already experiencing difficulties prior to the depression. The worsening situation was further complicated between 1919 and 1924 by persistent drought conditions which plagued farmers throughout Canada and lowered their crop yields even further.

Not everything was doom and gloom. There were personal as well as regional triumphs, but they went by unnoticed by the general public. For example, N. H. McTaggart, Progressive MP for Maple Creek in the arid south-western corner of Saskatchewan had between 450 and 500 soldier settlers in his constituency. Barnett informed him that ever since 1921, despite the economic downturn, the Maple Creek area had led Saskatchewan in the number of repayment collections. On a

national level, there were three SSB districts in McTaggart's constituency which compared extremely well with the rest of Canada in
regard to loan repayment, salvage and general prosperity. Only fourteen
or fifteen salvage cases had been reported and just as many had repaid
their loans in full. Barnett wrote McTaggart that 'the very fact that . . .
you have not heard from (any) of them indicates that they are happy,
contented, and prosperous'. Similar stories were reported in western
Ontario and the Maritimes.[142]

Farm diversification remained an important priority for the SSB as
cereal prices remained depressed. Settlers were encouraged to maintain
a small number of pigs, cows and poultry to offset expenses. In turn, any
income generated from grain receipts could be used to reduce financial
obligations. The dominion Department of Agriculture supported the
SSB's attempts to promote thrift, economy and diversification amongst
its settlers because it was 'essential to the prosperity and continued
success of the settler'.[143] It agreed with the SSB's conclusions that in the
short-term grain farming remained a gamble, especially in the prairies.
The Saskatoon district supervisor pointed out that farmers could
stabilise their family income and reduce the impact of a serious set-back
such as a crop failure simply by utilising all the sources of revenue that
mixed farming produced.[144] Ashton stressed another interesting point
concerning successful soldier settlers. 'It was very noticeable that
among our settlers the men who were succeeding best were the men
who, in addition to being good farmers, were good salesmen also.'[145]
Better farming denoted the application of modern scientific, managerial
and commercial techniques which ensured security and increased
returns. By 1925, however, it was too late to start advocating these
commonsensical ideas. The collapse of grain prices in 1920–21 had
already done the damage.

Indebtedness became a serious problem for the surviving soldier
settlers after 1921. Of the 5,203 adjustment cases processed in 1924, half
were located in Manitoba and Alberta. Alberta was also in the
embarrassing position of having the lowest collection record in the
country which averaged 38 per cent. Manitoba's 1,600 farm abandonments was considered extremely high as only 56 per cent of the
3,707 soldier settlers remained on their properties by 1926.[146] As the
number of salvage cases increased throughout the 1920s revaluation
became a highly contentious issue, a fact which highlighted the growing
political significance of soldier settlement.

The 1921 dominion election clearly demonstrated the degree of
veteran dissatisfaction with the Meighen government's apparent lack of
compassion and its inability to satisfy a variety of demands. The growing importance of the veteran issue in Canadian politics, and in

particular the question of soldier settlement, was reflected by the activities of the various veterans' organisations prior to the national election in December. But the real problem remained unemployment. Although it inflicted hardship on all sections of Canadian society, the plight of the returned man received an enormous amount of attention. In 1919 a special House of Commons committee was bombarded with letters, telegrams and evidence from a variety of individuals, boards of trade, municipalities and commercial associations warning the dominion government of the danger of veteran unemployment. It recommended that the eradication of veteran unemployment was a national undertaking and therefore a dominion responsibility; whereas civilian unemployment was strictly a municipal and provincial matter. The committee advised that steps be taken to meet the emergency both administratively and financially.[147] Meighen agreed that the dominion authorities had to play a key role in ameliorating unemployment, but 'the great thing to do . . . is to enforce with the least possible delay such a definite general policy as will get business going again and get our people back to work'. Meighen insisted that ex-servicemen could not be singled out or treated separately. Unemployment affected everyone and demanded national co-operation and bold solutions. Privately, Meighen had run out of patience with the veteran issue. At the beginning of the election campaign in September 1921 he told Sir Charles Hibbert Tupper, a prominent British Columbia conservative, that Canada's experience with the veterans over the last year 'amply demonstrates that the Government in its entire policy towards ex-service men reached the limit of generosity that the country could sustain'.[148]

However, the Canadian electorate, including a large number of ex-soldiers, had grown impatient with Meighen's government and he was soundly defeated at the polls. After his defeat, he readily admitted to Amery that unemployment and veteran discontent were contributory factors, but he pointed to the depression and the Conservative government's unpopular wartime activities as the prime reasons for the defeat.[149] However, the change of government did not bring about an improvement in the economic fortunes of many veterans. Unemployment continued to rise and the demands by the veterans' associations for resolute action grew louder.[150] Deflation and the phenomenal drop in prices for primary commodities had wiped out the equity of many soldier settler properties. According to one confidential report undertaken by the Liberals during the 1921 election campaign the situation bordered 'on a financial crisis for the loans advanced by the [Conservative] Government are in excess of what the farms are worth at 1922–1923 prices and valuations'. Losses between the 1919–20 price levels and the actual 1922–23 valuations was estimated at $10 million.[151]

The report severely criticised the previous government's financial management of the entire soldier settlement operation. It conceded that the economic situation had initially led to exorbitant prices, but it charged the SSB with carelessness in its selection and loan granting procedure. Overstaffing, it claimed, was another problem which contributed to high costs. The only solution, according to the report, was to increase the interest on the loans by 0.5 per cent and extend the repayment period by five years.[152] The Liberal government reopened the investigation into soldier settlement when it appointed a parliamentary inquiry in March 1922. A number of relief measures were suggested to ease veteran indebtedness. They included the revaluation of land, livestock and equipment, exemption of interest for a period of years, a reduction in the rate of interest and the extension of the redemption period on stock and equipment loans. The inquiry recommended that the original repayment period of four to six annual instalments on stock, equipment and building loans, as set out in the 1919 Act, be extended to twenty-five years. Barnett was forced to admit to the committee that under the old regime the SSB repayment scheme had been too heavy in 1919. Similarly, the committee suggested that a sliding scale of interest exemptions be granted to soldier settlers who had settled before the end of 1921. The government accepted both points and incorporated them as amendments to the legislation in 1922.[153]

Although the government wrote off over $10 million in interest under the 1922 amendments its optimistic forecast that 1923 would be a better year was quickly dispelled. The SSB reported at the year's end that over $88 million remained outstanding of a total of $107 million in loans and interest charges. In August the SSB was transferred to the Department of Immigration and Colonisation and became the Land Settlement Branch. The move was, in part, designed to rationalise settlement administration and operations in light of the latest attempt in Anglo-Canadian co-operative colonisation: the 3,000 British Family Scheme. In 1924 new regulations were introduced limiting the granting of new loans to soldiers who applied to purchase farms already owned by the SSB, or to those who owned land and could have applied for a loan but did not, or those to whom the SSB were committed because they had been recommended for training or had a justifiable claim to be dealt with. However, it was stated emphatically that no new applicants would be accepted for training or qualification.[154]

Deflation continued to afflict livestock prices: the SSB estimated in 1924 that livestock values had decreased by over 50 per cent. However, it was not until 1925 that remedial legislation was brought in to reduce indebtedness caused by the drastic fall in livestock values. In the end, close to $3 million was struck from soldiers' accounts.[155] The burning issue remained land revaluation. After travelling extensively throughout Manitoba, a leading provincial Liberal fund-raiser noted that land revaluation was the most important issue with soldier settlers: '[T]hese people will never attain any degree of success until the purchase price has been reduced and these people placed in a position where the land will earn enough to pay all the carrying charges and permit a profit to the individual.' In February 1925 the Manitoba provincial command of the GWVA, supported by the United Farmers of Manitoba, agreed. It insisted that all soldier settlement lands receive revaluation[156] and in the following month, at the annual conference of the provincial commands of the GWVA, demands were made that the government introduce amendments, including land revaluation, to the soldier settlement legislation to relieve the hardship being suffered by the majority of settlers.[157]

According to E. J. Garland, an Alberta MP and an outspoken champion of the veterans' cause, land revaluation was not only urgent but imperative. Since 1922 Garland had campaigned unsuccessfully for the necessary land revaluation legislation and in 1925 he once again failed.[158] However, time was on his side. Pressure mounted until eventually veterans succeeded in winning the necessary concessions from a minority Liberal government in 1926. The appropriate legislation was introduced but the constitutional crisis which ensued for most of that year prevented its passage. In January 1927 the newly elected Liberal government was reminded of its obligation to Canada's veterans by the newly formed Canadian Legion and the United Farmers of Alberta. Aware of their responsibilities, politicians on both sides of the House demanded fairness, leniency and compassion for Canada's soldier settlers, while the government duly promised to deal effectively with land revaluation.[159] Between July 1927 and the spring of 1930 the SSB laboured under the enormous burden of reappraising 8,103 applicants out of the 10,697 eligible to apply. By the end of 1929, 7,043 appraisals had received their final review. It was estimated that the aggregate sale price of the 7,043 properties was $26.5 million. The total adjustment granted in these cases was $6,379,930, representing an average reduction of 24 per cent. When revaluation was completed in 1930 a total of 8,047 farms had been revalued at $30.39 million with reductions estimated at $7.4 million. This was written off and was far below the estimated $10 million forecast by Robert Forke, Minister of Immigration and Colonisation, in March 1927.[160]

The agricultural situation stabilised by 1925–26. In 1927 Canada produced a record bumper crop, only to be surpassed by an even bigger yield in 1928.[161] Surely with revaluation and two excellent harvests soldier settlement was at last on a solid footing? The depression of 1929 wiped out any optimism that remained and brought greater disappointment and despair to those soldier settlers who survived. According to the 1931 SSB report, of the original 24,491 soldier settlers who had received loans from the SSB over half had abandoned their holdings by 1931. Just 11,612 remained and of these only 5,500 were judged to be in a secure position with a good chance of success. Approximately 4,500 veterans had a reasonable chance. It was this group upon which the SSB focused its attention and supervisory resources. The remaining 1,600 or so fell under the category 'likely to fail' but the SSB was determined not to abandon these cases and it was evident 'that dispossession of their farms under existing conditions would not be warranted'.[162]

The onslaught of a new depression forced the SSB to further alleviate the plight of the surviving soldier settlers. Yet another special committee was appointed in early 1930 by the Liberal government to examine pensions and returned soldiers' problems. In May its findings were presented to Parliament in which its most important recommendation was a 30 per cent reduction of the total outstanding indebtedness of all soldier settlers still occupying their farms. All livestock liens held by the SSB would be terminated and the stock reverted outright to the settler. No debate ensued and after just two days of procedural necessities its recommendations became law. With an impending national election that July it was not surprising that the committee's recommendations were legislated so quickly. By March 1931 a further $11.3 million was written off the soldier settler account.[163]

The SSB was officially abolished in 1931.[164] However, there were a few outstanding financial adjustments made for the remaining soldier settlers. Clearly, the depression hampered the newly elected Conservative Prime Minister's efforts to appease Canada's ailing soldier settlers. Wheat prices reached a record low and the burden of accumulated arrears forced R. B. Bennett to introduce additional remedial legislation in 1933 in the form of interest remission. A new feature was the bonus amendment. It was designed to reward the thrifty, hard-working settler who showed determination to make his repayments. Previously, remedial legislation had benefited the good, bad and indifferent settler. After detailed discussions with soldiers' organisations and settlers themselves the amendment was implemented in order to remedy the disparity of previous legislation. The measure established that for every dollar the settler contributed towards his arrears or instalments the government would equal that payment to relieve some of the burden. As a precondition settlers had for the first time to pay insurance premiums and local taxes on their holdings. Previously soldier settlement lands were considered Crown lands and therefore not subject to taxation. By

31 March 1935 soldier settlers had earned a bonus totalling $1.9 million.[165]

Ultimately, the financial cost to the nation was substantial. From its inception to March 1935 Canada's soldier settlement programme had cost $136.3 million. Repayments amounted to $52.2 million and approximately $35.2 million was written off through various remedial legislation inaugurated since 1922. This left $48.9 million outstanding. However, when compared to the cost of veterans' benefits paid out by the dominion government between 1914 and 1935, a sum of approximately $1 billion, the sums spent on soldier settlement were exorbitant in per capita terms. The equivalent of 13.6 per cent of veterans' benefits was spent on just over 4 per cent of the total number of *able-bodied* Canadian veterans!

But what of the survivors? Of the 24,998 soldier settlers who received loans from the SSB, 10,828 or 43 per cent were still in possession of their farms. The precariousness of the situation was reflected by the equity grading system adopted by government officials which measured the likelihood of a settler's success. The table demonstrated that 32 per cent of the settlers had an equity of 40 per cent or more in their farms; 17 per cent fell within the 20–40 per cent bracket; 15 per cent had less than 20 per cent equity and 36 per cent had no equity at all.[166]

What had gone wrong with Canada's soldier settlement policy? Undoubtedly, the international economic climate was a crucial factor which ultimately dictated the degree of 'success' or 'failure' of the scheme. The artificially high wheat prices created during the war and maintained by the immediate post-war boom, gave the policy's architects the illusion that their programme had been established on a secure and prosperous footing. Patriotism, a sense of national obligation to the returned man, and the relief of a return to normality clouded the minds of politicians, administrators and citizens alike to the dangers of establishing a national land settlement policy for a select few during an inflationary spiral of unprecedented proportions. The brave few who warned that high prices were no substitute for actual farming experience were unfortunately ignored.

To establish whether soldier settlement was a success or failure poses an interesting problem. As a policy it was an outright failure. The expenditure of approximately $145 million by 1935 and the large sums which were written off and remained outstanding were damning indictments. The 'failure' of 57 per cent of the SSB's clients points to a similar conclusion. However, there were individual successes. These figures ignore the 6,500 soldier settlers who claimed their soldier grant and farmed without SSB assistance. Even abandoned farms were not lost. Many were resold to neighbouring farmers or newly arrived immigrants and, in fact, resold land usually brought in a slight profit, especially before land prices slumped in 1923. Expansion did not stop despite the gloomy economic climate. The number of soldier grant entries which were claimed after the initial rush, although small, reflected that some soldier settlers were able to expand and make a comfortable living. In fact, the Royal Commission on Immigration and Settlement in Saskatchewan in 1930 recorded that very few of the successful soldier settlers operated on their minimum entitlement of 160 acres. Rather they had expanded to 320 acres. As Barnett astutely pointed out, everyone was aware of the failures but not the successes: 'very often your good man is not known even by neighbouring farmers'.[167]

Canada had tried to honour its obligation to its returned men by providing them with an opportunity to re-establish themselves within civilian life and contribute to the future prosperity of the nation. Unfortunately, the general public did not realise how costly their sacrifice had been. The fact that the resettlement of British ex-servicemen was a complete fiasco was still more disconcerting. In the final analysis, despite some individual successes, Canada's soldier settlement policy was a disappointing failure. It is to the other dominions which we must now turn our attention.

## Notes

1 NA, William Lyon Mackenzie King Papers (hereafter King Papers), J1 series, vol. 59, pp. 50968–9, Caroline Hope Crerar to King, 6 August 1921.
2 Howard Palmer, *Patterns of Prejudice*, Toronto, 1982, pp. 47–60; Avery, *'Dangerous Foreigners'*, pp. 65–115. For a discussion of Canadian attitudes, treatment and policies toward central European ethnic minorities during and after the war see John Herd Thompson, *The Harvests of War*, Toronto, 1978, pp. 73–94; Frances Swyripa, 'The Ukrainian image: loyal citizen or disloyal alien', in Frances Swyripa and J. H. Thompson, eds, *Loyalties in Conflict*, Edmonton, 1983, pp. 47–68; Donald Avery, 'Ethnic and class tensions in Canada, 1918–20: Anglo-Canadians and the alien worker', *ibid.*, pp. 79–98; Henry Drystek, 'The simplest and cheapest mode of dealing with them: deportation from Canada before World War II', *Histoire sociale – Social History*, XV, 1982, pp. 407–41; Barbara Roberts, 'Shovelling out the "mutinous": political deportation from Canada before 1936', *Labour/Le Travail*, XVIII, 1986, pp. 77–110; idem, *Whence They Came: Deportation from Canada 1900–1935*, Ottawa, 1988.
3 The term 'alien' is another term which was used to describe a foreign immigrant. During and after World War I it became more of a derogatory term used to describe immigrants from countries which Canada and the empire had been fighting against.
4 For the impact of Canadian servicemen on wartime politics see Desmond Morton, 'Polling the soldier vote: the overseas campaign in the Canadian general election of 1917', *Journal of Canadian Studies*, X, 1975, pp. 39–58.
5 SAB, Pamphlet file, 'Soldier and the land' by A. M. Forbes. Reprinted by the Canadian Council of Agriculture (c. 1919). For an examination of comparative soldier settlement policies in contemporary periodicals see the following: W. A. Baille-Grohman, 'A paradise for Canadian and American soldiers', *Nineteenth Century and*

*After*, LXXXIII, 1918, pp. 762–78; A. J. Hannan, 'Land settlement of ex-service men in Australia, Canada, and the United States', *Journal of Comparative Legislation and International Law*, 3rd series, II, 1920, pp. 225–37.

6 SAB, Pamphlet file, 'Soldier and the land', by Forbes.

7 John Herd Thompson and Allen Seager, *Canada 1922–1939: Decades of Discord*, Toronto, 1985, pp. 3–4 and 11.

8 Cole Harris, 'The myth of the land in Canadian nationalism', in P. Russell, ed., *Nationalism in Canada*, Toronto, 1966, pp. 27–43; Martin J. Weiner, *English Culture and Decline of the Industrial Spirit, 1850–1980*, Cambridge, 1981, p. 6.

9 Canada, *Debates*, 1919, IV, p. 3863.

10 *Ibid.*

11 *Canadian Annual Review*, 1918, p. 585.

12 M. J. Barber, 'The Assimilation of Immigrants in the Canadian Prairie Provinces, 1886–1918: Canadian Perception and Canadian Policies', unpublished Ph.D. thesis, University of London, 1975, pp. 288–9; Avery, *'Dangerous Foreigners'*, p. 88.

13 *Canadian Annual Review*, 1918, p. 585.

14 NA, Records of the Royal Canadian Legion (hereafter Legion Records), vol. 1, f. 4, pp. 56 and 137, minute book of the GWVA, 27 July 1918 and 3 March 1919; *Canadian Annual Review*, 1918, p. 586.

15 NA, Borden Papers, vol. 225, f. RLB 1824, p. 126305, Bonar Law to Borden, 13 February 1918; *The Veteran*, I, February 1918, pp. 8–9.

16 SAB, Meighen to H. A. Robson, 15 March 1918; NA, Borden Papers, vol. 225, f. RLB 1824, p. 126213, H. A. Kennedy to Borden, 5 October 1917; *ibid.*, p. 126264, Charles Stewart, Premier of Alberta, to Borden, 16 January 1918; *ibid.*, p. 126258, J. W. Mitchell, Provincial Secretary of the Alberta GWVA, to Borden, 15 January 1918; *ibid.*, pp. 126290–2, N. F. R. Knight, Secretary-Treasurer of GWVA, to Borden, 28 January 1918.

17 NA, RG 15, vol. 1127, f. 3850452, Maber to Meighen, 22 February 1918.

18 *Ibid.*, f. 3850452, Maber to Meighen, 19 March 1918.

19 *First Report of the Soldier Settlement Board of Canada*, 31 March 1921, p. 13.

20 *Canadian Annual Review*, 1918, p. 587.

21 Morton and Wright, *Winning the Second Battle*, p. 103; NA, Borden Papers, vol. 234, f. RLB 2198/1, pp. 130663–78a, H. A. Wright to Borden, 18 and 30 November 1919; *ibid.*, vol. 239, f. RLB 2418, p. 133330, Thomas Longworth, Secretary-Treasurer of the Lethbridge GWVA, to Borden, 18 February 1918; *ibid.*, pp. 133332–3, Mitchell to Borden, 19 February 1918 and W. A. Buchanan to Borden, 19 February 1918.

22 Quotation cited in Morton and Wright, *Winning the Second Battle*, p. 104.

23 NA, RG 15, H. E. Hume Papers, Deputy Commissioner of Dominion Lands (hereafter Hume Papers), vol. 4, f. 1, circular by L. Pereira, Secretary of the Department of the Interior, 16 April 1918; *ibid.*, memorandum of interview between Maber, a Mr Perrin and Hume, 16 May 1918; Maber to Cory, 28 May 1918; circular by Pereira, 31 May 1918.

24 PC 1805, 19 July 1918; PC 1658, 6 July 1918; NA, Hume Papers, vol. 4, f. 2, telephone message, Maber to Hume, 24 September 1918; NA, RG 15, vol. 1127, f. 3850452, Maber to Meighen, 14 November 1918.

25 NA, Records of the Department of Indian Affairs, RG 10, vol. 7530, f. 26001–1, vol. 1, F. D. Stewart, Secretary of the Saskatoon GWVA land settlement committee, to J. D. McLean, Assistant Departmental Secretary of Indian Affairs, 15 September 1917; R. C. Irving, Dominion Secretary of the Army and Navy Veterans of Canada (ANV), to the Superintendent-General of Indian Affairs, 17 December 1918; NA, Borden Papers, vol. 239, f. RLB 2418, p. 133330, Longworth to Borden, 18 February 1918.

26 NA, RG 10, vol. 7530, f. 26001–1, vol. 1, Meighen to D. C. Scott, 25 November 1918.

27 NA, Hume Papers, vol. 4, f. 2, D. C. Scott to Hume, 7 December 1918; NA, RG 10, vol. 7530, f. 26001–1, vol. 1, D. C. Scott to W. M. Graham, Indian Commissioner, Regina, 26 March 1919; D. C. Scott to Meighen, 9 December 1918.

28 NA, Hume Papers, vol. 4, f. 2, Provincial Conference, November 1918: memorandum as to soldier settlement; Paul M. Koroscil, 'Soldiers, settlement and development in

British Columbia, 1915–1930', *BC Studies*, no. 54, 1982, pp. 67–8; Morton and Wright, *Winning the Second Battle*, p. 143.

29 Roger Graham, *Arthur Meighen*, I, *The Door of Opportunity*, Toronto, 1960, pp. 161 and 176.

30 *Canadian Annual Review*, 1918, p. 426.

31 *Ibid.*, p. 427.

32 SAB, J. A. Calder Papers, M2–4, pp. 1344–6, undated memorandum by Calder entitled, 'Providing land for our returned soldiers'.

33 *Canadian Annual Review*, 1918, pp. 428–9.

34 M. Stuart Hunt, *Nova Scotia's Part in the Great War*, Halifax, 1920, pp. 328–9; *Canadian Annual Review*, 1918, p. 430; NA, Sir Arthur Currie Papers, vol. 3, colonisation file no. 8, 'Inspection tour of the maritime provinces, 11–27 November 1924'; McGill University Libraries, A. M. Forbes Papers, Box 1, f. 2, J. E. Richards to Lieutenant-Colonel Bruce F. Campbell, Supervisor, Soldier Settlement Board, Montreal, 29 October 1918.

35 NA, Borden Papers, vol. 244, f. RLB 2772, pp. 136614–15, Meighen to Borden, 11 December 1918; PC 299, 11 February 1919; Canada, *Debates*, 1919, IV, p. 3849.

36 PC 807, 3 April 1918; NA, RG 76, vol. 610, f. 901346, part 5, circular by Pereira to all agents of dominion lands in Manitoba, Saskatchewan, Alberta and the Railway Belt in British Columbia, 16 April 1918; W. D. Scott to Walker, 18 April 1918; Morgan, 'Soldier settlement in the prairies', p. 41.

37 *First Report of the SSB*, p. 152.

38 *Canada Year Book*, 1920, p. 32.

39 NA, Records of the Department of Militia and Defence, RG 9 III A1, series 10, vol. 93, f. 10–12–44, 'Soldier Settlement Board: instructions in agriculture, plans for procedure', 28 October 1918.

40 *Ibid.*, Meighen to Sir Edward Kemp, 5 November 1918; 'Agricultural training: Khaki University and demobilisation', 28 October 1918; *Report of the Ministry of Overseas Military Forces of Canada, 1918*, London, 1918, pp. 473–84.

41 W. J. Black, 'Agricultural training for returned soldiers', *Agricultural Gazette of Canada*, V, 1918, pp. 1123–7; C. W. Cavers, 'Selecting and training soldiers for agriculture', *Agricultural Gazette of Canada*, VI, 1919, pp. 426–8.

42 NA, RG 9 III A1, series 10, vol. 93, f. 10–12–44, Ministry of Militia to Lieutenant-General Sir Arthur Currie, Commander of the Canadian Corps, 19 December 1918.

43 NA, RG 38, vol. 225, Secretary of the Department of Veterans Affairs to J. G. Mitchell, Private Secretary's Office of the Department of the Interior, 11 February 1918; *Canadian Annual Review*, 1918, pp. 558–9; *ibid.*, 1919, pp. 599–600; E. L. Chicanot, 'The Canadian soldier on the land', *United Empire*, XIII, 1922, pp. 200–2.

44 NA, RG 76, vol. 610, f. 901346, part 8, copy of statement made by Meighen and released by C. W. Cavers, Director of Information, SSB, 15 November 1919.

45 Canada, *Debates*, 1919, first session, I, p. 3863.

46 NA, King Papers, J4 series, vol. 147, f. 1200, p. 107270, memorandum by Ashton for the Prime Minister, Minister of Finance and the Minister of the Interior entitled, 'Soldier settlers' problems', 7 April 1930; *ibid.*, vol. 147, f. 1199, p. 107215, memorandum entitled 'Future of the Soldier Settlement Board and the Land Settlement Branch', n.d.; PAO, RG 3, H. Ferguson Papers, Box 46, memorandum by Ashton entitled, 'Some aspects of land settlement', c. 1923; *Third Report of the Soldier Settlement Board*, 31 December 1924, p. 20. By the end of November 1924 reorganisation had reduced the staff to 600 and by 1930 some 500 remained employed. Morton and Wright cite the total number of employees as 1,594 but the sources cited did not mention that figure.

47 Morton and Wright, *Winning the Second Battle*, p. 145.

48 *First Report of the SSB*, pp. 7–9.

49 *Ibid.*, pp. 8 and 13; *Canadian Annual Review*, 1920, p. 460; *Canada Year Book*, 1920, p. 33. For the details on Indian reserve lands see NA, RG 10, vol. 7530, f. 26001–1, part 1, list showing unsold surrendered lands in Manitoba, Saskatchewan, Alberta and Ontario, May 1919; D. C. Scott, Deputy Superintendent General of the Department

of Indian Affairs, to W. M. Graham, Indian Commissioner, Regina, 7 October 1919. Scott listed nine western reserves in which the Department of Indian Affairs had received over $716,000 in payments from the SSB for surrendered Indian land. For a recent study of the Department of Indian Affairs including a brief description of the settlement of native soldiers see E. Brian Titley, *A Narrow Vision: Duncan Campbell Scott and the Administration of Indian Affairs in Canada*, Vancouver, 1986.

50 Quotation cited in Morton and Wright, *Winning the Second Battle*, p. 149; *Canadian Annual Review*, 1920, p. 459.

51 *Canadian Annual Review*, 1920, pp. 241 and 459–60; *First Report of the SSB*, p. 7; GAA, Garnet D. Ellis Papers, Ellis to his parents, 23 September 1918.

52 *First Report of the SSB*, p. 21. Also see C. R. Fay, 'Lessons of soldier settlement in the Canadian west', *United Empire*, XIV, 1923, pp. 202–8. According to the 1921 census the number of men employed in agriculture was 1,017,000. If the 25,000 soldier settlers are subtracted from the total (the SSB report was published before the census was conducted) the increase in the number of agriculturally employed is 2.5 per cent. Thompson, *Decades of Discord*, p. 348.

53 *First Report of the SSB*, p. 20; *Canada Year Book*, 1920, p. 35; Morton and Wright, *Winning the Second Battle*, p. 148.

54 *First Report of the SSB*, p. 22.

55 E. J. Ashton, 'Soldier land settlement in Canada', *Quarterly Journal of Economics*, XXXIX, 1925, p. 496; *Proceedings of the Special Committee appointed by Resolution of the House of Commons on the 10th of March, 1921, to consider questions relating to the Pensions, Insurance and Re-establishment of Returned soldiers . . . May 26th, 1921* (Ottawa 1921). Hereafter cited as *Special Committee, 1921*. The entire report gives an excellent insight into SSB operations, in particular Major John Barnett's evidence.

56 *Canada Year Book*, 1920, p. 34; *First Report of the SSB*, p. 20.

57 *Second Report of the Soldier Settlement Board*, 31 March 1923, pp. 7–10; *Tenth Report of the Soldier Settlement Board*, 31 March 1935, pp. 3–21; Ashton, 'Soldier settlement', pp. 496–7; Morgan, 'Soldier settlement in the prairies', pp. 44–50.

58 Ontario, *Sessional Papers*, LII, part VIII (1920), *Report of the Commission of Enquiry into the Kapuskasing Colony, 1920*; PAO, RG 3, E. C. Drury Papers, Boxes 27 and 44, general correspondence and evidence on Kapuskasing enquiry; Johnston, *Drury*, pp. 167–71; Koroscil, 'Settlement and development'.

59 SAB, W. M. Martin Papers, M4-I-85, pp. 25102–6, Ashton to Premier Martin of Saskatchewan, 15 November 1918; NA, Legion Records, vol. 1, f. 4, p. 105, minute book of the GWVA, 2 December 1918; Canada, *Debates*, 1919, IV, p. 3858; *First Report of the SSB*, p. 12; *The Veteran*, III, January 1920, pp. 21 and 46.

60 John McDonald, 'Soldier settlement and depression settlement in the forest fringe of Saskatchewan', *Prairie Forum*, VI, 1981, pp. 35–7.

61 *First Report of the SSB*, p. 10; *Proceedings of the Special Committee appointed by Resolution of the House of Commons on the 18th of September, 1919, and to whom was referred Bill No. 10, An Act to amend the Department of Soldier's Civil Re-establishment Act . . . 21 October 1919* (Ottawa 1919), p. 216. Hereafter cited as *Special Committee, 1919*; *Proceedings of the Special Committee Appointed to Consider Questions Relating to the Pensions, Insurance and Re-establishment of Returned Soldiers, 1924* (Ottawa 1924), p. 432. Hereafter cited as *Special Committee, 1924*.

62 NA, RG 15, vol. 1127, f. 3850452, memorandum by Maber for Meighen, 14 November 1918; *ibid.*, f. 3850452(1), memorandum by Maber for Meighen, 19 March 1919.

63 McDonald, 'Soldier settlement', p. 38; NA, King Papers, J1 series, vol. 54, pp. 46589–92, Lyne to King, 25 September 1920; King to Lyne, 13 October 1920.

64 *Special Committee, 1924*, pp. 68 and 90; Royal Commission on Immigration and Settlement (Saskatchewan) 1930, *Record of Proceedings*, testimony of Major John Barnett, vol. 23, p. 36.

65 PAM, Royal Canadian Legion, Manitoba Provincial Command Papers, MG 10 C67,

Box 11, Minute Book (1919–26), 7th meeting, 24 October 1919, p. 2; *ibid.*, Manitoba Department of Mines and Natural Resources, Land Branch Files, RG 17 D1, Box 19, f. 346, charts showing the number of unoccupied quarter sections in districts and municipalities east and west of Lake Manitoba, 1930; NA, Hume Papers, vol. 4, f. 3, memorandum by T. W. Dwight, Department of the Interior, Forest Branch, 19 June 1919.

66 R. W. Murchie and H. C. Grant, *Unused Lands of Manitoba*, Winnipeg, 1926, p. 61; McDonald, 'Soldier settlement', p. 39; NA, C. A. Magrath Papers, vol. 3, f. 8, memorandum by Ashton, 'Inspection tour of prairie provinces and British Columbia, 19 August-19 October 1924', 30 October 1924.

67 NA, Borden Papers, vol. 238, f. RLB 2389, pp. 133169–69a, Wilmot Yates to Borden, 6 March 1920; PAM, Valentine Winkler Papers, pp. 3309–12 and 3375A, Findlay to Winkler, Minister of Agriculture and Immigration (1915–20), 5 January 1920; S. M. Hayden to Winkler, 2 April 1920.

68 SAB, Calder Papers, M2–5, pp. 1463–4, G. Harmon Jones, Secretary of the Saskatchewan Military Hospitals Commission, to Calder, 22 February 1916.

69 SAB, S. J. Latta Papers, M5-IV-54, undated Saskatchewan Returned Soldiers Employment Commission memorandum (probably late 1918), Saskatchewan Returned Soldiers Employment Commission file, 1917–20.

70 SAB, papers of the Saskatchewan Returned Soldiers Employment Commission, G459.1, minutes of the 1918 annual meeting, 18 July 1918; *ibid.*, C. A. Dunning Papers, M6:X-204–7, pp. 43285–6, minutes of the meeting of the executive committee of the Saskatchewan Returned Soldiers Employment Commission, 5 September 1917.

71 SAB, Dunning Papers, M6:Y-3–5–0, p. 12062, Acting Deputy Minister of the Department of the Interior to Dunning, 1 September 1921. For Dunning's career see J. W. Brennan, 'C. A. Dunning, 1916–1930: The rise and fall of a western agrarian Liberal', in John E. Foster, ed., *The Developing West*, Edmonton, 1983, pp. 246–70.

72 GAA, Soldier Settlement Board file, W. Strojich, Superintendent, Farm Service Division, Department of Veterans Affairs, to Herbert R. Harris, 17 August 1966; PAO, RG 3, Ferguson Papers, memorandum by Ashton entitled 'Some aspects of land settlement', *c.* 1923.

73 Herbert R. Harris, *The Book of Memories and a History of the Porcupine Soldier Settlement and Adjacent Areas, 1919–1967*, Shand Agricultural Society, 1967, pp. 5–8.

74 *Sixth Report of the Soldier Settlement Board*, 31 December 1927, p. 8; GAA, SSB file, Strojich to Harris, 17 August 1966; Harris, *Book of Memories*, pp. 9–11; E. C. Morgan gives an interesting description of the balloting procedure at Prairie River, 'Soldier settlement in the prairies', p. 53.

75 Morgan, 'Soldier settlement in the prairies', pp. 53–4; SAB, transcript of interview with Mrs Mary McLenaghan by A. N. Nicolson, 13 January 1976, pp. 12–14.

76 *First Report of the SSB*, p. 94.

77 SAB, McLenaghan transcript, p. 12.

78 GAA, SSB file, Strojich to Harris, 17 August 1966.

79 *First Report of the SSB*, p. 94.

80 GAA, SSB file, Strojich to Harris, 17 August 1966; SAB, transcript of interview with William Howse conducted by D. H. Bocking, 12 June 1963, pp. 9–13; *ibid.*, R-E440, transcript of interview with J. H. Brockelbank compiled in January 1976. In his introduction to the Howse transcript, Bocking records the prices for certain farm produce during the depression years of the 1930s. The price of no. 2 Northern wheat, which averaged thiry cents a bushel, fell to seventeen cents. Barley, which cost seven cents a bushel to thresh, was sold for four cents a bushel. Dressed beef was one cent per pound and live prime steers fetched $9 to $10 each. Eggs sold for two or three cents a dozen. One wagon load of oats bought one pair of rubber boots.

81 SAB, transcript of interview with Mrs T. Mawhinney conducted by D. H. Bocking, 12 June 1963, pp. 8–9.

82 SAB, McLenaghan transcript, pp. 10 and 13.

83 *Book of Memories*, pp. 15 and 38; SAB, Howse transcript, p. 19.
84 PRO, CO 721/2/f. 17, Bedson to Macnaghten, 12 February 1919; *First Report of the SSB*, p. 27.
85 *Canadian Annual Review*, 1917, pp. 530–1; PRO, CO 721/2/f. 17, Ashton to Macnaghten, 12 January 1919. The announcement of the new SSB regulations was made in Ottawa on 14 February 1919 but no mention was made of conditions which applied to British veterans. A copy of the announcement was forwarded to the Colonial Office by Lieutenant-Colonel Pelletier, Agent-General for Quebec, 13 October 1919; Amery Papers, Box F.73, Meighen to Hamar Greenwood, 18 October 1919; Amery to Meighen, 25 November 1919.
86 PRO, CO 721/2/f. 17, Ashton to Macnaghten, 12 January 1919.
87 NA, RG 76, vol. 585, f. 821430, part 1, Bedson to Ashton, 3 April 1919.
88 *Ibid.*, Ashton to Calder, 15 May 1919.
89 PRO, CO 721/2/f. 17, Fiddes to Macnaghten, 20 February 1919.
90 NA, RG 76, vol. 585, f. 821430, part 1, Acting Deputy Minister of Immigration and Colonisation to Smith, 30 May 1919.
91 *Ibid.*; Desmond Morton, ' "Kicking and complaining": demobilisation riots in the Canadian Expeditionary Force, 1918–19', *Canadian Historical Review*, LXI, 1980, pp. 334–60.
92 NA, RG 76, vol. 585, f. 821340, part 1, Amery to Bedson, 16 April 1919.
93 Glynn, 'Assisted emigration to Canada', pp. 209–38.
94 PRO, BT 56/45/CIA/1958, memorandum by Wilfrid Eady, secretary of the Industrial Transference Board, 8 July 1929.
95 PRO, LAB 2/1235/EDO 220, Clark to Amery, 10 January 1929; Ministry of Labour memorandum, 4 March 1929. For Canadian attitudes to British immigration in the 1920s see John A. Schultz, 'Canadian attitudes toward empire settlement, 1919–1930', *Journal of Imperial and Commonwealth History*, I, 1973, pp. 237–51; *idem*, ' "Leaven for the lump": Canada and Empire settlement, 1918–1939', in Constantine, ed., *Emigrants and Empire*, pp. 150–73; Sir Clifford Sifton, 'The immigrants Canada wants', *MacLean's Magazine*, 1 April 1922.
96 PRO, CO 721/5/f. 82, conference between OSC, Agents-General and High Commissioners, 5 March 1919.
97 NA, RG 76, vol. 585, f. 821340, part 1, Blair to Cory, 30 June 1919.
98 *Ibid.*, part 2, Blair to Smith, 29 September 1919; Blair to Smith, 30 September 1919; Smith to Plant, 7 October 1919.
99 *Canadian Annual Review*, 1920, p. 243; *First Report of the SSB*, p. 27; PRO, CO 721/2/f. 17, Bedson to Macnaghten, 12 February 1919; NA, RG 76, vol. 610, f. 901346, part 8, information bulletins released by Cavers for SSB, 10 December 1919, 4 and 9 January 1920.
100 *Canadian Annual Review*, 1920, p. 243.
101 *Vancouver World*, 15 January 1920.
102 NA, RG 76, vol. 585, f. 821340, part 2, W. Butterworth to R. P. Porter, 9 December 1919; Jolliffe to Blair, 30 and 31 January 1920; *ibid.*, part 4, Jolliffe to Blair, 3 and 30 August and 3 September 1920.
103 *Ibid.*, part 2, regional reports submitted to the Deputy Minister of Immigration and Colonisation, January 1920; *ibid.*, part 4, Harold Buckle, Acting Secretary of the Ontario Soldiers' Aid Commission, to Blair, 15 September 1920.
104 *Ibid.*, part 2, regional reports submitted to the Deputy Minister of Immigration and Colonisation, January 1920.
105 *Ibid.*, part 4, Buckle to Blair, 15 September 1920.
106 *Ibid.*, Blair to Smith, 29 September 1920; PRO, CO 721/20/2478, W. H. Roberts to Wilson, 25 June 1920.
107 NA, RG 76, vol. 585, f. 821340, part 2, Blair to Jolliffe, 19 January 1920; Blair to Dr J. A. Amyot, Deputy Minister, Department of Public Health, 31 January 1920.
108 *Ibid.*, vol. 610, f. 901346, part 8, Maber to the Deputy Minister of Immigration and Colonisation, 26 July 1920; *ibid.*, vol. 585, f. 821340, part 3, memorandum by Maber, 18 March 1920.

109 *Ibid.*, vol. 585, f. 821340, part 4, Smith to Blair, 31 August 1920.
110 *Ibid.*, W. R. Little, Acting Secretary of Immigration and Colonisation, to F. A. Walpole, Office of Secretary-Treasurer, GWVA, 23 September 1920.
111 Amery Papers, Box F.73, Meighen to Greenwood, 18 October 1919; Amery to Meighen, 25 November 1919; NA, RG 76, vol. 585, f. 821340, part 4, Amery to Calder, 15 June 1920.
112 PRO, CO 721/13/2491, Milner to Devonshire, 1 October 1920.
113 PRO, CO 721/17/2491, Colonial Office memorandum dealing with the interviews between the Colonial Office, Calder and Smith at Brown's Hotel, 19 September 1920.
114 NA, RG 76, vol. 12, f. 72, part 12, Blair memorandum, 21 June 1921.
115 PRO, CO 721/19/3848, extract from the minutes of the 54th meeting of the OSC, 29 June 1920.
116 *Ibid.*, memorandum by Bedson, Scott and Wilson on 'Agricultural training centres for ex-Imperials in Canada', n.d.
117 PRO, CO 721/15/3848, Smith circular to all Canadian government emigration agents in Britain, 25 November 1920.
118 *First Report of the SSB*, p. 27.
119 PRO, CO 721/19/3848, Bedson to Plant, 27 November 1920.
120 PRO, CO 721/15/3848, OSC to Smith, 15 December 1920; minute by Malcolm Jones, junior Colonial Office official, 15 December 1920.
121 *Ibid.*, minute by Macnaghten, 9 December 1920.
122 NA, RG 76, vol. 585, f. 821340, part 7, overseas employment register for October–December 1921 compiled by the Ministery of Labour, 1 January 1922.
123 *First Report of the SSB*, p. 27; NA, RG 76, vol. 585, f. 821340, part 3, Ashton to Blair, 23 April 1920; PRO, CO 721/63/3848, Ashton to Plant, 18 June 1923; Plant to Ashton, 13 July 1923.
124 Thompson, *Harvests of War*, p. 61.
125 J. H. Thompson, ' "Permanently wasteful but immediately profitable": prairie agriculture and the Great War', *Canadian Historical Association Papers*, 1976, p. 193.
126 Thompson, *Harvests of War*, p. 59; R. MacGregor Dawson, *William Lyon Mackenzie King, 1874–1923*, I, *A Political Biography*, London, 1958, p. 393.
127 *Canada Year Book*, 1920, p. 6.
128 Thompson, *Harvests of War*, p. 61; *Canada Year Book*, 1920, p. 5. Thompson noted that in 1916 wheat and its support crop oats accounted for 90.3 per cent of the total prairie field crop acreage. Even more startling is the concentration of wheat production in the prairies in 1918.
129 Thompson, *Harvests of War*, p. 61.
130 *Ibid.*, pp. 69–70.
131 *Ibid.*, p. 68. The yield in 1916 was seventeen bushels per acre and dropped to eleven bushels per acre in 1918. (*Canada Year Book*, 1920, pp. 4–5.) Conversely, wheat in 1915 sold for eighty cents a bushel compared to the 1917 and 1918 harvests which sold at the fixed price of $2.21 per bushel. Despite the drastic reduction in yields between 1915 and 1917–18, the smaller 1917 harvest netted $405.7 million in revenue compared to the 1915 harvest revenues of $325 million.
132 Thompson, ' "Permanently wasteful" ', p. 198; *Canada Year Book*, 1920, p. 5.
133 NA, Meighen Papers, vol. 49, f. 199, p. 27686, Barnett to George Buskard, Meighen's private secretary, 22 January 1921.
134 *Ibid*; *Canadian Annual Review*, 1921, p. 345.
135 *Canada Year Book*, 1921, p. 810; *Canadian Annual Review*, 1921, p. 345.
136 NA, Meighen Papers, vol. 17, f. 29, p. 9644, Barnett to Sir Joseph Flavelle, Canadian industrialist, financier and millionaire, 6 October 1921. In per centages, the total number of soldiers who had made a contribution to their first instalment was 77 per cent. When the first SSB report was released in March 1921 the total had climbed to 82 per cent. *First Report of the SSB*, p. 19.
137 *First Report of the SSB*, p. 20.
138 *Ibid.*, p. 18.

139 Morton and Wright, *Winning the Second Battle,* p. 151.
140 *Second Report of the SSB,* p. 9; *Third Report of the SSB,* p. 8.
141 Dawson, *William Lyon Mackenzie King,* I, p. 393.
142 SAB, N. H. McTaggart Papers, microfilm, Reel 1, section 1, f. 15, Barnett to McTaggart, 10 April 1924; NA, Magrath Papers, vol. 3, f. 8, memorandum by Ashton on inspection tour of Middlesex, Huron, Perth, Oxford, Norfolk and Brent counties in Ontario, 10 June 1924; *ibid.,* memorandum by Ashton entitled, 'Western Canada inspection tour, 1925, with some notes on a visit to Simcoe and Muskoka areas in Ontario', 2 November 1925.
143 NA, Records of the Department of Agriculture, RG 17, vol. 3122, f. 61–1, ff. 278192, J. H. Grisdale, Deputy Minister of the Department of Agriculture, to Ashton, 6 April 1921.
144 *Ibid.,* Ashton to Grisdale, 31 March 1921; *Second Report of the SSB,* p. 14.
145 NA, RG 17, vol. 3122, f. 61–1, ff. 299791, Ashton to Grisdale, 30 December 1924.
146 *Third Report of the SSB,* p. 17; *Canada Year Book,* 1922–23, p. 938; Murchie and Grant, *Unused Lands,* pp. 61–2; PAM, John Bracken Papers, f. 138, eighth and last Annual Convention, Manitoba Provincial Command, GWVA, report of the Agricultural Committee, 17 March 1926.
147 *Special Committee, 1919,* p. 58.
148 NA, Meighen Papers, vol. 54, f. 226, p. 30437, Meighen to Tupper, 10 September 1921. For an examination of the battle between the veterans and the dominion government over gratuity payments and pensions see Desmond Morton and Glenn Wright, 'The bonus campaign, 1919–1921: veterans and the campaign for re-establishment', *Canadian Historical Review,* LXIV, 1983, pp. 147–67; Desmond Morton, 'Resisting the pension evil: bureaucracy, democracy, and Canada's board of pension commissioners, 1916–1933', *Canadian Historical Review,* LXVIII, 1987, pp. 199–224.
149 Amery Papers, Box F.74, Meighen to Amery, 14 December 1921. 'It is my contention', wrote Meighen, 'that only under very extraordinary circumstances can a War Government succeed in a post-war contest.' For an examination of the post-war unemployment issue see Struthers, *No Fault of Their Own,* pp. 12–43.
150 NA, King Papers, J1 series, vol. 72, pp. 61093–4, H. Coleburne, Dominion Secretary of the ANV, to King; Morton and Wright, *Winning the Second Battle,* pp. 152–4.
151 *Ibid.,* vol. 82, pp. 63903–4, King to Charles Stewart, Minister of the Interior, 15 May 1922, report included in letter.
152 *Ibid.*
153 *Second Report of the SSB,* pp. 16–19; Morton and Wright, *Winning the Second Battle,* pp. 152–3; *Sixth Report of the SSB,* pp. 18–19; *Canada Year Book,* 1921, pp. 809–10; *ibid.,* 1922–23, pp. 938–9.
154 *Third Report of the SSB,* p. 7; *Canada Year Book,* 1924, pp. 925–6.
155 *Third Report of the SSB,* pp. 8–9; *Sixth Report of the SSB,* p. 19.
156 NA, King Papers, J1 series, vol. 82, p. 69809, M. G. Walker to King, 9 December 1922; PAM, Bracken Papers, f. 36, 7th Annual Convention, Manitoba Provincial Command, GWVA, February 1925; NA, King Papers, J1 series, vol. 119, p. 101077, United Farmers of Manitoba to King, 28 February 1925.
157 NA, Legion Records, vol. 1, f. 4, pp. 302–3, minutes of the conference of provincial commands of the GWVA, 12–14 March 1925.
158 Canada, *Debates,* 1925, IV, p. 3553; *ibid.,* 1922, IV, p. 3349.
159 Morton and Wright, *Winning the Second Battle,* p. 204; PAM, Bracken Papers, f. 138, Report of the First Annual Convention of the Manitoba Provincial Command, Canadian Legion, 18–19 March 1926; NA, King Papers, J1 series, vol. 165, p. 119898, resolution on land revaluation passed at the annual convention of the United Farmers of Alberta, 18–21 January 1927; *ibid.,* vol. 130, pp. 110777–9, King to J. O. Davis, Secretary of the South Tisdale Soldier Settlers, n.d. (probably September 1926); Canada, *Debates,* 1926–27, I, pp. 15, 59 and 228–46.
160 *Eighth Report of the Soldier Settlement Board,* 31 December 1929, pp. 10–14; *Tenth Report of the SSB,* p. 14; *Canadian Annual Review,* 1930–31, p. 572; Canada,

*Debates*, 1926–27, I, p. 904. For the revaluation procedure see the *Sixth Report of the SSB*, pp. 18–20 and the *Seventh Report of the Soldier Settlement Board*, 31 December 1928, pp. 10–11. For an example of a revaluation case see GAA, A. H. Stewart Papers, diaries, accounts and correspondence, 1922–41. For detailed departmental procedure see PAM, Records of the Minister of Mines and Natural Resources, Manitoba, RG 17 A1, Box 1, f. 10, SSB lands file, 1929–31; *ibid.*, RG 17 D1, Box 19, f. 346, Land Branch files, 1930–52.

161 Canada, *Annual Departmental Reports*, II, 1926–27, Annual Report of the Department of the Interior, p. 5; *ibid.*, II, 1927–28, Annual Report of the Department of the Interior, statement by W. W. Cory, Deputy Minister, p. 5; *Seventh Report of the SSB*, p. 11.

162 *Ninth Report of the Soldier Settlement Board*, 31 December 1931, pp. 5–6.

163 *Canadian Annual Review*, 1930–31, p. 572; Canada, *Debates*, 1930, III, pp. 2471 and 2639; *Ninth Report of the SSB*, p. 10.

164 *Canadian Annual Review*, 1930–31, p. 573.

165 *Tenth Report of the SSB*, pp. 5 and 14. For the municipal taxation issue see above report, pp. 6–7 and NA, King Papers, J1 series, vol. 184, pp. 131328–30, J. J. McGurran, Acting Secretary of the Saskatchewan Association of Rural Municipalities, to King, 29 December 1929.

166 *Tenth Report of the SSB*, pp. 10–14; *Canadian Annual Review*, 1935 and 1936, p. 151. It is interesting to note that of the 10,273 active soldier settlers as of December 1928, 6,652 or 64 per cent had not received financial assistance when obtaining land, therefore relieving their initial burden of debt. *Seventh Report of the SSB*, p. 22.

167 Royal Commission on Immigration and Settlement, vol. 32, p. 28; *Special Committee, 1924*, p. 84.

# CHAPTER FIVE

# Anglicisation, soldier settlement and the politicisation of British immigration to South Africa

I have often told (the Nationalists) that the British Empire is not an octopus, whose feelers enwrap all to their doom; but something greater, whose benevolent embraces will hold them for ever; from them they will never escape, and in a very little while, never want to.

Sir Percy Fitzpatrick, author, politician and landowner, 5 May 1926[1]

The theme of anglicisation is a familiar one throughout late eighteenth and early nineteenth century British imperial history. For example, after the conquest of Canada in 1760, successive British governments embarked upon a series of spasmodic and half-hearted policies designed to assimilate French Canadians into English colonial society. The capture of the Cape colony in 1795 compounded the problem of how to rule another foreign people of European extraction when Dutch settlers were incorporated into Britain's expanding empire. Worried about the loyalty of these new subjects, administrators possessed a number of options which were employed to facilitate anglicisation in French Canada and South Africa during the first four decades of the nineteenth century. The most direct method was by the imposition of English institutions. According to one historian, 'direct' anglicisation referred primarily to political and structural changes in local government, the civil service and the legal system which were intended to have an immediate impact upon these colonial societies. In contrast, 'indirect' anglicisation referred to policies in the fields of education, immigration and religion which, with the aid of time, would exert a subtle but steady influence.[2]

Anglicisation was revived after the second Anglo-Boer War (1899–1902), motivated this time by the British government's attempt to foster white racial harmony and create a new rural order in South Africa. Once again, a key ingredient within that policy was immigration which was designed to bolster colonial defence, promote colonial development and sustain the British connection. However, as we have seen, the creation of a large, united and prosperous rural English-speaking community in the conquered Boer republics faced a host of obstacles. In January 1914 the fledgling Union government acknow-ledged that owing to the Anglo-Boer War, the shortage of unskilled labour, and recurrent labour unrest on the gold fields, there was little interest in emigration to South Africa. The 1921 census confirmed the inertia of post-Union immigration.[3] Yet, despite the modest numbers, British immigration to South Africa remained a highly contentious issue throughout the 1920s.

The politicisation of South African soldier settlement was not, how-ever, centred on the conflict between the dominion government and veterans' organisations for participation in and control of post-war policy. Rather, it was an integral part of the larger debate on British immigration to South Africa which was being waged between ultra-patriotic, English-speaking interests and Afrikaner nationalists in the dominion. In fact, it was the failure of Milner's reconstruction policies, in which a state-aided immigration programme spearheaded by the settlement of demobilised imperial troops was to restore British numbers and hence British political hegemony in the region, which contributed to the increased tension between the two white political communities after 1902. Indeed, political forces within South Africa had a direct bearing on policy formulation. Foremost amongst them was the resurgence of a militant strain of Afrikaner nationalism and the increased polarisation of the two white communities after 1914. But we must not forget the different roles played by the British and South African governments. How far was the British government prepared to go to accommodate and promote British immigration to, and land settlement in, South Africa? How did South African domestic politics complicate these issues?

It was to redress the growing numerical imbalance between Afrikaners and English that, in 1920, a small but determined group of individuals formed the 1820 Memorial Settlers' Association (hereafter 1820 Association), which was committed to bringing British immigrants into the country as settlers. Although it failed to achieve its ultimate objective – British political hegemony – an examination of this organisation provides a valuable insight into the struggle to maintain the imperial link in South Africa.

## 'Poor whiteism' and the outbreak of the Great War

What made land settlement and immigration in South Africa so politi-cally explosive? The answer can be found in the legacy of the reconstruction period after the Boer War, the growing political power of the *bywoners* or 'poor whites' and the impact of World War I on party politics in South Africa. Rural depopulation was becoming a major domestic problem. Ever since the 1880s rural whites, largely Afrikaners, were being forced off the land through speculation and the com-mercialisation of agriculture, and migrated to the urban and industrial centres in search of work. The rinderpest epidemic of 1896–97, the British army's scorched earth policy during the second Anglo-Boer War and poor yields due to sustained drought and disease between 1903 and 1908 dramatically increased an already alarming migratory trend, with the greatest exodus occurring between 1911 and 1921.[4] Impoverished, uneducated and unskilled, poor whites were put in direct competition with African labour. This led Afrikaners to argue that employment was hard enough to find without immigrants competing in the same job markets. Why help the poor of other countries to relocate, argued Afrikaner nationalists, when there were enough poor in South Africa?

The Dutch churches, instrumental in publicising the problem before the Boer War, advocated rehabilitation to stem the growing tide of poor whites. Their pleas were heard by the two leading Afrikaner political parties created in the aftermath of the Boer War, *Het Volk* and *Orangia Unie*, who endorsed a back-to-the-land policy. It included supervised rural settlements and an education system to safeguard the position of the poor whites *vis-à-vis* the non-white population.[5] Another important stimulus to Afrikaner political consciousness derived from the expansion of South Africa's industrial base, as the result of which Afrikaner workers were increasingly exposed to English-speaking workers and their methods of industrial organisation. They began to assimilate these techniques until eventually they assumed complete control of several industrial unions in the gold fields. From this power base the unions cultivated important links between urban and rural Afrikaners, strengthened the cultural bond between them and thus extended the political cohesion of a reinvigorated Afrikanerdom.[6] The Afrikaners' ability to organise industrially signified a growing political power which could not be ignored.

The Unionist Party of South Africa, which represented the majority of the English-speaking population and the mining interests, had made the promotion of land settlement with state assistance a major plank of its party platform since 1910. Repeatedly it urged the vigorous develop-ment of South Africa's farming potential through the initiation of an effective land settlement policy and introduction of suitable British immigrants. The party executive deemed it imperative to initiate state-aided immigration, provide land on reasonable terms, and, if need be, acquire land by the state for settlement purposes. Furthermore, it advocated a tax on unimproved land. The latter measure, though controversial, was essential because it would force the large speculative landowners and companies to unlock or develop their holdings, thereby promoting the general prosperity of the nation.[7]

Patrick Duncan, a former member of the reconstruction administration and a leading Unionist MP, advocated the establishment of a system of state-subsidised passages to promote the immigration and settlement of experienced agriculturalists in South Africa. He acknowledged, however, that the government of Louis Botha was not willing to take any positive action. If anything was to be done at all it would be by private effort.[8] Another Unionist MP, Sir Charles Crewe, was similarly convinced that the ruling South African Party (SAP) would not help immigrants at all. The issue was politically sensitive for Botha because his 'own people object and he is too afraid of losing [political] support to risk anything'.[9]

Indeed, the Prime Minister had to walk a fine line for fear of antagonising his Afrikaner support. Politicians from all bands of the political spectrum agreed that there was an urgent necessity to secure a larger white population on the land. The problem was who and from where. The Unionists supported state-aided immigration to reinforce the small, isolated white community in South Africa. The SAP remained non-committal because of its delicate position in the middle ground between the two white political communities. The Nationalists, a militant Afrikaner wing which had split from the SAP in January 1914, were vehemently opposed to any form of state-aided immigration on the grounds that the money was better spent helping the poor whites to relocate back to the land. They condemned state-aided immigration as 'political immigration . . . the thin end of the wedge inserted by the Unionists'.[10] Their condemnation was an astute political move. Not only did it allow the Nationalists to cultivate growing Afrikaner discontent and mould it into a firm political base, but it gave them political credibility within the Afrikaner community as the defenders of Afrikaner culture.

Afrikaner nationalism, accelerated by the war, enabled the Nationalists to gain important inroads within traditional SAP strongholds. The rebellion in September 1914 of hardline, anti-British Afrikaners who had remained uncomfortable under the yoke of British rule was easily suppressed, but it increased the polarisation within the Afrikaner community between the moderates and pro-war supporters of Botha and his political lieutenant J. C. Smuts, and the rebels and their sympathisers who supported the Nationalists led by General J. B. M. Hertzog. As the war intensified, the rift within the Afrikaner community widened as many more Afrikaners shifted allegiance from the SAP to the Nationalists because of South Africa's expanding commitment to the war and the support Botha and Smuts received from British interests in South Africa. Furthermore, Hertzog's cry of 'South Africa first' rekindled Afrikaner aspirations of republicanism and the goal of a new and independent South Africa outside the imperial framework.[11]

On the outbreak of war the majority of English-speaking South Africans were similarly swept up in a wave of patriotism which made loyalty to South Africa a constituent part of a wider loyalty to Britain and the empire. The Governor-General of South Africa, Lord Buxton, confirmed this in a confidential cable to the Colonial Office in 1917: 'The Unionists have always claimed to be the special guardians of the British connection and have taken every opportunity of pressing for a larger contribution to the cost of [empire].'[12] This was abhorrent to vast numbers of Afrikaners, who promptly rejected it and it merely contributed to resurgent republicanism. As nationalist attitudes hardened in both white communities it was evident that the breach between them and within the Afrikaner community itself had widened. Within this turbulent environment, the British government became anxious to see Botha kept in power because it was through him that British imperial interests, and hence the British connection, would be maintained.[13] British immigration was also seen as an important though sensitive means of sustaining the connection.

## Private initiative during the war

As predicted, the initiative was left to private enterprise during the war when a gigantic flood of prospective immigrants was expected to follow demobilisation.[14] The campaign for increased British immigration and land settlement after the war was led by a group of ultra-loyalists within the Unionist party. These men included some of the most prominent and active English-speaking politicians, financiers and newspaper proprietors in South Africa. Leadership was provided by the examples of Sir Percy Fitzpatrick and Sir Thomas Smartt, two wealthy and influential entrepreneurs who had developed an avid interest in capital intensive agriculture. The remaining members of the group included Duncan, Crewe and Sir Lionel Phillips. As managing director of the Johannesburg office of the Central Mining and Investment Corporation, one of the largest and most powerful gold mining conglomerates in South Africa, Phillips was able to employ his managerial skills in conjunction with his financial contacts to assist in the promotion of British emigration. The outspoken Crewe was a prominent Eastern Cape politician, soldier and journalist. Wholly committed to the imperial cause in South Africa, his power and influence stemmed from his part-ownership of the *East*

*London Daily Dispatch.* With the possible exception of Fitzpatrick, he was most vigorous in campaigning for an aggressive immigration policy to attract British settlers after the war.[15] As a former member of Milner's 'kindergarten', Duncan had firsthand knowledge of the aims and shortcomings of Milner's immigration and land settlement policies. Like most leading Unionists, he was deeply concerned about the relationship between the black and white races in South Africa and the ability of the European races to maintain their 'permanent preponderance' in the population.[16] In 1909 by way of the 'White Expansion Society' he proposed the placement of young emigrants possessing a limited amount of capital with South African farmers. After 1910 he became the Unionist party's leading exponent of the need for a state-aided land settlement and assisted migration policy.[17]

South African initiative was being observed from London by the Royal Colonial Institute. As mentioned above, Rider Haggard was despatched on a fact-finding mission to the dominions to investigate their attitude towards plans to assist ex-servicemen to settle in the overseas empire after the war. His visit to South Africa in February-March 1916 rekindled the immigration issue at a time when English-Afrikaner relations were at their lowest. Governor-General Buxton and J. X. Merriman, one of the Cape's shrewdest and most respected parliamentarians, warned Haggard while en route of the need for caution and tact in South Africa. Owing to the delicate political situation and Afrikaner sensitivity to immigration, he was strongly advised to avoid making public pronouncements regarding the settlement of British ex-servicemen in South Africa after the war. 'Now is like a magazine full of high explosives teeming with sedition and anti-English feeling,' explained Merriman. 'Any . . . advocacy of the introduction of British immigrants will be made the text for fiery appeals to the backveld . . . Such a crusade will render poor Botha's task doubly hard.'[18] Botha was all too aware of the problem, according to Fitzpatrick. It was better to work quietly, avoid publicity and not give the Nationalists a chance to attack the government.[19]

Haggard had no intention of creating political waves and heeded the advice. He too was alive to the danger that an ill-timed remark would do unending damage to the imperial migration cause in South Africa. Conceding that it was unlikely the South African government would initiate an immigration policy, he admitted that the prospects for land settlement were poor, especially for the ordinary British working-class migrant, because the uncapitalised immigrant farmer could not compete with his African counterpart. South African agriculture required capital, much more than in the other dominions, because of the emphasis on private investment and the need to develop new farming methods such as irrigation and other forms of water conservation. These circumstances were in part dictated by South Africa's climate, always demanding and sometimes inhospitable. Haggard concurred with leading Unionists that if anything was to be achieved it would be through private initiative. He therefore submitted that British half-pay and retired officers with capital provided a small but potentially useful class under the circumstances. Merriman agreed: 'The most we can hope for is for a special immigration of (half)-pay officers and the like with moderate means and no ambition beyond making a home instead of a fortune.'[20]

Despite the poor outlook in South Africa, Haggard's mission spurred the English-speaking immigration enthusiasts into action. J. W. Jagger, a successful Cape businessman, Unionist politician and educationist, formed the South African Settlers' Information Committee (SASIC) shortly after Haggard's visit. He was a keen and energetic promoter of settlement in the dominion and enlisted Smartt, Fitzpatrick, Duncan and several other prominent Unionist politicians to sit on the committee. A London committee was established soon afterwards. W. P. Schreiner, South African High Commissioner, was asked to sit on the London committee; although he fully supported the objects of the SASIC, he declined the invitation because of his official status. However, he saw no reason for the Trades Commissioner not to serve provided the Union government did not object. Meanwhile, the SASIC sought British governmental recognition in connection with work on a future central migration authority.[21]

Private enterprise in South Africa did not go unnoticed in Whitehall, and Milner, for one, fully appreciated the effort. 'Nobody knows better than I that South Africa is the weakest link in the Imperial chain, and that link has certainly not been strengthened by the war.' He still maintained that the only way to prevent the imperial link from snapping and to increase British influence was a 'steady flow of settlers' to South Africa after the war.[22] Leo Amery, a devout Milnerite, agreed. British immigration would contribute to the future unity of South Africa.

> If South African resources and agricultural possibilities are developed as they might be, there will be room for soldier settlers ... all over the country who will soon help to bring a different atmosphere into place. My faith in the future is based on the fundamental belief that a great region like South Africa will inevitably develop. At each phase of development it will call for immigrants, and those immigrants will reinforce the principle of equal rights, and of South African as against purely racial patriotism.[23]

Afrikaner nationalism was on the ascendancy during the latter part of the war and Afrikaner race patriotism was indeed becoming an increasingly worrisome issue within the English-speaking community which was put on the defensive. Their concern stemmed from increasing demands from militant Afrikaners for independence whose achievement became a major objective of the Nationalists in 1917. Fitzpatrick explained to Amery that it was not simply the rebellion of 1914 or republicanism which bonded the Nationalist party together: it was their anti-Botha, anti-Smuts feelings which gave them common ground. Afrikaner discontent was directed at Botha, Smuts and the SAP because they had 'given up the policy of a Dutch racial party'.[24]

Denying that they were attempting to swamp the Afrikaner population, many ultra-loyalists feared that the British element would itself be destroyed by these same Afrikaner supremacists if they got into power. As Crewe informed the Colonial Secretary, Walter Long, the Nationalists seemed to imagine that Afrikaner independence could be achieved using 'less dangerous methods' such as constitutional or parliamentary means rather than war or insurrection.[25] According to Crewe the only effective countermeasure was a steady stream of British immigrants, preferably soldiers, with assistance from the imperial government. 'Otherwise,' he lamented, 'the Britisher in S[outh] Africa whose endurance is being strained to its limits will give up hope and will gradually become absorbed or leave the country.'[26]

There was a sense of desperation which permeated the correspondence arriving in Britain from Unionists in South Africa throughout 1917, and this was reflected by Crewe and Fitzpatrick. Crewe was not optimistic about the immediate outlook for the English in South Africa unless a racial balance was struck in their favour.

I know them (the Boers) as a people and ultimately as individuals and there is going to be no fusion of races and the Boer who has not changed in sentiment in a hundred years will not alter in another hundred. There are already a great number of Englishmen out here who look upon the future of this country as certainly Dutch with Dutch government and who unless things . . . improve as the result of an active policy of introducing Englishmen after the War will sell out here . . .[27]

Fitzpatrick was much more succinct. The Boer 'will tolerate us, but we must be good: *They* will run the country. They own it. They are it.'[28]

## Soldier settlement and free passage, 1916–22

Haggard's visit forced the South African government to start thinking about its repatriation and post-war reconstruction policies. In August 1916, the very capable and determined Minister for Lands, Hendrik

Mentz, began to study in earnest the problem of post-war employment for discharged South African soldiers. Eager for ideas, he solicited the views of a number of local recruiting and employment committees. Suggestions ranged from public works programmes, education and railway administration to the civil service, police, forestry, posts and telegraphs, lands and irrigation. Preliminary indications revealed among those who had returned from the front that an agricultural career rated highly as a post-war occupation. The problem was that it was impossible to estimate how many were interested in farming because the government had not yet initiated a statistical survey with the local recruiting committees.[29]

When the British government first approached Pretoria in September 1916 concerning soldier settlement plans, the reply was polite but non-committal. No decision had yet been made, but indications were that when it was it would be strictly limited to helping South African veterans. This was confirmed in February 1917 when the High Commission was informed that it was impossible for South Africa to absorb considerable numbers of immigrants after the war because of a lack of resources.[30]

Apart from the financial and logistical questions, however, the Union government had a more deep-seated reason to be cautious: the perennial issue of the poor white, a more serious and seemingly insoluble problem. This resurfaced as a major political issue at the beginning of 1916. A severe drought had been raging since 1912, one of the worst in living memory. Pressure grew for the government to introduce a drought relief bill, a major component of which was the development of irrigation and water conservation projects. Not only would such legislation provide permanent relief in specific drought-stricken regions but it would give employment to whites. By August, the government decided that the drought relief schemes provided an excellent opportunity for resettling South African veterans. This immediately opened up a political Pandora's box which highlighted the worsening relations between the two white communities and demonstrated how sensitive and politically divisive the immigration issue had become.

Nationalist politicians saw the development of irrigation schemes as the country's salvation and the solution to the poor white problem. Arguing that charity began at home, they were convinced that these schemes provided much-needed employment for impoverished white South Africans and potentially formed the cornerstone to the nation's continued agricultural prosperity.[31] Similarly, Nationalists staunchly rejected Unionist calls for overseas immigrants, and dismissed the idea of assisted passage as political immigration, the subsidised importation of the poor of overseas nations.

Unionist members were quick to point out the continual failure of government-sponsored irrigation settlements since the 1880s. It was 'no use going in for a policy of false economy and settling third-class people on third-class lands'. Great care had to be taken as to the type and class of settler if taxpayers' money was not to be wasted and the policy defeated. The remedy lay in a system of government-sponsored agricultural education.[32] Furthermore, the cure for the poor white problem was not government hand-outs, preferential employment and high salaries on the railways or in the civil service. Development was the answer and immigration was the key in solving the problem. Unionists argued that there were not enough whites in South Africa to develop the country, and the majority of them lacked the experience or knowledge to accomplish the task. Immigrants, on the other hand, brought skill, initiative, fresh ideas and capital.[33]

The debate on the settlement provisions for returned soldiers created a furore in the House of Assembly in 1917. Unionists advocated preferential and generous treatment for ex-servicemen who had seen action and wanted to farm after demobilisation. The Nationalists expressed abhorrence at the suggestion, claiming that it favoured the ex-servicemen to the detriment of the poor white. Angrily, Mentz refused to be drawn on the issue of preference. Instead, he argued that the amendment to the 1912 Land Settlement Act, which increased the range of government assistance, was to help any and all South Africans interested in farming after the war. He emphatically denied that the government contemplated any special settlement legislation for veterans. The Nationalists remained dissatisfied and unconvinced.[34]

Throughout 1917 and 1918 the South African government remained resolute in its determination not to introduce special soldier settlement projects, state-aided migration programmes or participate in an imperial free passage scheme. Schreiner reported disconsolately that the other dominions were very active in promoting their own schemes in Britain. He pleaded with Botha to emulate their initiative, but the government was unmoved.[35] Nothing changed when Milner and Amery were appointed to the Colonial Office in 1919.[36] The news was disappointing but not unexpected. The Colonial Office, though aware of the delicacy of the immigration issue and the political reasons why the South Africans were never eager to discuss post-war emigration except in very general terms, continued to hope that South Africa would be able to participate more actively in the near future.[37] It was doubtful that this would happen. The very presence of Milner and Amery at the Colonial Office aggravated the problem by igniting Afrikaner opposition to immigration.[38]

Government paralysis resulted in confusion and frustration among

South African civil servants who found themselves lacking in clear policy directives, chains of command or resources to deal with the flood of applications that followed demobilisation. It also led private land companies and philanthropic agencies to play a much larger role in immigration matters than they would have done if Smuts, Botha's successor as Prime Minister in 1919, had pursued an aggressive immigration policy.[39] Led by Fitzpatrick, South African immigration enthusiasts discussed the need to establish an office in London to attract prospective settlers, preferably of the ex-officer class.[40] Into the breach stepped the SASIC. Phillips, who was in London doing war work for the Ministry of Munitions and the Imperial Mineral Resources Bureau, accepted the SASIC's offer of president in November 1918. The committee's first priority was to raise funds to enable it to work more effectively and Phillips suggested canvassing landowning companies based in London.[41] The next step was to safeguard prospective settlers against exploitation by unscrupulous agents who might induce them to purchase land at exorbitant prices or under impossible conditions. In March 1919 the SASIC outlined a series of guidelines for settlers and purchasers interested in South Africa. They ranged from pointers on title, water supply, rainfall and altitude to issues such as location, labour supply and soil type. The SASIC emphasised that it was an impartial body. 'While the committee cannot see their way to offer an opinion upon the merits or demerits of land offered to settlers or the price demanded, they are impelled to caution those who have under their consideration offers of this description not to make purchases without satisfying themselves on the following points.'[42]

It was sound advice because London was plagued by dubious and fraudulent South African land companies who misled prospective settlers about the quick and easy returns they could expect by farming in the dominion. South Africa had become 'a land for large landlords', according to one commentator, a land where 'speculation is the greatest of all our industries', complained another.[43] The companies which gave British and South African authorities constant trouble were those involved in irrigation and citriculture. For example, Letaba Orange Estates sought to entice soldier settlers and others to the Eastern Transvaal, although the region was notorious for malaria, blackwater fever and the dreaded tsetse fly.[44] Zebediela Estates, another citrus venture in the same area, aroused governmental suspicions. Founded in 1917, the company was suspected of using misleading advertising and making false claims about the scale of returns settlers could make in the first years of their investment. There was a host of smaller ventures scattered throughout the Transvaal and Eastern Cape promising an excellent lifestyle, easy returns and low risks. Most were unsound and unbusinesslike, aroused unending suspicion and soon disappeared with the 1920–22 depression.[45]

Meanwhile, the Department of Lands was coping as best it could with domestic soldier settlement. In August 1918 Mentz was told by his officials that the issue of returned soldier employment was proving entirely unsatisfactory. By the end of September 531 South African veterans had been placed on approximately 860,000 acres valued at £331,000.[46] Between 1918 and 1921 a plethora of grievances, demands and deputations requesting greater assistance for the returned man inundated the department. A variety of newly formed ex-servicemen's organisations made the most vocal demands. They requested that a soldier representative be appointed to each provincial Land Board in order that the returned man receive a more sympathetic hearing. A number of local recruiting committees and returned soldiers' employment committees grew anxious about government policy. They complained that an increasing number of discharged ex-servicemen from the rural districts were drifting into the towns swelling the ranks of the unemployed. Most of them had been brought up on farms and were well versed in farming practices. Could not the government see fit to take immediate steps to help these men secure suitable employment in a land settlement scheme, thus relieving the burden on the towns?[47]

In 1920 pressure for assistance increased as the international depression began to bite. J. Sommerville, Under-Secretary for Lands, was certain that his department would receive more applications for financial assistance from prospective soldier settlers than the budget allowed.[48] In January 1921 the government acceded to demands made by several veterans' organisations for a returned soldiers conference. Smuts was eager to allay the fears of many ex-servicemen and reassure them that the government was doing its utmost to help the returned man. Pension scales topped the list of priorities and it was expected that their examination would take up most of the conference's time. But the Department of Lands was aware that land settlement would play a crucial part in the remaining time allocated. There was also the problem of the press. Department officials were subsequently advised to be 'superlatively cautious', for if the position of the returned soldier with respect to land settlement was shown in 'too rosy a light' it would arouse Nationalist rebuke. The SAP was certainly not looking for another round of intense and acrimonious political wrangling involving soldier settlement and the poor white.[49]

The conference met in Johannesburg in May. Participants included representatives of a variety of ex-servicemen's organisations, regional advisory boards and government departments. Of the 130 resolutions passed, barely sixteen dealt with land settlement and, as predicted, pension issues dominated the conference agenda. The major thrust of the settlement proposals, however, was veteran representation on the provincial Land Boards and the development of a national group settlement scheme.[50] The government accepted the resolutions, but it was clear that nothing would be done regarding land settlement.

In 1919 enquiries from returned soldiers interested in land settlement averaged 100 per month. Of these 10 per cent were from men in the Witwatersrand area, 40 per cent from other urban areas, 30 per cent from the country and 20 per cent from the various fronts and military hospitals in South Africa and overseas. The figures included a negligible amount from British ex-servicemen. The enquirers were of three types: men with capital and farming experience (largely ex-officers), men with experience but little or no capital, and men with neither experience nor capital.[51] A large proportion of the returned soldier enquiries were from poor whites and this at least disproved the Nationalists' claim that soldiers were receiving preferential treatment when many soldiers had been poor whites prior to enlistment. Nevertheless, by March 1922 only 2,287, or 21.5 per cent of the applications received from South African soldiers, were settled under existing legislation, and by February 1923 one-sixth had cancelled, surrendered or ceded their holdings.[52] Ironically, those British ex-servicemen that arrived in South Africa under the auspices of the British government's free passage scheme outnumbered approximately three-fold the total number of South African veterans settled under the terms of Pretoria's own legislation. In addition, many of these British veterans embarked upon agriculture but bypassed the dominion government, using their own resources or the facilities of the 1820 Memorial Settlers' Association and private land companies. None the less, of the dominions, South Africa received the fewest number of British ex-servicemen and their families. Of the final total of 86,027 who participated in the imperial free passage scheme, South Africa received only 6,064 or 7 per cent.[53]

Private enterprise fared no better. In 1920 the Smartt Syndicate went public in an attempt to attract settlers to the estate and reap the benefit of a post-war boom in land prices. A tremendous amount of energy and investment capital was expended to prepare the estate for an expected rush, but it never materialised and thirteen soldier settlers eventually took possession of 775 acres of irrigable land. In 1925 one-half abandoned their holdings and by 1930 not one soldier settler remained.[54]

Fitzpatrick's Sundays River Settlement Scheme proved equally disappointing. In 1916 the project seemed financially sound with a share capital of £200,000. Both Haggard and the outspoken Director of Irrigation, F. E. Kanthack, strongly recommended it and firmly believed that it was one of the most promising land settlement schemes in the country – a showpiece of South African initiative and ingenuity.[55] Eager to push ahead during the war, Fitzpatrick endeavoured to enlist the weighty financial backing of the mining interests, but Otto Beit and the Central Mining and Investment Corporation declined. Although he did not want to leave an old friend in the lurch, Beit was already committed to Smartt's venture. An additional reason why Beit declined to help an old friend was the unreliability of Fitzpatrick's estimates and his expectations on the initial returns. Solly Joel, the mining magnate and owner of De Beers, was more encouraging. He intimated that De Beers was prepared to buy 500 acres at £50 per acre in order to provide for the settlement of its employees who had joined the colours.[56]

Fitzpatrick had always expressed that resolute action and pre-planning were essential to meet the expected rush of ex-service settlers once the war ended. In pursuit of this, he reserved 2,000 acres of prepared land for fruit growing in allotments ranging in size from ten to fifty acres and offered it to both South African and British ex-servicemen at a greatly reduced price. It was a sound strategy motivated by patriotism rather than profit, but the construction of new irrigation facilities was hopelessly behind schedule limiting the numbers of men who could be absorbed immediately.[57]

The predicted flood of settlers never took place. By 1920 there were sixty-five overseas settlers at Sundays River, but there is no indication of how many were ex-servicemen. In 1921–22, with the start of Britain's military retrenchment and naval disarmament programme, the original group was bolstered by an unspecified number of ex-officers, largely from the Royal Navy. They were a determined, articulate and highly organised group who worked closely with Fitzpatrick to promote Sundays River and encourage fellow officers to join them. A naval settlers' committee was formed in July 1922 and an option on 1,000 acres was obtained from Fitzpatrick. Eager to promote land settlement and liaise with interested officers in Britain, the naval settlers' committee proved a valuable adjunct to Fitzpatrick's efforts. In late 1922, he applauded the formation of a complementary military settlers' committee established to attract similarly redundant army officers to the valley. Unfortunately, it is impossible to estimate the number of ex-service settlers at Sundays River during this time.[58]

Problems continued to hamper Fitzpatrick's settlement work. The construction of a large irrigation dam fell behind schedule, its completion delayed until 1922. Prosperity seemed assured, but by this point the settlers had already experienced years of devastating drought. Even with the completion of Lake Mentz the drought persisted, pro-longing the settlers' suffering. Finally, in 1928 the irrigation facilities provided the settlers with the water they had been promised as early as

1918. But it was too little too late. In January 1923 the company had been forced into liquidation by the government who took control of the project.[59]

## Smuts and a belated attempt at a policy

In January 1921 the South African government launched a publicity campaign in London to attract prospective agricultural settlers with a minimum of £1,000 capital. Why the apparent and sudden shift in policy? Its implementation must be seen within the context of the merger between the Unionists and SAP the previous November and the general election scheduled for February 1921. Botha's successor as prime minister, General Jan Smuts, preoccupied with international events and policy making, had never paid much attention to the immigration issue. But with a critical election in the offing he realised that a positive move in this direction would earn him greater credibility with his new party allies and galvanise their support behind him. Some leading Unionists were encouraged by Smuts's initiative and saw the publicity campaign as a step in the right direction and a sign of positive state intervention. Writing before the February election, Lionel Phillips, a former Unionist, was hopeful that a victory for Smuts was a victory for the immigration lobby. He was certain that Smuts would be more sympathetic, if not more forthcoming with active government assistance.[60]

An encouraging step was taken in May with the appointment to the High Commission of Dirk Boshoff, the former inspector of settlements with the Department of Lands, as a settlers' information, land and agricultural officer.[61] The publicity campaign, however, was a limited success. It attracted a number of ex-officers with capital, the majority of whom wanted to pursue agriculture. Unfortunately for the government the overall numbers were small. In the first year of operation 244 men were encouraged to emigrate to South Africa bringing with them on average £6,000 each for a total of £1.6 million. By the end of March 1923, 1,030 settlers had taken approximately £4 million in investment capital to their new home. Boshoff was far from satisfied, arguing that a great deal more could be accomplished if 'a bolder more progressive immigration policy were adopted . . . with better organisation in South Africa'.[62] The lack of proper facilities to train and guide settlers in South Africa, coupled with persistent and harmful rumours about unscrupulous land companies, jeopardised the progress being achieved in London. Boshoff also complained that he was continually hampered by poor and irregular supplies of settlement literature.[63] Moreover, the government's minimum capital requirement introduced investors rather than farmers. As far as he was concerned, the only organisation which was doing anything constructive for the settler was the 1820 Association.[64]

## The 1820 Memorial Settlers' Association

The founding in 1920 of the 1820 Association marked a new chapter in British immigration to South Africa. It was founded, in part, to commemorate the centenary of the landing of the 3,500 British settlers at Algoa Bay in the Eastern Cape. The 1820 Association boasted that it could offer to those who had served during the war an opportunity to start a new and productive life in a country which possessed vast agricultural, industrial and economic potential.[65] Its real objective, however, was to restore British immigration to South Africa in an attempt to reinforce the English-speaking community. In that respect, it was an adjunct of Unionist party policy.

The first decade of the 1820 Association's history was spent catering to the half-pay officer and the British public school boy. It was a highly selective, socially exclusive policy and one which received its share of criticism. The 1820 Association attempted to attract men with capital 'represented either by money or training'. It clearly stipulated that single men were required to possess a minimum of £1,500 capital prior to emigrating and £2,000 was fixed for married men. These financial qualifications were above the minimum capital required by the government and were certainly more realistic considering the enormous expense incurred by settlers in adapting to new environmental conditions and farming practices.[66]

The 1820 Association aimed at governmental and popular support, settlers of the 'right sort' and financial solvency. The most immediate problem facing the fledgling movement was to enlist support, and Sir Charles Crewe, its first chairman between 1920 and 1934, wasted no time. Within the first year he compiled an impressive list of honorary vice-presidents encompassing (with the exception of General Hertzog's Nationalists) many within the mainstream of the political spectrum in South Africa. It was no surprise that Milner was offered and accepted the title of honorary president. Milner applauded Crewe's initiative but warned that the road ahead would be unyielding and the task a thankless one. 'I have no doubt', he told Crewe, 'British loyalists will have to continue to do all the work, and get few of the rewards. I am sure, by the way, that it is by your plan of quietly but steadily introducing men (of) good British blood that the position can alone be consolidated.'[67]

When Crewe solicited support from Merriman he revealed his intense desire to 'get together a really live body and get the ear of the Colonial Office' in London. This achievement would enable the 1820 Association 'not only to get . . . settlers but prevent exploitation by bogus (and) impossible schemes'.[68] However, the 1820 Association would 'rigidly abstain (from) embarking on any policy of land purchase for Settlement purposes'. Its primary concern was the scientific and 'systematic introduction of the old strain of British blood on a scale which (would) ensure the predominance of the white race' in South Africa.[69] Crewe, in extending an invitation to the Oversea Settlement Committee to attend the inaugural meeting of the London committee in August 1920, emphasised that the 1820 Association was 'neither political nor racial and presents an opportunity of assisting settlement in South Africa, which is not likely to occur again'.[70]

The active participation in the 1820 Association of many former Milnerites and Unionist politicians from Smuts's English-speaking phalanx within the SAP after the party merger in November 1920, raised an additional problem. Although the 1820 Association's leaders stressed that their organisation was non-racial and apolitical these claims were dismissed by the Afrikaner community. Instead, Nationalists charged that the 1820 Association was indeed trying to contain the Afrikaner by promoting British immigration. In fact, some Unionists took a more defensive view. The only salvation for a British South Africa was the maintenance of the political *status quo* between the two white communities. A steady and constant flow of British immigrants to South Africa would ensure a numerical balance between the two white races.

Initially, the applicants were largely ex-officers who possessed some capital and were interested in farming. Many settlers in this class had possessed a farm prior to leaving the mother country.[71] But Smartt, the Minister of Agriculture, agreed with Sir Edgar Walton, a leading Unionist and Schreiner's successor as High Commissioner, that these same British officers held many misconceptions about farming in South Africa. They seemed 'to imagine that stepping out of the Army and onto a farm is an easy process, whereas it is one that requires extremely close attention to nature and a good deal of hard work.'[72] Smartt argued that it would be better to have young experienced farmers with £600 than the inexperienced farmer with £1,500: 'Knowledge (and experience with) farm life would be likely to do better than a man with four times the am(oun)t who might be inclined to imagine farming was a life of ease, enlivened by sounds of sport.'[73]

The highly selective policy of the 1820 Association contained important social overtones. The enormous supply of cheap black labour ensured that white agricultural labour could not compete on the same level and the emphasis was on the settler with capital who could establish himself as a gentleman farmer. At the same time an English farmer could not go to South Africa and 'think that he could simply walk around and leave all the dirty work to be done by natives', warned the Earl of Leven and Melville, a member of the London executive.[74] Phillips similarly emphasised that discipline, respect, hard work and deference to one's place in society were vital qualities which had to be instilled into the native. Therefore it was essential to secure 'people of gentle breeding for the influence they (would) gradually exercise upon the native mind'.[75]

The maintenance of a social balance between the black and white races was considered essential for the Union's future social stability. The role of the native as the unskilled labourer and the dour, paternalistic white landowner as master remained a dominant theme in the social attitudes of the white South African farming community. And *baaskap* (or boss-ship) was not an Afrikaner monopoly in light of the class of immigrant the 1820 Association was hoping to attract.[76] However, the achievement of social stability also included striking a balance between the rural and urban communities. 'Domestic stability within the Union cannot be expected unless the normal unrest of industrial workers can be "ballasted" by a large stable agricultural population' preferably of Anglo-Saxon stock.[77] This was the motive for the 1820 Association's determination to resettle British ex-officers in rural South Africa: social, racial and political stability.

Crewe's attempt to gain a sympathetic ear at the Colonial Office proved successful. Amery was delighted, welcomed the invitation and raised no objections for closer co-operation with the organisation. However, the Colonial Office made it clear that its participation would be in an advisory capacity only.[78] The function of the 1820 Association as an 'honest broker' increased in importance, however, as it became clear to the Colonial Office that the political implications of British immigration to South Africa made it impossible for South Africa to participate officially in the imperial migration schemes which had caught the rest of the empire's imagination.[79]

The 1820 Association and the South African High Commission in London soon developed a harmonious and intimate working relationship. Part of the reason was the close personal friendship of Phillips, Schreiner and Walton and their commitment to sending the right type of settler to South Africa. Smartt, as Minister of Agriculture, provided an additional link in the network of influential and strategically placed personalities. He admitted that so far as the South African government was concerned, the 1820 Association was the most competent body to deal with prospective settlers. To have 'an organised body of disinterested people looking after settlers and seeing that they are not fleeced by designing speculators' was vital.[80]

The 1820 Association worked hard to maintain an untarnished

reputation. The decision not to become involved in realty or land speculation was a conscious step designed to give it greater flexibility and influence within government circles. Its voluntary nature, integrity, emphasis on sound advice and assistance rather than booking fees, commissions and land sales, elevated it above official reproach. Enquiries received by the Oversea Settlement Committee concerning the standard of living in South Africa, employment prospects, agricultural potential and opportunities, and the cost of passages were either forwarded directly to the London executive or via the South African High Commission. Although the High Commission had the final word on the suitability of a settler and was responsible for screening and approving his application, the High Commission lacked the facilities to cope with large numbers of enquiries. Therefore, it resorted to sending information enquiries directly to the 1820 Association. Even when a more vigorous Union government policy was initiated in London in January 1921 the High Commission preferred to work closely with the 1820 Association because of its reputation and experience.

Such a privileged position, however, exposed the 1820 Association to ridicule and attack from several private South African land settlement and colonisation companies jealous of its status. Charges of favouritism were levelled by some companies which complained that the 1820 Association basked in the 'sunshine of official recognition' and used its privileged position to steer settlers away from those private operations it deemed unsafe.[81] There was a grain of truth in these charges, but the 1820 Association had taken it upon itself to act as an immigration watch-dog. Complaints about misleading information and the purchase of worthless land continued to plague the organisation's efforts. This prompted the 1820 Association to monitor closely the activities of these companies in London and their operations in South Africa to ensure that any complaints about one company did not damage the honest and competent work of others. Similarly, Phillips emphasised that settlers brought out under the auspices of the 1820 Association must be supervised closely during their probationary period. 'In a movement of this kind considerable damage may result from reports spread by dissatisfied Settlers.'[82]

The role of the 1820 Association as an honest broker was appreciated by the British. During its first three years in London the persistent shortage of operating capital had plagued the 1820 Association's operations, but this problem was solved in August 1923. Under the terms of the Empire Settlement Act of 1922, enacted to promote and assist British emigration within the empire, the British government was entitled to negotiate settlement agreements with both public and private bodies. As a result, Crewe negotiated an agreement with the British government whereby a capitation grant of £10 per settler, or per head of household in the case of families, would be paid to the 1820 Association. The entire scheme was to be administered for five years and was not to exceed £10,000 per annum. The London executive was convinced that this grant would enable them to meet their operating expenses and maintain an active propaganda campaign to attract more settlers. The 1820 Association thus received a guaranteed supply of money to prime the propaganda pump.[83]

Supplementary agreements were signed over the next three years which included an increase of the capitation grant. With the 1820 Association's annual call for money after 1923 the Treasury began to question more seriously the London executive's financial practices and acumen. By 1926 one Treasury official saw the agreements as simply a stopgap measure employed by the 1820 Association to solve its ever worsening cash flow problem. The Colonial Office was quick to point out, however, that the 1820 Association had spent £70,000 on the promotion of British settlement between 1920 and 1926 whereas the British government had contributed to the organisation's coffers a mere £2,500 in subsidy grants. It was therefore inadvisable to quibble about procedure. The Treasury relented, agreeing with the Colonial Office that the task being met by the 1820 Association was, politically speaking, one of the most important in the empire.[84]

## Election of the Pact government

The SAP's defeat by Hertzog's Nationalists and their coalition or pact partners, the South African Labour Party, in June 1924 had a direct impact on South African immigration and land settlement policy. It also had a profound impact upon the work of the 1820 Association. Smuts had proved ineffective in combating the problems brought about by the post-war depression. While unemployment and poor whiteism had grown at a phenomenal rate he launched his electoral campaign aimed at accomplishing three objectives. Topping the list was the increased use of the country's natural resources through a greater utilisation of its agricultural potential. The introduction of European settlers and the improvement of the condition of the poor whites completed the election platform. These were sound objectives but the conditions required for their achievement were lacking. Depressed markets for primary produce, low prices and a three-year drought had certainly not helped farmers. Money was needed to educate and assist the poor white, but local authorities were hard pressed to meet their commitments. Unemployment was so severe that many South Africans were leaving the country to find work. In the circumstances what chance did an immigrant have of finding a job or embarking upon a career in agriculture?[85]

Political controversy in South Africa between 1925 and 1928 deterred many British immigrants from making the dominion their home. The controversy which burst open the old racial wounds between English and Afrikaner was the Nationality and Flag Bill first tabled in May 1926.[86] The issue rekindled the fires of race patriotism at a critical time when the 1820 Association was desperately trying to reorganise its resources and tap new sources of British immigrants. The Colonial Office was convinced that future negotiations concerning South African settlement schemes and settler subsidies would be held in abeyance for the time being. For the moment it was Africa for the Afrikaner, the Colonial Office being warned that it should not expect sympathy or assistance from the new government in immigration matters. Meanwhile, the only hope was for the Colonial Office to continue working through the 1820 Association until Smuts regained power.[87]

For Crewe and his associates it seemed that their worst fears had been realised. The poor white problem would receive Hertzog's undivided attention to the further detriment of the immigration cause in South Africa. Phillips, however, struck a note of cautious optimism.

> I quite understand that the Nationalist Government, for political reasons of its own, is not inclined to take a very open attitude regarding the encouragement of British settlers. At the same time, it cannot be oblivious to the danger to white civilisation in South Africa unless the stream of white emigration can be strengthened. Moreover, the Nationalist Government cannot be blind to the folly of attempting to re-establish the 'poor whites' on the land, though they must, of course, for political purposes advocate and perhaps support schemes with the object in view, even with their tongues in their cheeks! But, unless they are very ill-informed, they must also know . . . that it is the active Englishmen and the up-to-date European who have done the development up to now and in whom the hope of the future lies. It is of course very difficult for any of us to gauge the true mentality of the Boer: it is right to say that he has really no confirmed convictions and pursues a day to day policy according to the expediency of the moment.[88]

Undaunted, Crewe battled on. He set about reorganising and reinvigorating the Transvaal, Natal and London executives. He reported to Lady Milner that the settlement work was progressing 'swimmingly' despite the Pact government's legislation to facilitate for the rehabilitation of the poor white.[89]

Both Crewe and the British government remained unconvinced of the Pact government's sincerity to help the overseas immigrant as outlined in the Land Settlement Laws Further Amendment Bill of 1925. The Earl of Athlone, the newly appointed Governor-General, reported to the Colonial Office that the legislation at first glance appeared to indicate that the Nationalists were no longer opposed to immigration from overseas. However, this was not the case. The legislation was introduced to 'facilitate the rehabilitation of the "poor white" on the land which the government hold to be the true solution of that problem'.[90] Crewe's appraisal was more blunt: 'Hertzog is struggling (and) he knows that putting the poor whites back on the land is no real solution of that question, they won't make farmers in the days of competition, but he does it for political reasons.'[91]

Crewe's assessment was correct. The new South African government had no intention of embarking upon an intensive immigration policy in Europe. 'As state-aided immigration has never formed part of our policy,' stated C. I. Pienaar, South African Commissioner for Commerce in Milan, 'I presume there is no intention on the part of the state to undertake any intensive immigration campaign.'[92] There was not. Moreover, the close working relationship between the 1820 Association and the High Commission in London suddenly but not unexpectedly ended upon Walton's resignation as High Commissioner in 1925. He was replaced by the aggressive Nationalist, J. S. Smit. The London executive was prepared to co-operate with the new High Commissioner, but Crewe was adamant that it was better not to have any contact with him whatsoever. Quite simply, he did not trust Smit or his new personnel. Neither did R. A. Blankenburg, a long-serving member of the High Commission staff and an important link between the High Commission and the 1820 Association. Becoming fed up with the office under Smit, he resigned in early 1926.[93]

The 1820 Association still had a friend in Amery who had returned as Colonial Secretary in Stanley Baldwin's Conservative government in November 1924. Although concerned about the new outlook in South Africa and its bearing on the 1820 Association, he remained 'cautiously optimistic' about British immigration to South Africa.[94] Above all, he was determined to advance the cause of British immigration to South Africa through the machinery of the Empire Settlement Act. He praised the 1820 Association's settlement work as the 'most hopeful thing being done in South Africa at this moment'.[95] But moral support was not enough.

Despite the 1820 Association's valiant attempt to continue promoting British immigration, even the ever-optimistic Crewe could not deny the effect the lack of funds, settlers and domestic government support were having on its work. The severe shortage of cheap accessible land, the priority received by the poor whites after 1924 and the perennial battles with shady land companies also continued to restrict settlement.[96] From the political perspective the numbers game remained a central ideological principle in the race patriotism of Crewe and the 1820 Association. But as the 1920s progressed, revealing the political and economic realities which limited the number of British immigrants entering South Africa, they were forced to tone down the rhetoric. Instead, Crewe and his associates concentrated on the practical aspects of their policy such as publicity, fund-raising, training, settler support and aftercare.

By the late 1920s, Crewe had resigned himself to the fact that numbers would be small, dictated by financial necessities and the class and type of settler the 1820 Association attempted to cultivate. The 1820 Association readily admitted that it could always do with more settlers, but as they were not forthcoming it tried to hide behind the statement that quality was more important than quantity. But was it? The small numbers of settlers of the 'right type' were certainly not going to bring about the radical changes hoped for in the domestic political climate. By 1928, Crewe grudgingly accepted that the 1820 Association's contribution to maintaining the British connection was small but nevertheless vital. It was of 'such a kind that character and push count for much more than numbers, and there is no doubt they are making their mark'.[97] Maybe so, but large numbers of competent settlers would have made a greater impact on the domestic scene, and they had not materialised.

The failure to attract greater numbers of settlers must be attributed to the 1820 Association's highly selective, socially exclusive policy which prevented it from recruiting greater numbers of settlers. Rather than establishing an imperial yeomanry on the South African veldt, the 1820 Association had gone some way in creating an imperial gentry in rural South Africa. Indeed, the settlers were of a high standard and possessed an enormous amount of investment capital. However, the competition of an abundant, cheap black labour force and the demands inflicted upon agriculture by the region's climate and topography constantly militated against South Africa being a favoured destination for the average British emigrant. Plus there was the problem of farming on the veldt with its emphasis on substantial capital reserves. Nevertheless, given the political environment, the 1820 Association's achievements were impressive. Between 1921 and 1930 it introduced approximately 20 per cent of the total number of British immigrants who arrived in South Africa during the same period.[98]

Despite the 1820 Association's claim that it was non-racial and apolitical, its determination to introduce a large British element to counteract Afrikanerism smacked of Milnerism and British race patriotism. Many Afrikaners quite rightly distrusted the motives of the 1820 Association, and it was a foregone conclusion that when the Nationalists came to power the poor white would receive priority. Afrikaner race patriotism triumphed, eliminating the need for the Nationalists to attack British immigration as a tool of imperial interests. The onslaught of the depression in the early 1930s and the unification of Afrikanerdom through the establishment of a coalition government between Smuts and Hertzog in March 1933 effectively ended any hope of promoting large-scale British immigration to South Africa. Crewe for one certainly held no illusions over the lack of support the 1820 Association had received from the authorities in South Africa. Irritated by the immigration rhetoric employed by both Smuts and Hertzog to woo the English vote, he exclaimed, 'as far as settlement was concerned it did not matter which Gov(ernmen)t was in office for I had had no serious help from either! Smuts now talks about a strong immigration policy when he gets back to power, but he won't *do* anything. Plus ça change plus c'est la même chose.'[99]

In the final analysis, it was Afrikaner nationalism which defeated the promotion of large-scale British immigration to South Africa. Poor whiteism, an important symbol in the struggle to protect an Afrikaner identity, was the means by which the Nationalists dictated immigration policy after 1914. The polarisation of the two white communities, particularly between 1910 and 1924, did not give the ruling SAP much room to manoeuvre on issues over which English and Afrikaner interests were diametrically opposed. Forced to occupy the sensitive middle ground, 'official South African policy was characterised by platitudes or ritual incantations'.[100] Despite the constraints of the domestic political scene, serious doubt remains as to the sincerity of both Botha and Smuts to support British immigration. Their public pronouncements were guarded and vague, steeped in the knowledge that any commitment to empire migration would lose votes in the backveldt. Rhetoric aside, this determination to pursue a course of inaction for fear of antagonising Afrikaner support left many of Pretoria's bureaucrats in an untenable situation. In fact, it was the 1820 Association which carried out the only consistent and positive immigration strategy in South Africa throughout the inter-war period.

The politicisation of British immigration and land settlement emphasised both the delicacy and the awkwardness with which South African domestic politics had complicated these issues. It also highlighted and reinforced the 1820 Association's central position as the broker between London and Pretoria. Similarly, it demonstrated how far the Colonial and Dominions Offices were prepared to go to accommodate and promote British immigration to and land settlement in South

Africa. For even after the Nationalist victory in 1924 British settlers continued to be subsidised from the Imperial Exchequer until the outbreak of war in 1939. Ultimately, despite the efforts to sustain the British connection, it was Afrikaner nationalism which triumphed over imperial interests.

## Notes

1 Amery Papers, Box G.84, Fitzpatrick to Amery, 5 May 1926.
2 James Sturgis, 'Anglicisation as a theme in Lower Canadian history 1807–1843', *British Journal of Canadian Studies*, III, 1988, pp. 210–29; *idem*, 'Anglicisation at the Cape of Good Hope in the early nineteenth century', *Journal of Imperial and Commonwealth History*, XI, 1982, pp. 5–32. See also Johnston, *British Emigration Policy 1815–1830*.
3 British immigration to South Africa averaged only 10,000 annually before 1914, and after World War I it dropped to a mere 2,900 per year up to the outbreak of war in 1939. U.G. 12–1914, *Report of the Economic Commission*, p. 26; Edna Bradlow, 'Immigration into the Union 1910–1948: Policies and Attitudes', unpublished Ph.D. dissertation (2 vols) University of Cape Town, 1978, II, p. 441.
4 Davenport, *South Africa*, p. 319; Carnegie Commission, *Report of the Commission on the Poor White Problem in South Africa*, 5 vols, Stellenbosch, 1932, I, p. 7; Stanley Trapido, 'Landlord and tenant in a colonial economy: the Transvaal 1880–1910', *Journal of Southern African Studies*, V, 1978, pp. 26–58; *idem*, 'Reflections on land, office and wealth in the South African Republic, 1850–1900', in S. Marks and A. Atmore, eds, *Economy and Society in Pre-industrial South Africa*, London, 1980, pp. 350–68.
5 T. R. H. Davenport, *The Afrikaner Bond*, London, 1966, pp. 274–7.
6 Davenport, *South Africa*, p. 319; Charles van Onselen, *Studies in the Social and Economic History of the Witwatersrand 1886–1914*, 2 vols, Johannesburg, 1982, II, pp. 111–170.
7 Cory Library for Historical Research, Rhodes University, Grahamstown, Brigadier-General Sir Charles Crewe Papers, minutes of the Unionist Party Conferences, 1910–20, minutes of the party conference, 19 November 1912; minutes from the first day of the party conference held in Bloemfontein, 23 May 1910. The Unionist Party unanimously reaffirmed these resolutions in successive party conferences prior to World War I and in 1919 at the first party conference after the war. Also see South Africa, *House of Assembly Debates*, 1914, 24 April 1914, cols 1938–40 and 26 May 1914, cols 2806–14. For a more detailed examination of Unionist Party policy see A. A. Mawby, 'The Unionist Party of South Africa, from May 1910 to August 1914', unpublished B.A. (Honours) dissertation University of the Witwatersrand, 1965; Barlow Rand Archives (hereafter BRA), Johannesburg, Sir Lionel Phillips Papers, Land Settlement File 1911–25, A. C. Hershensohn to Phillips, 3 February 1911.
8 Jagger Library, University of Cape Town, Sir Patrick Duncan Papers, Duncan to Sir Thomas Smartt, 11 October 1912, D1.34.4; Duncan to Milner, 23 August 1915, D15.11.3.
9 WRO 947/545, Crewe to Long, 25 March 1917.
10 *Cape Times*, 17 February 1916.
11 Noel Garson, 'South Africa and World War I', in Hillmer and Wigley, eds, *First British Commonwealth*, pp. 80–1.
12 PRO, CO 551/95/31932, Buxton to Long, 25 May 1917.
13 Garson, 'South Africa and World War I', pp. 68–73. For the impact of the Afrikaner rebellion on British-South African relations see S. B. Spies, 'The outbreak of the First World War and the Botha government', *South African Historical Journal*, no. 1, 1969, pp. 47–57.

14 South African Library (hereafter SAL), Cape Town, J. X. Merriman Papers, Sir Graham Bower to Merriman, 20 May 1916; National English Literary Museum (hereafter NELM), Grahamstown, Sir Percy Fitzpatrick Papers, A/LC V 1052/48, Fitzpatrick to Phillips, 28 August 1918; BRA, Phillips Papers, Letter Book, PHI (1918–19), Phillips to Smartt, 14 November 1918.

15 *Dictionary of South African Biography*, III, p. 181.

16 Jagger Library, Duncan Papers, Duncan to Smartt, 11 October 1912, D1.34.4.

17 Bradlow, 'Immigration into the Union', II, p. 352; Mawby, 'Unionist Party of South Africa', pp. 45–52.

18 Higgins, *Private Diaries*, London, 1980, p. 53; RCSA, Haggard Mission file, Haggard to Wilson, 3 March 1916; SAL, Merriman Papers, Buxton to Merriman, 23 February 1916; HLRO, J. C. C. Davidson Papers, f. 28, Buxton to Bonar Law, 10 March 1916; Norfolk Record Office (hereafter NRO), Sir H. Rider Haggard Papers, MC 32/14, Merriman to Haggard, 26 February 1916.

19 NELM, Fitzpatrick Papers, D A/L III 565/41, Fitzpatrick to his wife, 25 February 1916.

20 Higgins, *Private Diaries*, p. 53; Haggard, *After-War Settlement*, pp. 5–8; NRO, Haggard Papers, MC 32/15, Merriman to Haggard, 11 March 1916.

21 Central Archives Depot (hereafter CAD), Union Buildings, Pretoria, Department of Lands, LDE 18349, Box 913, Jagger to Schreiner, 22 June 1916; Schreiner to W. Soper, secretary of London SASIC, 20 July 1916; Soper to Schreiner, 5 October 1916; Secretary for High Commission to Secretary for Lands, 27 November 1916; PRO, CO 532/90/49865, SASIC to Bonar Law, 17 October 1916.

22 Cory Library, Crewe Papers, Milner to Crewe, 19 March 1917.

23 Amery Papers, Box E.60, Amery to Fitzpatrick, 22 October 1917.

24 *Ibid.*, Box E.59, Fitzpatrick to Amery, 5 July 1917.

25 WRO 947/545, Crewe to Long, 25 March 1917.

26 *Ibid.*, Crewe to Long, 25 March and 15 May 1917.

27 *Ibid.*, Crewe to Long, 17 August 1917.

28 Amery Papers, Box E.59, Fitzpatrick to Amery, 5 July 1917.

29 Transvaal Archives Depot (hereafter TAD), Union Buildings, Pretoria, J. C. Smuts Papers, vol. 113, no. 174, memorandum by Mentz entitled, 'Employment of discharged troops at the end of the war', 31 August 1916; CAD, LDE 18370, I, Box 914, minutes by D. P. Liebenburg, junior departmental official, 1 March and 5 April 1917; Liebenburg to Mentz, 16 February 1917; Amery Papers, Box E.59, memorandum by Fitzpatrick on South African political situation (c. 1917).

30 WRO 947/601, Buxton to Long, 20 December 1916; CAD, LDE 18346, Box 913, H. G. Watson, secretary to the Prime Minister, to Schreiner, 19 February 1917.

31 *Cape Times*, 17 and 29 February 1916.

32 *Ibid.*, 17 February 1916. For an examination of government-sponsored irrigation schemes in South Africa prior to 1910 see A. J. Christopher, *The Crown Lands of British South Africa 1853–1914*, Kingston, 1984, pp. 98–109.

33 *Cape Times*, 1 May 1917.

34 *Ibid.*, 20 March, 12 and 15 May, 8 June 1917.

35 CAD, LDE 18346, Box 913, Schreiner to Botha, 27 June 1917; minute by Mentz, 27 August 1917.

36 CAD, LDE 20593, I, Box 1081, minute from the South African Prime Minister's Office, 14 March 1919; PRO, CO 532/134/5280, South African High Commission to Amery, 23 January 1919; CO 721/2/f. 39, minute by Fiddes, January 1919.

37 PRO, CO 532/91/4553, minute by unknown Colonial Office official, 27 January 1917; TAD, Smuts Papers, vol. 205, no. 7, Amery to Smuts, 4 October 1919. In February 1919, Amery recalled a conversation he had with Botha who was in Europe for the peace talks. Botha professed his eagerness to attract a good class of settler to South Africa so long as it was not 'too publicly advertised'. Barnes and Nicholson, *Amery Diaries*, I, p. 257.

38 Bradlow, 'Immigration into the Union', II, p. 412.

39 CAD, LDE 20593, II, Box 1082, F. E. Kanthack, Director of Irrigation, to G. H. Hughes,

Secretary for Lands, 15 April 1920; J. Sommerville, Under-Secretary for Lands, to Hughes, 21 July 1920; Hughes to Mentz, 4 August 1920; memorandum by Kanthack submitted to Mentz, n.d.; Schreiner to Botha, 23 March 1918; LDE 18346, Box 913, Schreiner to Mentz, 10 January 1918 and 12 March 1919; LDE 20953, I, Box 1081, Schreiner to Amery, 17 April 1919; Cory Library, Crewe Papers, Walton to Crewe, 24 July 1922.

40  SAL, Merriman Papers, E. I. D. Gordon to Merriman, 21 December 1918; NELM, Fitzpatrick Papers, A/LB X, Fitzpatrick to C. H. C. van Breda, 29 November 1918.

41  BRA, Phillips Papers, Letter Book, PHI (1918–19), Phillips to Soper, 21 November and 4 December 1918.

42  *Ibid.*, Phillips to Wilson, 23 April 1919.

43  CAD, LDE 20953, IX, Box 1085, C. W. Cousins, Secretary for Labour, to Robert Wigram, 21 February 1928; Rhodes House Library, Oxford, MSS. Afr. s. 132, Basil Williams Papers, Merriman to Williams, 20 February 1920.

44  PRO, CO 721/45/1959, Amery to Walton, 6 February 1922; CO 721/44/1827, *ibid.*, 28 February 1922.

45  PRO, CO 721/21/3824, Hughes to London High Commission concerning Mooi River Estates near Potchefstroom, 5 November 1920; CO 721/16/1965, minute by Macnaghten on Harmony Estates, 3 February 1920; CO 721/91/1966, meeting between Plant, W. Bankes Amery, OSC financial officer, the 1820 Memorial Settlers' Association and the Press Advertisement Manager's Association, 26 May 1924; William Cullen Library, University of the Witwatersrand, Johannesburg, Zebediela Citrus Estates File, A 1724.

46  CAD, LDE 18370/8, I, Box 918, minute by Hughes, 23 August 1918; Hughes to Secretary, Returned Soldiers Employment Committee, Pretoria, 23 January 1919.

47  *Ibid.*, Secretary of the Comrades of the Great War, Johannesburg, to Mentz, 8 May 1919; Secretary, Returned Soldiers' Employment Committee, Pretoria, to Sommerville, 11 January 1919; 'Memorandum to the settlement for returned soldiers submitted by the Returned Soldiers Advisory Board for the Witwatersrand', 27 October 1919.

48  South African Parliamentary Papers, *Select Committee Report, S.C. 4a* – '18, *Provision for South African Forces in the Present and Previous Wars*, p. 371; CAD, LDE 18370/26, Box 920, minute by Sommerville, 30 August 1920.

49  CAD, LDE 18370/29, Box 921, Smuts to Colonel Deneys Reitz, Minister of Lands, 23 March 1921; minute by Sommerville, 12 April 1921; departmental minute, 16 April 1921.

50  *Rand Daily Mail*, 5 and 7 May 1921.

51  CAD, LDE 18370, III, Box 915, departmental minute initialled PCB, 24 February 1919. One official's claim that the Union government was doing more for the returned soldier than any of the Allied governments was dismissed as ludicrous by one newspaper: 'Poor blind ostrich; he deserves an unofficial pension for loyalty to a lost cause.' *The South African Farm News, Exchange and Mart*, 11 November 1919.

52  CAD, LDE 18370/30, Box 921, A. D. Bridge, junior departmental official, to Reitz, 13 and 14 February 1923. For an excellent statistical breakdown of returned soldier allotments including names, region, nationality and placement at agricultural colleges see the various reports dated 1 January 1917 to 31 March 1921, LDE 18370 (volume number missing), Box 915.

53  Plant, *Oversea Settlement*, p. 74. The figure for South Africa is slightly exaggerated as it includes a minuscule but unspecified number of ex-servicemen who settled in Southern Rhodesia.

54  SAL, Smartt Syndicate Papers, File E-20, Mr Mugglestone to F. Hirschhorn, mining financier, 23 May 1936; U.G. 35–1920, *Annual Report of the Department of Justice for the calendar year 1919*, p. 21; U.G. 21–26, *Annual Department Reports (1924–25)*, Department of Justice.

55  William Cullen Library, Drummond Chaplin Papers (microfilm), reel 3, Fitzpatrick to Chaplin, 8 March 1916; Andrew Duminy and Bill Guest, *Interfering in Politics: A Biography of Sir Percy Fitzpatrick*, Johannesburg, 1987, p. 215; U.G. 29–17, *Reports*

on *Various Irrigation Projects (provided for in Loan Estimates for year ending 31 March 1918)*, p. 19; NELM, Fitzpatrick Papers, A/LC V 1052/148, Fitzpatrick to Phillips, 28 September 1918.

56  NELM, Fitzpatrick Papers, B/A VI 1068/101, Beit to Fitzpatrick, 30 May 1916; D Q1=A/L;III(a) 578/11, Fitzpatrick to his wife, 11 September 1917.

57  Cape Archives (hereafter KAB), Cape Town, A 671, vol. 13, annual shareholders meeting of the Cape Sundays River Settlement, 11 April 1917; NELM, A/LB X, Fitzpatrick to I. Tribolet, official at the Horticulture Division, Department of Agriculture, 25 June 1917.

58  U.G. 35–1920, *Department of Justice*, p. 39; NELM, Fitzpatrick Papers, A/LC V 1052/41, Fitzpatrick to Commander C. H. Petrie, 3 July 1922; A/LC VI 1053/18, Fitzpatrick to Smartt, 21 July 1922; A/LC V 1052/94, Fitzpatrick to Reitz, 24 July 1922; KAB, A 671, vol. 10, minutes of the naval settlers committee, 21 July 1922; Sundays River Military Committee to the Adjutant-General, War Office, 3 October 1922; Amery diaries, 13 and 22 September 1922.

59  Jane M. Meiring, *Sundays River Valley: Its History and Settlement*, Cape Town, 1959; Duminy and Guest, *Interfering in Politics*, p. 215; Amery diaries, 13 September 1927.

60  BRA, Phillips Papers, Letter Book, PHI(1909–21), Phillips to Geoffrey Dawson, editor of *The Times*, 7 February 1921.

61  CAD, LDE 20953, II, Box 1082, telegram, Walton to Smuts, 16 and 26 February 1921; *Rand Daily Mail*, 20 May 1921.

62  *Ibid.*, III, Box 1083, A. H. Tatlow, manager of the South African Railways and Harbours Publicity Department, to Secretary for Lands, 30 March 1922; Edna Bradlow, 'Empire settlement and South African immigration policy, 1910–1948', in Constantine, ed., *Emigrants and Empire*, p. 182; CAD, LDE 20953, IV, Box 1083, advertising campaign statistics, March 1923; Boshoff to Sommerville, Secretary for Lands, 3 May 1923.

63  *Ibid.*, IV, Box 1083, 'Propaganda and farm training', memorandum by Boshoff, 5 August 1922.

64  *The Farmer's Weekly*, 2 January 1924.

65  Cory Library, *South African Pamphlets*, XVIII, no. 9, 'The 1820 Memorial Settlers' Association: its aims, objects, constitution, organisation, etc', 1920, p. 6. There is no comprehensive study of the 1820 Association, an organisation which still exists today. For further insights see R. G. Morrell, 'Rural Transformations in the Transvaal: The Middelburg District, 1919 to 1930', unpublished M.A. thesis, University of the Witwatersrand, 1983; J. Stone, *Colonist or Uitlander? A Study of the British Immigrant in South Africa*, Oxford, 1973, pp. 124–7; Bradlow, 'South African immigration policy', pp. 184–8.

66  Stone, *Colonist or Uitlander?*, pp. 125–6; 'Aims, objects, constitution, organisation', p. 5; Cory Library, Pamphlet Box 25, 'The 1820 Memorial Settlers' Association: a brief account of the movement and a few plain reasons for supporting it', 1921, p. 3; A. J. Christopher, 'The European concept of a farm in southern Africa', *Historia*, XV, 1970, pp. 93–9.

67  Cory Library, Crewe Papers, Milner to Crewe, 24 April 1921.

68  SAL, Merriman Papers, Crewe to Merriman, 1 May 1920.

69  Cory Library, Pamphlet Box 25, 'A brief account of the movement', pp. 4–5.

70  PRO, CO 721/21/1936, Crewe to Oversea Settlement Committee, 30 July 1920. The SASIC was absorbed by the 1820 Association during the formation of its London executive in August 1920. For details of incorporation see CO 721/36/1936, first report of the London executive, 30 September 1921.

71  BRA, Box 485, f. 1, minutes of the 1820 Association Central Executive Committee, 12 April 1921.

72  Cory Library, Sir Edgar Walton Papers, Smartt to Walton, 13 April 1922.

73  Cory Library, Crewe Papers, Smartt to Crewe, 3 December 1921.

74  Quotation cited in Stone, *Colonists or Uitlanders?*, p. 126.

75  Cory Library, Crewe Papers, Phillips to Crewe, 7 October 1921.

76 Stone, *Colonists or Uitlanders?*, p. 127.
77 PRO, CO 532/99/51865, memorandum by Colonel J. J. Byron, October 1917.
78 PRO, CO 721/21/1936, Colonial Office to London Committee of 1820 Association, 11 August 1920; H. Handcock, secretary of London Committee, to Macnaghten, 13 August 1920.
79 PRO, CO 721/23/2441, minute by Plant, 11 January 1921.
80 TAD, Smuts Papers, vol. 210, nos 63 and 64, Crewe to Smuts, 5 April and 24 May 1923; Cory Library, Crewe Papers, Smartt to Crewe, 3 December 1921; Walton Papers, Smartt to Walton, 13 April, 19 May and 7 July 1922.
81 CAD, LDE 20593, III, Box 1082, interview between Mentz and Colonel Hartigan, chairman of the Associated Representatives of South African Land Selling Companies Ltd, 22 July 1921.
82 Cory Library, Crewe Papers, Phillips to Crewe, 7 October 1921.
83 PRO, T 161/735/S 21362/1, capitation grant agreement signed between the Duke of Devonshire, Colonial Secretary, and the 1820 Association on 17 August 1923; Bodleian Library, Viscount Milner Papers, Box 671, Crewe to Lady Milner, 31 March 1924.
84 PRO, T 161/967/S 21362/01/1, L. Cuthbertson, Treasury representative on Oversea Settlement Committee, to E. T. Crutchley, Oversea Settlement Committee finance officer, 5 June 1925; PRO, Dominions Office Papers (hereafter DO), DO 57/13/1937, Crutchley to Cuthbertson, 22 January 1926; Cuthbertson to Crutchley, 27 January 1926.
85 W. K. Hancock, *Smuts: The Fields of Force, 1919–1950*, London, 1968, p. 157.
86 Davenport, *South Africa*, pp. 288–9.
87 PRO, CO 721/83/0817/1, E. H. Farrar to Macnaghten, 4 September 1924; Macnaghten to Farrar, 21 October 1924.
88 Cory Library, Crewe Papers, Phillips to Crewe, 10 December 1924.
89 Bodleian, Milner Papers, Box 671, Crewe to Lady Milner, 26 November 1925; *ibid.*, Violet Milner Papers, C 243/1, Crewe to Lady Milner, 15 December 1924.
90 PRO, CO 721/83/0817/1, Athlone to Amery, 17 April 1925.
91 Bodleian, Violet Milner Papers, C 243/3, Crewe to Lady Milner, 30 May 1926.
92 CAD, LDE 20593/1, Box 1085, Pienaar to Secretary for Lands, 12 October 1925.
93 Bodleian, Milner Papers, Box 671, Crewe to Lady Milner, 12 April 1926. Before returning to South Africa Blankenburg confided to Amery that he found Smit 'tiresome [and] a bit of a cad to boot'. Amery diaries, 26 March 1926.
94 Amery diaries, 22 December 1926
95 Cory Library, Crewe Papers, Amery to Crewe, 31 January 1925.
96 Bodleian, Violet Milner Papers, C 243/11, Crewe to Lady Milner, 11 July 1929; Milner Papers, Box 671, Crewe to Lady Milner, 12 April 1926; Bradlow, 'Immigration into the Union', II, pp. 514–15.
97 Bodleian, Milner Papers, Box 671, Crewe to Lady Milner, 24 March 1927 and 10 January 1928.
98 Of the 5,414 British immigrants introduced since 1921, 4,810 still resided in the Union. Very few settlers failed, an achievement of which the 1820 Association was quite proud. Its failure rate was only 7.5 per cent, which was a tribute to its emphasis on thorough screening and settler aftercare. More importantly, they were the type who distinguished the 1820 Association's efforts from the immigration policies of the other dominions. By August 1930 the settler total had climbed to 5,800. Statistics also revealed the cost effectiveness of the 1820 Association's work. Between January 1921 and January 1925, 1,179 adult settlers and 698 dependents arrived possessing £3 million of investment capital or approximately £2,544 per adult. The total cost incurred by the 1820 Association was £21,585 or £11.10s per person. CAD, Governor-General's Archive, Box 2253, f. 1/27, 'Report from the general manager for settlement for the year ending 30th June 1929', pp. 1–2; *The 1820*, II, August 1930, p. 17.
99 Bodleian, Milner Papers, Box 671, Crewe to Lady Milner, 3 December 1925.
100 Bradlow, 'South African immigration policy', p. 188.

# CHAPTER SIX

# Australia and New Zealand:
# the failure of the Anzac legend

'Our duty', proclaimed Senator E. D. Millen, Australia's Minister of Repatriation, 'is . . . to labour together and build, even upon the initial mistakes and apparent failure inevitable in a national undertaking of this magnitude, that in the final analysis our work shall be proven solvent, sound, and justified by its achievements.'[1] The Australian experience of resettling ex-servicemen on the land after World War I proved contrary to Millen's patriotic but misplaced optimism. In the final analysis, Australia's 'achievements' were a series of regional disasters whose overall failure plagued state and Commonwealth administrations throughout the inter-war period. What differentiated Australian efforts from those of her sister dominions was the range, direction and variety of schemes undertaken.[2]

Land settlement had always been an integral part of the Australian experience and a necessary feature of state politics. According to one observer, soldier settlement 'was a policy which carried with it no implications that were either revolutionary or experimental. It simply meant that whereas the primary producers of the pre-war period were civilians, a large number of the primary producers of the post-war era would be civilians' who had served in the Australian Imperial Force (AIF). Soldier settlement was therefore not an innovation but simply a phase of Australian land settlement which was itself a key aspect of Australia's repatriation programme.[3] This may be true in general, but it glosses over the social and political implications inherent in soldier settlement. It also ignores the imperial element: the intended contribution of British ex-servicemen who settled in Australia, the role played by British capital which provided the financial basis of many soldier settlement projects and the utilisation of soldier settlement as a patriotic vehicle for ideas in social planning, economic regeneration and imperial solidarity.

Soldier settlement was seen as a national obligation, a patriotic gesture designed to demonstrate Australia's gratitude for the sacrifices her manhood had made in protecting individual freedom, international democracy and the empire. It was an emotional response sparked by a deep-seated sense of responsibility for the returned man. Furthermore, it was a constructive policy which would contribute to the continued economic prosperity and social well-being of both the individual and the state. Of central importance to this basic premise was the concept of the yeoman farmer and its centrality to the Australian agrarian myth.

The ideological basis of Australia's agrarian myth was two-fold and was firmly embedded in a neo-mercantilist doctrine which was rigorously endorsed during the 1920s under the banner 'Men, money and markets'. It was based on the exploitation and diversification of Australia's extensive and seemingly infinite land resources which, it was thought, could best be developed by small, independent farmers. Generated surpluses would be exported to Great Britain while the small farmer would provide a market for British manufactured goods.[4] Complementing the economic strand was the 'romantic, populist and arcadian idea that farming represented an idealistic way of life because it was "close to nature", and was therefore in some way morally superior to urban industrial life'.[5] In Australia's concept of rural arcadia the yeoman farmer was industrious, autonomous, dedicated and hardworking. He was the mainstay of society and his vocation was the life-blood of the nation. According to this notion the maintenance of a large class of stalwart primary producers guaranteed Australia's economic, social, political, military and moral security because a healthy rural community ensured a vibrant and prosperous nation.[6] The yeoman farmer was therefore both progenitor and protector of that legacy.

During World War I a new legend and tradition emerged which not only paralleled the agrarian myth and the yeoman ideal but shared some of their salient features. The 'Anzac' legend or 'digger' tradition was created during the unsuccessful Gallipoli campaign. For Australians, Gallipoli signified not just the first major test of its military prowess, but more importantly a coming of age. Australians believed that their country had indeed achieved nationhood.[7] The campaign created the Anzac '[o]ne of the most powerful and influential images in the [Australian] national consciousness'; one that was extremely important in moulding a distinctive national identity and character.[8]

What were the qualities of the Anzac myth? What were its origins? And how did they relate to the agrarian myth and the yeoman ideal? The Australian public saw the Anzac as 'tough and inventive, loyal to [his] mates beyond the call of duty, a bit undisciplined . . . chivalrous, gallant, sardonic'.[9] Mateship, 'that strange blend of individualism and interdependence', was an important quality which was reinforced time and time again under the stressful conditions of battle.[10] But these attributes were not created at Anzac Cove. Rather, the Australian experience of war heightened these sentiments, ingraining the Anzac myth more deeply into the national character. The Anzac myth was born of a truly Australian phenomenon which had been transformed into a credo in its own right – the tradition of the bush or 'outback'. Resourcefulness, initiative, perseverance, trustworthiness, manliness and mateship were values highly praised. Rekindled by the war this tradition and its values found fertile ground in the exploits of the Anzacs. For the Australian historian Geoffrey Serle, the Australian soldier or 'digger was only a new version of the bushmen'.[11] Conversely, these same attributes were central to the yeoman ideal and had significant overtones for the soldier settler. For if the Anzac stereotype can be equated with a wartime version of the bushmen, then the soldier settler provides continuity between the pre-war concept of the yeoman ideal with the post-war concepts of the agrarian myth and the modern yeoman farmer.

The cross-fertilisation of the outback, yeoman and Anzac traditions had important political implications during the post-war era. Prior to 1914, the independent, free thinking and self-sufficient yeoman symbolised stability, achievement and democracy. He was enshrined as the ideal Australian. During the war the digger became a role model because he too incorporated the best qualities of Australian character, manhood, egalitarianism and citizenship. Once again, the soldier settler combined the ideals of the yeoman farmer with the Anzac tradition to become a symbol of post-war political stability. This was particularly important for conservative Australian political opinion which wholeheartedly embraced soldier settlement because it was seen as a method of reinforcing traditional Australian society against what they saw as the socially destructive forces of syndicalism, Bolshevism and militant trade unionism.[12]

## A debt of honour

In July 1915, when the first casualties began arriving in Australia from Gallipoli, the Commonwealth government had still to formulate a repatriation policy. Prime Minister Andrew Fisher was attacked for the shabby reception accorded to Australia's first group of returning heroes. He was eager to make amends, and at the end of July he announced his government's commitment to give returned ex-servicemen preference in government employment.[13] By the beginning of August, the Commonwealth government produced a preliminary outline of a scheme to provide employment for returned servicemen. A Federal Parliamentary War Committee was established to supervise and co-ordinate work between the federal executive, the state governments, municipal authorities, commercial and industrial interests. A state Council would be set up in each state to liaise with the federal executive and the local authorities. The great fear was 'that a number of separately controlled organisations may spring up, and that confusion, inefficiency, and over-lapping may result'.[14] It was obvious that the responsibility for the returned soldier was a national obligation which had to be met. More importantly, this marked a recognition that the state had to intervene positively in areas of social policy hitherto the realm of private initiative and philanthropy.

However, there was a more immediate political consideration inextricably woven into Australia's war effort. As Marilyn Lake demonstrates in her recent study of soldier settlement in Victoria:

> The discharged soldiers were highly visible in Australia's cities and if unemployed, destitute or in other ways seemingly ill used, became a hindrance to recruiting. Australians relied on voluntary recruiting and from the beginning of the war, government spokesmen felt obliged to promise material rewards to prospective soldiers to entice them to enlist.[15]

As the slaughter in France stretched AIF manpower requirements, recruiters were faced with a daunting task. The need to maintain recruitment levels while at the same time mollifying the returned soldier became a delicate political conundrum. Pension plans, promises of preferential treatment in employment and land settlement schemes were designed to solve the problem. The haste with which Australian administrators jumped at the idea of land settlement as a solution to the recruitment problem signified an emotional response to a problem that actually demanded cool, calm and careful consideration. Recruits who went to the front believing that they would get farms under generous conditions after the war were being deceived by a government which had not properly examined the issue.[16] The recruits were also deceiving themselves, blinded by their patriotism and sense of duty.

In February 1915 Prime Minister Fisher canvassed the state premiers regarding the establishment of a soldier settlement policy for returning Australian veterans once the war was over. Sympathetic responses were received, Premier Earle of Tasmania replying that he did not see any 'insuperable difficulty' in giving effect to the suggestions outlined.[17] In July, Victoria and New South Wales announced that returned soldiers would be given preferential treatment under their respective Land Acts. However, New South Wales went one step further and outlined its intention to reserve special soldier settlement areas. The Governor of Western Australia, Major-General Sir Harry Barron, reported to the Colonial Office that immigration and especially soldier settlement were 'receiving the serious consideration of the [State] Government'.[18] South Australia, which had been formulating a policy as early as June, also announced its intentions in July but warned that its chief obstacle would be to acquire enough land. Tasmania was slower to respond. Governor Sir William Macartney was informed by his ministers that the issue would be discussed at cabinet level once the Tasmanian Parliamentary War Council was constituted.[19] Queensland, just as patriotic, was prepared to make definite arrangements assuming, however, that the imperial government co-operated by providing railway facilities to serve land designated for soldier settlement. The Colonial Office was unsure if this meant building the railways or providing the capital. In any case, a non-committal answer was despatched to Queensland's Labor government.[20]

Meanwhile, the Federal Parliamentary War Committee slowly mobilised its administrative resources. At the end of August, J. C. Watson, a former Labor Prime Minister (April-August 1904), accepted the position as the committee's honorary organiser. On 17 September, Watson released a suggested plan of action which would ensure employment and land settlement opportunities for returned soldiers after the war. 'The problem of settling returned soldiers on the land', he explained, 'is, in the main, the problem of settling the moneyless man in a calling which requires capital, and presents some aspects of peculiar difficulty.' For example, apart from in Western Australia and Queensland, good and accessible Crown land suitable for settlement was in short supply. State War Councils would have to rely on purchasing privately owned land conveniently located to railway facilities. The scarcity and high prices of live stock complicated the matter, but Watson was cheerfully confident that these obstacles could be surmounted by enlisting the benevolence of the patriotic and public-spirited community.[21]

What about the extension of the land settlement privileges to British ex-servicemen desirous of settling in Australia after the war? Preliminary indications were that nothing had been decided. South Australia reported that large areas of land were available for Australian and British ex-soldiers, but for the time being no allowance could be made for British ex-servicemen until domestic requirements had been fulfilled. The New South Wales government concurred. Privately, however, the New South Wales Minister for Lands, W. G. Ashford, hoped that his government would not extend soldier settlement privileges to British ex-servicemen. 'I trust', he implored Premier W. A. Holman, 'that no such assurance will be given so far as New South Wales is concerned.'[22] Queensland, on the other hand, had made its offer conditional on financial support from the Imperial Exchequer. Once again, Watson was confident that more land would be offered than was necessary to meet the requirements for Australian soldiers, and that the excess would be held at the disposal of discharged British ex-servicemen. 'Of these latter there is every reason to believe there will be a large number, and if they can be provided for they will represent a most desirable accession to the national strength of the Commonwealth.'[23]

Haggard arrived in Australia at the beginning of April 1916, at exactly the moment Commonwealth and state officials were formulating a repatriation policy. Although all the states had promised concessions for returning soldiers in 1915 only South Australia had acted upon its earlier promises and formulated a somewhat limited policy. The remaining states proved very reluctant to initiate their own soldier settlement programmes. Premier John Scaddan of Western Australia dismissed state responsibility altogether believing that the initiative rested solely with the Commonwealth government. Apart from preferential treatment and a few minor concessions, at the beginning of 1916 there was no general scheme which gave tangible form to the promises offered by the states in 1915. The difficulty was capital provision.

An essential prerequisite was a financial programme which clearly delineated responsibility between the Commonwealth and state governments.[24] In mid-February 1916 an inter-state conference of Premiers and Ministers for Lands was convened in Melbourne to discuss the settlement of returned men on the land. A sense of urgency shrouded the entire conference and everyone concerned agreed that the necessary repatriation machinery had to be in place before the war ended in order to minimise social distress and economic dislocation. More significantly, an immediate and substantive policy had to be formulated to meet certain social and political considerations. The Victorian government was especially apprehensive about the political implications of delay because of the harmful effects it could have on recruitment. As a result, it was important to 'settle and launch the scheme as soon as possible'. Watson stressed that in light of the recent and violent disturbances involving returned men in Melbourne it was crucial to get the returned soldiers away from the urban areas and on to the land at the earliest possible moment.[25] He advocated this approach for several reasons. Organised labour was becoming increasingly restless and began to question seriously the extent of Australia's participation in the war. Conservative politicians feared that the growing number of returned men might be tempted to join forces with organised labour as a means of voicing their own grievances which in turn would affect recruitment and morale. Something had to done to prevent this situation from developing and to make the returned man an ally rather than a potential enemy of the state. As Marilyn Lake suggests, Australia was panicked into soldier settlement by the fear of 'cities . . . congested with idle men'.[26]

The conference eventually agreed on a general plan based on the recommendations laid down by Watson and a sub-committee of the Federal Parliamentary War Committee which had presented its report in mid-January. The Commonwealth and State governments pledged their co-operation in the promotion of soldier settlement, but the states remained hesitant and cautious about their role. It was made very clear that the provision of land rested solely upon the states, therefore making them responsible for the administration and organisation of settlement policy. The Commonwealth provided the funds by means of loans to the states who, in turn advanced the money to the settler through their respective agricultural banks. Furthermore, to meet the special requirements of the soldier settler the states agreed to liberalise the conditions of repayment and charge reduced rates of interest. The establishment of training farms and settler qualification committees was stressed to ensure proper selection and screening of applicants.[27]

## British perceptions of Australian responses, 1916–20

Meanwhile, Sir Ronald Munro-Ferguson, Governor-General of Australia, was asked to monitor Haggard's progress. Munro-Ferguson was sceptical of Australian land settlement schemes and the RCI initiative. When he first heard of Grey's imperial soldier settlement scheme he informed the Colonial Office that the situation in Australia was discouraging. The depressing feature was government incompetence to promote an effective and co-ordinated land utilisation policy. It was this indifference to inter-governmental co-operation, which according to Munro-Ferguson, 'discourages agriculture and concentrates upon wasteful and wild-cat projects all the available resources of the country – and renders labour the chief burden on the State instead of its main support'.[28] The trade unions, he noted, had always been hostile toward immigration, white and coloured. Although some sections of Australian public opinion recognised the need to bolster the white population against the expanding Asian populations to the north, he believed Haggard's tour would aggravate trade union militancy against British immigration. '[T]he Unions control [immigration] Policy [which] is selfish, urban and short-sighted, arrogant, to an almost inconceivable degree. Haggard is quite likely to stir up this sleeping dog in the manger and bring this antagonism into organised activity.' More-over, Munro-Ferguson placed little confidence in Haggard's abilities or usefulness.[29]

To the surprise and chagrin of Colonial Office officials in London and several British plenipotentiaries in Australia, Haggard's tour of Australia was a resounding success.[30] Haggard knew how vital it was to score an initial success because he realised that if one of the larger states like Victoria refused assistance the others might be inclined to follow. There were anxious moments, especially in Labor-controlled New South Wales and Queensland, but the tremendous popular enthusiasm which his mission generated made it very difficult for the states not to offer some concessions to British soldier settlers.[31] 'Thanks partly to Sir Rider Haggard who found public opinion on the turn', Munro-Ferguson informed Bonar Law, 'there has been a change in public sentiment on the subject' of immigration.[32] His timing had been critical. Haggard cabled the RCI from Adelaide in May, advising that there 'is an open door throughout Australia for our ex-servicemen'. This endorsement was received at the Premiers' Conference, attended by Haggard, in which the participants resolved 'to treat . . . returned British soldiers in a manner similar to that in which returned Australian soldiers are treated'. Of course, the various promises of land and equal treatment for British soldier settlers would depend upon how the British government reacted to Australian generosity. 'It is quite a toss up, with odds against,' recorded Haggard, 'as the [British] Government or the permanent officials . . . are sure to be openly or secretly obstructive, unless distress and tumult force them to action.'[33]

Money remained the chief difficulty. 'The amount of assistance to be given to returned soldiers is only controlled by the readiness and ability of the taxpayer to find the money,' remarked the Tasmanian Minister of Lands, Works and Agriculture, J. B. Hayes.[34] True enough, but the states' attitude towards the Commonwealth's role as the financial arbi-ter varied. Naturally, they were anxious to get as much out of the federal authorities as possible. W. Hutchinson, Victoria's Minister of Crown Lands and Survey, reminded his colleagues that to make land available railways would have to be built. He hinted that the Commonwealth should assist in building the necessary communications infrastructure if the states were to be responsible for organising and administering soldier settlement. The Assistant Treasurer for New South Wales, H. C. Hoyle, pointed out that buying land would involve considerable expenditure at a time when money markets were stagnant. If the money was obtained for soldier settlement it might prove impossible to get money for other public works projects. This rational approach to the problem was contrasted with the 'strangely confident' mood of Western

Australia and Queensland who submitted expensive estimates and claimed that their ambitious projects could be fulfilled provided that the money was made available. W. D. Johnson, Minister of Lands and Agriculture for Western Australia, boasted that his state could easily settle 40,000 veterans. The difficulty would be finding them.[35]

By mid-1916 the Commonwealth faced a fast increasing war debt. The financial strain on the London money market was enormous, forcing the British Exchequer to close the market-place to small short-term borrowers such as the Australian states. The imperial government now regarded the Commonwealth as the sole Australian borrower on the London market, a view which the state governments had reluctantly accepted in the previous November. W. G. Higgs, the Commonwealth Treasurer, reassured his state colleagues that the Australian government would attempt to raise money for public works on their behalf, but he warned that the markets were extremely tight.[36] How then were the state governments going to honour their promises?

The imperial government posed the same question. It recognised that the speed of land settlement was dictated by the states' ability to borrow money to facilitate road and railway construction. Colonial Office officials were convinced that the money supply would remain tight after the war limiting the scope of these projects. In their estimation, Western Australia, Queensland and Tasmania were the only states to which substantial numbers of British ex-servicemen were likely to migrate because of a genuine desire on the part of those States to encourage their settlement.[37] Moreover, snapped one permanent official, 'the Australians are too much inclined already to spend money and energy on public works which would be better devoted to carrying on the war'.[38] But this was precisely the point which British authorities only partially recognised. As the war dragged on further limiting the sources of capital available to the states, it emerged that the states' support for soldier settlement was really an indirect means of getting development capital in wartime for a host of road, rail and irrigation schemes. A keen migration enthusiast, C. G. Wade, the New South Wales Agent-General, was even more forthright. The provision of huge sums of capital for soldier settlement and other public works projects in Australia lay squarely with the imperial authorities. The Australian Agents-General were unanimous 'that [imperial soldier settlement] was not a matter of emigration in the ordinary sense . . . but rather a matter of Empire cooperation, and that if the States welcome these ex-soldiers from the United Kingdom to the land the Imperial Government should provide money for the beneficent purpose.'[39]

There were other reservations. Farming was a heartbreaking endeavour for most settlers and the idea of an inexperienced British soldier clearing his own farm, unaccustomed to the tedious, heavy manual labour required and meanwhile carrying an enormous long-term debt, made British officials doubt the practicality of the exercise.[40] Besides, the Colonial Office insisted on maintaining a wait-and-see attitude in 1916 *vis-à-vis* post-war migration. 'We are still ignorant of what the post-war conditions will be, and whether it will be right to encourage or discourage emigration, or simply to pursue the neutral policy of the period before the war.'[41]

The promise of a farm was a valuable recruiting tool in 1916. During the state election in New South Wales, Governor Sir Gerald Strickland observed that both political parties were cultivating the votes of the returned man. Although recruitment had increased Strickland took exception to the expenditure involved in fulfilling the election promises: 'I have warned Ministers that ardour to win the General Election should not be carried too far, and I have asked them to reflect on the financial consequences of their promises.'[42] For the remainder of 1916 the political arena was dominated by the conscription referendum. This overshadowed all other issues in Australia and soldier settlement therefore remained in limbo. Tasmania and New South Wales did pass legislation but the numbers of returned men eager to take up farming were small and usually unfit. Some states, particularly Queensland, Western Australia and Victoria, came to realise that financial questions would govern a scheme's ultimate success. This was hammered home when the Commonwealth advances promised in February and May were not forthcoming because of the Commonwealth government's failure to raise the money in Britain.[43]

It was resolved at the Premiers' Conference of January 1917 that British veterans would be granted unconditionally the same soldier settlement facilities as Australians. The Commonwealth was prepared to advance a total of £2 million for soldier settlement in 1917 which comprised an advance to the states of a grant to a maximum of £500 per settler. The states complained that this figure was inadequate and wanted it raised to £700.[44] On the other hand, Munro-Ferguson questioned both the sincerity of their commitment to put British soldier settlers on an equal footing and the feasibility of the settlement projects open to British settlers. He believed that the general opinion in the dominion was that Australia was not bound to provide the same terms for overseas immigrants. Repatriation would be a costly affair and Munro-Ferguson realised that the £10 million already earmarked for public works was inadequate for Australian veterans. It was also clear that the estimates for the settler advance were too low and would soon have to be raised. He concluded that such gloomy prospects did not inspire much confidence in Australia for prospective overseas candidates.[45] 'One effect of the high cost of settlement', wrote the Governor-General, 'will be that the British Tommy will not have a look in (and) that all hope of strengthening Australia by immigration is once more lost. It sometimes seems to me as if Australia were determined to commit Harri Kari.'[46]

Munro-Ferguson was equally outspoken regarding the type of soldier settlement which Australia should undertake. He told Walter Long in late 1917 that the development by New South Wales and South Australia of large-scale wheat settlements for ex-servicemen carried enormous financial liabilities which they were ill-prepared to meet. Canada, which 'had an immense start in land settlement over Australia because of her zeal and success in that undertaking', was better prepared to implement an economically viable wheat settlement programme for returning veterans. In his opinion, intensive cultivation, which required close supervision and significant capital investment was much cheaper and better suited to Australian conditions.[47] The key to successful settlement, however, was sound financial management. But Munro-Ferguson was sceptical, despite attempts by some state governments to reduce expenditure, he complained that 'extravagance in many forms is rife'. With the election of W. M. Hughes as Prime Minister in October 1915 the Governor-General became more optimistic. 'He (Hughes) is seriously alarmed by the condition of the finances, and considers that the one object of the Government should be to restrict unnecessary expenditure so as to be able to concentrate his efforts on Repatriation and Land Settlement.'[48]

Problems associated with domestic demobilisation and repatriation absorbed the attention of both the Commonwealth and state governments between 1917 and 1920. As 1917 unfolded it grew painfully obvious that soldier settlement would become ensnared in the perennial battle over states' rights. The battle lines were drawn during the Premiers' Conference of January 1917. National defence was a Commonwealth matter and as such the Commonwealth was responsible for the recruitment, training and outfitting of Australia's troops. Naturally, this included their subsequent repatriation and Prime Minister Hughes reaffirmed this pledge to the returned soldier during the conference. But he attempted unsuccessfully to give the Commonwealth a more positive and constructive role in the formulation of a uniform soldier settlement policy which would guarantee equal treatment for the returned man nationwide. He argued that while the Commonwealth was required to find the money to pay for repatriation and soldier settlement it was entitled to know what measures the states were proposing to implement. He did not go as far as to demand that the Commonwealth should directly intervene in state administration.

Rather, he pleaded for the establishment of a central authority to monitor and co-ordinate the various state activities.

Alarmed, the states interpreted Hughes's demands as a claim for central control and would have none of it. They refused to be bullied by Hughes's financial strong-arm tactics. Land settlement was clearly a state responsibility and the premiers ensured that it, and hence soldier settlement, remained separate from the general repatriation policy.[49] Intolerant of Commonwealth interference, each state embarked on its own soldier settlement scheme. The result, according to the historical geographer J. M. Powell, 'was a bewildering variety of approaches in which the distinctive common ingredient was this jealously protected unequal alliance with the federal government.'[50] Furthermore, the fragility of the alliance was intensified as the states, who regarded the Commonwealth as simply 'a mere lending machine', tried to squeeze the maximum amount of subsidy money from the federal partner.[51]

But Hughes was no fool. He clearly recognised that the Commonwealth's negotiating position *vis-à-vis* the states on inter-government financial matters had been substantially enhanced by Britain's decision to restrict the London money market to the Commonwealth for the duration of the war. This presented Hughes with an opportunity to bring the states into line and ensure greater central control in specific policy areas such as 'national development'. During the conference he re-emphasised the precariousness of Australia's financial situation, in particular the states' desire to continue their public works programmes. 'I should like to get this matter quite clear,' he reminded his state counterparts. 'Our chances of getting money largely depend upon the extent of the facilities we will offer British soldiers to take up land in Australia.'[52] The extension of soldier settlement privileges to British ex-servicemen therefore must not be seen simply as a patriotic gesture. Politically, it was a means by which the Commonwealth government could assert itself in the federal arena. More importantly, British ex-servicemen became a vehicle which allowed access to British capital.

Meanwhile, Munro-Ferguson was concerned that the Commonwealth government was unprepared to deal with the problems of repatriation. He was extremely doubtful that the Commonwealth could provide the resources for the contemplated resettlement of 40,000 Australian soldier settlers at an estimated cost of £60 million. And he was alarmed by Senator Millen's apparent nonchalance towards the cost.[53] The initial enthusiasm for resettling British ex-servicemen had also begun to wane. South Australia, which was the first state to extend an invitation to British ex-servicemen and the first to initiate a soldier settlement policy, was the first to overturn its previous offer owing to the difficulties it experienced in establishing its own returned men. It was forced to suspend its offer to British ex-servicemen until arrangements for South Australian veterans were completed. Only Western Australia remained steadfast in its determination to assist British veterans, but even here there was concern as to how expensive the invitation would prove to be and who would pay for it.[54]

William Macartney, now Governor of Western Australia, advised the British government to treat post-war soldier settlement in Australia with 'great caution'. He warned that there were better chances, more opportunities and less risk for the small farmer in Britain than in Western Australia.[55] Much of the land targeted for development was of inferior quality and heavily forested, and would require an enormous amount of capital and back-breaking work to bring it under cultivation. According to Macartney's sources, the optimum size of a farm which ensured the best possibility of success was 1,000 acres. However, cost made this type of settlement impossible on a large scale and out of reach for the vast majority of British ex-servicemen. The governor also discounted the enthusiastic claims made by Premier James Mitchell, himself a large and successful farmer, that mixed farming could be conducted by soldier settlers in the south-west on a profitable basis with holdings of just fifty acres. Macartney doubted the soundness of Mitchell's claims because of the cost, isolation and limited amount of suitable farm land in the region.[56] On the other hand, men with capital could 'no doubt find plenty of land fit for cattle raising or sheep on a large scale but the small man would be beaten by the high cost of handling the great distances and the absence of local markets.' Labour costs and railway rates were high, exacerbated by a cumbersome, inflexible and irksome Lands administration. Without sheep or cattle rearing to ballast the farmer's revenue, agriculture was an enterprise Macartney advised British soldiers not to undertake in Western Australia. 'At the present moment the position is very unsatisfactory and contains the elements of much future trouble.' Macartney therefore advised careful scrutiny of each proposed soldier settlement scheme before ex-imperials were encouraged to come out.[57]

There was another problem, which according to Macartney and Sir H. L. Galway, Governor of South Australia, was just as serious and potentially more dangerous than extravagant state expenditure. It was the 'human' factor. 'The average returned soldier is not an easy individual to handle,' wrote Galway.[58] Macartney agreed. War service had definitely unsettled a large number of returned men which rendered them 'unfit or unwilling to resume what they now look upon as a very monotonous and dreary life, devoid of any excitement and also necessitating steady and continuous work.'[59]

## The Returned Servicemen's League and free passage

Rather than being a threat to the state, most returned soldiers were loyal, trustworthy defenders of the *status quo*. Although some returned soldiers proved to be an increasingly disruptive element in Australian society after 1915, the majority of veterans staunchly supported the Hughes government and its prosecution of the war. Represented by the influential Returned Soldiers' and Sailors' Imperial League of Australia (the national body established in 1916 out of the various state Returned Servicemen's Associations and better known as the Returned Servicemen's League or RSL), the returned soldier movement became an important ally of the government. The Commonwealth government realised the need to maintain RSL support for its wartime policies because it appreciated the RSL's importance in furthering its repatriation programme. The government's willingness to recognise the RSL as the official representative body of returned soldiers, and the announcement in September 1917 that the government was prepared to offer it financial assistance, confirmed the RSL's role as chief arbiter between the Commonwealth and the vast majority of Australian ex-servicemen.[60] In addition, the RSL was directed by men of moderate views, it being anxious to build a reputation as a responsible and disciplined body. As a result, the political power and influence of the RSL grew steadily and, although the RSL made a conscious effort to remain apolitical, it exerted a powerful political influence during recruitment drives and for the 'Yes' vote during the conscription referenda.

There was little indication of soldiers joining revolutionary Soldiers' and Workers' Councils. According to Sir F. A. Newdegate, Macartney's successor as Governor of Western Australia, '[t]he root idea of the League is to combat "Bolshevism" and individually to put the same energy into the development of Australia as their service at the Front, and be a power for good in Australia.'[61] Very few disputed the loyalty of the majority of the veterans. This was reiterated in March 1920 by the former commander of the Australian and New Zealand Army Corps, Lieutenant-General Sir W. R. Birdwood, who stated that the Australian government regarded the returned soldier as its 'best asset against [the] terrible Bolshevists'.[62] However, there were radical elements among the returned soldiery and within the RSL itself. Although essentially an organisation of the right, the government's recognition of the RSL as the official voice of the returned soldier was designed in part to keep it in line. The federal authorities also monitored the political activity of many returned soldiers, in particular, Labor's efforts to organise them. As industrial militancy spread in 1917 and class divisions widened,

Hughes's Nationalist government became increasingly worried about the loyalty of the returned man. The factionalism and disharmony among the returned soldiers in 1919 seemed to confirm the government's worst fears as some actively supported striking trade unionists.[63] However, most diggers were a force for law and order who would, if called upon, keep the peace during times of civil disobedience. Indeed, there were violent clashes involving returned soldiers representing right-wing nationalist opinion and militant trade unionists, the most serious occurring in 1918 and 1919. But the RSL worked hard to prevent violence and divert its nationalist energies into constructive not destructive channels so avoiding embarrassment to either itself or the government.[64]

It was not until 1920 that the first wave of British ex-servicemen began arriving in Australia under the auspices of the imperial government's free passage scheme. Throughout 1919 discussions between the OSC and Australian representatives focused on passage rates, fare equalisation and shipping accommodation. Once the free passage scheme was in full swing the scarcity of shipping severely hampered Australian operations and Munro-Ferguson called upon the Colonial Office to discuss the problem with the Ministry of Shipping. The Australians were anxious that if the free passage scheme were terminated at the end of 1920 hardly any advantage would have accrued to Australia. The Commonwealth government thus put tremendous pressure on Amery to extend the scheme.[65] It was this pressure in concert with British domestic considerations which gave Amery the leverage to secure Treasury agreement to an extension of the scheme for another year. When it was terminated at the end of 1921, it was Australia that received the largest share of British ex-servicemen, their wives and families. Of the final total of 86,027, Australia received 37,576 or 43.7 per cent.[66]

## Commonwealth versus states' rights

Australia proved at once the most energetic and yet the most frustrating dominion with which the British government had to deal. Unlike Canada, Australia did not have a paternalistic and centralised immigration or land settlement administration. Furthermore, it failed to develop a national soldier settlement or economic development strategy. In London, both the Commonwealth and the states possessed separate immigration offices and conducted their own propaganda campaigns to attract prospective settlers. Lack of co-operation and co-ordination between the states and the Commonwealth led to fierce competition. Friction increased as wealthier states like New South Wales and Victoria offered larger inducements, thus enticing more immigrants to the detriment of their weaker, poorer and less organised state rivals. The same was true within Australia itself. The lack of inter-state co-operation and the unnecessary competition between the states and Commonwealth spoilt any chance of formulating a harmonious national land settlement policy.[67]

Attempts were made in 1920 to rationalise the selection process in London and the immigration procedure in general. At the Premiers' Conferences held in Melbourne in May and July, Prime Minister Hughes hammered out a series of proposals, approved by the state representatives and implemented by Millen during a trip to London later that year. The Commonwealth would have full control of immigration operations overseas which included administration and organisation of transport facilities. The Commonwealth also assumed full financial responsibility. The primary objective was to settle these immigrants on the land in large settlement projects with the backing of the imperial government. The Australian Agents-General in London would form a consultive committee to co-ordinate efforts between the states and Commonwealth. Upon arrival in Australia, the states assumed complete responsibility for the settlement and employment of the immigrants; the definite and detailed financial arrangements of which would be negotiated between state and Commonwealth authorities.[68]

The immigration agreement of 1920 was a victory for Hughes in his battle with the states over control of immigration policy. He followed up this success with another in 1921 when he succeeded in pressing for Commonwealth control of loan money in agreements negotiated between Australia and Britain under the Empire Settlement Act. Proponents of states' rights grew anxious as they feared that the relationship between immigration and farm settlement forged by Hughes was a ploy to gain control over land policy, which was strictly a state jurisdiction.[69] The incident harked back to Hughes's bullying tactics at the Premiers' Conference of 1916. These anxieties increased as the Commonwealth and state governments became embroiled in the question of increased funding for the soldier settlement programme in 1920 and 1921.

At the conference of Commonwealth and state ministers held in Melbourne in October-November 1921 the states were accused by Senator Millen of evading their responsibility for ordinary settlement which they had shouldered willingly prior to the war. 'They have been making it all soldier settlement, and looking to the Commonwealth for an undue proportion of the financial responsibility associated with it,' he declared.[70] This angered the Minister of Lands for New South Wales, P.

F. Loughlin, whose state was singled out by Millen as backward precisely because it had fulfilled only 75 per cent of its soldier settlement quota. Loughlin countered by stating that if the Commonwealth wanted to share in the control of soldier settlement policy it should also shoulder some of the responsibility and not simply act as the financial broker. Hughes tried to calm the troubled waters, pointing out that the Commonwealth did not want to 'poach on State preserves'. However,

> we want to have a fair and reasonable proposition from the States. We must guarantee that the money will be used for the purpose for which it is borrowed. The Commonwealth will borrow the money, and therefore the Commonwealth must have some system of joint control.[71]

The reason for Hughes's request was the mounting cost of soldier settlement. The original figure of £28 million agreed upon in 1916 to settle 21,000 veterans at £500 per soldier settler had risen to £35 million and 23,000 men at £625 per man by 1919. During the 1920 conference the subsidy was further raised to £48 million to assist 36,000 veterans at £1,000 each.

Although eventually successful, it took a great deal of effort to bring the states into line over the financial issue. As mentioned above, part of the problem was that co-operation over repatriation and land settlement soon gave way to confrontation between the federal and state governments. The situation was exacerbated further by the huge numbers of returning servicemen who demanded immediate attention from unprepared and overstretched state authorities. Hard-pressed by the sheer number of veterans, many states were not only forced to spend more money to meet increased veteran demand, but also to request additional advances from the Commonwealth. This, in turn, intensified the conflict between the two levels of government. For example, in September 1917 the Victorian Premier asked Hughes whether the Commonwealth could advance the money necessary to purchase land for returned soldiers, as demand had become 'so great that the amount required cannot be provided at the rate at which the purchases are now being made'. The Prime Minister replied that the provision of land rested with the states. He also reminded the premier of the alternative strategy which had been discussed at the 1917 Premiers' Conference: that bonds could be used for the purchase of land thereby avoiding the initial outlay of large amounts of capital. In addition, the 'resources of the Commonwealth are very severely taxed to find the money necessary for the great and increasing obligations brought about by the war'.[72]

The problem of insufficient capital continued to haunt Australian soldier settlement in the immediate post-war period as limited financial resources were marshalled to deal with the multifarious demands of post-war reconstruction. State administrations made repeated and often desperate appeals for advances above those negotiated during the 1919 and 1920 Premiers' Conferences. For instance, in September 1921 the Victorian government pleaded for more money for its soldier settlement programme, a total of £2,285,000 over twelve months.[73] Tasmania made similar appeals. The State Treasurer, N. E. Lewis, reported to Premier Lee that extra funds were urgently needed to meet the overdraft at the Commonwealth Bank which had once more reached its limit. The overdraft had been incurred primarily in connection with the unforeseen pressures of soldier settlement. The swiftness of demobilisation had 'necessitated the expenditure of moneys upon the settlement of the returned men much earlier than was at first anticipated'. In other words, money envisaged to last for three to four years had been exhausted in less than two.[74]

The best illustration of the intense conflict between the Commonwealth and states over soldier settlement finances occurred in 1920 during and immediately after a series of top level inter-government conferences convened between May and July. In an attempt to control spending and ensure an equitable distribution of funds, it was agreed in 1919 to institute a quota system for soldier settlement in each state. Based on the number of enlistments which each state had provided for the AIF during the war, the following system was formulated (Table 1).

*Table 1  Soldier settlement quota*

| State | Enlistments | Quota |
| --- | --- | --- |
| New South Wales | 164,030 | 7,875 |
| Victoria | 112,399 | 5,395 |
| Queensland | 57,765 | 2,764 |
| South Australia | 34,959 | 1,678 |
| Western Australia | 32,231 | 1,545 |
| Tasmania | 15,458 | 743 |
| Total | 416,842 | 20,000 |

*Source*: AA CRS A571, item 23/7447, circular to state premiers by Acting Prime Minister, 14 February 1919.

These estimates, however, were to prove grossly inaccurate. As early as March 1919, South Australia's superintendent for soldier settlement, F. C. Grace, complained bitterly that unless more land was rapidly procured it was useless approving men for training since there was no land available upon completion of their training period. 'The numbers of returned men likely to apply for land will, I am confident, greatly exceed early estimates, and will reach several thousands.' By July 1920 the state

Minister of Repatriation had revised upward the total number of Australian veterans wanting to participate in South Australia's scheme to 4,000.[75] The picture was the same throughout the Commonwealth. Premier James Mitchell of Western Australia informed Acting Prime Minister Watt that his government was facing an equally difficult situation. Since taking office, Mitchell's government had settled 2,000 Australian veterans out of a total to date of 2,360, which was far beyond the quota which had been set at 1,545 in February 1919. In fact, according to the premier, between fifty and sixty men were still being settled every week. He added that his government expected to settle a further 2,500 and more money was urgently needed. 'The time has come', proclaimed Mitchell, 'when the development of this State needs the whole-hearted and sympathetic co-operation of Federal and State governments.'[76]

A number of senior officials in several states argued that the federal authorities were being obstructive, 'devising means of delay . . . even to refuse the payment of the money necessary' for settlement projects and public works programmes. Premier Mitchell was particularly scathing towards Senator Millen who, he alleged, was antagonistic towards the states, and whose attitude was 'discreditable' to Prime Minister Hughes's government and the nation.[77] The first half of 1920 witnessed continued deadlock between the states and the Commonwealth over finances. At a conference convened in Melbourne between Millen and the state Ministers of Repatriation to discuss new financial arrangements 'little progress was made', the issue being deferred to the forthcoming Premiers' Conference.[78]

It emerged, however, that some states were deliberately exceeding their authority regarding soldier settlement expenditure because of the heavy demand exerted by returning veterans (Table 2). For example, Tasmania was reprimanded by Hughes who expressed surprise that without Commonwealth authority, it had seen 'fit to enter into great obligations in expectation that the Commonwealth (would) lend the necessary sums'. Premier Lee was reminded that before a state could overspend its soldier settlement allocation it had to give the Commonwealth government an opportunity to consider additional funds. 'I feel obliged to point out that such procedure is calculated to embarrass my government, and, if followed generally by the States, might be accompanied by consequences of a serious character.'[79] Western Australia received an even stiffer rebuke from the Commonwealth government. Money had to be expended within the guidelines established at the 1919 Premiers' Conference. However, the Commonwealth government accused Western Australia of violating these agreements, and until money was expended in accordance with these agreements and proper statements were submitted to the Commonwealth, no further money would be forthcoming. 'It would appear that your Government desires to spend what it likes, and in whatever manner it likes, without due regard to the responsibility of the Commonwealth, and this view cannot be accepted.'[80]

Table 2  Soldier land settlement expenditure 1920/21

| State | Amount advanced to 15/12/20 |
| --- | --- |
| Victoria | £3,435,852 |
| New South Wales | £2,931,049 |
| Western Australia | £1,232,584 |
| South Australia | £1,183,654 |
| Queensland | £900,000 |
| Tasmania | £441,451 |
| Total | £10,124,590 |

Provision on estimates for 1920/21 – £16 million
Balance available – £5,875,410

Source:  AA CRS A571, item 22/24222.

What of the British ex-servicemen? The news was not encouraging. Owing to the overall increase in expenditure, Hughes announced that the Commonwealth would *not* now subsidise British ex-servicemen in Australian soldier settlement projects. He argued that it was unfair, given the present financial uncertainties, for these men to travel thousands of miles under promises that the Australian government could not fulfil. However, those men who had arrived or were coming under arrangements previously made would be treated under existing legislation, and Millen reiterated this point in the Australian Senate in late 1921. The government's primary obligation was to meet the demand of Australian veterans and until that obligation was fulfilled, warned Millen, Australia would be extremely cautious about making 'indiscriminate promises even to our cousins from the Old Country'.[81] What of the promise made to Haggard in 1916, asked Premier Lawson of Victoria? 'Fair and nebulous words, that is all,' replied Millen.[82] The onus therefore remained on the states to decide how many British ex-servicemen they wanted to assist.

But like the Canadians, Australians soon complained about the number of ex-imperials who arrived physically unfit and unable to undertake employment of any kind. Conversely, reports emerged that several state authorities were not looking after the ex-imperials as promised. 'So many of the men you have sent out are wandering the streets here workless and destitute', pleaded a representative of the

Imperial Service Men's Association to the Colonial Office, 'that something ought to be done.'[83] Some Australians began to wonder about the wisdom of the free passage scheme, and as the depression of 1920–22 deepened and unemployment steadily rose, popular opposition to assisted immigrants hardened, most notably within the trade union movement.

British ex-servicemen also began to question the wisdom of participating in the free passage scheme. Writing from Melbourne, William Fleming wrote that there was indeed no place like home. He and his family landed in Australia with £300 and with that sum soon obtained limited farming experience. 'But alas,' he lamented, 'Australia here [and] Australia as advertised at home are two different countries [and] very soon we had the experience but Australia had the money.' According to Fleming his was not an isolated case.

> I have met dozens of home people out here (and) they all tell the same story, a home man gets a bit of a surprise when he sees what the Lands department here call a grand farm. Try (and) imagine 100 acres of very steep country covered with dead gum trees [and] bracken 6 feet high, no roads (and) a wooden hut to live in not fit for beasts in some cases [and] the price anything from £20 to £40 an acre [and] that is what some of us has had to tackle. The typical settlers homes as advertised by Australia House are few (and) far between. Nevertheless the experience has been good (and) maybe some fairy will wave her wand (and) our ambition of having a farm on which we can settle [and] have an honest living will be realised.[84]

He warned the OSC to prepare those wishing to take up soldier settlement blocks in Australia of the possible disappointments. Settlers should not be duped into believing the propaganda or pronouncements of Australian government ministers and their officials and it was essential for prospective emigrants to 'get in touch with the men who have had the real test [of] . . . working and slaving to make a living on the land.'[85]

There were many others like Fleming. S. G. Blythe, a former private in the 1st Queens regiment who emigrated to Australia in April 1921, wrote to Premier Lee of Tasmania stating that he now wanted to return home. Regretting his participation in the scheme, he noted that his original intention had been to give his children a chance to the see the world and to better their prospects. Now unemployed, Blythe had also been diagnosed as having a heart condition which precluded him from heavy manual labour. Destitute, he pleaded with state officials that his only salvation was a return passage to England for himself and his family. He concluded that because Australian veterans received priority in employment and settlement, 'it is hopeless for an ex-Imperial soldier'.[86]

Nine months later, having received no response from the Tasmanian government, Blythe vented his spleen: 'I have been greatly deceived and my life blighted' he told the OSC. He thought it extremely unfair for a man who had fought in South Africa during the second Anglo-Boer War, and had served five years with the Colours between 1914 and 1919, three of them in France, that the authorities refused to pay his passage home. The Tasmanian authorities were unimpressed. According to their records, Blythe, a vulcanite turner by profession, had been offered a position as a caretaker at a golf course but did not get it because he did not 'understand the game'. Soon after this, he found a job at the Cadbury's chocolate factory in Hobart, but gave it up after just a fortnight because the work was too demanding. Once again, he tried the caretaker's job at the same golf course but left ten weeks later claiming that the long hours and working seven days a week was too much. Premier J. A. Lyons, Lee's successor, concluded that temperamentally, Blythe was 'unsuited to altered conditions which every migrant must necessarily face'.[87]

Leslie Brookes was another case in point. He had forfeited his pension to pay for his family's passage to Australia. 'I was led to understand that there was someone this end to put me right when I arrived but I was disappointed.' He had been in Tasmania for fifteen months but during that time had only worked a few weeks. Out of work, with a wife in hospital and two children to support, he requested a return passage: 'as we can starve just as well in our own country as in a strange one'.[88] The situation was equally desperate for wounded British veterans like Stanley Ottley and H. G. Day, men who had recovered sufficiently to be declared fit for a free passage but who became incapacitated when their health deteriorated after their arrival in Australia. What little pension they had was grossly inadequate, and although both men were receiving charitable relief they were anxious to return. 'I have practically given my life for the Empire', explained Ottley, '[and] at the present time being ill in bed due to wounds . . . [am] stranded here in a strange land amongst strange people trying to exist . . . on a pittance.'[89] Fortunately for Ottley and his family, the state government relented and paid for their return passage. Not so for the young Harry Day. Suffering from melancholy, he was admitted to the Hobart general hospital where he tragically committed suicide.[90]

In light of the growing number of complaints and demands for return passage, the Tasmanian authorities immediately tightened their immigration procedures, especially those concerning British ex-servicemen. The state government informed A. H. Ashbolt, its Agent-

General in London, that it could not assist any more destitute British ex-servicemen or help them return to the United Kingdom. For it had been only under very exceptional circumstances that assistance was given to Ottley in the first place. Ashbolt regretted these new instructions and hoped that the conditions which necessitated them would soon pass so that Tasmania could once again 'avail itself of the opportunity for increasing its population largely at the expense of the British Government'.[91]

The problem of stranded and destitute British ex-service migrants was not confined to Tasmania. All states reported an increase in hardship cases and demanded assistance from the Commonwealth and imperial governments. One of the biggest complaints lodged by the states concerned the large numbers of British veterans with 'permanently broken health'.[92] Why were they being given free passage in the first place? Greater supervision and closer scrutiny in London was needed. British observers, such as Field Marshal Lord Haig, were equally concerned about the plight of British veterans, particularly those in Australia, and condemned the inadequate arrangements for settlers overseas. Feelings ran high, Haig strongly advised British ex-servicemen not to emigrate to the dominions until, as he stated, 'the Dominion Governments have set their own house in order'.[93]

## Private enterprise and scandal in Victoria

Assistance under the free passage scheme stopped at the end of 1921, although people were allowed to sail until March 1923 provided their applications had been submitted prior to the December 1921 deadline. However, this did not stop British ex-servicemen from coming to Australia nor did it prevent them from participating in specific settlement schemes. There were two particularly scandalous schemes, one initiated by the private company Australian Farms Limited (AFL) and the other by the Victorian government. Settlers were enticed to a land which promised easy returns, bountiful harvests and some of the best supervision, settler support and aftercare possible. Instead, they found an ill-equipped company which had no idea of how to run a settlement operation. Even worse, they encountered an uncaring, uncooperative state government and the majority of settlers experienced years of hardship and deprivation. Despite the award of compensation for some participants in 1933, it was a hollow victory when set against the tragic circumstances these people had endured.

Headquartered in Melbourne and founded in 1912, the AFL wanted to tap what it thought was an excellent type of settler – the public school man and the British ex-officer with limited capital. Its secretary, R. V.

Billis, was despatched to London in late 1919 to seek moral and financial support not only from the imperial government, but from British shipping and banking interests in Australia, the small but influential Imperial Ex-Officers' Association and the Public Schools' Association.[94]

The AFL's settlement strategy was two-fold. Openings were available in Victoria for 100 ex-officers on prepared fruit-growing allotments under irrigation. Applicants were required to possess a minimum of £500 and accept company supervision until they were well established on their holding. The company also reserved the right to decide what types of fruit tree and vine were planted on at least 40 per cent of each holding and controlled the type of instruction each settler received. The AFL stated that these measures were necessary to ensure the production of sufficient quantities of specific fruit on a regular basis. Provisions were also made by the company for the packing and marketing of produce. Similarly, it maintained that it would co-operate closely with its clients, but, if possible, would not interfere with the interests of individual settlers.[95]

The cost of a fifteen-acre plot was £1,275 of which £700 was due in the first six months of operation. The remainder was to be paid over a period of twenty years at no more than 7 per cent interest. The company recognised that it took at least three years for a holding to start bearing fruit. It therefore decided to advance the sum of £75 per annum for living expenses to each settler for a period of three years. Applicants were reminded that they were eligible for assistance under the Victorian soldier settlement scheme.[96]

The second part of the AFL's settlement operation was wool production and sheep fattening on large grazing areas established in Victoria and New South Wales, and there were additional plans to expand grazing operations into South and Western Australia. The minimum capital requirement was £1,500 with each estate accommodating between ten and twenty-five men. A skilled supervisor was allocated to each estate and the company agreed to supply the equipment, buy and sell stock, and arrange for shearing, wool grading and packing. It was estimated that each settler could operate between 600 and 800 sheep. A series of financial arrangements and repayment schedules were outlined including a supervision fee of £50 per annum.[97]

Billis succeeded in getting the backing of the Ex-Officers' Association which committed £12,500 to the venture. In May the joint committee of the OSC and the National Relief Fund (a fund raised from public subscriptions during the war to help people who suffered material damage as a result of war) earmarked £25,000 for the benefit of ex-servicemen accepted by the company.[98] Billis was pleased, but Sir George Murray, a member of the National Relief Fund, was not. He pointed out that the Fund had exposed itself to criticism since a grant had been made to a company whose business it was to make a profit. He quickly denied responsibility on the grounds that he was absent when the decision was made.

The Treasury voiced its displeasure on the same grounds and emphasised the importance for the OSC not to commit the government to the scheme. Macnaghten replied testily that it was satisfying to know that the Treasury was taking an active interest in OSC business. He tried to reassure the Treasury, however, that the company commanded an exceptional measure of support throughout Australia. Among its 'special sponsors' was W. A. Watt, the Commonwealth Treasurer.[99] As Amery informed the shipping magnate, Lord Inchcape, Billis and Watt represented the 'Imperial School of thought in Australia which is engaged in combatting the powerful Bolshevist and Sinn Fein elements' in the dominion.[100] Here was a crucial admission. Amery and the OSC were favourably inclined to the company not simply because of its settlement plans but because of the political benefits involved. Macnaghten reinforced this idea.

> It is generally recognised that the extreme labour, Sinn Fein and Catholic elements are a serious menace in Australia. We may hope – and there is some evidence – that the extremists are losing ground there as here. The OSC hope that a forward settlement policy may have a considerable effect in weakening the extreme elements.[101]

Billis left Britain in July 1920 thoroughly satisfied with the support and co-operation he had received and the first group of four settlers arrived in Western Australia in September. At first, the state government was unreceptive to the idea of a private company encroaching on what it believed was a government responsibility. J. D. Connolly, Agent-General for Western Australia, thought the money was better spent through a dominion government rather than a private company no matter how altruistic its motives. Why should a company receive preferential treatment over a sovereign state? These objections were quickly cast aside as Premier Mitchell, with a modicum of pressure from Governor Newdegate, welcomed the advent of the company and assured it that the government would assist its operations in every possible way.[102]

It was in Victoria, however, where the company laid its most ambitious plans establishing two types of settlement for two different groups of ex-officer. The settlements at Melville Forest, Leslie Manor and Kongbool were set up as co-operative sheep stations designed to attract ex-officers from the Indian Army. With assistance from the imperial government and the Ex-Officers Association a fruit-growing settlement was established at Tresco West aimed at settling ex-officers from the British Army.[103]

It was in 1921 that Edwin Montagu, Secretary of State for India, first approached the AFL concerning the settlement of surplus India Army officers in Victoria. Both the company and the Victorian government were eager to attract these men. They were young, healthy, well-educated and possessed the necessary financial means. For the Victorian authorities these officers were a particularly important source of emigrant because they would be the foundation of a new and ambitious settlement programme currently under negotiation with the British government. Major Alan Currie, a retired officer and a director of the AFL, was despatched to India on behalf of the company and with the tacit approval of the Victorian government. His mission was to travel to all the major military centres in India to generate interest and promote the benefits of settlement in Victoria. As a trial exercise, he was to recruit a minimum of 200 settlers.[104]

Currie's mission was a success. He not only caught the attention of retiring officers but he also succeeded in attracting a number still on active service. For its part, the Victorian government agreed to make land available to the settlers through the AFL. The company undertook to provide housing, stock, implements and training for a three-year period. It guaranteed that the settlement estates would be well watered and possessed all the necessary outbuildings, fencing and other suitable improvements. Furthermore, 'no land will be offered which has not been inspected and approved by the Company whose Directors are experts in land values. Under this scheme settlers are not only assured of a first-class training, but will receive returns from the outset'. The ease with which settlers could turn an immediate profit was substantiated by Currie who proclaimed that settlers were assured of a return of between £500 and £1,000 per annum.[105]

Currie returned to Melbourne to discover that in fact the Victorian government had failed to honour its promises and had not acquired the properties as arranged. The situation was urgent as the first group of settlers were due to arrive in September 1922. The government immediately offered to purchase alternative properties, two of which were distinctly inferior to the original estates of Woolongoon and Challicum. The government admitted that the substitute estates of Melville Forest and Kongbool could support only one sheep for every three acres as opposed to much better figures for the original estates. Currie explained the grim situation to the settlers, admitting that the land was not that upon which he had based his projections and he would understand should they decide to refuse it.[106] The men, however, were victims of a *fait accompli*. They had invested heavily, committing most if not all of their compensatory gratuity in the form of a bond to the company. They certainly could not return to the army in view of Britain's commitment to military retrenchment. What choice did they have but to stick it out?

The estates were hurriedly purchased in late November 1922 but they were not subdivided into individual allotments until June 1923. When they were at last subdivided the Victorian government charged each settler an adjustment fee of £200 stating that until the allotment was surveyed the land was still the property of the government. The settlers cried foul but the stubborn W. McIver, state director of the Closer Settlement Board (CSB), ignored them.[107] This was not the final setback as, though it was originally envisaged as a joint venture, the Victorian government was forced to withdraw its support shortly afterwards. An amendment to the Closer Settlement Act of 1922, enacted in 1923, precluded the Victorian government from co-operating with any private organisation in connection with settlement work. This turn of events severely hampered the company's efforts and forced it to limit its operations to land already acquired. It was an ominous start to what became an ill-fated venture.

During the three-year period in which the AFL administered the co-operative-based sheep rearing estates there were profits to be shared but not at the levels originally envisaged by Currie. The price of wool had remained high and because a return was generated the settlements were considered a success. Problems surfaced immediately, however, when the company's agreement expired and the estates were dissolved. Buoyant wool markets had disguised the fact that the settlers had not acquired the proper practical experience in sheep raising and breeding. Once cast adrift they could not cope and the subsequent drop in wool prices compounded the hardship and destitution.[108] Furthermore, the AFL was liquidated shortly after the termination of its agreement in 1926. The Victorian government agreed to place the settlers under the supervision of the CSB but for those who had survived enough was enough. Many felt that they could neither work with nor under the draconian CSB and they refused the government's terms and left. Others sought compensation.

Take the case of ex-India Army Captain B. Godly, a Melville Forest settler. At considerable personal expense to the young settler it took the company eight months to place him on his holding. He testified to the ridiculous adjustment charges the state government insisted on extracting from its new settlers. Godly considered these fees were the single largest cause of disappointment among the ex-India Army settlers and fostered bitter resentment among the settlers who grew frustrated because they had no way of airing their grievances. Even more galling was their characterisation in certain sections of the Australian press: 'We are dubbed by certain rags as "Society pets", morning coated Farmers etc., whilst Cartoons have appeared of us in Silk hats dipping sheep and so on.'[109]

Similar complaints were voiced by settlers at Kongbool, probably the poorest and worst off of the three AFL sheep properties. The acreage was just too small to support the number of settlers and their stock. Holdings were abandoned and those settlers who remained eked out a living, all the while complaining that the pledges given at the time of their settlement, notably regarding advance preparation, had not been fulfilled.[110] At Leslie Manor, established as a mixed farming proposition, settlers were in a similar predicament and again testified to the inadequacies of the scheme. Captain C. R. Jessop was struck by the AFL's determination to push the Melville Forest operation and ignore the promotion of Leslie Manor. In his opinion, Leslie Manor was better situated for sheep rearing because the general quality of the land was better. His criticisms were directed at the company. There was no organised system of instruction or demonstration and the settlement had not been prepared in advance. The estate's management also left much to be desired. For example, the first manager on the estate was ignorant of cultivation techniques; he was even unable to adjust a plough or a reaper and binder. The second manager was incompetent and lost 100 sheep in one day by dipping them in unfavourable weather. The third manager was no better. When entrusted by Jessop to purchase 500 sheep he returned with a shipment of tick-infested animals which had to be dipped out of season at the risk of considerable loss.[111] Although Jessop admitted that he was lucky to have selected a good allotment he was one of the first settlers to leave once his property had been revalued.

The irrigated fruit farming operation at Tresco West suffered a similar fate. It was described by one Victorian MLA, F. E. Old, an experienced farmer who championed the cause of many impoverished soldier farmers, as 'one of the most ghastly failures perpetrated on unsuspecting settlers'.[112] As with wool, the markets for fruit were extremely depressed. This was compounded by the fact that orchards needed time to mature. Hence, the financial burden proved enormous in the early stages of fruit farming because it demanded a large injection of capital with little or no return. But the area was anyway unsuitable for profitable fruit production. In 1925 the majority report of the Victorian Royal Commission on soldier settlement attributed the low citrus yield across the region to poor drainage, but Old went further in his condemnation of the project. The entire settlement was unsuitable for irrigation because of the soil's high salinity. It may have been a legitimate endeavour but it was a proposition founded on the wrong principles. The AFL directors knew nothing of land settlement, particularly irrigation, and therefore never gave their clients a proper chance. Another problem was poor supervision and management. By March 1927 only twenty-two of the original sixty-two ex-British Army officers were still settled or employed on Tresco West in rural occupations. Twenty-one had left their holdings for more secure employment in business and commerce, five had returned to Britain, three had emigrated to New Zealand, four had joined the Royal Australian Air Force and the local constabulary, six had disappeared and one was dead.[113] The situation in Victoria worsened.

In 1923 Victoria embarked upon its own overly ambitious project to establish 10,000 British settlers on their own farms. The scheme aimed to attract men who possessed approximately £1,000 of their own capital and the Victorian government once again looked to India for potential investors. The projected cost, excluding passage, was £3 million. The Commonwealth government raised the loan and the interest was shared equally between the imperial, federal and state governments. The first stage of the programme was to settle 2,000 immigrants and their dependents, and state authorities estimated that they would have to provide an additional £1,500 per farm in the way of loans repayable under generous terms. The settlers were promised complete financial control and twelve months practical experience before taking over their holding.[114]

The scheme was an absolute fiasco. Only 814 British settlers, of which 75 per cent were ex-servicemen, entered Australia between 1923 and 1927. After examining the districts where land was available, 455 decided not to embark upon the venture.[115] The biggest complaint was that the price of land was too high and that there was not much freedom of choice. Fears were raised by William Bankes Amery, Britain's migration representative in Australia (1925–28), that British settlers tended to receive blocks of land rejected or abandoned by native Australians. His claim was substantiated as more complaints arrived condemning the land as uneconomic, second-rate and unsuitable for agriculture. Of the remaining 361, only a paltry fifty achieved partial success.[116]

Some settler accounts have survived giving a startling picture of what many ex-officers in this particular scheme encountered. In September 1923 Frank Thompson, a former lieutenant in the Royal Engineers, settled on the Red Cliffs estate, a soldier settlement scheme originally established for Australian veterans. The land was over-valued, not properly drained and therefore unsuitable for fruit farming. Thompson charged that he did not receive equal treatment and did not receive wages during the first two years of operation. The four acres planted in citrus yielded nothing but poor returns and an £800 deficit. The remaining twelve acres were much more promising but only because Thompson, at enormous expense, drained the land. Land purchased at £20 per acre had cost an additional £15 per acre to drain.

And what had he achieved? In four years he had produced sixty-eight and a half tons of dried fruit, twenty-five tons of currants and forty-three and one-half tons of sultanas. He had worked the holding for six years and estimated that his financial return over the same period was a mere £120. All he had to show for his hard work and determination was a bank statement showing a debit of £500. During 1927–28 the state board of inquiry visited his holding and agreed that it was over-capitalised and advised revaluation. The absurdity of the revaluation process, according to Thompson, was that one of the valuers was a former area supervisor who had given him a steady stream of misleading advice. Even more damning was Thompson's claim that during the three years Mr Brynes was area supervisor he had visited him once for three minutes! For a state that prided itself on its claims of expert advice and close supervision this was indeed damaging. But Thompson's censure was principally directed against the conduct of certain individuals and he admitted that he found no specific reason to complain against the Victorian government.[117]

Another ex-officer, W. H. Voyle, certainly had grounds to complain. He arrived in the wheat-growing Mallee district in 1925, an area targeted for soldier settlement during the war. It became painfully obvious to him that the area could not grow wheat in sufficient quantities, 'and that the settlers had been made the victims of an unjustifiable and disastrous experiment'. He charged that the Victorian government was guilty of 'a colossal blunder and sheer incompetence' and that they had deliberately gambled with the lives of innocent men, women and children. Similarly, he insisted that the state government bear the costs – moral, legal and financial – of official misrepresentation and inefficiency. What really annoyed him was the obstinacy, inflexibility and lack of compassion displayed by the Victorian Lands department. He had sunk all his capital into the venture but the two years of hard work on his 727-acre block had been all for nought. Despite encouraging reports from the regional inspectors, who noted Voyle's good progress and hard work, when his financial circumstances worsened the state authorities were not prepared to increase their assistance. 'I earnestly ask for your indulgence and sympathy,' pleaded Voyle in March 1928. 'My record and a report of my progress made will I think, bear witness that we have not been idle.' The direct appeal to McIver failed. 'Horses can, apparently be maintained,' exclaimed the frustrated settler, 'but human beings are being denied the necessities of life.' Voyle was not alone in his condemnations.[118]

Charges of misrepresentation and breach of faith were levelled against the Victorian government by the remaining survivors of both the AFL and government schemes. Legal proceedings were launched in 1927 with the full support of the British and Indian governments. Victoria's Governor, Baron Somers, reported to the Dominions Office that nothing short of a Royal Commission would solve the parlous state of affairs in Victoria.[119] But he warned his superiors that it would be difficult to resolve the matter as the state politicians had quickly absolved themselves from any responsibility on the grounds that some of the ex-officer settlements were conducted under the auspices of a private company and were therefore outside the parameters of the Empire Settlement Act. If there was to be an investigation into the entire gamut of settlement issues in Victoria, explained McIver of the CSB, it was strictly a state matter. The imperial and Commonwealth governments were politely but effectively told to mind their own business.[120]

Pressure for a full and impartial enquiry mounted throughout 1927 and 1928. Governor Somers reported that the new Labor government was growing increasingly uncomfortable under the strain of persistent pressure, and the unpopular McIver was doing his utmost to wriggle out of the sticky situation. Determined to press home the claims of British ex-officers, both Somers and Bankes Amery refused to give up. Lord Lovat, Parliamentary Under-Secretary of State for the Dominions, was equally adamant that the matter be properly and carefully investigated and that a satisfactory conclusion be obtained. He reminded them: 'the complete failure of this scheme would have unfortunate repercussions on the migration to Australia as a whole.'[121] However, the damage to future assisted migration programmes had already been done. By 1927 animosity ran so high that according to one Colonial Office report the Labor governments of Victoria and New South Wales were 'anxious to hinder British settlement in Australia'.[122]

In the face of mounting pressure the Victorian government finally relented and appointed a board of inquiry to investigate the complaints of the ex-Indian Army officers. Somers was far from satisfied. He cabled London that the membership of the board of inquiry was weighted heavily in favour of the CSB. When the inquiry's findings were completed its report indicated a strong claim for compensation against the state government. Unfortunately for the settlers the board had no power to make recommendations and it appeared that the issue would be shelved.[123] Disappointed, Somers maintained the pressure on the Labor Premier E. J. Hogan to take more direct action and appoint a Royal Commission. The government remained intransigent and ignored the pleas for compensation from the settlers and the imperial authorities.

It was not until Hogan regained the premiership in December 1929 that constructive steps were taken. In 1930 a Royal Commission was finally appointed, although the actual recommendations were carried out by a Nationalist government. In its report released in 1933 it found that of the 311 complaints lodged by the British settlers all but seventeen were justified. The findings were willingly accepted by the state government and compensation was paid to 284 claimants, of whom 116 promptly returned to Britain. The cost of settling fifty British settlers and compensating approximately 300 more was an astronomical £5 million.[124] However, compensation was granted only to those British immigrants who been assisted by the Victorian government under the auspices of the 1923 settlement agreement. Those men, such as the ex-Indian Army officers who had been settled by the AFL were excluded because the British government had not been financially involved in the scheme.[125]

What had gone wrong with Australian soldier settlement and the attempts to establish a permanent and productive landed imperial yeomanry? The fact that 71 per cent of Australia's soldier settlers were still on the land in 1929 would suggest a successful policy. However, these figures were tabulated before the Great Depression. As Marilyn Lake's analysis for Victoria demonstrates, the dire economic circumstances of 1929–33 did take their toll of that state's soldier settlers. Of the 11,140 who originally embarked upon the scheme, approximately 60 per cent or 6,677 had abandoned farming by 1938. According to one Commonwealth government report 1,891 Victorians had abandoned their properties in 1929. By 1932 this figure had risen to 5,756, an increase of 3,865 in just four years (Table 3).[126]

Table 3   Australian soldier settlers remaining in 1929

| State | Original settlers | Remaining (1929) | |
|---|---|---|---|
| Victoria | 11,140 | 9,249 | 83% |
| New South Wales | 9,302 | 6,649 | 71% |
| Queensland | 6,031 | 3,617 | 60% |
| Western Australia | 5,030 | 3,345 | 70% |
| South Australia | 4,082 | 2,735 | 67% |
| Tasmania | 1,976 | 777 | 39% |
| Total | 37,561 | 26,591 | 71% |

Source: Pike report, CPP 1929, 2, part 2, Appendix XI, p. 59.

Obviously, economic factors played a key role. Fuelled by wartime speculation and post-war inflation the states were forced to buy land at extremely high prices. The shortage of livestock, building materials and farm equipment compounded the problem by raising operating costs. Those soldier settlers who were encouraged to settle in fruit-growing areas or irrigation settlements had the extra burden of having to buy specialised equipment for which they had no training. Besides the need for additional capital, the problem with these types of settlement lay in the exceptionally long period to be endured before settlers could realise a return on their investment when compared with the rapid rewards for soldier settlers who took up grain farming or sheep rearing. But it was the depression of 1920–22 which exposed the vulnerability of the entire policy. Administrators incorrectly assumed that the prices for primary products would remain buoyant throughout the initial stages of soldier settlement allowing the settler to reap the benefits of high prices and establish his operations on a strong footing. However, plummeting commodity prices hit many soldier settlers just as they were moving into full production. The result was that the soldier settlers were caught in a vicious cost-price squeeze which forced many to abandon their farms and condemned the survivors to a long period of indebtedness.[127]

Many of the settlers were hopelessly unsuited for the heavy manual labour required. The rush to satisfy as many applicants as quickly as possible led to poor settler selection. Veterans returned from Europe with a variety of physical and mental disorders which recurred or were aggravated by intense physical exertion and the British veterans had the added handicap of trying to farm in a foreign, often hostile environment with new and different techniques. The root of the problem, however, was the haste, and the general lack of forethought which characterised the implementation of Australia's soldier settlement policy. Munro-Ferguson's prediction that the Australian government's lack of pre-planning would slow down the repatriation process and hamper post-war reconstruction was correct. In 1925 the Victorian government, in its report of the Royal Commission on soldier settlement, admitted that it was 'common knowledge that there was a great rush of returned men in 1919 and 1920, and the machinery for handling them was taxed to the breaking point.'[128] What was worse for the British ex-service settlers was that they arrived at the peak of the screening process, adding to the strain, and at the time when land prices were at their highest. The promises of expert supervision and agricultural training never materialised. There was a glaring absence of a variety of preparatory scientific surveys on land reserved for soldier settlement. This resulted in the development of marginal land by inexperienced settlers with little or no knowledge of soil conditions, climate, drainage and other physical, seasonal or economic characteristics of the settlement region.[129]

The blame for the 'failure' of Australia's soldier settlement policy must lie with the Commonwealth and state governments. The decentralised nature of Australia's soldier settlement administration which led to the constant bickering over areas of Commonwealth-state jurisdiction, and the states' parasitic attitude toward Commonwealth subsidies 'exposed the fragility of [Australia's] immature federal system'.[130] It was impossible to apportion blame between the two levels of government and according to Justice Pike's report of 1929 which examined the losses due to soldier settlement, the relative responsibilities of the Commonwealth and state governments remained unclear.[131] The rationale behind the entire policy also became confused. What had begun as a debt of gratitude became an expensive and politically motivated exercise to create another sturdy yeoman class on Australian soil. In reality, the attempt to establish a new yeomanry in Australia was based on romantic illusions of the past generated by over-optimistic and misplaced assumptions of the potential of the returned man.[132]

What of the imperial element? Australia proved to be as enthusiastic as the rest of the empire in its attempt to resettle British ex-servicemen. But its eagerness to participate also highlighted and reinforced both Australia's dependence on British investment and the closer, less diversified commercial relationship between the two countries. According to sketchy official sources, Australia settled more British ex-servicemen than any other dominion, between one and two thousand in all, but at a greater financial and social cost.[133] Australian insistence that land alone held the key to continued prosperity and its refusal to give up the yeoman ideal made for some very extravagant experiments in the face of a changing imperial relationship. It was an expensive and trying lesson.

## New Zealand: a most disappointing result

The most patriotic and 'British' of the dominions, New Zealand was the first dominion to initiate and enact soldier settlement legislation in October 1915. The Discharged Soldier Settlement Act empowered the Minister of Finance to raise £50,000 for settlement purposes. In a series of amendments between 1916 and 1919 the initial sum was increased to £1.5 million. The Bill was to provide for two types of soldier, those who returned fit and well and those who returned partially disabled but able to do light farm work. Legislators envisaged settlement on Crown land and on land obtained by the government under the Land for Settlement Act of 1908. In 1917 an amendment was passed extending financial assistance to soldier settlers to help them clear, fence and drain land. It also provided them with assistance to purchase private farm land and gave the Minister of Lands authority to reserve land in urban areas for the construction of veterans' housing. More importantly, soldier settlers were not allowed to transfer lands acquired under the scheme for ten years, except with the permission of the local Land Board and the Minister of Lands. This measure was incorporated to inject an element of stability and prevent settlers from selling their holdings to hungry land speculators eager to turn a quick profit and benefit from wartime inflation.[134]

W. F. Massey's Reform government, which was heavily dependent upon rural support, was wholeheartedly committed to helping the returned man. Its quick legislative response was proof of its intent. When the Prime Minister, acting in his dual capacity as Minister of Lands, introduced the 1915 legislation, he equated New Zealand's efforts with those of ancient Rome. Just as the Roman legionnaire possessed the patriotic traditions of Rome, claimed Massey, it was New Zealand's soldier citizens who were the modern day heirs to those most noble and democratic ideals.[135] There was a great deal of discussion and support for the soldier settlement legislation right across the New Zealand political spectrum. However, numerous speakers warned that the land had to be purchased at a fair and decent price. They did not want the soldiers to be permanently dependent on borrowed money. Nor did they want to see these men gouged by profiteers demanding high prices for land that could make any type of settlement prohibitive.[136]

Land settlement was a prominent feature of party politics in New Zealand, and after World War I was seen as an indispensable component of its reconstruction strategy. In this respect, official attitudes were similarly centralist to those of their Canadian counterparts, and, like Australia, involved the active support of the local conservative-orientated Agricultural and Pastoral Associations. Sir Francis Bell, who administered New Zealand's land policy during several of Massey's absences in London during the war, was especially aware of the government's responsibility. He steadfastly refused to open up any Crown land which was suitable for civilian settlement, insisting that it be reserved for ex-servicemen.[137] In 1919–20 soldier settlement reached its peak. Prior to demobilisation, approximately 1,700 New Zealand ex-servicemen were authorised to settle on 508,000 acres at a cost of £1.15 million. Two years later the government responded to veteran demand and settled 9,041 ex-servicemen on 3.1 million acres at a cost of £12 million. Despite the enormous expenditure, it has been claimed that the Massey government failed to cope with the volume of returning veterans, exposing it to hostile attacks from the press, the New Zealand Farmers' Union and an impatient New Zealand Returned Soldiers' Association (NZRSA).[138]

These critics bitterly complained that the government was wasting money buying cultivated land at highly inflated prices when large areas of Crown land remained undeveloped. Indeed, the scale of land speculation in New Zealand during World War I was frenetic. It was estimated that half of the rural land in the dominion changed hands between 1916 and 1924.[139] What was the government to do? Crown land suitable for agricultural development was scattered, isolated and scarce. Committed to reserving its meagre land resources for New Zealand veterans, Massey's government was forced to buy private land at prices inflated by wartime speculation in order to meet veteran demand. Clearly, Massey's administration faced a dilemma. It was a conflict between the government's desire to take advantage of the agricultural prosperity fostered by secure wartime markets on the one hand, and the huge financial burden of buying land at grossly inflated prices on the other.[140]

What were the implications for British ex-servicemen wanting to emigrate after the war? The granting of equal treatment to ex-imperials was restricted by New Zealand's limited resources and its commitment to its own troops. Only after these claims had been honoured was the New Zealand government willing to consider applications from British veterans. During the Haggard mission, Massey reiterated this point. Haggard recorded that Massey was most sympathetic and generally eager to help but far from definite on the form or substance of the assistance to be offered.[141] When hostilities ended and the free passage scheme was formulated the New Zealand government once again stressed its desire to help British ex-servicemen settle in New Zealand on the same terms as New Zealand veterans, but only after New Zealand claims had been satisfied. Furthermore, it would not allow the conveyance of British ex-servicemen to New Zealand until all New Zealand troops had been repatriated. And at that point, it warned there was a strong possibility that there would be no government land available beyond the needs of domestic requirements.[142]

A shortage of shipping throughout 1920–21 further aggravated a frustrating situation for prospective British ex-service migrants and a dominion keen on restocking its Anglo-Saxon heritage. There was another, even more serious problem: a severe housing shortage in 1920 that threatened to stifle all British migration to the dominion. The problem became more acute in 1921 as the world's economy slumped, inflation spiralled and unemployment sharply increased. In March 1921, the Massey government informed the OSC that after examining New Zealand's commercial, industrial and financial outlook in relation to the depressed labour market, the free passage scheme would have to be curtailed. The OSC was instructed 'that no approved Imperial Overseas Settlement applicant, whether single or married, be allowed to proceed to New Zealand unless employment and accommodation await him on arrival.'[143] This was a critical blow to those who advocated an unrestricted 'white' immigration policy. There was unrelenting hostility in some sections of New Zealand society, including elements of the NZRSA towards the entry and influx of Asiatics. Equally strident warnings emanated from the same quarters predicting that, from a racial and strategic view to limit the flow of immigrants from Britain was at once dangerous, unnecessary and unpatriotic.[144] Cooler heads prevailed, however. After a vigorous debate at the 1922 NZRSA annual conference the association agreed to support the government's temporary restriction of the free passage scheme. The recent dumping of hundreds of unemployed, homeless and destitute ex-imperials in Auckland emphasised the necessity for such action. Confident that the economic downturn was a passing phase, the NZRSA endorsed the government's policy.[145] At the conclusion of the free passage scheme New Zealand had received 15.5 per cent or 13,349 British ex-servicemen and their families.[146]

Land offered for civilian settlement remained limited throughout 1921 as the New Zealand authorities maintained their policy of preference for the returned man. However, there were signs that demand among ex-servicemen, especially for pastoral properties, was slackening. The fall in wool and mutton prices made soldier settlement less attractive thereby allowing the government to throw open previously reserved areas to civilian settlement. By January 1922 there was little demand for any class of farm land by ex-servicemen and the proclamations which had reserved these specific settlement areas were annulled. The worsening depression, however, made civilian settlement less attractive and the disposal of the previously reserved 340,000 acres difficult.[147]

The depression of 1920–22 and the consequent fall in prices of primary produce severely tested the resolve and determination of the bulk of the settlers, particularly the pastoralists. The government found it necessary to postpone soldiers' rent payments and give interest relief on their mortgages. Nevertheless, it confidently expected prices would recover in the near future and it was willing to temporarily forego payments due from soldier settlers in an attempt to relieve the financial pressure. The NZRSA were far from satisfied and demanded a full inquiry into the plight of the soldier settlers. As the number of distressed cases multiplied and agricultural prices failed to recover the government appointed special Boards of Inquiry in 1923 to report on the matter.[148]

The Boards of Inquiry conducted a comprehensive investigation but mistakenly concluded that the depression was the principal cause of settler failure. Well before the economic downturn many soldier settlers were experiencing severe difficulties largely attributable to inflated land prices. The depression simply 'hastened and accentuated a process already begun'.[149] The New Zealand government remained steadfast in its determination to help the soldier settler and its response to the crisis was similar to that of the other dominions. However, the generous gesture of postponing rent and interest payments during the depression, and keeping the number of foreclosures to an absolute minimum, was unheard of in the other dominions. It was evident, however, that despite an exceptionally sympathetic stance a more permanent form of relief was needed. Led by the NZRSA, the cry went up for the initiation of revaluation proceedings. The Boards of Inquiry duly recommended such action and the government reacted quickly by establishing twenty-four district revaluation committees. Of the total of 5,347 who applied by mid-1925, 5,284 had been dealt with. In March 1928 reductions totalled £2.68 million.[150]

What was the final cost to the New Zealand government? The entire repatriation process cost New Zealand just over £31 million. The losses accrued to soldier settlement, including revaluations, remissions and outstanding debts, was £7 million or 25 per cent of the total amount expended.[151] Despite these losses the government were satisfied with its 'success' on behalf of the returned soldier. The figures were certainly in line with those written off by Canada and Australia and as one commentator writes:

> Considering the [New Zealand] Government's adoption of an ill-advised policy of settling soldiers on improved lands bought at inflated prices, and its insistence on carrying on with such policy despite widespread and constructive criticism; and taking into account the inefficient administration of this policy by the Lands Department, the inexperience of the soldier settlers, the faulty subdivision of many of the estates, the second class quality of much of the supposedly first class land, the inadequacy of financial advances, and finally the effects of the slump, it is quite remarkable that the loss of 25 per cent sustained by the Government was not much greater.[152]

And what of the British ex-service migrant? As far as soldier settlement is concerned, he made no impact. The exhaustive and detailed soldier settlement reports compiled by the Department of Lands between 1921 and 1930 fail to record one case of a British soldier settler.[153] So what happened to those who participated in the free passage scheme? When the scheme was launched the New Zealand government emphasised that the greatest demand was for single female domestics and single male farm labourers. At first, families were encouraged to immigrate but the chronic housing shortage in 1920 forced the New Zealand authorities to discourage them. Instead, efforts were confined to the able-bodied single ex-servicemen, both skilled and unskilled, and the single woman or war widow without encumbrances, able to take up domestic service.[154] Moreover, the New Zealand government's warning that New Zealand veterans would receive preferential treatment and placement on the land, and that it was highly unlikely that there remained enough land to satisfy domestic requirements, no doubt intimidated all but the most determined or financially independent British soldier settlers. Even then, it would have been a very small number indeed. It must therefore be assumed that the vast majority found employment in secondary and tertiary industries or as unskilled labour.[155]

New Zealanders soon complained that many of the British immigrants, in particular the ex-imperials, arrived destitute and penniless adding to an already serious unemployment problem. Hence the government's curtailment of the free passage scheme except for those who had both assured employment and accommodation. Once these restrictions were in place very few British ex-servicemen embarked for New Zealand.[156] New Zealand's response to the free passage scheme was undoubtedly as patriotic as Canada's and Australia's. However, despite the fact that the country was the third largest beneficiary under the scheme, the final results were exceedingly disappointing. Local economic conditions certainly had a more immediate impact on the government's repatriation programme than in the other dominions and had a greater bearing on the fortunes of the British participants. Similarly, the disappointing results demonstrated New Zealand's vulnerability to outside economic factors, its increased dependence on imperial trading links, especially the overseas markets for its primary produce, and its lack of industrial diversification.[157] Finally, New Zealand's efforts to settle her own veterans on the land may have been a mixed success, but the concomitant reinforcement of its landed yeomanry with an imperial component was an unmitigated failure.

## Notes

1 Imperial War Museum, London, *Repatriation*, I, March 1919, p. 2. *Repatriation*, whose motto was 'Help the Man with the Medal', was a monthly magazine published for returning Australian veterans by the Ministry of Repatriation. Senator Millen was Minister of Defence in Sir Joseph Cook's administration between June 1913 and September 1914. He was given the repatriation portfolio in September 1917 until his retirement in February 1923. Millen also promoted government assisted immigration and was responsible for reorganising Australian immigration operations in London in 1920.
2 J. M. Powell, *An Historical Geography of Modern Australia*, Cambridge, 1988, pp. 92–120. R. A. Hawkins, 'Socialism at work? Corporatism, soldier settlers, and the

canned pineapple industry in south-eastern Queensland, 1917–39', *Australian Studies*, no. 4, 1990, pp. 35–59. One of the richest sources of post-World War I soldier settlement conducted on a regional and local context has been undertaken by Australian undergraduates in which useful material has been accumulated but over-looked by most scholars. See bibliography.

3 L. J. Pryor, 'The Origins of Australia's Repatriation Policy, 1914–1930', unpublished M.A. thesis, University of Melbourne, 1932, pp. 177–8.

4 Macintyre, *The Oxford History of Australia*, pp. 198–217. Schevdin, *Great Depression*, pp. 62–3; David Clark, 'Australia: victim or partner of British imperial-ism?', in E. L. Wheelwright and Ken Buckley, eds, *Essays in the Political Economy of Australian Capitalism*, I, Sydney, 1975, p. 63; Drummond, *Imperial Economic Policy*, pp. 43–144; W. H. Richmond, 'S. M. Bruce and Australian economic policy 1923–9', *Australian Economic History Review*, XXIII, 1983, pp. 238–57; N. Cain, 'The economists and Australian population strategy in the twenties', *Australian Journal of Politics and History*, XX, 1974, pp. 346–59; Kosmas Tsokhas, 'People or money? Empire settlement and British emigration to Australia, 1919–34', *Immigrants and Minorities*, IX, 1990, pp. 1–20; idem, 'Protection, imperial preference and Australian conservative politics, 1923–39', *Journal of Imperial and Commonwealth History*, XX, 1992, pp. 65–87.

5 Ken Fry, 'Soldier settlement and the Australian agrarian myth after the First World War', *Labour History*, no. 48, 1985, p. 41.

6 Russel Ward, *The Australian Legend*, Melbourne, 1958; J. B. Hirst, 'The pioneer legend', *Historical Studies*, XVIII, 1978–79, pp. 316–37; Russel Ward, 'The Australian legend re-visited', *Historical Studies*, XVIII, 1978–79, pp. 171–90; J. M. Powell, *Mirrors of the New World*, Folkstone, 1977, pp. 74–83; Lake, *Limits of Hope*, pp. 11–24. Marilyn Lake's book has sparked an interesting historiographical debate in some Australian social history circles. See J. Templeton, 'Set up to fail? Soldier settlers in Victoria', *Victorian Historical Journal*, LIX, 1988, pp. 42–50; book review by R. Wright in *Journal of Australian Studies*, no. 23, 1988, pp. 111–13; book review by Charles Fahey in *Australian Historical Studies*, XXIII, 1988, pp. 140–1; Alan Atkinson, 'Communication', *Australian Historical Studies*, XXIII, 1989, p. 337.

7 Geoffrey Serle, 'The digger tradition and Australian nationalism', *Meanjin*, XXIV, 1965, p. 149.

8 D. A. Kent, 'The Anzac book and the Anzac legend: C. E. W. Bean as editor and image-maker', *Historical Studies*, XXI, 1985, p. 376; K. S. Inglis, 'The Anzac legend', *Meanjin*, XXIV, 1965, pp. 25–44; Kevin Fewster, 'Ellis Ashmead Bartlett and the making of the Anzac legend', *Journal of Australian Studies*, VII, 1982, pp. 17–30; Noel McLachlan, 'Nationalism and the divisive digger', *Meanjin*, XXVII, 1968, pp. 302–9; Bill Gammage, 'The crucible: the establishment of the Anzac tradition', in M. McKernan and M. Browne, eds, *Australia: Two Centuries of War and Peace*, Sydney, 1988, pp. 147–66. Also see Jane Ross, *The Myth of the Digger: The Australian Soldier in Two World Wars*, Sydney, 1985.

9 W. F. Mandle, *Going It Alone*, Ringwood, 1978, p. 4. For the impact of the Gallipoli campaign and the imprint it left on the Australian public and national character see K. S. Inglis, 'The Australians at Gallipoli', Part I, *Historical Studies*, XIV, 1970, pp. 219–30; idem, Part II, XIV, 1970, pp. 361–375.

10 Mandle, *Alone*, p. 8.

11 W. Gammage, 'Anzac', in J. Carroll, ed., *Intruders in the Bush: The Australian Quest For Identity*, Melbourne, 1982, p. 62; Kent, 'Anzac book', p. 379; Inglis, 'The Anzac legend', p. 27; L. L. Robson, 'The Australian soldier: formation of a stereotype', in McKernan and Browne, eds, *War and Peace*, pp. 313–37; Serle, 'Digger tradition', p. 152.

12 Ward, *Australian Legend*; Hirst, 'The pioneer legend', pp. 316–37; Ward, 'The Australian legend re-visited', pp. 171–90; Inglis, 'The Anzac legend', pp. 30–1; Serle, 'Digger tradition', p. 156; McQueen, 'Shoot the Bolshevik', pp. 185–193.

13 Lake, *Limits of Hope*, p. 27.

14 *Commonwealth Parliamentary Papers* (hereafter *CPP*), 1914–15–16–17, V, no. 243,

Federal Parliamentary War Committee, Employment of Returned Soldiers, 1915; National Library of Australia (hereafter NLA), J. C. Watson Papers, MS 451/series 3/f. 30, notes on duties of Honorary Organiser, 27 August 1915; PRO, CO 532/78/52167, Munro-Ferguson to the Secretary of State for the Colonies, 29 September 1915, announcing the formation of the Federal Parliamentary War Committee.

15 Lake, *Limits of Hope*, p. 25.

16 Pryor, 'Australia's Repatriation Policy', pp. 178–9.

17 Australian Archives (hereafter AA), AA, CRS A2, item 15/3659, Fisher circular to state premiers, 13 February 1915; Earle to Fisher, 3 March 1915.

18 PRO, CO 532/79/36749, extract from a secret despatch from Barron to Bonar Law, 1 July 1915.

19 PRO, CO 532/78/35815, Lieutenant-Colonel Sir H. L. Galway, Governor of South Australia, to Bonar Law, 18 June 1915; CO 532/78/49553, *ibid.*, 10 September 1915; *South Australian Parliamentary Debates* (hereafter *SAPD*), 1915, II, p. 2063; CO 532/78/49553, Acting Premier of Tasmania to Macartney, 14 September 1915.

20 PRO, CO 532/79/36749, minute by Harding, 13 August 1915. During the debate on Queensland's soldier settlement legislation in 1917 the invitation to British ex-servicemen was maintained. *Queensland Parliamentary Debates*, 1917, p. 3100.

21 PRO, CO 532/78/52167, J. C. Watson, 'Returned soldiers. employment and settlement', 17 September 1915, p. 3; Lake, *Limits of Hope*, p. 28.

22 PRO, CO 532/78/35815, Galway to Colonial Secretary, 18 June 1915; CO 532/78/49553, *ibid.*, 10 September 1915; *SAPD*, 1917, pp. 1136–8; CO 532/78/42675, Sir Gerald Strickland, Governor of New South Wales, to Colonial Office, 30 July 1915; Archives Office of New South Wales (hereafter AONSW), Premier's Department, 4/6248, Ashford to Holman, 20 April 1916.

23 PRO, CO 532/78/52167, 'Employment and settlement', p. 4.

24 Pryor, 'Australia's Repatriation Policy', pp. 180–4; PRO, CO 418/150/62279, Barron to Bonar Law, 1 October 1916.

25 *CPP*, 1914–15–16–17, V, no. 299, Conference of Commonwealth and State Governments 17–19 February 1916, Report of Debates, pp. 11–13 and p. 28; Lake, *Limits of Hope*, pp. 32–6.

26 Lake, *Limits of Hope*, p. 36. In Western Australia Premier Scaddan reported in 1916 that there was plenty of work in the country districts but veterans could not be enticed to go. Two years later the situation was more urgent as thousands more veterans had returned. 'The returned soldier should not be allowed to remain in the City without occupation', implored another MLA. A South Australian deputy agreed but warned that employment in the city was much more congenial to the majority of returned men than settling on an isolated block of farm land. *Western Australian Parliamentary Debates* (hereafter *WAPD*), 1916, p. 359; *ibid.*, 1918, p. 1899; *SAPD*, 1916, I, p. 233.

27 *CPP*, Conference of Commonwealth and State Governments, 17–19 February 1916, p. 5.

28 Bodleian, Lewis Harcourt Papers, Box 479, Munro-Ferguson to Harcourt, 10 March 1915. For an analysis of Munro-Ferguson's career as Australia's Governor-General see C. Cunneen, *The Kings' Men*, London, 1983, pp. 106–50.

29 HLRO, Davidson Papers, f. 15, Munro-Ferguson to Bonar Law, 7 March 1916 and 22 December 1915; PRO, CO 418/144/9028, Munro-Ferguson to Bonar Law, 18 January 1916. Munro-Ferguson wrote to the fourth Earl Grey that he had worked with the celebrated author on a government commission before the war. Haggard 'didn't strike me as very practical but then his business is writing and he will no doubt be helpful'. Durham University, Department of Palaeography and Diplomatic, the Fourth Earl Grey Papers, Munro-Ferguson to Grey, 24 January 1916.

30 Peter Pierce, 'Rider Haggard in Australia', *Meanjin*, XXXVI, 1977, pp. 200–8; HLRO, Davidson Papers, f. 15, Munro-Ferguson to Bonar Law, 24 May 1916; PRO, CO 532/84/27819, minute by Macnaghten, 20 June 1916; CO 418/149/40464, Galway to Bonar Law, 1 July 1916; CO 418/150/40465, Sir Arthur Stanley, Governor of Victoria, to Bonar Law, 10 July 1916.

31 Haggard, *After-War Settlement*, pp. 11–22. For his personal views on the Australian leg of the tour see Higgins, *Private Diaries*, pp. 57–64.
32 PRO, CO 532/84/42220, Munro-Ferguson to Bonar Law, 19 July 1916.
33 Higgins, *Private Diaries*, p. 63; *Victorian Parliamentary Papers* (hereafter *VPP*), II, Inter-State Conference, Adelaide, May 1916, Report of Resolutions, Proceedings and Debates, vi and Appendix C, p. 116.
34 Archive Office of Tasmania (hereafter AOT), Closer Settlement Board files, AB 1/1, Hayes to a group of Scottsdale soldier settlers, 6 June 1917.
35 *CPP*, Conference of Commonwealth and State Governments, 17–19 February 1916, pp. 24 and 36; Pryor, 'Australia's Repatriation policy', p. 189.
36 *CPP*, Conference of Commonwealth and State Governments, 17–19 February 1916, p. 16. For the problems of wartime finance, state expenditure and Australian borrowing in London see Bernard Attard, 'Politics, finance and Anglo-Australian relations: Australian borrowing in London, 1914–1920', *Australian Journal of Politics and History*, XXXV, 1989, pp. 142–63.
37 WRO 947/616, Macartney to Bonar Law, 29 July 1916; PRO, CO 532/85/56089, minute by Macnaghten, 24 November 1916.
38 PRO, CO 532/125/5864, minute by H. Lambert, 11 February 1918.
39 AONSW, Premier's Department, 4/6248, Wade to Premier Holman, 18 April 1917.
40 PRO, CO 532/85/56089, minute by Lambert, 24 November 1916.
41 PRO, CO 532/89/26194, minute by Macnaghten, 5 June 1916.
42 PRO, CO 418/147/39679, Strickland to Bonar Law, 30 June 1916; L. L. Robson, 'The origin and character of the first A.I.F., 1914–1918: some statistical evidence', *Historical Studies*, XV, 1973, pp. 737–49.
43 Pryor, 'Australia's Repatriation Policy', p. 200; Australian War Memorial (hereafter AWM), G. F. Pearce Papers, 3 DRL/2222, bundle 3, folder 3, item 40, decoded cable, Hughes to Pearce, 8 June 1916.
44 PRO, CO 532/91/6463, Munro-Ferguson to Long, 3 February 1917; CO 532/92/36162, Munro-Ferguson to Long, 18 July 1917. The £2 million was divided between the states as follows: £500,000 each for Queensland, New South Wales and Western Australia, £250,000 for South Australia, £150,000 for Victoria and £100,000 for Tasmania. AA, CRS A2, item 18/888, Prime Minister's Department to Secretary, Board of Trustees, Australian Soldiers Repatriation Fund, 9 March 1917.
45 PRO, CO 418/157/10816, Munro-Ferguson to Long, 3 January 1917; WRO 947/624, Munro-Ferguson to Long, 23 January and 23 July 1917.
46 WRO 947/625, Munro-Ferguson to Long, 23 September 1917.
47 AWM, Lieutenant-General W. R. Birdwood Papers, 3 DRL/3376 item 30, Munro-Ferguson to Birdwood, 25 September 1917; NLA, Viscount Novar Papers, MS 696/964–9 and 976–82, Munro-Ferguson to Long, 5 October and 30 November 1917.
48 NLA, Novar Papers, MS 696/733–6, Munro-Ferguson to Bonar Law, 4 August 1915 and MS 696/1139–42, Munro-Ferguson to Milner, 4 February 1919.
49 Pryor, 'Australia's Repatriation Policy', pp. 201–2.
50 J. M. Powell, 'The debt of honour: soldier settlement in the dominions, 1915–1940', *Journal of Australian Studies*, V, 1980, p. 68.
51 Pryor, 'Australia's Repatriation Policy', p. 202; Powell, 'Debt of honour', p. 68.
52 Quotation cited in Lake, *Limits of Hope*, p. 32.
53 PRO, CO 418/170/9506, Munro-Ferguson to Long, 2 December 1918; CO 418/158/47624, Munro-Ferguson to Long, 31 July 1917.
54 PRO, CO 532/85/53930, Galway to Bonar Law, 10 November 1916; CO 532/110/23730, Galway to Long, 25 March 1918; CO 532/113/59865, Secretary for the South Australian Agent-General to W. A. S. Hewins, Under-Secretary of State for Colonies, 9 December 1918; *WAPD*, 1918, pp. 740–3; *ibid.*, 1920, pp. 25 and 1337–8.
55 WRO 947/617, Macartney to Long, 3 June 1917.
56 Bodleian, Milner Papers, MSS. Eng. hist., c. 707, ff. 99–100, Macartney to Milner, 19 February 1919.
57 WRO 947/617, Macartney to Long, 3 June 1917; Bodleian, Milner Papers, MSS. Eng. hist., c. 707, ff. 119–22, Macartney to Milner, 9 June 1919; *ibid.*, ff. 103, Macartney to

Milner, 25 March 1919; PRO, CO 418/181/14505, Macartney to Long, 1 January 1919.

58 PRO, CO 418/161/10765, Galway to Long, 5 January 1917.

59 PRO, CO 418/181/14505, Macartney to Long, 1 January 1919.

60 G. L. Kristianson, *The Politics of Patriotism*, Canberra, 1966, p. 12; Russel Ward, *The History of Australia 1901–1975*, London, 1978, pp. 138–42; Mary Wilson, 'The making of Melbourne's Anzac day', *Australian Journal of Politics and History*, XX, 1974, pp. 197–209; M. Mrdak, ' "Soldier-citizen": returned Servicemen and the R.S.L. 1916–1929', unpublished B.A. Honours dissertation, University of New England, 1986.

61 PRO, CO 418/179/22856, Sir W. E. Davidson, Governor of New South Wales, to Milner, 25 January 1919; CO 418/195/28735, Newdegate to Milner, 1 May 1920; G. C. Bolton, *A Fine Country to Starve In*, Nedlands, 1972, p. 11; Amery Papers, Box F.74, Newdegate to Amery, 30 May 1921.

62 British Library, Add. MSS. 62425, Walter Long Papers, Birdwood to Long, Secretary of State for the Admiralty, March 1920.

63 Marilyn Lake, 'The power of Anzac', in McKernan and Browne, eds, *War and Peace*, pp. 194–222; F. Cain, *The Origins of Political Surveillance in Australia*, Sydney, 1983.

64 Marilyn Lake, *A Divided Society*, Melbourne, 1975, pp. 145–53 and 172–5; Ross Fitzgerald, *A History of Queensland*, St. Lucia, 1984, p. 16; Kristianson, *Politics of Patriotism*, p. 13; Raymond Evans, ' "Some furious outbursts of riot": returned soldiers and Queensland's "Red Flag" disturbances, 1918–1919', *War and Society*, III, 1985, pp. 75–98; David Hood, 'Adelaide's first "taste of Bolshevism": returned soldiers and the 1918 peace day riots', *Journal of the Historical Society of South Australia*, no. 15, 1987, pp. 42–53.

65 PRO, CO 418/186/13070, Munro-Ferguson to Milner, 10 March 1920; *ibid.*, minute by Macnaghten, 16 March 1920; PRO, T 161/24/S 1237, Harding to F. Skevington, junior Treasury official, 12 August 1920; CO 721/14/2478, meeting of Australian Agents-General, 14 April 1920 and Amery's reply, 4 May 1920.

66 Plant, *Oversea Settlement*, p. 74.

67 PRO, CO 418/158/47624, Munro-Ferguson to Bonar Law, 31 July 1917; CO 721/39/2489, Munro-Ferguson to Churchill, 6 April 1922; J. M. Powell, 'Australia's "failed" soldier settlers, 1914–23: towards a demographic profile', *Australian Geographer*, XVI, 1985, pp. 225–9; *idem*, 'Debt of honour', pp. 64–87.

68 PRO, CO 721/13/2489, Munro-Ferguson to Milner, 10 August 1920; CO 721/14/2500, copy of Australian immigration proposals approved at Premiers' Conference, Melbourne, 24 May 1920; *New South Wales Parliamentary Papers* (hereafter *NSWPP*), 1920–1, joint volume I, 'Report of the Resolutions, Proceedings, and Debates of the Premiers' Conference . . . May 1920'; *ibid.*, 'Conference of Commonwealth and State Prime Ministers . . . July, 1920'; L. F. Fitzhardinge, *William Morris Hughes: A Political Biography*, II, *The Little Digger 1914–1952*, London, 1979, p. 441; D. Pope, 'Assisted immigration and federal-state relations: 1901–1930', *Australian Journal of Politics and History*, XXVIII, 1982, pp. 21–31.

69 M. Roe, ' "We can die just as easy out here": Australia and British immigration, 1916–1939', in Constantine, ed., *Emigrants and Empire*, p. 100.

70 *NSWPP*, 1922, joint volume I, 'Conference of Commonwealth and State Ministers . . . October-November 1921', p. 18.

71 *Ibid.*, p. 26.

72 AA, CRS A571, item 17/30298, [?] to Hughes, 29 September 1917 and Hughes's reply, 29 October 1917.

73 *Ibid.*, item 22/24222, H. W. Lawson to Cook, 1 September 1921.

74 AOT, Premier's Department (hereafter PD), PD 1/176/5/20, Lewis to Premier Lee, 17 January 1920.

75 State Records of South Australia (hereafter SRSA), Government Record Group (hereafter GRG), GRG 35/209, minute books of the State Land Settlement Committee (November 1918 to November 1920), I, report by Superintendent Grace, 18

March 1919 and minutes of 2 July 1920.

76 Battye Library, Western Australian Archive (hereafter WAA), WAA 26, item 324/20, Mitchell to Watt, 19 March 1920 and Mitchell to Hughes, 28 June 1920.

77 *Ibid.*, item 324/20, telegram, Mitchell to a Mr McKinnon, 28 June 1920; Mitchell to Hughes, 28 June 1920.

78 SRSA, GRG 35/209, I, minutes of Land Settlement Committee, 2 July 1920.

79 AOT, PD 1/176/5/20, Prime Minister's Department to Lee, 20 February 1920.

80 Battye Library, WAA 26, item 324/20, Secretary Russell to Mitchell, 14 July 1920.

81 Roe, 'Australia and British immigration'; *NSWPP*, 1920, joint volume I, p. 48; *Commonwealth Parliamentary Debates*, XCVIII, 1921, p. 13266.

82 *NSWPP*, 1920, joint volume I, p. 48.

83 PRO, CO 721/25/2452, Millen to Amery, 4 January 1921; CO 721/36/3819, E. Radford, Secretary of the New South Wales branch of the Imperial Service Men's Association, to Plant, 6 April 1921.

84 PRO, T 161/216/S 21713, Fleming to OSC, 12 June 1923. I would like to thank Professor Michael Roe for this reference.

85 *Ibid.*

86 AOT, PD 1/55/2/22, Blythe to Lee, 29 May 1922; Blythe to Chief Secretary, 30 September 1922.

87 *Ibid.*, PD 1/55/14/23, Blythe to OSC, 26 June 1923; memorandum by L. A. Evans for Tasmanian Ministry of Agriculture, 31 October 1923; Lyons to Tasmanian Agent-General, 2 November 1923.

88 *Ibid.*, PD 1/55/17/21, Brookes to Lee, n.d. (probably early 1921).

89 *Ibid.*, PD 1/55/21/21, for the 1921 correspondence on Ottley and Day cases.

90 *The Mercury*, 31 August 1921.

91 *Ibid.*, PD 1/55/21/21, minute by Hayes, 10 October 1921; Ashbolt to Lee, 20 October 1921.

92 AA, CRS A457, item E213/2, part 1, H. S. Gullett, Superintendent of Immigration, to Prime Minister's Department, 30 May 1921; A458, item F394/2, Mitchell to Prime Minister S. M. Bruce, 20 July 1923; CRS A461, item A349/1/6, Mitchell to Acting Prime Minister, 22 June 1921; *ibid.*, Gullett to Prime Minister's Department, 17 December 1920.

93 Paul Suckling, 'British Migration to Australia in the 1920s and the Role of the New Settlers' League', unpublished B.A. Honours dissertation, University of the West of England, Bristol, 1993, p. 26. Original source, PRO, CO 721/49/103778, Haig's statement on oversea settlement, 14 December 1922.

94 C. Turnor, *Land Settlement for Ex-Service Men in the Overseas Dominions*, London, 1920, p. 42; PRO, CO 721/19/2480, Billis to Macnaghten, 31 December 1919; CO 721/16/2480, minute by Macnaghten, 4 March 1920; *Melbourne Age*, 16 April 1920.

95 PRO, CO 721/19/2480, memorandum on fruit settlement by Major H. Hely-Pounds submitted to the OSC by Billis, 3 July 1920.

96 *Ibid.*

97 *Ibid.*, memorandum on sheep and wool growing by Major Hely-Pounds submitted to OSC by Billis, 3 July 1920.

98 PRO, CO 721/16/2480, minute by Macnaghten, 5 May 1920; CO 721/19/2480, minutes of the joint committee, 18 May 1920.

99 PRO, CO 721/14/2480, minute by Macnaghten, 9 June 1920; CO 721/16/2480, Treasury to Macnaghten, 30 March 1920; Macnaghten to Treasury, 1 April 1920 and Treasury reply, 3 April 1920.

100 PRO, CO 721/16/2480, Amery to Lord Inchcape, 7 May 1920.

101 PRO, CO 418/211/56799, minute by Macnaghten, 5 December 1921.

102 PRO, CO 721/19/2480, Billis to Macnaghten, 6 July and 8 September 1920; CO 721/14/2480, Connolly to Macnaghten, 30 June and 23 July 1920; CO 721/21/2480, Newdegate to Amery, 3 September, 13 October and 17 October 1920.

103 PRO, DO 57/34/0568, Euan Wallace to Sir Victor Warrender MP, 26 May 1927.

104 PRO, CO 418/220/5826, memorandum by Currie, 6 October 1922.

105 PRO, DO 57/34/0568, 'Introductory note by the Government of India, regarding a scheme for the Settlement of British Officers of the Indian Army in Victoria, Australia', no author, n.d.; Captain C. R. Jessop to the Military Secretary, Army Headquarters, India, 13 February 1927.

106 PRO, DO 57/54/0568/5, extract from an unidentified Australian newspaper, n.d. (probably 1927).

107 *Ibid.*

108 PRO, DO 57/34/0568, Wallace to Warrender, 26 May 1927.

109 PRO, DO 57/50/0568/1, extract from a letter from B. Godly to his parents forwarded by them to Lady Bennett, 5 February 1927.

110 PRO, DO 57/54/0568/5, Major-General C. Fasken to Dominions Office, 21 February and 18 March 1921; DO 57/62/0568, Oversea Settlement Department memorandum, January 1928.

111 PRO, DO 57/34/0568, Jessop to Military Secretary, India, 13 February 1927.

112 *Victorian Parliamentary Debates* (hereafter *VPD*), CLXXI, 27 July 1926, p. 448.

113 PRO, DO 35/23, quarterly secret report by Baron Somers, Governor of Victoria, 15 December 1926; *VPP*, 1925, II, no. 32, Report of the Royal Commission on Soldier Settlement, p. 50; *VPD*, CLXXI, 27 July 1926, pp. 448–50; DO 57/50/0567, list of Tresco West settlers, 31 March 1927.

114 S. McDonald, 'Victoria's immigration scandal of the thirties', *Victorian Historical Magazine*, XLIX, 1978, pp. 100–13; I. L. Hunt, 'Group settlement in Western Australia', *University Studies in History and Economics*, VIII, 1958, p. 41.

115 *Ibid.*

116 PRO, DO 57/4/011/3, memorandum by Captain Marshall Wood, assistant to Bankes Amery, 12 May 1926; DO 57/4/0085/4, Bankes Amery to Macnaghten, 18 May 1926; DO 57/34/0568, minute by J. R. S. Macleod, assistant principal, 14 May 1927; Hunt, 'Group settlement', p. 41.

117 PRO, DO 57/156/2702/14, sworn statement of Frank Thompson (c. 1929).

118 *Ibid.*, sworn statement of W. H. Voyle. Victorian Public Record Office, VPRS 749, item 327, f. 5025/101, Voyle's correspondence with Lands department, inspection reports and departmental minutes, 1927–29. Also see DO 57/156/2702/14 for those of Charles Clarke and F. G. Trigg.

119 PRO, DO 35/45, quarterly secret report by Somers, 31 July 1928. For the imperial government's involvement in legal assistance see DO 57/64/0569/18, 19, 21 and 24.

120 PRO, DO 57/64/0569/27, Somers to Amery, 12 March 1928; DO 57/62/0568, H. Farrands, Acting Secretary of the Development and Migration Commission, to Bankes Amery, 9 November 1927.

121 PRO, DO 35/45, quarterly secret report by Somers, 31 July 1928; DO 57/62/0568, Lovat to Somers, 31 January 1928.

122 Macintyre, *Oxford History of Australia*, pp. 207–11; G. Sherington, *Australia's Immigrants 1788–1978*, London, 1980, pp. 104–14; PRO, DO 57/32/OSO 4065 (old file number), minute by Macnaghten, 24 June 1927.

123 PRO, DO 35/45, quarterly secret reports by Somers, 28 January, 2 April and 31 July 1929; DO 57/98/0569/52, telegram from Crutchley, Bankes Amery's successor as migration representative, to Dominions Office, 23 March 1929.

124 *VPP*, 1933, no. 3, Report of the Royal Commission on Migrant Land Settlement; Hunt, 'Group settlement', p. 41; McDonald, 'Victoria's immigration scandal', pp. 232–5.

125 India Office Library and Archive, L/MIL/7/5592, W. Garnett, junior Colonial Office official, to MacLeod, 22 September 1933; L/MIL/7/5592/M491, minute by J. A. Simpson, India Office junior clerk, 19 January 1934.

126 Lake, *Limits of Hope*, pp. 136–8.

127 Powell, 'Debt of honour', pp. 65–6; For information on specific regions or settlement schemes see the following: Quentin Beresford, 'The World War One soldier settlement scheme in Tasmania', *Tasmanian Historical Research Association Papers and Proceedings*, XXX, 1983, pp. 90–100; Lloyd Robson, *A Short History of Tasmania*, Melbourne, 1985, pp. 188–20; J. M. Powell, 'The mapping of "soldier

settlement": a note for Victoria, 1917–1929', *Journal of Australian Studies*, III, 1978, pp. 44–51; Sean Glynn, 'Government policy and agricultural development: Western Australia, 1900–1930', *Australian Economic History Review*, VII, 1967, pp. 115–41; Leith McGillivray, 'Land and People. European Land Settlement in the South East of South Australia 1840–1940', unpublished Ph.D. thesis, University of Adelaide, 1982, pp. 375–452.

128 *VPP*, 1925, II, no. 32, Report of the Royal Commission on Soldier Settlement, p. 6. For the reasons for delay in Australia's repatriation policy see C. E. W. Bean, *The Official History of Australia in the War of 1914–1918*, VI, Sydney, 1942, pp. 1054–6; Fitzhardinge, *Little Digger*, pp. 351–3.

129 Powell, 'Debt of honour', pp. 66–7.

130 *Ibid.*, p. 84.

131 *CPP*, 1929, II, no. 46, Report on the Losses Due to Soldier Settlement by Mr Justice Pike, p. 8; L. F. Giblin, 'Losses due to soldier settlement. Report by Mr Justice Pike', *Economic Record*, V, 1929, pp. 337–9; Fry, 'Agrarian myth', p. 39; *CPP*, 1926–27–28, V, no. 119, Conference of Commonwealth and State Ministers . . . June and July 1927, pp. 67–8.

132 'Agricultural development in Western Australia', p. 138; Powell, 'Mapping of "soldier settlement" ', p. 47; Fry, 'Agrarian myth', p. 43.

133 Western Australia recorded 403 ex-imperials who had participated in its various settlement schemes. Of these only 235 remained on the land by 1925. Despite aggressive advertising, Queensland received only thirty-nine of an expected 1,600 ex-imperials. In Victoria rough estimates put their figure between six to eight hundred. Figures are not available for the remaining states. *Western Australia Parliamentary Papers*, 1925, I, no. 5, Report of the Royal Commission on Group Settlements, xxviii; D. J. Murphy, R. B. Joyce and Colin A. Hughes, eds, *Labor in Power: The Labor Party and Governments in Queensland 1915–57*, St. Lucia, 1980, p. 228; Victorian estimates were gathered from archival papers and McDonald, 'Victoria's immigration scandal'.

134 Jourdain, *Land Legislation*, pp. 46–9 and 189–99; J. O. Melling, 'The New Zealand Returned Soldiers Association, 1916–23', unpublished M.A. thesis, Victoria University College, 1952, pp. 78–98; J. M. Powell, 'Soldier settlement in New Zealand, 1915–1923', *Australian Geographical Studies*, IX, 1971, pp. 144–60; *The New Zealand Official Year Book* (hereafter *NZYB*), 1917, pp. 433–5.

135 Powell, 'Debt of honour', p. 64.

136 *NZPD*, 1917, CLXXVIII, pp. 247 and 367; *ibid.*, 1919, CLXXXIV, p. 343.

137 *NZPD*, 1917, CLXXVIII, p. 631; Mayhew, 'Soldiers' Association, 1916–1943', p. 24; Melling, 'New Zealand Soldiers' Association', p. 82; 'New Zealand I. Immigration', *Round Table*, XII, 1921–22, pp. 913–17; M. Fairburn, 'The rural myth and the new urban frontier', *New Zealand Journal of History*, IX, 1975, pp. 3–21. In October 1916, Lord Liverpool, Governor of New Zealand, informed Bonar Law that the Tuwharetoa tribe near Napier on the eastern coast of the North Island had reserved 25,000 acres of native land for Maori veterans irrespective of the tribe or tribes to which they belonged. Both Liverpool and the British government were impressed with this patriotic gesture. PRO, CO 209/289/55606, Liverpool to Bonar Law, 5 October 1916. Maoris soldier settlement was discussed regularly in the New Zealand Parliament. For example, see *NZPD*, 1917, CLXXVIII, p. 731.

138 Mayhew, 'Soldiers' Association, 1916–1943', p. 136; *Appendix, Journals of the House of Representatives* (hereafter *AJHR*), 1921–22, C-9, pp. 1–2; PRO, CO 209/309/41033, Lord Jellicoe, Governor-General of New Zealand, to Churchill, Colonial Secretary, 11 July 1921; Melling, 'New Zealand Soldiers' Association', pp. 80–93; D. J. George, 'The Depression of 1921–22 in New Zealand', unpublished M.A. thesis, University of Auckland, 1969, pp. 146–70; M. R. Sharpe, 'Anzac day in New Zealand 1916–1939', *New Zealand Journal of History*, XV, 1981, pp. 97–114.

139 W. H. Oliver, ed., *The Oxford History of New Zealand*, Oxford, 1981, p. 232.

140 Melling, 'Soldiers' Association, 1916–23', pp. 80–1; *NZPD*, 1921, CXCII, pp. 467–77 and 630–1. For an analysis of the problems of rural depression which persisted

throughout New Zealand in the inter-war period see Barrie MacDonald and David Thompson, 'Mortgage relief, farm finance, and rural depression in New Zealand in the 1930s', *New Zealand Journal of History*, XXI, 1987, pp. 228–50.

141  Oliver, *Oxford History of New Zealand*, p. 232; Haggard, *After-War Settlement*, pp. 22–4; Higgins, *Private Diaries*, pp. 65–6; PRO, CO 532/84/33878, Liverpool to Bonar Law, 9 June 1916.

142  Turnor, *Land Settlement*, pp. 29–30; PRO, CO 721/5/f. 82, New Zealand government to J. Allen, New Zealand High Commissioner, 13 March 1919, tabled at meeting of OSC advisory committee, 14 March 1919; PRO, CO 209/303/24178, Liverpool to Milner, 31 March 1920.

143  PRO, CO 721/26/3825, Allen to Amery, 2 April 1921; CO 721/25/3825, Cameron to Plant, 30 March 1921.

144  *Quick March*, monthly magazine of the NZRSA, 10 March 1921, p. 36; *ibid.*, 11 July 1921, pp. 55, 57 and 59; P. S. O'Connor, 'Keeping New Zealand white, 1908–1920', *New Zealand Journal of History*, II, 1968, pp. 47–65.

145  PRO, CO 721/25/3825, Allen to Macnaghten, 4 January 1921; CO 721/40/OSO 95447, Jellicoe to Churchill, 27 July 1922; *Quick March*, 10 July 1922, pp. 33–4.

146  Plant, *Oversea Settlement*, p. 74.

147  PRO, CO 209/309/56217, Jellicoe to Churchill, 28 September 1921; CO 209/312/9200, *ibid.*, 13 January 1922.

148  PRO, CO 209/312/9200, Jellicoe to Churchill, 13 January 1922; Jourdain, *Land Legislation*, p. 48; *AJHR*, 1923, C-9a, p. 3.

149  *AJHR*, 1923, C-9, p. 5; George, 'Depression', pp. 160–3.

150  *AJHR*, 1924, C-9, p. 2; George, 'Depression', p. 167; 'New Zealand I. the twenty-second session of Parliament', *Round Table*, XIV, 1923–24, pp. 187–9.

151  George, 'Depression', p. 168.

152  *Ibid.*, pp. 169–70. Of all the dominions, the quarterly secret reports from the New Zealand Governors-General between 1917 and 1930 provided some of the most informative and up-to-date material on land settlement, repatriation and immigration. Even after reserved lands had been thrown open to civilian settlement the statistical progress of New Zealand repatriation was maintained. Of particular interest are those of Governor-General C. Fergusson (1924–30). For example, see his quarterly secret reports between 1926 and 1930 in DO 35/4, 24, 48 and 69.

153  No statistics exist for British soldier settlers in the annual reports contained in the *AJHR* or the *NZYB* from 1921 to 1930 and 1915 to 1931 respectively.

154  National Archives of New Zealand, Wellington (hereafter NANZ), L1 Burnt File, Box 130, 1920/533, memorandum by H. Thomson, Secretary, Immigration Department, to Minister of Immigration, 4 August 1920. I am deeply indebted to Dr. Stephen Constantine for the use of these sources and notes. For an assessment of British immigration to New Zealand in the inter-war period see his article 'Immigration and the making of New Zealand, 1918–1939', in Constantine, ed., *Emigrants and Empire*, pp. 121–49.

155  During the 1930s the Empire Settlement League of New Zealand initiated a scheme to assist unemployed British ex-servicemen in New Zealand by placing them on small farms. Mrs T. Phillips wrote to the president of the League, Mrs Jones Neilson requesting that her husband be allowed to register. He had come to New Zealand in 1921 from Scotland under the auspices of the soldier settlement scheme. Evidently he had abandoned farming and was currently on relief work but had decided that it was time to try farming again. Department of Palaeography and Diplomatic, Durham University, Malcolm MacDonald Papers, 8/1/15, Phillips to Jones Neilson, 21 January 1932.

156  NANZ, L1 Burnt File, Box 130, 1920/533, telegram to High Commission, 20 October 1921; High Commissioner to Massey, 22 August 1922.

157  G. R. Hawke, *The Making of New Zealand: An Economic History*, Cambridge, 1985, pp. 7–17.

# CONCLUSION

# Foredoomed to failure?

In a survey of the British government's migration policy conducted in 1930, the Overseas Settlement Department concluded that assisted migration since World War I had been 'fostered largely for social and political reasons, and that the economic aspects of it [had] been more or less secondary'.[1] This was undeniably true. Although important economic arguments were used to popularise and justify soldier settlement, free passage and empire settlement, it was the parallel objectives of political stability and social cohesion which lay at the root of these policies designed to reinforce the physical and emotional bonds of empire. Whereas strategic motives had governed the pursuit of military colonisation in the past, it was the political necessity of shoring up society's ramparts against the allegedly destructive forces of socialism released by the war which underscored dominion governmental policy in the 1920s. Ironically, the economic uncertainties of the 1920s, in particular the onset of the Great Depression in 1929, rather than any threat of social breakdown ultimately defeated soldier settlement, assisted migration and overseas settlement.

Was soldier settlement policy an outright failure? Within the dominions analysed, the attempt to create a landed imperial yeomanry was a spectacular disaster. Officially, Australia established between one and two thousand ex-imperials on the land, Canada less than 300, and South Africa and New Zealand none. Even with the inclusion of perhaps 1,000 ex-officers settled by private initiative in South Africa and Australia, a liberal estimate of the total number of landed ex-imperials in the self-governing dominions would be a maximum of no more than 3,500. Considering that Britain demobilised four million men after World War I, of which 750,000 expressed an initial interest in agriculture, the gulf between official estimates and actual results is staggering. Of course, the picture is somewhat distorted as it excludes those ex-servicemen who settled in the Crown colonies, such as Kenya and Southern Rhodesia. Similarly, it ignores those who established themselves on the land independent of government or philanthropic agencies, and it remains impossible to estimate the number of independently settled ex-servicemen. Arriving as ordinary immigrants they were quickly absorbed into their new economic and social environments, making them effectively untraceable. Nevertheless, one may confidently surmise that the numbers were minuscule because this category of soldier settler would have needed large amounts of private capital to discount the variety of state assistance which was offered. Once again, with regard to those who settled in the Crown colonies and mandated territories, the numbers were small. Kenya, however, proved to be the exception. For as C. J. Duder has ably demonstrated, between 650 and 700 soldier settlers, mostly ex-officers who became an integral part of the Kenyan colonial elite, invested in large-scale farming operations. But like their brother officers in the dominions, many abandoned or sold their properties preferring to speculate rather than settle.[2]

Britain's free passage scheme for ex-service personnel provides another illustration of the gulf between imperial expectations and actual results. Ultimately, free passage was an administrative landmark which provided the cornerstone for the expansion of assisted migration encompassed in the Empire Settlement Act of 1922, itself a 'major revolution of policy'.[3] Statistically, its architects regarded the free passage scheme as a tremendous success. Just over 86,000 people were assisted at approximately £28 per head at a total cost of £2,418,263 between April 1919 and March 1923. The scheme accounted for 12 per cent of the total number of British emigrants who settled in the empire between 1919 and 1922.[4] For the emigrants themselves it provided the chance for a new life overseas; an opportunity that may never have existed had they been reliant upon their own means. This was particularly important for those who embarked for Australia and New Zealand as under normal circumstances these fares would have been the highest, deterring many who instead might have travelled to Canada. Fare equalisation through government subsidisation allowed for cheaper access to the Antipodes, somewhat nullifying Canada's geographical advantage.

Nevertheless, the final tally was a far cry from the initial estimates of early 1919. While the shortage of shipping during the first eighteen months hampered efforts, the onset of the short, sharp post-war depression of 1920–22 paradoxically both made and broke the scheme. Had unemployment not been such a serious problem the British government would neither have supported the idea of free passage nor its subsequent extension. But at the same time the dominions were suffering equivalent economic and social problems created by the post-war depression. The inability of the dominion governments to satiate the demands from their own veterans for jobs and housing led to the growing animosity toward the ex-imperial and the subsequent tightening of immigration regulations.

The underlying problem, however, was the neo-mercantilist rationale behind imperial soldier settlement. The emphasis on agricultural settlement in the dominions and the eagerness to create a landed imperial yeomanry which would strengthen imperial defence, enhance primary production and act as a protected market for British manu-factured goods, ignored the profound economic and social changes which were transforming the imperial relationship. The empire 'as an organic system, harmoniously balanced between industrial metropole and agricultural periphery' was quietly dissolving as the dominions continued to expand and intensify their own industrial base.[5] The failure of the numerous soldier settlement policies throughout the empire had as much to do with the incorrect presuppositions in Britain and the dominions about the economic relationship between them than it did with over-optimistic administrators settling inexperienced settlers on marginal land at a time of depressed prices for primary produce.

Economic factors aside, the failure to establish a landed imperial yeomanry was in part attributable to the growth of a 'sturdy' dominion nationalism. E. T. Crutchley, Bankes Amery's successor as Britain's migration representative in Australia, reported in 1932 that the growth of dominion nationalism in the 1920s, itself strengthened by the equality of status conferred by the Imperial Conference of 1926 and confirmed in the Statute of Westminster in 1931, revealed 'a manifest determination to view questions of population and migration from the national point of view only'.[6] No longer would the needs of the mother country dictate migration policy unless these needs coincided with conditions in the dominions which favoured a large incursion of British subjects.

This signal, which was being sounded in the late 1920s, was heard loud and clear by British policy makers during the severe depression of 1929–33. Similarly, it emerged that these same British policy makers were becoming increasingly sensitive to the dominions' viewpoint regarding British immigration and overseas settlement. Previously, the dominions had bitterly complained that they were being used as the dumping ground for Britain's impoverished and urban unemployed; that the British government was, in effect, transferring its domestic respon-sibilities and difficulties to their shoulders. As the economic uncertainties of the 1920s and early 1930s intensified, the dominions felt justified in imposing tighter entry regulations which restricted access to those immigrants able to contribute immediately to dominion industries which suffered from a shortage of experienced manpower. The policy of 'passing all immigrants through a fine sieve' was also designed to allay the fears of dominion labour which ardently believed that British immigrants competed for jobs, lowered wages and increased unemployment. In July 1928, Amery explained to Prime Minister Stanley Baldwin that there was a 'considerable divergence between the national situation and outlook in Great Britain and in the Dominions in connection with oversea settlement. We cannot hope to bridge that gulf except by a policy of conciliation and forbearance.'[7]

The depression of 1929–33 effectively ended assisted migration to the dominions. It did not, however, stifle the debate on the pros and cons of imperial migration. Throughout the 1930s and indeed during World War II, the political issues raised by imperial migration, particularly *vis-à-vis* the white dominions, remained central to British policy making. The intractability of the migration problem eventually forced a re-examination of the entire issue. For example, Whitehall concluded that British public opinion would be more exacting in future as it was vital to ensure a proper continuity of policy in this respect. 'On the other hand, the support of a Dominion Government for migration into that Dominion is contingent upon public opinion there and this is influenced very largely by current economic issues.'[8] A realistic economic appraisal was thus required before the incubation of a new migration scheme; something that was never done during the 1920s.[9] This last point was continually emphasised by post-war reconstruction planners throughout World War II. As one senior Colonial Office official reminded the Governor of Kenya in early 1943, the 'success of any [soldier] settlement scheme must depend on the settler obtaining a market for his products'.

> The economic situation at the end of the war is so uncertain that it is at the moment quite impossible to say in what countries there will be room for fresh settlement and what such settlers could produce. Again, most of the Empire countries overseas in which European settlement is possible will be very much pre-occupied with the resettlement of members of their own population who have been serving in the Forces. This is likely to be a substantial problem in itself, and I imagine will make Governments reluctant to agree to large-scale immigration until it is disposed of.

The same official also noted that there had been a 'progressive cooling' towards proposals for large-scale group settlement, mainly as it had been found that the number of people who could be settled under such schemes was entirely disproportionate to the expenditure involved. Indeed, the risks of failure were great in group settlement projects:

'Settlement on the land or otherwise of single individuals or families in existing communities seems to offer much less risk of failure . . .'[10]

It was also recognised that migration should neither be used simply as a bargaining tool in Anglo-dominion relations nor be solely governed by the complementary issues of how to increase dominion productivity, expand markets for dominion produce and safeguard markets for British manufacturing. Imperial migration was a joint venture which required active support and encouragement on both sides. Co-operation not confrontation was the new watchword. Conversely, the dominions could not have it all their own way and British officials argued that in future assisted settlement schemes the dominions would have to be prepared to contribute on an equal share financially. More importantly, the onus was on the dominions to provide better settler support and aftercare.[11]

What of the various dominion soldier settlement policies established after World War I? Although they varied in type from dominion to dominion, the various schemes were nevertheless a resounding and collective failure. Just over one million dominion men and women enlisted during World War I. Of this total, approximately 80,000 or 7.6 per cent embarked upon agriculture under the auspices of their respective soldier settlement schemes. By 1930 less than half were still in possession of their homesteads and of these many were barely holding their own. Combined with the number of British veterans who were settled in the mother country, the final total of landed ex-servicemen throughout Britain and the white dominions barely reached 100,000.

The depression of 1920–22 was a critical factor in the failure of many soldier settlers. Depressed prices for primary produce made it extremely difficult for many of these new producers to make a return on their investment. However, the depression cannot be blamed exclusively for the failure of the policy as many settlers were already experiencing problems during the post-war boom. It was post-war inflation rather than the depression which laid the foundation for the settlers' future difficulties. Over-inflated prices for land, livestock and equipment forced many settlers to invest all of their capital and any immediate returns they may have accrued from the first harvest. Since many were carrying a 100 per cent debt load, a sharp drop in prices for primary products was bound to demonstrate their extreme vulnerability.

Why then did the dominions embrace the idea of soldier settlement so willingly, when, with decades of settlement experience, they knew that soldiers made poor settlers? The patriotic hysteria created by the war and the subsequent public pressure for a coherent policy was one factor. The soldiers deserved a reward for the hardships and sacrifices they had endured defending 'King, Country and Empire' and most politicians, except the most foolhardy, were understandably reluctant to oppose such a noble cause given their wish to remain in office after the war. Patriotism also dulled the memory of many civil servants and policy makers who had previously opposed or had remained sceptical about the usefulness of soldier farmers before the war. Besides, the war had presented social planners and politicians alike with an opportunity to start afresh and build a new society. Maybe, just maybe, the soldier farmer could redeem himself if given the proper supervision and state assistance.

But this was precisely the complaint lodged by many Canadian soldiers; that they did not receive the proper supervision or support that had been promised. Although Canada possessed the most centralised soldier settlement administration backed by a central government which was prepared to take the initiative in policy formulation, many settlers harboured an acute dislike for the early activities of the Soldier Settlement Board. It was derided as overbearing, inflexible, coercive and bureaucratically sluggish. Moreover, supervision had become 'subservient to the collection of dues . . . which was scarcely assisted by the knowledge that the Board had powers of seizure and sale far exceeding those of normal business practice'.[12] Ottawa's claim that it would conduct soldier settlement along normal business principles was misleading and incorrect. Moreover, while wheat remained the primary cash crop, soldiers were unlikely to heed the government's advice that farm diversification was the safer course of action. When the bottom fell out of the grain markets in September 1920 it was too late for many settlers to shift the focus of their operations. Heavily indebted, it proved impossible for the majority of Canada's surviving soldier settlers to change to mixed farming, and those that did found the going very difficult. Even if a degree of success was obtained the prices for their produce were equally poor.

Yet, when contrasted with Australia, Canada's soldier settlement strategy seemed relatively simple and straightforward. Unlike Canada, Australia did not have a national or centralised soldier settlement policy and, similarly, Australia did not have a unified national development strategy. However, Australian soldier settlers encountered the same problems with bureaucratic red-tape, post-war inflationary pressures, depressed markets and prices, and harsh climatic fluctuations. But unlike their Canadian or New Zealand counterparts, Australian veterans suffered from the vagaries of an evolving and immature federal system. The profound lack of inter-state co-operation and the harmful competition which fostered unnecessary political friction between the Commonwealth and states was certainly more significant in Australia than in her sister dominions. There was also a 'marked inequality in treatment' of the returned man. They may have fought as Australians but pre-war partisanship and regionalism resurfaced after hostilities ceased. Men were settled as Victorians, Western Australians and Tasmanians not Australians.[13]

Like Canada, New Zealand developed a centralised approach to soldier settlement, but owing to regional environmental differences, there was a degree of parochialism which resembled the deeply divisive Australian example. And unlike the senior dominion, where the central authority kept a firm administrative grip on all aspects of policy, a pivotal role was played by the eleven regional Land Boards. As one observer suggests, New Zealand's approach was a 'decentralised system under national coordination'.[14] New Zealand was as generous and determined as Canada and Australia in its provision of assistance to its ex-servicemen, but its policy suffered from a fundamental flaw which did not seriously handicap the efforts of her dominion colleagues. Most of New Zealand's best farm land was privately owned and this forced the government to buy land at exorbitantly inflated prices. What little Crown land was available was isolated, thickly forested and expensive to clear. When once subdivided, the allotments were too small for viable farming and subsequently uneconomical and the problem was compounded by New Zealand's utter dependence upon British markets for its primary produce. Of all the dominions, New Zealand had the least diversified economy: it was therefore the most dependent upon the mother country for capital to develop its primary resource base. As one historian remarks, the Antipodean dominions were 'bound closely to Britain by preference and necessity'.[15] Only Canada was diversifying internationally and, of course, developing closer ties with the United States.

South Africa was a unique case because of the political sensitivity of both the immigration and land settlement issues. Its persistent refusal to participate in the free passage scheme or any empire settlement project, or give its own veterans preferential treatment, was testimony to the delicate nature of South Africa's domestic political scene. It might be argued that dominion nationalism played a much more significant role in the defeat of the imperial dream than in any of the other dominions. More precisely, it was Afrikaner nationalism, as represented by the poor white problem, which triumphed over British interests. Yet, in the face of such obstacles the 1820 Memorial Settlers' Association was able to make some notable achievements and contribute, albeit in small measure, to the flow of British immigration to South Africa.

The pressure exerted by the RCI throughout the war and the popular enthusiasm generated by the Haggard mission in 1916 was deeply significant. But even popular enthusiasm had its role to play in the failure of soldier settlement. The citizens of empire *expected* that something would be done for their returned men. With the abrupt end of the war in November 1918, the hasty implementation of a policy based on over-optimistic and misplaced assumptions about the soldier as the 'right type' of settler and the economic capacity of the 'new' lands were pivotal to the eventual failure of soldier settlement. Even more fundamental was the mystique that land settlement offered political, social and economic security. Though powerful, the 'agrarian myth' was archaic. In some ways it hindered rather than promoted development because it blinded many people to the economic realities of a new, industrial and increasingly urbanised age. Some grudgingly renounced the dream. For others the fog never lifted.[16]

Was the establishment of a yeoman class moulded from the survivors of World War I nothing more than a chimeric dream? The answer must be a resounding 'yes', despite the hopes expressed by conservative elements throughout the empire that the yeoman was a viable solution to post-war economic dislocation and social unrest. In the final analysis, soldier settlement neither solved unemployment nor produced untold national wealth. Instead, it created indebtedness, hardship and disappointment. Unemployment remained a seemingly insoluble problem and ex-servicemen and their families suffered more than their share of misery. Equally, the War Office noted that the economic value of the ex-soldier was 'practically nil in many industries whilst that of his civilian confreres [had] been rising with experience'.[17] Even reservists who had served with the colours for seven years found that serving their country was a serious handicap from the perspective of post-service employment. Out of touch with the market-place, their skills had grown rusty and outdated. Once again, the promise to provide adequate industrial and technical training had fallen through because of a lack of preparation, funding and resources. In Britain, by the late 1920s veterans comprised 80 per cent of the unemployed between the ages of thirty and thirty-four, and 58 per cent of the total unemployed.[18]

Of course, no one could have predicted the depression of 1920–22 which did so much to shatter the dreams and quash the honest endeavours of thousands of soldier settlers. The fact remains, however, that the entire policy contained inherent and fundamental structural defects – ideological, political and administrative. Those brave souls who succeeded despite the low prices, hollow promises and bureaucratic bungling did so either because of their good fortune or their determination to succeed or a happy coincidence of the two. But the vast majority had been foredoomed to failure.

# Notes

1 PRO, BT 56/30/CIA/1641, minute by Board of Trade official, 14 May 1930.
2 C. J. D. Duder, ' "Men of the officer class": The participants in the 1919 soldier settlement scheme in Kenya', *African Affairs*, XCII, 1993, pp. 69–87. During the early 1920s the ex-service settlers presented an acute political crisis for the imperial government. See Duder, 'The settler response to the Indian crisis of 1923 in Kenya: Brigadier General Philip Wheatley and "direct action" ', *Journal of Imperial and Commonwealth History*, XVII, 1989, pp. 349–73.
3 Drummond, *Imperial Economic Policy*, p. 43.
4 Plant, *Oversea Settlement*, pp. 74–5.
5 Kennedy, 'Reconstruction', p. 417; Vernon C. Fowke, *The National Policy and the Wheat Economy*, Toronto, 1957, pp. 177–95.
6 PRO, T 161/531/S 34376/02, report by Crutchley entitled, 'Migration to Australia', 1932, p. 2. For an examination of dominion nationalism and British policy making in the inter-war period see John Darwin, 'Imperialism in decline? Tendencies in British imperial policy between the wars', *Historical Journal*, XXIII, 1980, pp. 657–79; Max Beloff, 'Britain and Canada between the wars: a British view', in Peter Lyon, ed., *Britain and Canada: Survey of a Changing Relationship*, London, 1976, pp. 50–60; John B. O'Brien, 'Empire v. national interests in Australian-British relations during the 1930s', *Historical Studies*, XXII, 1987, pp. 569–86; Macintyre, *Oxford History of Australia*, pp. 198–221.
7 PRO, DO 57/72/OSO 5747, Amery memorandum for Baldwin, 'Unemployment and migration', 24 July 1928.
8 PRO, DO 131/35, Dominions Office memorandum on migration policy, 13 October 1942.
9 PRO, CO 852/505/4, memorandum by Sir Alan Pim, former Colonial Office official and African specialist, entitled 'European settlement in the dependent empire', n.d. However, the summary by Lord Hailey, chairman of the Colonial Research Committee, is dated 1 October 1942.
10 PRO, CO 967/161, A. J. Dawe, Assistant Under-Secretary of State for the Colonies, to Sir Henry Monck-Mason Moore, 29 March 1943.
11 BPP, Cmd. 4689, *Report to the Secretary of State for Dominion Affairs of the Inter-Departmental Committee on Migration Policy, 1934*, p. 22; Cmd. 5766, *Report of the Oversea Settlement Board, May 1938*, pp. 16–19 and 36.
12 Powell, 'Debt of honour', p. 83.
13 *Ibid.*, p. 84.
14 *Ibid.*, p. 72.
15 Macintyre, *Oxford History of Australia*, p. 205.
16 Premier James Mitchell of Western Australia best represents the stubborn determination to keep the agrarian myth alive. In 1930 he wrote to George Lansbury, Commissioner of Works in Ramsay MacDonald's Labour government, that Australia's decision to halt state-aided imperial migration was a regrettable one. 'To me it is unthinkable that we should much longer drift along in the aimless fashion of recent years. Australia is in trouble because of being woefully under-peopled and because too much of her energy has been devoted to the factory instead of the farm.' PRO 30/69, Ramsay Macdonald Papers, 1/340, Mitchell to Lansbury, 13 August 1930.
17 PRO, WO 32/4222/31/General 2713, 'Note on the employment question', 14 July 1924.
18 Ward, *The War Generation*, p. 30.

# APPENDIX 1

*Number of ex-service migrants granted free passage under
the imperial ex-service free passage scheme, 1919–1922*

| COUNTRY | MEN | WOMEN | CHILDREN | TOTAL 1 | TOTAL 2 |
|---|---|---|---|---|---|
| AUSTRALIA | 16,514 | 8,316 | 9,923 | 34,753 | 37,576 |
| CANADA | 11,539 | 7,522 | 7,499 | 26,560 | 26,905 |
| NEW ZEALAND | 5,467 | 3,391 | 4,032 | 12,890 | 13,349 |
| SOUTH AFRICA | 2,688 | 1,777 | 1,429 | 5,894 | 6,064 |
| OTHER | 991 | 666 | 442 | 2,099 | 2,133 |
| TOTAL | 37,199 | 21,672 | 23,325 | 82,196 | 86,027 |

*TOTAL 1* Totals of ex-service migrants assisted between 1919 and 1922.
*TOTAL 2* Final totals, without gender or adult/children breakdowns, as of 23
May 1924.

*Source*: G. F. Plant, *Oversea Settlement*, London, 1951, p. 74.

# APPENDIX 2

*Number of dominion and United Kingdom soldiers who received assistance to settle on the land\**

| COUNTRY | NUMBER |
|---|---|
| AUSTRALIA | 37,561 |
| CANADA | 24,998 |
| NEW ZEALAND | 9,041 |
| SOUTH AFRICA | 2,287 |
| UNITED KINGDOM | 23,770\*\* |
| TOTAL | 97,657 |

\* This does not include British ex-servicemen who emigrated and settled in the overseas empire under the imperial ex-service free passage scheme.

\*\* The United Kingdom figure includes Scotland, England and Wales. In the case of Scotland an unspecified number of allotments for civilian settlement were included.

These statistics give an estimate of the number of soldiers given state assistance to settle on the land. Figures were obtained from a variety of UK and dominion official sources. Please see relevant footnotes for the specific references.

# BIBLIOGRAPHY

## *Unpublished primary sources*
### *United Kingdom*

Government records
*Public Record Office (Kew, London)*

Board of Trade

| | |
|---|---|
| BT 13 | Establishment Division: Correspondence and Papers |
| BT 56 | Chief Industrial Adviser's Department |
| BT 65 | Power, Transport and Economic Department: Correspondence and Papers |
| BT 70 | Statistical Department/Statistics Division: Correspondence and Papers |

Cabinet Papers

| | |
|---|---|
| CAB 23 | War Cabinet Minutes |
| CAB 24 | Memoranda |
| CAB 26 | Home Affairs Committee |
| CAB 27 | Cabinet Committees |
| CAB 37 | Photographic Copies of Cabinet Papers |
| CAB 41 | Photographic Copies of Cabinet Correspondence: Letters in Royal Archive |
| CAB 117 | Reconstruction Secretariat Files |

Colonial Office

| | |
|---|---|
| CO 42 | Canada: Original Correspondence |
| CO 43 | Canada: Entry Books |
| CO 209 | New Zealand: Original Correspondence |
| CO 323 | Colonies (General): Original Correspondence |
| CO 418 | Australia: Original Correspondence |
| CO 532 | Dominions: Original Correspondence |
| CO 537 | Supplementary Correspondence |
| CO 551 | Union of South Africa: Original Correspondence |
| CO 721 | Oversea Settlement: Original Correspondence |
| CO 852 | Economic: Original Correspondence |
| CO 885 | Confidential Print (Miscellaneous) |
| CO 886 | Confidential Print: Dominions |
| CO 967 | Private Office Papers |

Dominions Office

| | |
|---|---|
| DO 35 | Dominions: Original Correspondence |
| DO 57 | Oversea Settlement: Original Correspondence |
| DO 131 | Childrens Overseas Reception Board |

Ministry of Labour
      LAB 2          Correspondence and Papers

Ministry of Agriculture, Fisheries and Food
      MAF 48      Land: Correspondence and Papers
      MAF 53      Secretariat and Parliamentary Branch: Correspondence and
                        Papers
      MAF 60      Ministry of Food and Food Departments of the Board of
                        Trade: Records

Prime Minister's Office
      PREM 1      Correspondence and Papers

Ministry of Reconstruction
      RECO 1      Records

Treasury
      T 1            Treasury Board Papers
      T 161        Supply Files
      T 172        Chancellor of Exchequer's Office: Miscellaneous Papers
      T 176        Otto Niemeyer Papers

Treasury Solicitor and HM Procurator General (Chancery Lane)
      TS 27        Registered Files: Treasury and Miscellaneous Files

War Office
      WO 32      Registered Papers: General Series
      WO 33      O and A Papers
      WO 43      Old Series Papers
      WO 163    War Office Council and Army Council

## Manuscript collections

### United Kingdom

Julian Amery, MP, Eaton Square, London (private residence)
      Leo Amery Papers

Bodleian Library (Oxford)
      H. H. Asquith Papers
      Lionel Curtis Papers
      Lewis Harcourt Papers
      Viscount Milner Papers
      Lady Violet Milner Papers
      Round Table Papers
      Selborne Papers

British Museum
      William Ashley Papers
      Walter Long Papers

Durham University
      Fourth Earl Grey Papers
      Malcolm MacDonald Papers

House of Lords Record Office
 Beaverbrook Papers
 A. Bonar Law Papers
 David Lloyd George Papers
 J. C. C. Davidson Papers
 John St Loe Stratchey Papers

Institute of Commonwealth Studies
 Richard Jebb Papers

Norfolk Record Office
 H. Rider Haggard Papers

Public Record Office
 Ramsay MacDonald Papers

Rhodes House Library (Oxford)
 J. X. Merriman Papers
 Basil Williams Papers

Royal Commonwealth Society Archives
 E. J. Harding Papers
 T. E. Sedgwick Papers

University of Sheffield
 W. A. S. Hewins Papers

University of Warwick
 Leslie Scott Papers

Wiltshire Record Office
 Walter Long Papers

*Miscellaneous primary sources – other UK archives*

Greater London Council Record Office
Imperial War Museum
India Office Library and Archive
British Library of Political and Economic Science

## Australia

*Australian Archives* (Canberra)
Government records

| | | |
|---|---|---|
| CRS A2 | Prime Minister's Department, General Correspondence Files, Annual Single Number Series, Immigration (1901–20) | |
| CRS A457 | Prime Minister's Department, Correspondence Files (1907–23) | |
| CRS A458 | Prime Minister's Department, Correspondence Files (1916–29) | |
| CRS A461 | Prime Minister's Department, Correspondence Files (1934–50) | |
| CRS A571 | Department of the Treasury, Correspondence Files, Annual Single Number Series (1901–76) | |

*Archives of New South Wales* (Sydney)
    Premier's Department
*Archives of Tasmania* (Hobart)
    AB 1          Closer Settlement Board Files
    PD 1          Premier's Department
*Battye Library, Western Australian Archive* (Perth)
    WAA 26     Premier's Department
*State Records of South Australia*
    GRG 35     Department of Lands
*Victorian Public Record Office* (Melbourne)
    VPRS 749   Advance files, Mallee
*Australian War Memorial* (Canberra)
    Lieutenant-General W. R. Birdwood Papers
    G. F. Pearce Papers
*Mitchell Library* (Sydney)
    MSS 302    Papers of the British Immmigration League of Australia
*National Library of Australia* (Canberra)
    MS 451     J. C. Watson Papers
    MS 696     Viscount Novar Papers (Munro-Ferguson)
    MS 6609    Returned Services League Papers


### Canada

*National Archives of Canada* (Ottawa)

Government records
    Department of Agriculture (RG 17)
    Department of External Affairs (RG 25)
    Department of Immigration and Colonisation (RG 76)
    Department of Indian Affairs (RG 10)
    Department of the Interior (RG 15)
    Department of Militia and Defence (RG 9)
    Department of Veterans Affairs (RG 38)
    Governor-General's Office (RG 7)

Private papers and records
    R. B. Bennett Papers (MG 26 K)
    Robert Borden Papers (MG 26 H)
    Arthur Currie Papers (MG 30 E100)
    4th Earl Grey Papers (MG 27 II B2)
    H. E. Hume Papers (RG 15)
    Edward Kemp Papers (MG 27 II D9)
    W. L. M. King Papers (MG 26 J)
    C. A. Magrath Papers (MG 30 E82)
    Arthur Meighen Papers (MG 26 I)
    George Perley Papers (MG 27 II D12)
    Royal Canadian Legion Papers (MG 28 I298)
    Clifford Sifton Papers (MG 27 II D15)

*Glenbow-Alberta Institute* (Calgary)
    W. D. Albright Papers
    Canadian Pacific Railway – Advisory Committee Papers
    Garnet D. Ellis Papers
    Dr. G. R. Johnson Papers
    A. H. Stewart Papers

*Provincial Archives of Manitoba* (Winnipeg)

Government records
    Department of Mines and Natural Resources (RG 17)

Private papers and records
    John Bracken Papers (MG 13 I 2)
    T. C. Norris Papers (MG 13 H 1)
    Royal Canadian Legion – Manitoba and Northwestern Ontario Command
    Papers (MG 10 C67)
    Frederick G. Thompson Papers (MG 14 C46)
    Valentine Winkler Papers (MG 14 B45)

*McGill University Libraries – Department of Rare Books and Special
Collections* (Montreal)
    W. D. Lighthall Papers
    A. M. Forbes Papers

*Provincial Archives of Ontario* (Toronto)

Government records
    Premiers' Papers (RG 3)
        William Hearst
        E. C. Drury
        H. Ferguson

*Saskatchewan Archives Board* (Regina and Saskatoon)

Private papers and records
    J. A. Calder Papers (M2)
    C. A. Dunning Papers (M6)
    S. J. Latta Papers (M5)
    W. M. Martin Papers (M4)
    N. H. McTaggart Papers
    Walter Scott Papers (M1)

## Republic of South Africa
*Barlow Rand Archives* (Johannesburg)
    Lionel Phillips Papers
*Central Archives Depot* (Pretoria)

Government records
    Department of Agriculture
    Department of Lands
    Governor-Generals Archive
    Secretary for Justice

Private papers and records
　　J. C. Smuts Papers
*Killie-Campbell Africana Library, University of Natal* (Durban)
　　J. S. Marwick Papers
　　A. M. Miller Papers
*National English Literary Museum* (Grahamstown)
　　Percy Fitzpatrick Papers
*Rhodes University* (Grahamstown)
　　Charles Crewe Papers (microfilm)
　　Edgar Walton Papers
*South African Library* (Cape Town)
　　J. X. Merriman Papers
　　Thomas Smartt Papers
*University of Cape Town*
　　Patrick Duncan Papers
*William Cullen Library, University of the Witwatersrand* (Johannesburg)
　　Drummond Chaplin Papers (microfilm)
*Miscellaneous primary sources – other South African archives*

Cape Archive Depot　　　　　　　　National War Fund
Johannesburg Public Library　　　　Transvaal Archive Depot


## Published primary sources

### United Kingdom

*Hansard and other official publications*
Colonial Office Lists and Dominions and Colonial Office Lists
House of Commons Debates, Fifth Series, 1915–1931
House of Lords Debates, Fifth Series, 1916–1919
Who's Who
Who Was Who


*Parliamentary Papers*
C.356, Report of the Select Committee on the Employment of Soldiers, Sailors, and Marines in Civil Departments of the Public Service (1876).
C.383, Report of the Select Committee on the Employment of Soldiers, Sailors, and Marines in Civil Departments of the Public Service (1877).
C.4751, Correspondence on the Proposed Formation of an Emigrants' Information Office (1886).
C.274, Report from the Select Committee on Colonisation (1889).
C.152, Report from the Select Committee on Colonisation (1891).
C.258, Report of the Select Committee on Retired Soldiers' and Sailors' Employment (1894).
C.338, Report of the Select Committee on Retired Soldiers' and Sailors' Employment (1895).
Cd. 2978, Departmental Committee on Agricultural Settlements in British

Colonies: Report of the Departmental Committee Appointed to Consider Mr Rider Haggard's Report on Agricultural Settlements in British Colonies I (1906).

Cd. 2991, Report of the Committee on Civil Employment of Ex-Soldiers and Sailors; together with Appendix (1906).

Cd. 2992, Minutes of Evidence taken before the Committee on Civil Employment of Ex-Soldiers and Sailors; together with Digest and Index (1906).

Cd. 3404, Published Proceedings and Precis of the Colonial Conference, 15th to 26th April (1907).

Cd. 3407, Memorandum on the History and Functions of the Emigrants' Information Office (1907).

Cd. 3523, Minutes of Proceedings of the Colonial Conference (1907).

Cd. 5741, Precis of the Proceedings of the Imperial Conference (1911).

Cd. 5745, Minutes of Proceedings of the Imperial Conference (1911).

Cd. 7915, Report of the Disabled Sailors and Soldiers Committee Appointed by the President of the Local Government Board (1915).

Cd. 8048, Interim Report of the Departmental Committee Appointed by the President of the Board of Agriculture and Fisheries to consider the Production of Food in England and Wales (1915).

Cd. 8182, Introduction and Part I of the Final Report of the Departmental Committee appointed by the President of the Board of Agriculture and Fisheries to consider the Settlement or Employment on the Land in England and Wales of Discharged Soldiers and Sailors (1916).

Cd. 8277, Part II of the Departmental Committee appointed by the President of the Board of Agriculture and Fisheries to consider the Settlement or Employment on the Land in England and Wales of Discharged Sailors and Soldiers (1916).

Cd. 8397, Farm of Borgie. Memorandum respecting the Farm of Borgie which has been presented to the State by the Duke of Sutherland (1916).

Cd. 8462, Final Report of the Royal Commission on the Natural Resources, Trade and Legislation of Certain Portions of His Majesty's Dominions (1917).

Cd. 8506, Reconstruction Committee. Part I of the Report of the Agricultural Policy Sub-Committee Appointed in August, 1916 to consider and report upon the methods of effecting an increase in the home-grown food supplies, having regard to the need of such increase in the interest of National Security (1917).

Cd. 8566, Imperial War Conference, 1917. Extracts from Minutes of Proceedings and Papers Laid before the Conference (1917).

Cd. 8672, Report to the Secretary of State for the Colonies of the Committee appointed to consider the measures to be taken for settling within the Empire Ex-Service Men who may desire to emigrate after the War (1917).

Cd. 9173, Correspondence as to the Emigration Bill, 1918 (1918).

Cd. 9177, Imperial War Conference, 1918. Extracts from Minutes of Proceedings and Papers laid before the Committee (1918).

Cd. 9231, Ministry of Reconstruction. Report on the Work of the Ministry for the period Ending 31st December, 1918 (1919).

Cmd. 317, Report of the Inter-Departmental Committee appointed to consider and report upon the Immediate Practical Steps which should be taken for the Provision of Residential Treatment for Discharged Soldiers and Sailors Suffering from Pulmonary Tuberculosis and for their Re-Introduction in Employment, Especially on the Land (1919).

Cmd. 325, The War Cabinet. Report for the Year 1918 (1919).

Cmd. 573, Report of the Oversea Settlement Committee for the year ended 31st December, 1919 (1920).

Cmd. 851, Ministry of Agriculture and Fisheries. Report of the Committee appointed by the Minister of Agriculture and Fisheries to enquire into the Pembrey Farm Settlement (1920).

Cmd. 1134, Report of the Oversea Settlement Committee for the year ended 31st December, 1920 (1921).

Cmd. 1184, Report of the Proceedings under the Small Holding Colonies Acts, 1916 and 1918, for the period ended 31st March 1920 (1921).

Cmd. 1474, Conference of Prime Ministers and Representatives of the United Kingdom, the Dominions, and India, held in June, July and August 1921. Summary of Proceedings and Documents (1921).

Cmd. 1580, Report of the Oversea Settlement Committee for the year ended 31st December, 1921 (1922).

Cmd. 1804, Report of the Oversea Settlement Committee for the year ended 31st December, 1922 (1923).

Cmd. 2009, Imperial Economic Conference of Representatives of Great Britain, the Dominions, India, and the Colonies and Protectorates, held in October and November, 1923. Report of Proceedings and Documents (1924).

Cmd. 2107, Report of the Oversea Settlement Committee for the year ended 31st December, 1923 (1924).

Cmd. 2132, Report to the President of the Oversea Settlement Committee from the Delegation Appointed to Enquire into Conditions affecting British Settlers in Australia (1924).

Cmd. 2167, Report to the President of the Oversea Settlement Committee from the Delegation Appointed to enquire into the Conditions affecting British Settlers in New Zealand (1924).

Cmd. 2383, Report of the Oversea Settlement Committee for the Year ended 31st December, 1924 (1925).

Cmd. 2581, Agricultural Policy (1926).

Cmd. 2608, Report to the Secretary of State for Dominion Affairs of the Inter-Departmental Committee Appointed to consider the Effect on Migration of Schemes of Social Insurance (1926).

Cmd. 2640, Report of the Oversea Settlement Committee for the year ended 31st December, 1925 (1926).

Cmd. 2673, Report on the Group Settlements in Western Australia (1926).

Cmd. 2697, Ministry of Agriculture and Fisheries. Small Holdings and Allotments. Memorandum on Financial Position (1926).

Cmd. 2751, Ministry of Agriculture and Fisheries. Small Holdings and Allotments Bill. Explanatory Memorandum (1926).

Cmd. 2760, Report by the Right Hon. the Earl of Clarendon, Chairman, and Mr

T. C. Macnaghten, C.M.G., C.B.E., Vice-Chairman of the Oversea Settlement Committee, on their visit to Canada in connection with British Settlement (1926).

Cmd. 2768, Imperial Conference, 1926. Summary of Proceedings (1926).

Cmd. 2847, Report of the Oversea Settlement Committee for the year ended 31st December, 1926 (1927).

Cmd. 3088, Report of the Oversea Settlement Committee for the year ended 31st December, 1927 (1928).

Cmd. 3308, Report of the Oversea Settlement Committee for the year ended 31st December, 1928 (1929).

Cmd. 3589, Report of the Oversea Settlement Committee for the year ended 31st December, 1929 (1930).

Cmd. 3717, Imperial Conference, 1930. Summary of Proceedings (1930).

Cmd. 3887, Report of the Oversea Settlement Committee for the period 1st January, 1930, to 31st March, 1931 (1931).

Cmd. 4075, Economic Advisory Council Committee on Empire Migration. Report (1932).

Cmd. 4689, Report to the Secretary of State for Dominion Affairs of the Inter-Departmental Committee on Migration Policy (1934).

Cmd. 5766, Report of the Oversea Settlement Board, May, 1938.

## Australia

*Hansard* (Commonwealth and State)
Commonwealth Parliamentary Debates
New South Wales Parliamentary Debates
Queensland Parliamentary Debates
South Australia Parliamentary Debates
Victorian Parliamentary Debates
Western Australia Parliamentary Debates

*Parliamentary Papers*
Commonwealth Parliamentary Papers
Federal Parliamentary War Committee, Employment of Returned Soldiers, 1915.

J. C. Watson, Returned Soldiers. Employment and Settlement, 1915.

Federal Parliamentary War Committee, Sub-Committee to consider the question of Settling Returned Soldiers upon the Land, Report and Recommendations, 1916.

Conference of Commonwealth and State Governments, February 1916, Report of Resolutions, Proceedings and Debates, 1916.

Conference of Commonwealth and State Ministers . . . June and July 1927.

Justice Pike, Report on the Losses Due to Soldier Settlement, 1929.

Rural Reconstruction Commission, Settlement and Employment of Returned Men on the Land, Second Report, 18 January 1944.

State Parliamentary Papers
New South Wales, Report of the Resolutions, Proceedings, and Debates of the Premiers' Conference . . . May 1920.

New South Wales, Conference of Commonwealth and State Prime Ministers . . . July, 1920.

Victoria, Royal Commission on Soldier Settlement, Majority and Minority Reports, 1925.

Victoria, Inter-State Conference, Adelaide, May 1916, Report of Resolutions, Proceedings and Debates.

Western Australia, Report of the Royal Commission on Group Settlements, 1925.

## Canada

*Hansard*
House of Commons, Debates (1915–1930)
House of Commons, Sessional Papers
House of Commons, Journals of the House of Commons
House of Commons, Appendices, Journals of the House of Commons
Senate, Debates (1915–1930)
*Federal and Provincial Parliamentary Papers and Publications*
Canada Year Book (1914–1935)
Canadian Annual Review (1914–1935)
Commission of Conservation. *Rural Planning and Development.* Thomas Adams, ed., Ottawa, 1917.

Commission of Conservation. *Urban and Rural Development in Canada.* Report of Conference held at Winnipeg, 28–30 May 1917, Ottawa, 1917.

Department of Agriculture, *A Guide Book: Information for Intending Settlers,* 5th ed. Ottawa, 1884.

Department of Soldiers' Civil Re-establishment, Annual Reports (1919–1927).

Department of the Interior, Annual Reports (1900–1930).

Hawkes, Arthur. *Special Report on Immigration dealing mainly with Co-operation Between the Dominion and Provincial Governments and the Movement of People from the United Kingdom to Canada.* Ottawa: Government Printing Bureau, 1912.

Military Hospitals Commission. *The Soldier's Return: From 'Down and Out' to 'Up and In Again': A Little Chat With Private Pat* (Ottawa, 1917).

Murchie, R. W. and H. C. Grant. *Unused Lands of Manitoba.* Winnipeg: Ministry of Agriculture and Immigration, 1926.

Ontario Legislative Assembly, *Sessional Papers*, Report of the Ontario Unemployment Commission, 1916.

Overseas Military Forces of Canada, *Report,* 1918 (London, 1918).

Proceedings of the Special Committee Appointed to Consider and Report upon the Rates of Pensions to be Paid to Disabled Soldiers and the Establishment of a Permanent Pensions Board (Ottawa, May 1916).

Proceedings of the Special Committee Appointed to Consider, Inquire into, and Report upon the Reception, Treatment, Care, Training and Re-education of the Wounded, Disabled and Convalescent who have served in the Canadian Expeditionary Force . . . 1917 (Ottawa, 1918).

Proceedings of the Special Committee appointed by Resolution of the House of Commons on the 18th of September, 1919, and to whom was referred Bill No.

10, An Act to amend the Department of Soldiers' Civil Re-establishment Act . . . 21 October 1919 (Ottawa, 1919).

Proceedings of the Special committee appointed by Resolution of the House of Commons to consider the question of continuing the War Bonus to Pensioners, and any Amendments to the Pension Law which may be proposed . . . 18 June 1920 (Ottawa, 1921).

Proceedings of the Special Committee appointed by Resolution of the House of Commons on the 10th of March, 1921, to consider questions relating to the Pensions, Insurance and Re-establishment of Returned Soldiers . . . May 26th, 1921 (Ottawa, 1921).

Report and Proceedings of the Special Committee Appointed by Resolution of the House of Commons of Canada on the 30th March 1922 to consider Questions Relating to Pensions, Insurance and Re-establishment of Returned Soldiers (Ottawa, 1922).

Proceedings of the Special Committee Appointed to Consider Questions Relating to the Pensions, Insurance and Re-establishment of Returned Soldiers, 1924 (Ottawa, 1924).

Royal Commission on Employment and Immigration (Saskatchewan) 1930.

Scammell, Ernest. *The Provision of Employment for Members of the Canadian Expeditionary Force on Their Return to Canada and the Re-Education of Those Who Are Unable to Follow Their Previous Occupations Because of Disability* (Ottawa, 1916).

Soldier Settlement Board, Annual Reports (1921–1936).

## New Zealand

*Hansard*

New Zealand Parliamentary Debates, 1900–1930

The New Zealand Year Book

*Parliamentary Reports*

Department of Lands and Surveys. Discharged Soldiers Settlement. Annual Reports (1921–31), C-9 series.

Department of Lands and Surveys. Soldier Settlement (1923), C-9a series.

Jourdain, W. R. *Land Legislation and Settlement in New Zealand* Wellington: Government Printer, 1925.

## Union of South Africa

*Hansard*

House of Assembly Debates, 1915–1923 (Cape Times)

House of Assembly Debates, 1924–1930 (new series)

*Select Committee Reports*

S.C. 4 – '12. On Land Settlement Bill.

S.C. 4 – '18. Provision for South African Forces in Present and Previous Wars.

S.C. 4a – '18. Provision for South African Forces in Present and Previous Wars.

S.C. 5 – '19. Provision for South African Forces in Present and Previous Wars.

S.C. 3 – '20. War Pensions and Returned Soldiers, First and Second Reports, July 1920.

S.C. 3a – '20. War Pensions and Returned Soldiers, Third (and Final) Report, 1920.

*Union Government Reports*
U.G. 12–1914. Report of the Economic Commission.
U.G. 29–1917. Reports on Various Irrigation Projects.
U.G. 19–1918. Report of the Director of Irrigation.
U.G. 28–1920. Report of the Director of Irrigation.
U.G. 35–1920. Annual Report of the Department of Justice for the calendar year 1919.
U.G. 56–1920. Census of the European or White Races of the Union of South Africa 1918.
U.G. 8–1922. Annual Departmental Reports (1920–21).
U.G. 14–1923. Annual Departmental Reports (1921–22).
U.G. 15–1923. Third Census of the Population of the Union of South Africa.
U.G. 42–1923. Third Census of the Population of the Union of South Africa, Part V (Birthplaces).
U.G. 9–1924. Annual Departmental Reports (1922–23).
U.G. 15–1925. Annual Departmental Reports (1923–24).
U.G. 14–1926. Report of the Economic and Wage Commission 1925.
U.G. 21–1926. Annual Departmental Reports (1924–25).
U.G. 38–1929. Annual Report on Statistics of Migration, 1927.
U.G. 19–1930. Annual Report on Statistics of Migration, 1928.
U.G. 37–1930. Annual Report on Statistics of Migration, 1929.
U.G. 29–1931. Annual Report on Statistics of Migration, 1930.

## Newspapers, journals and periodicals

### United Kingdom

*Morning Post*
*The Standard of Empire*
*Pall Mall Gazette*
*The Times*

### Australia

*Melbourne Age*
*Argus*
*Sydney Morning Herald*
*The Mercury*

### Canada

*Canada*
*Edmonton Journal*
*Manitoba Free Press*
*Montreal Gazette*
*Ottawa Citizen*
*Daily Colonist*
*Saskatoon Phoenix*
*Vancouver World*
*Toronto Evening Telegram*
*Regina Leader*

*The Record*
*Toronto Star*

## Union of South Africa

*Cape Times*
*Johannesburg Star*
*Natal Mercury*
*The South African Farm News, Exchange and Mart*
*Natal Witness*
*Rand Daily Mail*
*The Farmer's Weekly*

## Contemporary books and articles

### Books

Begbie, Harold. *Albert, Fourth Earl Grey, A Last Word*. London: Hodder and Stoughton, 1917.

Buxton, Earl of. *General Botha*. London: John Murray, 1924.

Cairns, Alex and A. H. Yeatman. *The Manitoba Veteran: History of the Veteran Movement 1916 to 1925 and of the Canadian Legion, 1926 to 1935*. Winnipeg: Veterans Press, 1961.

Clifford, W. G. *The Ex-Soldier By Himself*. London: A. & C. Black, 1916.

Darrell, Frederick. *Should I Succeed in South Africa. By a Successful Colonist*. London: Simpkin, Marshall, Hamilton, Kent and Co., 1900.

Fiddes, Sir George. *The Dominions and Colonial Offices*. London: G. P. Putnam's Sons, 1926.

Haggard, H. Rider. *A Farmer's Year*. London: Longmans, Green and Co., 1899.

—— *Rural England*. London: Longmans, Green and Co., 1902.

—— *The Poor and the Land*. London: Longmans, Green and Co., 1905.

—— *Regeneration*. London: Longmans, Green and Co., 1910.

Hall, A. D. *Agriculture After the War*. London: John Murray, 1916.

Hunt, M. Stuart. *Nova Scotia's Part in the Great War*. Halifax: The Nova Scotia Veteran Publishing Co., 1920.

Parkinson, Sir Cosmo. *The Colonial Office From Within 1909–1945*. London: Faber and Faber Limited, 1947.

Pearson, Sir Arthur. *Victory Over Blindness*. London: Hodder and Stoughton, *c.* 1920.

Pilkington, Col. Henry. *Land Settlement for Soldiers*. London: William Clowes and Sons, 1911.

Seeley, J. R. *The Expansion of England*. London: Macmillan and Co., 1885.

Stead, R. J. C. *The Empire Builders and Other Poems*. Toronto: William Briggs, 1908.

Warman, W. H. *The Soldier Colonists*. London: Chatto and Windus, 1918.

### Articles

Arthur, R. 'Imperial emigration and its problems'. *Proceedings of the Royal Colonial Institute*, XL (1908–09), 314–40.

Ashton, E. J. 'Soldier land settlement in Canada'. *Quarterly Journal of Economics*, XXXIX (1925), 488–98.

—— 'Some colonisation problems: a Canadian view'. *United Empire*, XXI (1930), 420–4.

'Australia: the British settlers in Victoria'. *Round Table*, XXIV (1933–34), 203–8.

Baille-Grohman, William A. 'A paradise for Canadian and American soldiers'. *Nineteenth Century and After*, LXXXIII (1918), 762–78.

Bathurst, Charles. 'The land settlement of ex-service men'. *Nineteenth Century and After*, LXXVIII (1915), 1097–1113.

Black, W. J. 'Agricultural training for returned soldiers'. *Agricultural Gazette of Canada*, V (1918), 1123–7.

Brown, George. 'Western problems and immigration after the war'. *Proceedings of the Canadian Club*, Toronto, XIII (1915–16), 183–99.

'Canada I. The immigration problem'. *Round Table*, XIII (1922), 157–71.

*The Carnegie Report on the Poor White Problem in South Africa*. 5 vols. Stellenbosch, 1932.

Cavers, C. W. 'Selecting and training soldiers for agriculture'. *Agricultural Gazette of Canada*, VI (1919), 426–8.

Chicanot, E. L. 'The Canadian soldier on the land'. *United Empire*, XIII (1922), 200–2.

Chidell, Fleetwood. 'Imperial migration and the clash of races'. *Quarterly Review*, CCXXXIII (1920), 359–74.

Cormie, J. A. 'The war and immigration'. *Westminster Advertiser* (1916), 129–32.

Dawson, W. H. 'Empire settlement and unemployment'. *Contemporary Review*, CXXVII (1925), 576–83.

Dennis, J. S. 'Some of Canada's problems'. *Addresses Delivered before the Canadian Club of Montreal* (1916–17), 147–55.

Ernle, Lord. 'A great agriculturalist – Edward Strutt'. *Nineteenth Century and After*, CIX (1931), 473–83.

'Farm settlements for ex-service men'. *Journal of the Ministry of Agriculture*, XXXI (1924), 783–5.

'Farm and small holdings settlements of the ministry'. *Journal of the Ministry of Agriculture*, XXXIII (1927), 882–6.

Fay, C. R. 'Lessons of soldier settlement in the Canadian west'. *United Empire*, XIV (1923), 202–8.

Fisher, L. 'Canada and British immigration'. *Contemporary Review*, CXXVIII (1925), 601–5.

Flumerfelt, A. C. ' "The landless man" and "the manless land" of Canada'. *Addresses Delivered before the Canadian Club of Montreal* (1916–17), 179–83.

Fox, Frank. 'A way out of our troubles – Empire resettlement'. *National Review* (1922), 562–7.

Giblin, L. F. 'Losses due to soldier settlement. Report by Mr Justice Pike'. *Economic Record*, V (1929), 337–9.

Green, F. E. 'Home colonisation by soldiers and sailors'. *Nineteenth Century and After*, LXXIX (1916), 888–905.

Haggard, H. Rider. *The After-War Settlement and Employment of Ex-Service Men in the Oversea Dominions* (pamphlet), London, 1916.

Hannan, A. J. 'Land settlement of ex-service men in Australia, Canada, and the United States'. *Journal of Comparative Legislation and International Law*, 3rd series, II (1920), 225–37.

Kidner, T. B. 'The disabled soldier'. *Addresses Delivered before the Canadian Club of Montreal* (1916–17), 111–22.

Kinloch-Cooke, Sir Clement. 'An Empire migration policy'. *The Empire Review and Journal of British Trade*, XXXI (1917), 49–59.

—— 'Land settlement after the war'. *Fortnightly Review*, XCIX (1916), 691–8.

Kirchner, W. H. 'Canada's immigration policy after the war'. *Canada Monthly* (1916), 334–6.

'Land settlement'. *Journal of the Ministry of Agriculture*, XXVI (1919), 327–8.

'Land settlement after the war'. *Round Table*, VI (1915), 120–5.

Leacock, Stephen. 'Empire settlement'. *United Empire*, XIII (1922), 30–2.

Mappin, Godfrey. 'Migration as a paying proposition'. *United Empire*, XII (1921), 591–4.

'New Zealand I. Immigration'. *Round Table*, XII (1921–22), 913–17.

'New Zealand I. The twenty-second session of Parliament'. *Round Table*, XIV (1923–24), 187–204.

'Position and prospects of ex-service small holders'. *Journal of the Ministry of Agriculture*, XXX (1923), 246–50.

Redmayne, J. S. 'The problem of successful migration'. *United Empire*, X (1919), 550–5.

Rogers, Robert. 'Canada's problems during and after the war'. *Addresses Delivered before the Canadian Club of Montreal* (1916–17), 79–86.

'Sailors and soldiers on the land'. *Quarterly Review*, CCXXVI (1916), 135–51.

'Scheme for the land settlement of ex-service men'. *Journal of the Ministry of Agriculture*, XXIV (1917), 326–8.

'Settlement plans in Canada'. *Empire Review*, XXXI (1917), 59.

Shann, E. 'Group settlement of migrants in Western Australia'. *Economic Record*, I (1925), 73–93.

Sifton, Sir Clifford. 'The immigrants Canada wants', *MacLean's Magazine*, 1 April 1922.

Smith, J. Obed. 'Canada the land of opportunity'. *Empire Review*, XXXVI (1922), 173–5.

Todd, J. L. 'Returned soldiers and the medical profession'. *Canadian Medical Association Journal*, VII (1917), 1–13.

Turnor, C. 'The organisation of migration and settlement within the empire'. *United Empire*, XI (1920), 247–54.

—— *Land Settlement for Ex-Service Men in the Oversea Dominions* (pamphlet), London, 1920.

Wade, C. G. and F. C. 'Overseas settlement'. *Empire Review and Journal of British Trade* (1919), 127–31.

Wade, C. G. 'Post-war settlement of soldiers and imperial migration'. *Nineteenth Century and After*, LXXXII (1917), 1156–70.

Wade, F. C. 'Migration within the empire'. *Empire Review*, XXXVI (1922), 124–7.
Woodhouse, C. G. 'Returning the soldier to civilian life'. *South Atlantic Quarterly*, XVII (1918), 265–89.

## Memoirs, diaries and letters

Addison, C. *Four and a Half Years*. 2 vols. London: Hutchinson, 1934.
Amery, L. S. *My Political Life*. London: Hutchinson, 1953.
Barnes, John and D. Nicholson, eds. *The Leo Amery Diaries*. 2 vols. London: Hutchinson, 1980 and 1988.
Buchan, John. *The African Colony*. London: William Blackwood and Sons, 1903.
—— *Memory Hold-The-Door*. London: Hodder and Stoughton, 1940.
Clark, Alan, ed. *'A Good Innings': The Private Papers of Viscount Lee of Fareham*. London: John Murray, 1974.
Ernle, Lord. *Whippingham to Westminster*. London: John Murray, 1938.
Fraser, Maryna and Alan Jeeves, eds. *All That Glittered*. Cape Town: Oxford University Press, 1977.
Haggard, H. Rider. *The Days of My Life*. 2 vols. London: Longmans, Green and Co., 1926.
Higgins, D. S., ed. *The Private Diaries of Sir H. Rider Haggard 1914–1925*. New York: Stein and Day Publishers, 1980.
James, R. R. *Memoirs of a Conservative: J. C. C. Davidson's Memoirs and Papers, 1910–1937*. London: Weidenfeld and Nicolson, 1969.
Lewsen, Phyllis. *Selections from the Correspondence of J. X. Merriman, 1905–1924*. Cape Town: The Van Riebeck Society, 1969.
Long, Walter. *Memories*. London: Hutchinson and Co., 1923.
Middlemas, K., ed. *Thomas Jones: Whitehall Diary*. London: Oxford University Press, 1969.

## Secondary sources (works)

### Books

Adams, R. J. Q. and Philip P. Pourier. *The Conscription Controversy in Great Britain, 1900–18*. London: Macmillan, 1987.
Andrew, Christopher. *Her Majesty's Secret Service*. New York: Viking, 1986.
Andrews, E. M. *The Anzac Illusion. Anglo-Australian Relations during World War I*. Cambridge: Cambridge University Press, 1993.
Appleyard, R. T. *British Emigration to Australia*. London: George Weidenfeld and Nicolson, 1964.
Artibise, A. F. J. *Winnipeg: A Social History of Urban Growth 1874–1914*. Montreal: McGill-Queen's University Press, 1975.
Avery, Donald. *'Dangerous Foreigners'*. Toronto: McClelland and Stewart, 1979.
Baker, H. C. *Homes for Heroes*. Saskatoon: Early Mailing Service, 1979.

Barnett, Correlli. *The Collapse of British Power*. Gloucester: Alan Sutton Publishing, 1984.

Barrett, John. *Falling In. Australians and 'Boy Conscription', 1911–15*. Sydney: Hale & Iremonger, 1979.

Bean, C. E. W. *The Official History of Australia in the War of 1914–1918*, VI. Sydney: Angus & Robertson, 1942.

Becket, Ian F. W. and Keith Simpson, eds, *A Nation in Arms*. Manchester: Manchester University Press, 1985.

Belich, James. *The New Zealand Wars and the Victorian Interpretation of Racial Conflict*. Auckland: Penguin Books, 1988.

Berger, Carl. *The Sense of Power: Studies in the Ideas of Canadian Imperialism 1867–1914*. Toronto: University of Toronto Press, 1970.

Blake, Robert. *The Unknown Prime Minister*. London: Eyre and Spottiswoode, 1955.

Bolton, G. C. *A Fine Country To Starve In*. Nedlands: University of Western Australia, 1972.

Bond, Brian. *British Military Policy between the Two World Wars*. Oxford: Clarendon Press, 1980.

Bothwell, Robert, Ian Drummond and John English. *Canada, 1900–1945*. Toronto: University of Toronto Press, 1987.

Boyce, R. W. D. *British Capitalism at the Crossroads 1919–1932*. Cambridge: Cambridge University Press, 1987.

Bozzoli, Belinda, ed. *Town and Countryside in the Transvaal*. Johannesburg: Ravan Press, 1983.

Brown, Robert Craig. *Robert Laird Borden: A Biography*. I. *1854–1914*. Toronto: McClelland and Stewart, 1975.

Brown, Robert Craig and Ramsay Cook. *Canada 1896–1921: A Nation Transformed*. Toronto: McClelland and Stewart, 1974.

Butler, David and Anne Sloman. *British Political Facts 1900–1979*. 5th ed. London: Macmillan Press, 1980.

Burk, Kathleen, ed. *War and the State*. London: George Allen and Unwin, 1982.

Cain, F. *The Origins of Political Surveillance in Australia*. Sydney: Angus and Robertson Publishers, 1983.

Campbell, John, *F. E. Smith First Earl of Birkenhead*. London: Jonathon Cape, 1983.

Careless, J. M. S., and R. Craig Brown, eds. *The Canadians 1867–1967*. Toronto: Macmillan of Canada, 1967.

Carrothers, W. A. *Emigration from the British Isles*. London: D. S. King and Son, 1929.

Christie, R. *Electricity, Industry and Class in South Africa*. London: Macmillan Press, 1984.

Christopher, A. J. *The Crown Lands of British South Africa 1853–1914*. Kingston, Ontario: Limestone Press, 1984.

Colls, Robert and Philip Dodd, eds. *Englishness: Politics and Culture 1880–1920*. London: Croom Helm, 1986.

Constantine, S. *Unemployment in Britain between the Wars*. London: Longman Group, 1980.

—— *The Making of British Colonial Development Policy 1914–1940*. London: Frank Cass and Co., 1984.

—— ed. *Emigrants and Empire*. Manchester: Manchester University Press, 1990.

Cooper, A. F. *British Agricultural Policy, 1912–36*. Manchester: Manchester University Press, 1989.

Corbett, David C. *Canada's Immigration Policy: A Critique*. Toronto: University of Toronto Press, 1957.

Cowan, Helen I. *British Emigration to North America, 1783–1837*. Toronto: University of Toronto Library, 1928.

Crowley, F. K., ed. *A New History of Australia*. Melbourne: William Heinemann, 1974.

Cunneen, C. *The Kings' Men*. London: Allen and Unwin, 1983.

Davenport, T. R. H. *The Afrikaner Bond*. London: Oxford University Press, 1966.

—— *South Africa: A Modern History*. 3rd ed. London: Macmillan Press, 1987.

Dawson, R. MacGregor. *William Lyon Mackenzie King*. I. *A Political Biography 1874–1923*. London: Methuen and Co., 1958.

Dennis, Peter. *The Territorial Army, 1906–1940*. Woodbridge, Suffolk: Boydell and Brewer, 1987.

Denoon, Donald. *A Grand Illusion*. London: Longman Group, 1973.

Drummond, Ian M. *Imperial Economic Policy 1917–1939*. London: George Allen and Unwin, 1974.

Duminy, Andrew and Bill Guest. *Interfering in Politics: A Biography of Sir Percy Fitzpatrick*. Johannesburg: Lowry Publishers, 1987.

Dunae, Patrick A. *Gentlemen Emigrants*. Toronto: Douglas and MacIntyre, 1981.

Eayrs, James. *In Defence of Canada: From the Great War to the Great Depression*. Toronto: University of Toronto Press, 1964.

Eccles, W. J. *Canada Under Louis XIV 1663–1701*. Toronto: McClelland and Stewart, 1964.

Edwards, I. E. *The 1820 Settlers in South Africa*. London: Longmans, Green and Co., 1934.

Edwards, P. G. *Prime Ministers and Diplomats*. Melbourne: Oxford University Press, 1983.

England, R. *Discharged: A Commentary on Civil Re-establishment of Veterans in Canada*. Toronto: The Macmillan Company of Canada, 1943.

Erickson, Charlotte, ed. *Emigration From Europe 1815–1914*. London: Adam and Charles Black, 1976.

Field, H. John. *Toward a Programme of Imperial Life*. Westport, Conn.: Greenwood Press, 1982.

Fieldhouse, D. K. *Economics and Empire 1830–1914*. London: Macmillan Publishers, 1984.

Fitzgerald, Ross. *A History of Queensland: From 1915 to the 1980s*. St Lucia: University of Queensland Press, 1984.

Fitzhardinge, L. F. *William Morris Hughes*. II. *The Little Digger 1914–52*. London: Angus and Robertson, 1979.

Forster, Colin. *Industrial Development in Australia 1920–1930*. Canberra: The Australian National University, 1964.

Foster, John E., ed. *The Developing West*. Edmonton: University of Alberta Press, 1983.

Fowke, Vernon C. *The National Policy and the Wheat Economy*. Toronto: University of Toronto Press, 1957.

French, David. *British Economic and Strategic Planning 1905–1915*. London: George Allen and Unwin, 1982.

Friesen, Gerald. *The Canadian Prairies*. Toronto: University of Toronto Press, 1984.

Gabeddy, J. P. *Group Settlement*. 2 vols. Perth: University of Western Australia Press, 1988.

Garden, Donald S. *Albany*. Melbourne: Thomas Nelson Australia, 1977.

Gilbert, B. B. *The Evolution of National Insurance in Great Britain*. London: Michael Joseph, 1966.

Gilbert, Martin. *Winston S. Churchill. IV. 1917–1922*. London: Heinemann, 1975.

Gordon, D. C. *The Dominion Partnership in Imperial Defence, 1870–1914*. Baltimore: The Johns Hopkins University Press, 1965.

Graham, B. D. *The Formation of the Australian Country Parties*. Canberra: Australian National University Press, 1966.

Graham, Roger. *Arthur Meighen. I. The Door of Opportunity. II. And Fortune Fled*. Toronto: Clarke, Irwin and Company, 1960 and 1963.

Grey, Jeffery. *A Military History of Australia*. Cambridge: Cambridge University Press, 1990.

Grigg, John. *Lloyd George: From Peace to War 1912–1916*. London: Methuen, 1985.

Hall, D. J. *Clifford Sifton. I. The Young Napoleon 1861–1900. II. The Lonely Eminence 1901–1929*. Vancouver: University of British Columbia Press, 1981 and 1985.

Hammerton, A. J. *Emigrant Gentlewomen: Genteel Poverty and Female Emigration, 1830–1914*. London: Croom Helm, 1979.

Hancock, W. K. *Survey of British Commonwealth Affairs 1918–1939*. II, part 1. London: Oxford University Press, 1940.

—— *Smuts. I. The Sanguine Years, 1870–1919. II. The Fields of Force, 1919–1950*. Cambridge: Cambridge University Press, 1962 and 1968.

Hancock, W. K., and Jean van der Poel, eds. *Selections from the Smuts Papers*. 7 vols. London: Cambridge University Press, 1966 and 1973.

Harries-Jenkins, Gwyn. *The Army in Victorian Society*. London: Routledge and Kegan Paul, 1977.

Harris, Herbert R. *Book of Memories and a History of the Porcupine Soldier Settlement*. Sponsored and published by the Shand Agricultural Society, 1967.

Hawke, G. R. *The Making of New Zealand: An Economic History*. Cambridge: Cambridge University Press, 1985.

Hawkins, Freda. *Critical Years in Immigration: Canada and Australia Compared*. Montreal: McGill-Queen's University Press, 1989.

Hodder-Williams, Richard. *White Farmers in Rhodesia 1890–1965*. London: Macmillan, 1983.

Holland, R. F. *Britain and the Commonwealth Alliance 1918–1939*. London: Macmillan, 1981.

Hughes, Colin A. and B. D. Graham. *A Handbook of Australian Government and Politics 1890–1964*. Canberra: Australian National University Press, 1968.

Huttenback, R. A. *Racism and Empire*. London: Cornell University Press, 1976.

Hyam, R. *Elgin and Churchill at the Colonial Office 1905–1908*. London: Macmillan and Co., 1968.

Hynes, S. *The Edwardian Turn of Mind*. London: Oxford University Press, 1968.

Ingham, Kenneth. *Jan Christian Smuts*. Johannesburg: Jonathon Ball Publishers, 1986.

Johnson, P. B. *A Land Fit For Heroes*. Chicago: University of Chicago Press, 1968.

Johnston, C. M. *E. C. Drury: Agrarian Idealist*. Toronto: University of Toronto Press, 1986.

Johnston, H. J. M. *British Emigration Policy 1815–1830*. Oxford: Clarendon Press, 1972.

Johnstone, F. A. *Class, Race and Gold*. London: Routledge and Kegan Paul, 1976.

Judd, D. *Balfour and the British Empire*. London: Macmillan, 1968.

—— *Radical Joe*. London: Hamish Hamilton, 1977.

Kealey, Linda, ed. *A Not Unreasonable Claim*. Toronto: The Women's Press, 1978.

Kendle, John E. *The Colonial and Imperial Conferences 1887–1911*. London: Longmans, Green and Co., 1967.

Kendall, W., *The Revolutionary Movement in Britain 1900–21*. London: Weidenfeld and Nicolson, 1969.

—— *The Round Table Movement and Imperial Union*. Toronto: University of Toronto Press, 1975.

—— *John Bracken: A Political Biography*. Toronto: University of Toronto Press, 1979.

Kennedy, P. and Anthony Nicholls, eds. *Nationalist and Racialist Movements in Britain Before 1914*. London: Macmillan, 1981.

Koebner, R. *Empire*. Cambridge: Cambridge University Press, 1961.

Kristianson, G. L. *The Politics of Patriotism*. Canberra: Australian National University Press, 1966.

Lake, Marilyn. *A Divided Society*. Melbourne: Melbourne University Press, 1975.

—— *The Limits of Hope*. Melbourne: Oxford University Press, 1987.

Leneman, Leah. *Fit for Heroes! Land Settlement in Scotland after World War I*. Aberdeen: Aberdeen University Press, 1989.

Lewsen, Phyllis. *John X. Merriman*. Johannesburg: A. D. Donker, 1982.

Liddle, Peter. *Home Fires and Foreign Fields*. London: Brassey's Defence Publishers, 1985.

[ 221 ]

Long, B. K. *Drummond Chaplin*. London: Oxford University Press, 1941.

Louis, W. R. *In the Name of God, Go! Leo Amery and the British Empire in the Age of Churchill*. London: W. W. Norton, 1992.

Lowe, Rodney. *Adjusting to Democracy: The Role of the Ministry of Labour in British Politics 1916–1939*. Oxford: Clarendon Press, 1986.

Lyon, Peter, ed. *Britain and Canada: Survey of a Changing Relationship*. London: Frank Cass and Co., 1976.

Macdonald, Norman. *Canada, 1763–1841 Immigration and Settlement*. Toronto: Longmans, Green, 1939.

—— *Canada: Immigration and Colonisation 1841–1903*. Aberdeen: Aberdeen University Press, 1966.

Macintyre, Stuart. *The Oxford History of Australia, IV. 1901–1942*. Melbourne: Oxford University Press, 1986.

MacKenzie, John M. *Propaganda and Empire*. Manchester: Manchester University Press, 1984.

—— ed. *Imperialism and Popular Culture*. Manchester: Manchester University Press, 1986.

Mackenzie, S. P. *Politics and Military Morale*. Oxford: Clarendon Press, 1992.

McKernan, M. and M. Browne, eds. *Australia: Two Centuries of War and Peace*. Sydney: Allen and Unwin Australia, 1988.

McNaught, Kenneth. *The Pelican History of Canada*. London: Allen Lane, 1978.

Malarek, V. *Haven's Gate*. Toronto: Macmillan of Canada, 1987.

Malchow, H. L. *Population Pressures: Emigration and Government in Late Nineteenth-Century Britain*. Palo Alto, California: The Society for the Promotion of Science and Scholarship Inc., 1979.

Mandle, W. F. *Going It Alone*. Ringwood: Allen Lane, Penguin Press, 1978.

Mansergh, Nicholas. *The Commonwealth Experience*. 2 vols. London: Macmillan, 1982.

Marks, S. and A. Atmore, eds. *Economy and Society in Pre-industrial South Africa*. London: Longman Group, 1980.

Marlowe, John. *Milner: Apostle of Empire*. London: Hamish Hamilton, 1976.

Marsh, Jan. *Back to the Land*. London: Quartet Books, 1982.

Marwick, Arthur. *The Deluge: British Society and the First World War*. London: Penguin Books, 1967.

Meiring, J. M. *Sundays River Valley: Its History and Settlement*. Cape Town: A. A. Balkema, 1959.

Miller, Carman. *Painting the Map Red: Canada and the South Africa War, 1899–1902*. Montreal: McGill-Queen's University Press, 1993.

Moore, Christopher. *The Loyalists: Revolution, Exile, Settlement*. Toronto: Macmillan, 1984.

Morgan, Kenneth O. *Consensus and Disunity: The Lloyd George Coalition Government 1918–1922*. Oxford: Clarendon Press, 1979.

Morton, A. S. *A History of the Canadian West to 1870–71*. Toronto: Thomas Nelson and Sons, n.d.

Morton, A. S. and Chester Martin. *History of Prairie Settlement and 'Dominion Lands' Policy*. Toronto: The Macmillan Company of Canada,

1938.

Morton, Desmond. *A Peculiar Kind of Politics: Canada's Overseas Ministry in the First World War.* Toronto: University of Toronto Press, 1982.

—— *A Military History of Canada.* Edmonton: Hertig Publishers, 1985.

Morton, Desmond and Glenn Wright. *Winning the Second Battle.* Toronto: University of Toronto Press, 1987.

Morton, W. L. *The Kingdom of Canada.* Toronto: McClelland and Stewart, 1963.

—— *The Critical Years.* Toronto: McClelland and Stewart, 1964.

Moyles, R. G. and Doug Owram. *Imperial Dreams and Colonial Realities: British Views of Canada, 1880–1914.* Toronto: University of Toronto Press, 1988.

Murphy, D. J., R. B. Joyce and Colin A. Hughes, eds. *Labor in Power: The Labor Party and Governments in Queensland 1915–1957.* St Lucia: Queensland University Press, 1980.

Murray, Colin. *Black Mountain: Land, Class and Power in the Eastern Orange Free State, 1880s to 1980s.* Edinburgh: Edinburgh University Press, 1992.

Neatby, H. Blair. *William Lyon Mackenzie King.* II. *The Lonely Heights 1924–1932.* London: Methuen and Co., 1963.

Nimocks, W. *Milner's Young Men: The 'Kindergarten' in Edwardian Imperial Affairs.* Durham, NC: Duke University Press, 1968.

Offer, Avner. *The First World War: An Agrarian Interpretation.* Oxford: Clarendon Press, 1989.

Oliver, W. H., ed. *The Oxford History of New Zealand.* Oxford: Clarendon Press, 1981.

Ollivier, Maurice, ed. *The Colonial and Imperial Conferences From 1887 to 1937.* 3 vols. Ottawa: Queen's Printer and Controller of Stationery, 1954.

Orbach, L. *Homes for Heroes.* London: Seeley, Service and Co., 1977.

Palmer, Howard. *Immigration and the Rise of Multiculturalism.* Toronto: Copp Clark Publishing, 1975.

—— ed. *The Settlement of the West.* Calgary: University of Calgary Press, 1977.

—— *Patterns of Prejudice.* Toronto: McClelland and Stewart, 1982.

Parr, J. *Labouring Children. British Immigrant Apprentices to Canada, 1869–1924.* Montreal: McGill-Queen's University Press, 1980.

Perry, P. J. *British Farming in The Great Depression 1870–1914.* Newton Abbot, Devon: David and Charles, 1974.

Phillips, G. D. *The Diehards.* Cambridge, Mass.: Harvard University Press, 1979.

Plant, G. F. *Oversea Settlement.* London: Oxford University Press, 1951.

Pooley, Colin G. and Ian D. Whyte, eds. *Migrants, Emigrants and Immigrants: A Social History of Migration.* London: Routledge, 1991.

Porter, B. *The Lion's Share.* London: Longman Group, 1975.

Powell, J. M. *Mirrors of the New World.* Folkstone: Wm. Dawson and Son, 1977.

—— *An Historical Geography of Modern Australia.* Cambridge: Cambridge University Press, 1988.

Preston, Adrian and Peter Dennis, eds. *Swords and Covenants.* London: Croom

Helm, 1976.

Preston, Richard A. *Canada and 'Imperial Defense'. A Study of the Origins of the British Commonwealth's Defense Organisation, 1867–1919*. Durham, NC: Duke University Press, 1965.

Prost, Antoine. *In the Wake of War: 'Les Anciens Combattants' and French Society 1914–1939*. Oxford: Berg, 1992.

Rasporich, A. W. and H. C. Klassen, eds. *Prairie Perspectives II*. Toronto: Holt, Reinhart and Winston of Canada, 1973.

Read, Donald. *Edwardian England*. London: Harrap and Co., 1972.

Reese, Peter. *Homecoming Heroes*. London: Leo Cooper, 1992.

Reese, Trevor. *The History of the Royal Commonwealth Society, 1868–1968*. London: Oxford University Press, 1968.

Reynolds, Lloyd G. *The British Immigrant*. Toronto: Oxford University Press, 1935.

Roberts, Barbara. *Whence They Came: Deportation from Canada 1900–1935*. Ottawa: Ottawa University Press, 1988.

Robson, Lloyd. *A Short History of Tasmania*. Melbourne: Oxford University Press, 1985.

Rose, Kenneth. *King George V*. London: Weidenfeld and Nicolson, 1983.

Ross, Jane. *The Myth of the Digger: The Australian Soldier in Two World Wars*. Sydney: Hale & Iremonger, 1985.

Russell, P., ed. *Nationalism in Canada*. Toronto: McGraw-Hill Company of Canada, 1966.

Sawer, G. *Australian Federal Politics and Law 1901–1929*. Melbourne: Melbourne University Press, 1956.

Scally, Robert J. *The Origins of the Lloyd George Coalition*. Princeton, NJ: Princeton University Press, 1975.

Schevdin, C. B. *Australia and the Great Depression*. Sydney: Sydney University Press, 1970.

Schull, Joseph. *Ontario Since 1867*. Toronto: McClelland and Stewart, 1978.

Searle, G. R. *The Quest for National Efficiency*. Oxford: Basil Blackwell, 1971.

Semmel, B. *Imperialism and Social Reform*. London: Allen and Unwin, 1960.

Sherington, G. *Australia's Immigrants 1788–1978*. London: George Allen and Unwin, 1980.

Skelley, A. R. *The Victorian Army at Home*. London: Croom Helm, 1977.

Smith, T. E. *Commonwealth Migration: Flows and Policies*. London: Macmillan, 1981.

Spiers, Eward M. *The Army and Society, 1815–1914*. London: Longman, 1980.

Stacey, C. P. *Canada and the British Army*. London: Longmans, Green and Co., 1938.

—— *Canada and the Age of Conflict*. 2 vols. Toronto: University of Toronto Press, 1977 and 1981.

Stone, John. *Colonist or Uitlander?* London: Oxford University Press, 1973.

Streak, M. *Lord Milner's Immigration Policy for the Transvaal 1897–1905*. Johannesburg: Rand Afrikaans University, 1970.

Struthers, James. *No Fault of Their Own*. Toronto: University of Toronto Press, 1983.

Swenarton, M. *Homes Fit For Heroes*. London: Heinemann Educational Books, 1981.

Swyripa, Frances and J. H. Thompson, eds. *Loyalties in Conflict*. Edmonton: Printing Services, University of Alberta, 1983.

Taylor, A. J. P. *Beaverbrook*. London: Hamish Hamilton, 1972.

Thompson, J. H. *The Harvests of War*. Toronto: McClelland and Stewart, 1978.

Thompson, J. H., with Allen Seager. *Canada 1922–1939: Decades of Discord*. Toronto: McClelland and Stewart, 1985.

Thornton, A. P. *The Imperial Idea and Its Enemies*. 2nd ed. London: Macmillan, 1985.

Titley, E. Brian. *A Narrow Vision: Duncan Campbell Scott and the Administration of the Indian Affairs in Canada*. Vancouver: University of British Columbia Press, 1986.

Troper, Harold. *Only Farmers Need Apply*. Toronto: Griffin Press, 1972.

Turner, I. *Industrial Labour and Politics*. Sydney: Hale and Iremonger, 1979.

van Onselen, Charles. *Studies in the Social and Economic History of the Witwatersrand 1886–1914*. 2 vols. Johannesburg: Ravan Press, 1982.

Verney, Jack. *The Good Regiment: The Carignan-Salières Regiment in Canada, 1665–1668*. London: McGill-Queen's University Press, 1991.

de Villiers, André, ed. *English Speaking South Africa Today*. Cape Town: Oxford University Press, 1976.

Wallis, J. P. R. *Fitz: The Story of Sir Percy Fitzpatrick*. London: Macmillan, 1954.

Ward, Russel. *The Australian Legend*. Melbourne: Oxford University Press, 1958.

—— *The History of Australia*. London: Heinemann Educational Books, 1978.

Ward, Stephen R., ed. *The War Generation*. Port Washington, NY: Kennikat Press, 1975.

Weiner, Martin J. *English Culture and the Decline of the Industrial Spirit 1850–1980*. Cambridge: Cambridge University Press, 1981.

Wheatcroft, Geoffrey. *The Randlords*. London: Weidenfeld and Nicolson, 1986.

Wheelwright, E. L. and Ken Buckley, eds. *Essays in the Political Economy of Australian Capitalism*. I-II. Sydney: ANZ Book Company, 1975 and 1978.

Whetham, Edith H. *The Agrarian History of England and Wales. VIII. 1914–1939*. Cambridge: Cambridge University Press, 1978.

Wigley, P. G. *Canada and the Transition to Commonwealth*. Cambridge: Cambridge University Press, 1977.

Williams, Jeffrey. *Byng of Vimy*. London: Secker and Warburg, 1983.

Wilson, Barbara. *Ontario and the First World War*. Toronto: The Champlain Society, 1977.

Wilson, Monica and Leonard Thompson, eds. *The Oxford History of South Africa*. I. Oxford: Clarendon Press, 1969.

Wootton, G. *The Official History of the British Legion*. London: Macdonald and Evans, 1956.

—— *The Politics of Influence*. London: Routledge and Kegan Paul, 1963.

Yudelman, David. *The Emergence of Modern South Africa*. Cape Town: David Philip, 1984.

## Articles

Attard, Bernard. 'Politics, finance and Anglo-Australian borrowing in London, 1914–1920'. *Australian Journal of Politics and History*, XXXV (1989), 142–63.

Avery, Donald. 'Ethnic and class tensions in Canada, 1918–20: Anglo-Canadians and the alien worker', in Frances Swyripa and J. H. Thompson, eds, *Loyalties in Conflict*. Edmonton: Printing Services, University of Alberta, 1983, 79–98.

Beloff, Max. 'Britain and Canada between the wars: a British view', in Peter Lyon, ed., *Britain and Canada: Survey of a Changing Relationship*. London: Frank Cass and Co., 1976, 50–60.

Beresford, Quentin. 'The World War One soldier settlement scheme in Tasmania'. *Tasmanian Historical Research Association Papers and Proceedings*, XXX (1983), 90–100.

Berger, Carl. 'The true north strong and free', in P. Russell, ed., *Nationalism in Canada*. Toronto: McGraw-Hill Company of Canada 1966, 3–26.

Blakeley, Brian L. 'Women and imperialism: the Colonial Office and female emigration to South Africa, 1901–1910'. *Albion*, XIII (1981), 131–49.

—— 'The Society for the Oversea Settlement of British Women and the problems of Empire settlement, 1917–1936'. *Albion*, XX (1988), 421–44.

Black, David. 'Party politics in turmoil 1911–1924', in C. T. Stannage, ed., *A New History of Western Australia*. Perth: University of Western Australia Press, 1987, 381–405.

Bolton, G. 'Sir James Mitchell: the optimist', in Lyall Hunt, ed., *Westralian Portraits*. Perth: University of Western Australia Press, 1979, 159–67.

Bond, Brian. 'Recruiting the Victorian army, 1870–92'. *Victorian Studies*, V (1962), 331–8.

—— 'The effect of the Cardwell reforms in army organisation, 1874–1904'. *Journal of the Royal United Services Institute*, CV (1960), 515–24.

Bray, R. M. ' "Fighting as an ally": the English Canadian patriotic response to the Great War'. *Canadian Historical Review*, LXI (1980), 141–68.

Brennan, J. William. 'C. A. Dunning, 1916–30: the rise and fall of a western agrarian Liberal', in John E. Foster, ed., *The Developing West*. Edmonton: University of Alberta Press, 1983, 243–70.

Buckley, S. 'The Colonial Office and the establishment of an Imperial Development Board: the impact of World War I'. *Journal of Imperial and Commonwealth History*, II (1973–74), 308–17.

—— 'Attempts at imperial economic co-operation, 1912–1918: Sir Robert Borden's role'. *Canadian Historical Review*, LV (1974), 292–306.

Burley, Kevin H. 'The Imperial Shipping Committee'. *Journal of Imperial and Commonwealth History*, II (1973–74), 206–25.

Burroughs, Peter. 'Promoting thrift, sobriety and discipline in the British army: the establishment of military savings banks'. *Histoire sociale – Social History*, XIV (1981), 323–37.

Cain, Neville. 'The economists and Australian population strategy in the twenties'. *Australian Journal of Politics and History*, XX (1974), 246–59.

Cherwinski, W. J. C. 'Wooden horses and rubber cows: training British agricultural labour for the Canadian prairies, 1890–1930'. *Canadian Historical Association Papers* (1980), 133–54.

—— 'The incredible harvest excursion of 1908'. *Labour/le travailleur*, V (1980), 57–79.

—— ' "Misfits," "malingerers", and "malcontents": the British harvester movement of 1928', in John E. Foster, ed., *The Developing West*. Edmonton: University of Alberta Press, 1983, 271–302.

Christopher, A. J. 'The European concept of a farm in southern Africa'. *Historia*, XV (1970), 93–9.

Clark, David. 'Australia: victim or partner of British imperialism', in E. L. Wheelwright and Ken Buckley, eds, *Essays in the Political Economy of Australian Capitalism*, I. Sydney: ANZ Book Company, 1975, 47–71.

Cline, Peter. 'Winding down the war economy: British plans for peacetime recovery, 1916–19', in Kathleen Burk, ed., *War and the State*, London: George Allen and Unwin, 1982, 157–81.

Cole, D. L. 'The problem of 'Nationalism' and 'Imperialism' in British settlement colonies'. *Journal of British Studies*, X (1971), 160–82.

Cole, Douglas. '"The crimson thread of kinship": ethnic ideas in Australia, 1870–1914'. *Historical Studies*, XIV (1971), 511–25.

Constantine, Stephen. 'Empire migration and social reform 1880–1950', in Colin G. Pooley and Ian D. Whyte, eds, *Migrants, Emigrants and Immigrants: A Social History of Migration*. London: Routledge, 1991, 62–83.

Cook, A. J. 'Irish settlers in the Eastern Cape in the early nineteenth century'. *Southern African-Irish Studies*, I (1991), 100–12.

Corry, J. A. 'The growth of government activities in Canada 1914–1921'. *Historical Papers* (1940), 63–73.

Cross, J. A. 'The Colonial Office and the dominions before 1914'. *Journal of Commonwealth Political Studies*, IV (1966), 138–48.

Crowley, F. K. 'The British contribution to the Australian population: 1860–1919'. *University Studies in History and Economics*, II (1954), 55–88.

Cunningham, Hugh. 'The Conservative party and patriotism', in Robert Colls and Philip Dodd, eds, *Englishness: Politics and Culture 1880–1920*. London: Croom Helm, 1986, 283–307.

Darwin, J. 'Imperialism in decline? Tendencies in British policy between the wars'. *Historical Journal*, XXIII (1980), 657–79.

Davies, A. J. 'Australian federalism and national development'. *Australian Journal of Politics and History*, XIV (1968), 37–51.

Dickson, Paul Douglas. '"We prefer trade to dominion": imperial policy and the settlement of the King's Royal Regiment'. *Ontario History*, LXXXII (1990), 129–48.

Douglas, W. A. B. 'The blessings of the land: naval officers in Upper Canada, 1815–1841', in Adrian Preston and Peter Dennis, eds, *Swords and Covenants*. London: Croom Helm, 1976, 42–73.

Drystek, Henry. 'The simplest and cheapest mode of dealing with them: deportation from Canada before World War II'. *Histoire sociale – Social History*, XV (1982), 407–41.

Duder, C. J. D. 'The settler response to the Indian crisis of 1923 in Kenya:

Brigadier General Philip Wheatley and "direct action"'. *Journal of Imperial and Commonwealth History*, XVII (1989), 349–73.

—— 'Beadoc – the British East Africa disabled officers' colony and the white frontier in Kenya'. *Agricultural History Review*, XL (1992), 142–50.

—— ' "Men of the officer class": the participants in the 1919 soldier settlement scheme in Kenya'. *African Affairs*, XCII (1993), 69–87.

Emy, H. V. 'The impact of financial policy on English party politics before 1914'. *Historical Journal*, XV (1972), 103–31.

England, R. 'Discharged and disbanded soldiers in Canada prior to 1914'. *Canadian Historical Review*, XXVII (1946), 1–18.

Englander, David. 'Troops and trade unions, 1919'. *History Today*, XXXVII (1987), 8–13.

—— 'The National Union of Ex-Servicemen and the labour movement, 1918–1920'. *History*, LXXVI (1991), 24–42.

Englander, David and James Osborne. 'Jack, Tommy, and Henry Dubb: the armed forces and the working class'. *Historical Journal*, XXI (1978), 593–621.

Erickson, Charlotte. 'Agrarian myths of English immigrants', in O. F. Ander, ed., *In the Trek of Immigrants*. Rock Island, Illinois: Augustana College Library, 1964, 59–80.

Evans, Raymond. ' "Some furious outbursts of riot": returned soldiers and Queensland's "Red Flag" disturbances, 1918–1919'. *War and Society*, III (1985), 75–98.

Fairburn, M. 'The rural myth and the new urban frontier: an approach to New Zealand social history, 1879–1940'. *New Zealand Journal of History*, IX (1975), 3–21.

Fedorowich, E. K. 'The assisted emigration of British ex-servicemen to the dominions 1914–1922', in Stephen Constantine, ed., *Emigrants and Empire*, Manchester: Manchester University Press, 1990, 45–71.

—— ' "Society pets and morning coated farmers": Australian soldier settlement and the participation of British ex-servicemen, 1915–1929'. *War and Society*, VIII (1990), 38–56.

—— 'Anglicisation and the politicisation of British immigration to South Africa, 1899–1929'. *Journal of Imperial and Commonwealth History*, XIX (1991), 222–46.

—— 'The migration of British ex-servicemen to Canada and the role of the Naval and Military Emigration League, 1899–1914'. *Histoire sociale – Social History*, XXV (1992), 75–99.

Fewster, Joseph M. 'Documentary sources concerning Australia in Durham University'. *Durham University Journal*, new series, L (1988), 59–69.

Fewster, Kevin. 'Ellis Ashmead Bartlett and the making of the Anzac legend'. *Journal of Australian Studies*, VII (1982), 17–30.

Ford, Arthur R. 'Some notes on the formation of the Union government in 1917'. *Canadian Historical Review*, XIX (1938), 357–64.

Fry, K. 'Soldier settlement and the Australian agrarian myth after the First World War'. *Labour History*, no. 48 (1985), 29–43.

Gammage, Bill. 'Australians and the Great War'. *Journal of Australian Studies*, VI (1980), 26–37.

—— 'The crucible: the establishment of the Anzac tradition', in M. McKernan and M. Browne, eds, *Australia: Two Centuries of War and Peace*. Sydney: Allen and Unwin Australia, 1988, 147–66.

Garson, N. G. 'English-speaking South Africans and the British connection: 1820–1961', in André de Villiers, ed., *English Speaking South Africa Today*. Cape Town: Oxford University Press, 1976, 17–39.

—— 'South Africa and World War I', in Norman Hillmer and Philip Wigley, eds, *The First British Commonwealth: Essays in Honour of Nicholas Mansergh*. London: Frank Cass and Co., 1980, 68–85.

Gates, P. W. 'Official encouragement to immigration by the province of Canada'. *Canadian Historical Review*, XV (1934), 24–38.

Gilbert, A. D. 'The conscription referenda, 1916–17: the impact of the Irish crisis'. *Historical Studies*, XIV (1969), 54–72.

Glynn, Desmond. ' "Exporting outcast London": assisted emigration to Canada, 1886–1914'. *Histoire sociale – Social History*, XV (1982), 209–38.

Glynn, Sean. 'Government policy and agricultural development: Western Australia, 1900–1930'. *Australian Economic History Review*, VII (1967), 115–41.

Gough, A. 'The repatriation of the first Australian Imperial Force'. *Queensland Historical Review*, VII (1978), 58–69.

Graubard, S. R. 'Military demobilisation in Great Britain following the First World War'. *Journal of Modern History*, XIX (1947), 297–311.

Hall, D. J. 'Clifford Sifton: immigration and settlement policy, 1896–1905', in Howard Palmer, ed., *The Settlement of the West*. Calgary: University of Calgary Press, 1977, 60–85.

Hancock, K. J. 'The reduction of unemployment as a problem of public policy, 1920–29'. *Economic History Review*, 2nd series, XV (1962–63), 328–43.

Harris, Cole. 'The myth of the land in Canadian nationalism', in P. Russell, ed., *Nationalism in Canada*. Toronto: McGraw-Hill Company of Canada 1966, 27–43.

Hawkins, R. A. 'Socialism at work? Corporatism, soldier settlers, and the canned pineapple industry in south eastern Queensland, 1917–39'. *Australian Studies*, no. 4 (1990), 35–59.

Hirst, J. B. 'The pioneer legend'. *Historical Studies*, XVIII (1978–79), 316–37.

Hood, David. 'Adelaide's first "taste of Bolshevism": returned soldiers and the 1918 Peace Day riots'. *Historical Society of South Australia*, no. 15 (1987), 42–53.

Hunt, I. L. 'Group settlement in Western Australia'. *University Studies in History and Economics*, VIII (1958), 5–42.

Huttenback, R. 'No strangers within the gates: attitudes and policies towards the non-white residents of the British Empire of settlement'. *Journal of Imperial and Commonwealth History*, I (1973), 271–302.

—— 'The British Empire as a 'White Man's country' – racial attitudes and immigration legislation in the colonies of white settlement'. *Journal of British Studies*, I (1973), 108–37.

Hyam, R. 'The Colonial Office mind 1900–1914'. *Journal of Imperial and Commonwealth History*, VIII (1979), 30–52.

Inglis, K. S. 'The Anzac tradition'. *Meanjin*, XXIV (1965), 25–44.

—— 'The Australians at Gallipoli'. Part I, *Historical Studies*, XIV, 54 (1970), 219–30; *ibid.*, Part II, XIV, 55 (1970), 361–75.

Jarvis, Eric. 'Military land granting in Upper Canada following the War of 1812'. *Ontario History*, LXVII (1975), 121–34.

Johnson, J. K. 'The Chelsea pensioners in Upper Canada'. *Ontario History*, LIII (1961), 273–89.

Kennedy, Dane. 'Empire migration in post-war reconstruction: the role of the Oversea Settlement Committee'. *Albion*, XX (1988), 403–19.

Kent, D. A. 'The Anzac book and the Anzac legend: C. E. W. Bean as editor and image-maker'. *Historical Studies*, XXI (1985), 376–90.

Killingray, David. 'The Empire Resources Development Committee and West Africa 1916–1920'. *Journal of Imperial and Commonwealth History*, X (1982), 194–210.

Kirk-Greene, A. H. M. 'Taking Canada into partnership in "the White Man's burden": the British colonial service and the dominion selection scheme of 1923'. *Canadian Journal of African Studies*, XV (1983), 33–46.

Koroscil, Paul M. 'Soldiers, settlement and development in British Columbia, 1915–1930'. *BC Studies*, no. 54 (1982), 63–87.

Lake, Marilyn. 'Annie Smith: "soldier settler"', in Marilyn Lake and Farley Kelly, eds, *Double Time: Women in Victoria – 150 Years*. London: Penguin Books, 1985, 297–304.

—— 'The power of Anzac', in M. McKernan and M. Browne, eds, *Australia: Two Centuries of War and Peace*. Sydney: Allen and Unwin Australia, 1988, 194–222.

de Lepervanche, Marie. 'Australian immigrants, 1788–1940', in E. L. Wheelwright and Ken Buckley, eds, *Political Economy of Australian Capitalism*, I. Sydney: ANZ Book Company, 1975, 72–104.

Lockwood, P. A. 'Milner's entry into the War Cabinet, December 1916'. *Historical Journal*, VII (1964), 120–34.

Lowe, Rodney. 'The Ministry of Labour, 1916–19: a still, small voice?', in Kathleen Burk, ed., *War and the State*. London: George Allen and Unwin, 1982, 108–34.

Lower, A. R. M. 'Immigration and settlement in Canada, 1812–1820'. *Canadian Historical Review*, III (1922), 37–42.

McCormack, A. Ross. 'Cloth caps and jobs: the ethnicity of English immigrants in Canada 1900–1914', in Jorgen Dahlie and Tissa Fernando, eds, *Ethnicity, Power and Politics in Canada*, Toronto: Methuen Publications, 1981, 38–55.

—— 'Networks among British immigrants and accommodation to Canadian society: Winnipeg, 1900–1914'. *Histoire sociale – Social History*, XVII (1984), 357–74.

MacDonald, Barrie and David Thompson. 'Mortgage relief, farm finance, and rural depression in New Zealand in the 1930s', *New Zealand Journal of History*, XXI (1987), 228–50.

McDonald, John. 'Soldier settlement and depression settlement in the forest fringe of Saskatchewan'. *Prairie Forum*, VI (1981), 35–55.

McDonald, S. R. 'Victoria's immigration scandal of the thirties'. *Victorian*

*Historical Journal*, XLIX (1978), 228–37.

McDougall, Duncan M. 'Immigration into Canada, 1851–1920'. *Canadian Journal of Economics and Political Science*, XXVII (1961), 162–75.

McKernan, M. 'Catholics, conscription and Archbishop Mannix'. *Historical Studies*, XVII (1976–77), 299–314.

McLachlan, Noel. 'Nationalism and the divisive digger'. *Meanjin*, XXVII (1968), 302–8.

McQueen, Humphrey. 'Shoot the Bolshevik! Hang the profiteer! reconstructing Australian capitalism, 1918–21', in E. L. Wheelwright and Ken Buckley, eds, *Political Economy of Australian Capitalism*, II. Sydney: ANZ Book Company, 1978, 185–206.

Malchow, H. L. 'Trade unions and emigration in late Victorian England: a national lobby for state aid'. *Journal of British Studies*, XV (1976), 92–116.

Marks, Shula and Stanley Trapido. 'Lord Milner and the South African state'. *History Workshop Journal*, issue 8 (1979), 50–80.

Martell, J. S. 'Military settlements in Nova Scotia after the War of 1812'. *Collections of the Nova Scotia Historical Society*, XXIV (1938), 75–105.

Miller, Carman. 'Sir Frederick William Borden and military reform, 1896–1911'. *Canadian Historical Review*, L (1969), 265–84.

Moore, Christopher. 'The disposition to settle: the Royal Highland emigrants and Loyalist settlement in Upper Canada, 1784'. *Ontario History*, LXXVI (1984), 306–25.

Morgan, E. C. 'Soldier settlement in the prairie provinces'. *Saskatchewan History*, XXI (1968), 41–55.

Morton, D. 'Sir William Otter and internment operations in Canada during the First World War'. *Canadian Historical Review*, LV (1974), 32–58.

—— 'Polling the soldier vote: the overseas campaign in the Canadian general election of 1917'. *Journal of Canadian Studies*, X (1975), 39–58.

—— 'Noblest and best: retraining Canada's war disabled, 1915–1923'. *Journal of Canadian Studies*, XVI (1981–82), 75–85.

—— ' "Kicking and complaining": demobilisation riots in the Canadian Expeditionary Force, 1918–19'. *Canadian Historical Review*, LXI (1980), 334–60.

—— ' "Junior but sovereign allies": the transformation of the Canadian Expeditionary Force, 1914–1918', in Norman Hillmer and Philip Wigley, eds, *The First British Commonwealth: Essays in Honour of Nicholas Mansergh*. London: Frank Cass and Co., 1980, 56–67.

—— 'Resisting the pension evil: bureaucracy, democracy, and Canada's Board of Pension commissioners, 1916–33'. *Canadian Historical Review*, LXVIII (1987), 199–224.

—— 'The Canadian military experience in the First World War, 1914–1918', in R. J. Q. Adams, ed., *The Great War, 1914–18*. London, Macmillan, 1990, 79–100.

Morton, D. and Glenn Wright. 'The bonus campaign, 1919–1921: veterans and the campaign for re-establishment'. *Canadian Historical Review*, LXIV (1983), 147–67.

Morton, W. L. 'The 1920's', in J. M. S. Careless and R. Craig Brown, eds, *The*

*Canadians 1867–1967*. Toronto: Macmillan of Canada, 1967, 205–35.

Murphy, D. J. 'Religion, race and conscription in World War I'. *Australian Journal of Politics and History*, XX (1974), 151–63.

Newbury, C. 'Labour migration in the imperial phase: an essay in interpretation'. *Journal of Imperial and Commonwealth History*, III (1975), 234–56.

O'Brien, John B. 'Empire v. national intersets in Australian-British relations during the 1930s'. *Historical Studies*, XXII (1987), 569–86.

O'Connor, P. S. 'Keeping New Zealand white, 1908–1920'. *New Zealand Journal of History*, II (1968), 47–65.

O'Dowd, C. E. M. 'The general election of 1924'. *South African Historical Journal*, no. 2 (1970), 54–76.

Oliver, Bobbie. 'Disputes, diggers and disillusionment: social and industrial unrest in Perth and Kalgoorlie 1918–1924', in Jenny Gregory, ed., *Western Australia Between the Wars 1919–1939. Studies in Western Australian History XI*. Perth: University of Western Australia Press, 1990, 19–28.

Pierce, Peter. 'Rider Haggard in Australia'. *Meanjin*, XXXVI (1977), 200–8.

Playter, George F. 'An account of three military settlements in eastern Ontario – Perth, Lanark and Richmond, 1815–1820'. Ontario Historical Society, *Papers and Records*, XX (1923), 98–104.

Pope, D. H. 'Contours of Australian immigration, 1901–30'. *Australian Economic History Review*, XXI (1981), 29–52.

—— 'Assisted immigration and federal-state relations: 1901–1930'. *Australian Journal of Politics and History*, XXVIII (1982), 21–31.

Powell, J. M. 'Soldier settlement in New Zealand, 1915–1923'. *Australian Geographical Studies*, IX (1971), 144–60.

—— 'The mapping of "soldier settlement": a note for Victoria, 1917–29'. *Journal of Australian Studies*, III (1978), 44–51.

—— 'The debt of honour: soldier settlement in the dominions, 1915–1940'. *Journal of Australian Studies*, V (1980), 64–87.

—— 'Elwood Mead and California's state colonies: An episode in Australasian-American contacts, 1915–1931'. *Journal of the Royal Australian Historical Society*, LXVII (1982), 328–53.

—— 'Australia's "failed" soldier settlers, 1914–23: towards a demographic profile'. *Australian Geographer*, XVI (1985), 225–9.

Pugh, R. B. 'The Colonial Office, 1801–1925', in *The Cambridge History of the British Empire*, III, 711–68.

Radi, Heather. '1920–29', in F. K. Crowley, ed., *A New History of Australia*. Melbourne: William Heinemann, 1974, 357–414.

Raudzens, George. 'A successful military settlement: Earl Grey's enrolled pensioners of 1846 in Canada'. *Canadian Historical Review*, LII (1971), 389–403.

Reid, Bill G. 'Franklin K. Lane's idea for veterans' colonisation, 1918–1921'. *Pacific Historical Review*, XXXIII (1964), 447–61.

Rich, Paul. ' "Milnerism and a ripping yarn": Transvaal land settlement and John Buchan's novel "Prester John" 1901–1910', in Belinda Bozzoli, ed., *Town and Countryside in the Transvaal*. Johannesburg: Ravan Press, 1983, 412–33.

Richmond, K. 'Reaction to radicalism: non-labour movements, 1920–9'. *Journal of Australian Studies*, V (1979), 50–63.

Richmond, W. H. 'S. M. Bruce and Australian economic policy 1923–29'. *Australian Economic History Review*, XXIII (1983), 238–57.

Riddell, R. G. 'A study in the land policy of the Colonial Office, 1763–1855'. *Canadian Historical Review*, XVIII (1937), 385–405.

Roberts, Barbara. 'A work of empire: Canadian reformers and British female immigration', in Linda Kealey, ed., *A Not Unreasonable Claim*. Toronto: The Women's Press, 1978, 185–201.

—— 'Shovelling out the "mutinous": political deportation from Canada before 1936'. *Labour/Le Travail*, XVIII (1986), 77–110.

Robson, L. L. 'The origins and character of the first AIF, 1914–1918: some statistical evidence'. *Historical Studies*, XV (1973), 737–49.

—— 'The Australian soldier: formation of a stereotype', in M. McKernan and M. Browne, eds, *Australia: Two Centuries of War and Peace*. Sydney: Allen and Unwin Australia, 1988, 313–37.

Roe, M. 'Britain's debate on migration to Australia, 1917–39'. *Journal of the Royal Australian Historical Society*, LXXV (1989), 13–32.

—— ' "We can die just as easy out here": Australia and British immigration, 1916–39', in Stephen Constantine, ed., *Emigrants and Empire*. Manchester: Manchester University Press, 1990, 96–120.

Royal Commonwealth Society, 'Sir Rider Haggard's mission', *Library Notes*, new series, no. 190 (1973).

Saul, S. B. 'The economic significance of constructive imperialism'. *Journal of Economic History*, XVII (1957), 173–92.

Saunders, David. 'Aliens in Britain and Empire during the First World War', in Frances Swyripa and J. H. Thompson, eds, *Loyalties in Conflict*. Edmonton: Printing Services, University of Alberta, 1983, 99–124.

Schultz, J. A. 'Canadian attitudes toward Empire settlement, 1919–1930'. *Journal of Imperial and Commonwealth History*, I (1973), 237–51.

—— 'Finding homes fit for heroes: the Great War and Empire settlement'. *Canadian Journal of History*, XVIII (1983), 99–110.

Serle, Geoffrey. 'The digger tradition and Australian nationalism'. *Meanjin*, XXIV (1965), 149–58.

Sharpe, Maureen. 'Anzac day in New Zealand 1916–1939'. *New Zealand Journal of History*, XV (1981), 97–114.

Smith, David. 'Instilling British values in the prairie provinces'. *Prairie Forum*, VI (1981), 129–41.

Snelling R. C. and T. J. Barron. 'The Colonial Office and its permanent officials 1801–1914', in G. Sutherland, ed., *Studies in the Growth of Nineteenth-Century Government*. London: Routledge and Kegan Paul, 1972, 139–66.

Spies, S. B. 'The outbreak of the First World War and the Botha government'. *South African Historical Journal*, no. 1 (1969), 47–57.

Stacey, C. P. 'Halifax as an international strategic factor, 1749–1949'. Canadian Historical Association, *Report*, 1949, 46–55.

Struthers, James. 'Prelude to depression: the federal government and unemployment, 1918–1929'. *Canadian Historical Review*, LVII (1977),

278–94.

Stubbs, J. O. 'Lord Milner and patriotic labour 1914–1918'. *English Historical Review*, LXXXVII (1972), 717–54.

Sturgis, James. 'Anglicisation at the Cape of Good Hope in the early nineteenth century'. *Journal of Imperial and Commonwealth History*, XI (1982), 5–32.

—— 'Anglicisation as a theme in Lower Canadian history 1807–1843'. *British Journal of Canadian Studies*, III (1988), 210–29.

Summers, Ann. 'Militarism in Britain before the Great War'. *History Workshop*, issue 2 (1976), 104–23.

Swyripa, Frances. 'The Ukrainian image: loyal citizen or disloyal alien', in Frances Swyripa and J. H. Thompson, eds, *Loyalties in Conflict*. Edmonton: Printing Services, University of Alberta, 1983, 47–68.

Tankard, K. P. T. 'Effects of Irish versus German immigration on the eastern frontier, 1857–1858'. *Southern African-Irish Studies*, I (1991), 113–21.

—— 'The Lady Kennaway girls'. *Southern African-Irish Studies*, II (1992), 278–86.

Tawney, R. H. 'The abolition of economic controls, 1918–1921'. *Economic History Review*, XIII (1943), 1–30.

Templeton, Jacqueline. 'Set up to fail? Soldier settlers in Victoria'. *Victorian Historical Journal*, LIX (1988), 42–50.

Thomas, Lewis H. 'British visitors' perceptions of the west, 1885–1914', in A. W. Rasporich and H. C. Klassen, eds, *Prairie Perspectives II*. Toronto: Holt, Reinhart and Winston of Canada, 1973, 181–96.

Thompson, John H. ' "Permanently wasteful but immediately profitable": prairie agriculture and the Great War'. *Canadian Historical Association Papers* (1976), 193–206.

—— 'Bringing in the sheaves: the harvest excursionists, 1890–1929'. *Canadian Historical Review*, LIX (1978), 467–89.

Timlin, Mabel F. 'Canada's immigration policy, 1896–1910'. *Canadian Journal of Economics and Political Science*, XXVI (1960), 517–32.

Trapido, Stanley. 'Landlord and tenant in a colonial economy: the Transvaal 1880–1910'. *Journal of Southern African Studies*, V (1978), 26–58.

—— 'Reflections on land, office and wealth in the South African Republic', in S. Marks and A. Atmore, eds. *Economy and Society in Pre-industrial South Africa*. London: Longman Group, 1980, 350–68.

Tsokhas, Kosmas. 'People or money? Empire settlement and British emigration to Australia, 1919–34'. *Immigrants and Minorities*, IX (1990), 1–20.

—— 'Protection, imperial preference and Australian conservative politics, 1923–39'. *Journal of Imperial and Commonwealth History*, XX (1992), 65–87.

Tucker, A. V. 'Army and society in England, 1870–1904: a reassessment of the Cardwell reforms'. *Journal of British Studies*, II (1963), 100–41.

Turner, Ian. '1914–1919', in F. K. Crowley, ed., *A New History of Australia* Melbourne: William Heinemann, 1974, 312–56.

Van-Helten, J. J. and Keith Williams. ' "The crying need of South Africa": the emigration of single British women to the Transvaal, 1901–10'. *Journal of Southern African Studies*, X (1983), 17–38.

[ 234 ]

Voisey, Paul. 'The urbanisation of the Canadian prairies, 1871–1916'. *Histoire sociale – Social History*, VIII (1975), 77–101.

Waites, B. 'The government of the home front and the "moral economy" of the working class', in Peter Liddle, ed., *Homes Fires and Foreign Fields*. London: Brassey's Defence Publishers, 1985, 175–93.

Ward, Russel. 'The Australian legend re-visited'. *Historical Studies*, XXVIII (1978–79), 171–90.

Ward, S. 'The British veterans' ticket of 1918'. *Journal of British Studies*, VIII (1968), 155–69.

—— 'Intelligence surveillance of British ex-servicemen, 1918–1920'. *Historical Journal*, XVI (1973), 179–88.

—— 'Great Britain: land fit for heroes lost', in Stephen Ward, ed., *The War Generation*. Port Washington, NY: Kennikat Press, 1975, 10–37.

Whetham, Edith H. 'The agriculture act, 1920 and its repeal – the "Great Betrayal" '. *Agricultural History Review*, XXII (1974), 36–49.

Wigley, Philip. 'Whitehall and the 1923 Imperial Conference'. *Journal of Imperial and Commonwealth History*, I (1973), 223–35.

Williams, Keith. ' "A way out of our troubles": the politics of Empire Settlement, 1900–22', in Stephen Constantine, ed., *Emigrants and Empire*, Manchester: Manchester University Press, 1990.

Wilson, Mary. 'The making of Melbourne's Anzac day'. *Australian Journal of Politics and History*, XX (1974), 197–209.

Wright, M. 'Treasury control 1854–1914', in G. Sutherland, ed., *Studies in the Growth of Nineteenth-Century Government*. London: Routledge and Kegan Paul, 1972, 195–226.

## Unpublished theses, dissertations and papers

Barber, M. J. 'The Assimilation of Immigrants in the Canadian Prairie Provinces, 1896–1918: Canadian Perception and Canadian Policies'. Ph.D. thesis. University of London, 1975.

Barwick, W. E. 'The Murrumbidgee Irrigation Areas: A History of Irrigation Development in New South Wales from 1884, with special emphasis on the Murrumbidgee Irrigation Areas from 1906–1916'. B.Litt. thesis. University of New England, Armidale, 1979.

Bradlow, Edna. 'Immigration into the Union 1910–1948: Policies and Attitudes'. Ph.D. dissertation 2 vols. University of Cape Town, 1978.

Bottomley, John. ' "Barren spaces and terrible gnawing hunger": The Milner Government and Reconstruction, 1902–1905'. Paper presented to the Fourth Biennial General Meeting of the Economic History Society of Southern Africa. Rhodes University, Grahamstown, July 1986.

Brownell, F. C. 'British Immigration to South Africa, 1946–1970'. M.A. thesis. University of South Africa, 1977.

Duder, C. J. D. 'Soldier and Empire Settlement: An Imperial Perspective'. Essay. Royal Commonwealth Society Library, 1975.

—— 'The Soldier Settlement Scheme of 1919 in Kenya'. Ph.D. thesis. Aberdeen

University, 1978.

Evans, R. ' "Some Furious Outbursts of Riot": Returned Soldiers and Queensland's "Red Flag" Disturbances, 1918–19'. Seminar paper. Institute of Commonwealth Studies, University of London, 1984.

Fedorowich, E. K. 'H. Rider Haggard: the Spirit of Empire'. M.A. Thesis. University of Saskatchewan, 1983.

—— ' "A Truly Lamentable Affair": The Resettlement of Ex-Indian Army Personnel in Australia and Canada, 1919–1934'. Unpublished manuscript.

George, D. J. 'The Depression of 1921–22 in New Zealand'. M.A. thesis. University of Auckland, 1969.

Grushman, A. 'Empire Settlement: British Migration to Canada, 1919–1931'. Seminar paper. Institute of Commonwealth Studies, University of London, 1980.

Guest, W. R. 'The Political Career of Sir Percy Fitzpatrick 1907–1920'. Ph.D. dissertation. University of Natal (Durban), 1980.

Hallett, Mary E. 'The Fourth Earl Grey as Governor-General of Canada'. Ph.D. thesis. University of London, 1969.

Hopgood, Donald J. 'A Psephological Examination of the South Australian Labor Party from World War One to the Depression'. Ph.D. thesis. Flinders University, 1973.

LeLacheur, H. 'War Service Land Settlement in South Australia'. M.A. thesis. University of Adelaide, 1968.

McGillivray, Leith G. 'Land and People. European Land Settlement in the South East of South Australia 1840–1940. Ph.D. thesis. University of Adelaide, 1982.

Martin, C. 'The Huon 1914–1926'. M.A. thesis. University of Tasmania, 1992.

Mawby, A. A. 'The Unionist Party of South Africa, from May 1910 to August 1914'. B.A. (Hons) dissertation. University of the Witwatersrand, 1965.

Mayhew, W. R. 'The New Zealand Returned Soldiers' Association 1916–1943'. B.A. (Hons) thesis. Otago University, 1943.

Melling, J. O. 'The New Zealand Returned Soldiers' Association, 1916–23'. M.A. thesis. Victoria University College, 1952.

Milton, E. 'Soldier Settlement in Queensland After World War I'. B.A. (Hons) dissertation. University of Queensland, 1968.

Morrell, R. G. 'Rural Transformations in the Transvaal: The Middelburg District, 1919 to 1930'. M.A. thesis. University of the Witwatersrand, 1983.

Mott, Morris K. 'The "Foreign Peril": Nativism in Winnipeg, 1916–1923'. M.A. thesis. University of Manitoba, 1970.

Mrdak, M. ' "Soldier-Citizen": Returned Servicemen and the R.S.L. 1916–1929'. B.A. (Hons) thesis. University of New England, Armidale, 1986.

O'Sullivan, J. 'A New South Wales Land Settlement Policy. Kentucky Soldiers' Settlement, 1917–75, with Special Reference on the Period to 1940'. B.Litt. thesis. University of New England, Armidale, 1982.

Parker, D. 'An Assessment of Stanthorpe Soldier Settlement 1915–1930'. B.A. (Hons) thesis. University of New England, Armidale, 1982.

Pryor, L. J. 'The Origins of Australia's Repatriation Policy, 1914–1930'. M.A. thesis. University of Melbourne, 1932.

Regan, P. M. 'A War-Memoried Land – Some Aspects of Australia's Transition from War to Peace in 1919'. M.Litt. thesis. University of New England, 1985.

Reid, Bill. 'Proposed American Plans for Soldier Settlement During World War I'. Ph.D. thesis. University of Oklahoma, 1963.

Reynolds, M. 'The Noble Failure: King Island Soldier Settlement, 1918–1930'. B.Ed. dissertation. University of Tasmania, 1982.

Schultz, J. A. 'Canadian Attitudes Toward the Empire, 1919–1939'. Ph.D. thesis. Dalhousie University, 1975.

Suckling, P. G. E. 'British Migration to Australia in the 1920s and the Role of the New Settlers' League'. BA (Hons) thesis. University of the West of England, Bristol, 1993.

Wertimer, S. 'Migration from the United Kingdom to the Dominions in the Interwar Period, with Special Reference to the Empire Settlement Act of 1922'. Ph.D. thesis. University of London, 1952.

Williams, Keith. 'Labour Migration as Social Imperialism: The Ideology of Empire Settlement'. Seminar Paper. Institute of Commonwealth Studies, University of London, 1980.

—— 'The British State, Social Imperialism and Emigration From Britain, 1900–22: The Ideology and Antecedents of the Empire Settlement Act'. Ph.D. thesis. University of London, 1985.

## Biographical references

Dictionary of Australian Biography

Dictionary of National Biography

Dictionary of South African Biography

Morgan, Henry J. *Canadian Men and Women of the Time.* 2nd ed. Toronto: William Briggs, 1912.

Wallace, W. D. *The Macmillan Dictionary of Canadian Biography.* 3rd ed. Toronto: Macmillan Company of Canada, 1963.

# INDEX